Religions and Nonviolence

Religions and Nonviolence

The Rise of Effective Advocacy for Peace

RACHEL M. MACNAIR

BLOOMSBURY ACADEMIC
NEW YORK • LONDON • OXFORD • NEW DELHI • SYDNEY

BLOOMSBURY ACADEMIC
Bloomsbury Publishing Inc
1385 Broadway, New York, NY 10018, USA
50 Bedford Square, London, WC1B 3DP, UK
29 Earlsfort Terrace, Dublin 2, Ireland

BLOOMSBURY, BLOOMSBURY ACADEMIC and the Diana logo
are trademarks of Bloomsbury Publishing Plc

First published in the United States of America by ABC-CLIO 2015
Paperback edition published by Bloomsbury Academic 2024

Copyright © Bloomsbury Publishing Inc, 2024

Cover photos: Dove. (loliputa/Thinkstock); Abstract water sunset. (Acik/Thinkstock)
Cover design by Silverander Communications

All rights reserved. No part of this publication may be reproduced or transmitted in any form or by any means, electronic or mechanical, including photocopying, recording, or any information storage or retrieval system, without prior permission in writing from the publishers.

Bloomsbury Publishing Inc does not have any control over, or responsibility for, any third-party websites referred to or in this book. All internet addresses given in this book were correct at the time of going to press. The author and publisher regret any inconvenience caused if addresses have changed or sites have ceased to exist, but can accept no responsibility for any such changes.

Library of Congress Cataloging-in-Publication Data
MacNair, Rachel.
Religions and nonviolence: the rise of effective advocacy
for peace / Rachel M. MacNair.
pages cm
Includes bibliographical references and index.
ISBN 978-1-4408-3538-4 (alk. paper) — ISBN 978-1-4408-3539-1
1. Nonviolence—Religious aspects. 2. Peace—Religious
aspects. 3. Religions. I. Title.
BL65.V55M33 2015
205'.697—dc23   2015009255

ISBN: HB: 978-1-4408-3538-4
PB: 979-8-7651-2365-2
ePDF: 978-1-4408-3539-1
eBook: 979-8-2161-3814-3

To find out more about our authors and books visit www.bloomsbury.com
and sign up for our newsletters.

Contents

Introduction	1
Part I: Nonviolence in Religious Traditions	**15**
1 Judaism: Shalom	17
2 Hinduism: Ahimsa	39
3 Buddhism: Metta	62
4 Zoroastrianism: Good Conscience	81
5 Ancient Times and Religious Revolutions	94
6 Christianity: Blessed Are the Peacemakers	106
7 Islam: Salaam	128
8 First Nations of North America	151
9 The Sikhs	168
10 Bahá'ís: Unity	177
11 Revived Paganism	187
12 Tenrikyo: Joyous Life	194
13 Ethical Atheism and Humanism	206
Part II: Religion in Nonviolence Traditions	**215**
14 Sins: Religious Critiques of Societal Injustices	217
15 Virtues: Religious Character-Building for Nonviolent Discipline	232

16 Conflict Transformation	246
17 Campaigns and Active Confrontations	255
18 Coping and Healing	272
19 Building a Nonviolent Society	282
References	*297*
Subject Index	*307*
Scripture Index	*317*

Introduction

Buddhism: Anger must be overcome by the absence of anger; Evil must be overcome by good; Greed must be overcome by generosity; Lies must be overcome by truth. (Dhammapada 17:3)

Christianity: You have heard that it was said, "Love your neighbor and hate your enemy." But I tell you: Love your enemies and pray for those who persecute you. (Matthew 5:43–44)

Hinduism: The essence of non-violent technique is that it seeks to liquidate antagonisms but not the antagonists. (Mohandas Gandhi)

Islam: Good and evil are not equal; repair the evil done to you with something that is better. Then the enemy who did evil to you may turn into a close and true friend. (Qur'an 41:34)

Judaism: While a person may be individually pious, such good will pale in the face of the sin of not protesting against an emerging communal evil . . . such a pious person will be accountable for having been able to prevent it and did not. (Maharal of Prague)

WHAT IS NONVIOLENCE, AND HOW DOES IT WORK?

"Nonviolence" is a word that asserts what it is not—it is not violence. Since most things are not violent, it could cover more than we mean to cover here. Crimes, for instances, can be divided into those that are violent and those that are not (assault vs. shoplifting), and while this can be useful in some contexts, we mean something more positive here. In large part, we mean actions that counter violence or are alternatives to using violence for achieving worthy goals. This can be societywide or in personal lifestyles.

The Hindu word for nonviolence is ahimsa; *himsa* means violence, *a* means not, so ahimsa is "not violence." Because of Gandhi's pioneering work, the translation of this into English was popularized, and despite its negative nature—being "not" something—it has persevered. This is in large part because what it is not is so very important. Life is sacred, to be loved and respected, yet those that assert so can and do make an argument for taking life in some cases to preserve it elsewhere. Peace is to be pursued, but "just war" doctrines commonly declare specific wars as necessary for peace. Saying what an action must *not* be communicates something more.

There have been other words suggested that would be positive. Mohandas Gandhi proposed "satyagraha," which translates to "truth power." It is still a word that is common in some places, but neither the original word nor its translation have become commonplace. Other terms have come into common use to cover different aspects of nonviolence.

People Power

"People Power" is a very satisfying term in that it is positive and clear. It communicates immediately that we are discussing an assertive phenomenon with actual power. It states what kind of power it is in a way that people understand once they see how it works. It covers that aspect of nonviolence involving coordinated campaigns trying to achieve a very specific goal against an identifiable violent opponent. The term started in the Philippines in 1986 when a dictatorial leader tried to steal an election, and the achieved goal was for the dictator to leave and the person actually elected to take office. People Power happens when a large group of people refuse to cooperate with what they object to and set up viable alternatives.

It is based on an understanding of power as a psychological phenomenon: power exists because people decide it does. When people respect the decision-makers, then the decision-makers have power. When people do not respect them, but the decision-makers use violence to keep people in line, then the decision-makers have power. But if people refuse to cooperate even in the face of such violence, then the decision-makers' power disappears. That power was always based on cooperation, and enough noncooperation dissolves it.

Techniques of People Power include:

- *Strikes*. A refusal of a specific group to do specific work on behalf of specific (sometimes negotiable) demands.
- *General strikes*. The entire society deciding to stop work. Sometimes this is for just one day as a demonstration, and sometimes

Introduction 3

this is for the duration in response to a coup d'etat or a stolen election.
- *Boycotts.* Refusal to purchase specified products in the hopes of convincing those who sell them to alter their behavior.
- *Demonstrations.* These can range from an individual spray-painting graffiti to massive rallies. A greater number of people is far more effective, but smaller demonstrations can be the catalyst for creating larger ones. Whether or not they do so, they at least constitute a presence rather than an absence of objection.
- *Withdrawal.* People removing themselves from where those people need to be in order for the powerful to hold sway is often very effective.
- *Building alternative institutions.* Ranging from establishing good schools to providing alternative governments, this is a positive building up to replace the negative.

Creative variations on these and similar techniques can be considered to suit the situation.

Moral Jiu-Jitsu/Power of Conscience

"Jiu-jitsu" is a martial art that works by keeping opponents off-balance and using their own motions against them. Converting a martial term to a nonviolent one (which is commonly done), *moral jiu-jitsu* is when the opponents' understanding of themselves as doing the moral thing becomes unbalanced as the nonviolent activists convince them that the most moral thing to do is something different. Appeals to conscience are a major feature of nonviolent action. When successful, they will serve to help any campaign or other situation.

The helpfulness of the Power of Conscience includes:

- *Reaching a regime's officials.* Many times, while large demonstrations, strikes, or boycotts are occurring, individuals in the leadership structure of the violent institution have pangs of conscience. They can take helpful action ranging from giving out needed information to publicly announcing their own withdrawal.
- *Whistle-blowers.* Whether in leadership or one of the workers with access to material, just one person can release information. For example, one worker at the U.S. military headquarters, Daniel Ellsberg, released the Pentagon Papers in 1971; he has served as foundational inspiration for many other whistle-blowers.
- *Conscientious objection.* When done by massive numbers, objection to joining a required violent institution will be a form of People Power. If not many people feel called upon to do so, however, it

becomes a matter of individual witness for those who do. This is especially common for military drafts, but can also apply to such things as job requirements.
- *Conscience within violent situations.* Many government officials and soldiers with sound principles have intervened in effective ways in the midst of violence. A Nazi government official gave the Danes information about when the Jews would be rounded up so that the Danes could get them out safely first (see chapter 17). A Soviet submarine soldier under great social pressure nevertheless refused permission to launch a nuclear weapon during the Cuban Missile Crisis (see chapter 13).

Other Forms of Nonviolence

- Conflict resolution, which strives to bring willing parties to an agreement and can be quite creative
- Educational and advocacy efforts through various forms of speaking and writing
- Nonviolent communication in social interactions with others
- Social responsibility in purchasing decisions—avoiding the support of weapons production, worker mistreatment, environmental degradation, cruelty to animals, and so on
- Lifestyle choices
- Many, many other things

Courage Required

By opposing violence, nonviolence must necessarily also oppose apathy and cowardice. Both apathy and cowardice are major supports for the violence of others. Therefore, those who oppose violence oppose both apathy and cowardice every bit as much—perhaps more so. A person whose violence is based on a passion for social justice can be talked into using nonviolence instead on grounds of effectiveness, but a person who just does not care or is too afraid to do anything will not be able to handle the caring and courage that assertive nonviolence requires.

As Mohandas Gandhi put it,

> My nonviolence does not admit of running away from danger and leaving dear ones unprotected. Between violence and cowardly flight, I can only prefer violence to cowardice. I can no more preach nonviolence to a coward than I can tempt a blind man to enjoy healthy scenes. (Gandhi, 1924)

Introduction 5

It is frequent that the arguments in favor of violent action are based on the understanding that the alternatives of cowardice or of apathy are outrageous when injustices happen or when defense is needed against attacks. Throughout Part I we will see that it is common for religions or sections of religions otherwise based on nonviolence to use this reasoning to engage in defensive wars with no sense that they are being inconsistent. Their nonviolence was a matter of personal lifestyle and social interactions, but not of leaving themselves or innocent others vulnerable to attack.

Nonviolence then becomes a "third way": neither fight nor flight, but a way of fighting that does not involve injury and ideally one that appeals to consciences. Nonviolence advocates are as disdainful of cowards or those who do not care as are advocates of violence understood to be justified.

Nonviolence Is Effective

Gene Sharp is a prominent scholar who has written extensively on the historical cases of nonviolence (see the book list at the end).

More recently, due to the fact that so many campaigns have now happened that a statistical analysis on them can be run, scholar Erica Chenoweth (2012) has done an empirical study. She compares violent and nonviolent uprisings with clearly stated goals. She finds that 26% of the violent campaigns achieved their stated goal—but for nonviolent campaigns, 53% achieved their stated goal. So while almost half are not succeeding, nonviolent campaigns are roughly twice as likely to succeed as violent ones are.

This is made more remarkable upon the consideration that both forms require sound strategic thinking and well-thought-out tactics, and military science has been more focused on developing those well. Adding such discipline and learning from experience bids fair to improve the success rate for nonviolence in the future.

COVERING RELIGIONS

Religions Defined

Religion has been defined in a large number of ways, but for the purposes of this book, we are looking at organized religion and using the specific organizations that have been defined as individual religions.

The world's current major religions as defined by the largest number of adherents—hundreds of millions—are (in chronological order of age) Hinduism, Buddhism, Christianity, and Islam. They each get their own chapter in Part I. Other religions having millions of adherents include Judaism, which is ancient and foundational to other religions and to concepts needed for nonviolence, and the more recent Sikhism, Bahai, Tenrikyo, and revived Paganism (such as Wicca), all of which get complete chapters.

There are two which get chapters in spite of the fact that they have lower numbers of adherents currently, probably only in the hundreds of thousands. They are covered anyway because of having such a huge influence. Zoroastrianism is an ancient reaction against a violent society and influenced other monotheistic religions. The First Nations of North America had many religions, but as a category had an influence that far outpaces their current numbers.

Chapter 5 covers several different ancient religions. The philosophers Mo Tse in ancient China and Pythagoras in ancient Greece founded wisdom schools that are long gone, and some would argue whether they were actual religions. They are covered to show the deep roots in history that nonviolence advocacy has. This is important in a world where coverage of history often overemphasizes the wars that occurred and leaves us with the sense that this is all that history has been composed of. This gives the impression that the human race is more violent, and less nonviolent, than it really is. For that reason, we include some notable nonviolent actions from ancient times whose participants appealed to their gods and goddesses. Taoism is also covered here.

Ethical atheism is actually more an antireligion than a religion, but will be covered because there are insights about nonviolence and religion there as well.

Both Nonviolence and Violence

All of the religions have traditions of nonviolence, and all of them have traditions of violence as well, with the exception of ones that are fairly young. Jainism was founded on the principle of ahimsa, which means nonviolence, and criticized Hindus and Buddhists for failing to practice it sufficiently. Yet Jain rulers did engage in executions and aggressive wars. The Buddha offered ahimsa as a major principle, yet Buddhist rulers have done the same. Christianity was founded by a man who was tortured to death rather than offer violence to those committing injustice, and yet there has been plenty of shocking violence committed in its name.

Deterioration from founding principles is common, for at least four reasons:

1. The appeal of the argument that violence is necessary for defense of the religion and of innocent people.
2. The combination of religion and state, so that the interests of the state with its asserted monopoly on violence override and manipulate the religion's actual tenets.
3. Whenever the religion was imposed on a specific population because a ruler accepted it, there will be problems with sincerity and with understanding the tenets of the religion.
4. Massive violence needs justification in order to induce massive numbers of people to participate in it. Religion is conscripted to serve the purpose.

Yet the history of religion shows that nonviolence has historical roots that are quite deep. Many were founded on nonviolence principles, and the remainder developed them. Indigenous polytheistic religions (sometimes called "pagan") have wisdom traditions from which a nonviolence tradition can be drawn. The first reason for violence—defense of the religion or the innocent—can be addressed by understanding how techniques of nonviolence are in most cases superior for the purpose.

The only religions that do not have nonviolence as a possibility are (1) the ones where divine beings or inevitable forces are seen entirely as aids to conquest or (2) the ones with emperor worship, which was especially common in ancient times. In current times, Nazism—inasmuch as it could be seen as a religion—was a form of emperor worship; this is also seen now in North Korea. In these cases, alternative religions must be appealed to.

Religions that have no such conquering deities or emperors are often nevertheless conscripted to serve philosophies of violence. This is to be expected. The human mind does not function as a cartoon villain who laughs when dastardly deeds are done, knowing full well that they are dastardly. The human mind prefers to assert its own goodness. Therefore, it will appeal to cosmic forces to establish its own preferences.

As English poet J.C. Squire wrote when war clouds were gathering in Europe for World War I:

God heard the embattled nations sing and shout
"Gott strafe England!" and "God save the King!"
God this, God that, and God the other thing
"Good God!" said God, "I've got my work cut out." (Squire, 1916, p. 57)

Nevertheless, as long as people supporting violent institutions belong to a religion that has traditions of nonviolence, as will be true in almost all cases, an appeal can be made to them based on that religion. An appeal can also be made to observers, people whose method of supporting the violence is entirely by acquiescing and not by active participation. Such people are much more easily convinced, and when that happens, a movement grows.

Interfaith Dialogue and Action

When religious people get involved in nonviolent activism, they often notice that they must cooperate with people of other religions, or of other denominations, in order to get anything done. In the 1960s, U.S. Civil Rights Movement, for example, Jews and atheists were active with the predominant Christians, and everyone's participation was welcome. Though it fell apart afterward, the Indian independence movement required Hindus and Muslims to act together, and nonviolent activists in that area to this day emphasize the importance of harmony between the two religions, along with the other religions in the area.

There is a tendency toward ecumenism and even celebration of diversity, as this very book attests. People who remain strictly exclusive about their own religion are quite capable of engaging in nonviolent action and do all the time, but there is a tendency for reaching out in interfaith ways—especially when nonviolent activists note that violent conflict often comes with rigid doctrines and are therefore more inclined to avoid those.

However, doctrines themselves can vary widely in their applicability. While doctrines that allow or encourage violence are one thing and doctrines that insist on or encourage nonviolence are another, there are many doctrines that do not address nonviolence or violence that can be used either way, depending on the predilections of the people holding them.

For example, the doctrine of reincarnation with karma can mean we should be kind even to lowly animals because they may have been human beings before or may become so in the future. Vegetarian practice tends to be more prominent in those religions that believe in reincarnation. However, reincarnation can also be understood to be a perfect blame-the-victim strategy—whatever circumstances of poverty or injustice that people might find themselves in are ones they earned through previous lifetimes. Killing means only that one is sending someone on to another rebirth, and this can actually be a favor to them if it helps them expend some bad karma and avoid accruing more.

Similarly, the Christian doctrine of Original Sin could mean that nobody is perfect. The burden of trying to be so and castigation for not succeeding is lifted. Humility for one's self and tolerance and understanding for others becomes greater as judgmentalism diminishes. On the other hand—the violent hand—it could mean that judgmentalism instead increases, that all people deserve to have bad things to happen to them, and that congregants are constantly beaten down with what sinners they are and threats of "hellfire and brimstone."

In both cases, it is not the doctrine itself, but how it is used, that indicates whether nonviolence or violence will result.

Great Diversity

When not relevant, we are not including the multiple ways religions have divided up, beyond major groupings. Finer points of creed and outright arguments are not of interest to nonviolence. There are ample resources for covering the details of those divisions, and this book is focused entirely on the nonviolence tradition in each.

Importantly for nonviolence: a case could be made that rather than seeing these as "divisions," we could see them as *multiplications*. Different people have different ideas about what religious approach is best for them. Some cherish tradition, and others want to adapt to current circumstances or new insights. Some people want very formal ritual, others want rather informal ritual, and yet others want meditation or contemplation in addition to or instead of ritual. Some wish to appeal to reason, others are more mystical. Some want very strict rules for behavior, and others want looser and less rigid guidelines. Some want a sophisticated organizational structure, and others are more interested in spirituality that knows no such boundaries. Styles of worship and levels of individual or group discipline are bound to vary widely, and they do so within each religion.

Therefore, having multiple approaches allows everyone to find a home in that religion somewhere. This multiplies the number of adherents.

We will also not be covering critiques that religions could make of each other on the basis of violence and nonviolence. This could be a fertile ground for much commentary, but it is for a different book. The comments on forms of violence are ones that nonviolent adherents of each religion are already quite familiar with as a matter of critiquing their own religion.

OUTLINE OF THE CHAPTERS

Part I: Nonviolence in Religious Traditions

In Part I, the order of the chapters is roughly chronological, except that Judaism and Hinduism are both quite ancient and without clear-cut beginning points in terms of historical dates. Both are the progenitors of other religions, setting up the two most common groupings of religions in the world now.

Part I will consider the nonviolence tradition in each of the world's defined religions, one by one. We give basic background on each, including their overall histories and scriptures. Many will find these worth reading even if already familiar with the religion, since the understanding of nonviolence underlies the selection of coverage and editorial comments.

Next come the beliefs and practices related to nonviolence, followed by some of the history of nonviolent campaigns. These are the heart of the chapters.

We then mention a set list of forms of violence and the positions and practice each religion has for these forms. There are two reasons for this. One is simply to give background on those forms of violence the religion has been or has become good about opposing, thus explaining more about its nonviolent stance. The other is to have a clear-eyed view of where religions have failed. The main thrust of the book is to focus on the positive; the negative has received so much attention and distorts the reality. However, painting too rosy a picture amounts to a cover-up. Nonviolent activists who belong to any specific religion are keenly aware of the problems of violence within their own religion.

This starts with ancient forms not nearly as advocated now: blood sacrifice and slavery. Current widespread forms are war, the death penalty, infanticide and feticide, meat consumption and poverty. Finally, we cover violence that *must* relate to religion: violence in that religion's scriptures, and how they treat what they understand to be "heresy."

Finally, each chapter will end with the relationships of that religion to other religions and sometimes mention smaller related religions. Some of this will be information that is simply interesting, but most of it may be helpful in interfaith understandings. Interfaith actions are included here since in some situations they can be nonviolent actions. Worldwide peace depends on interreligious harmony.

Part II: Religions in Nonviolence Traditions

The first chapter of Part II looks at social problems utilizing the religious word "sin." There will be nonviolent activists who shy away from the word because of callous hellfire-and-brimstone connotations, but here we are simply referring to the religious critique of violence and social injustices. Labeling the problems is the first step.

The next chapter deals with solutions in terms of good character: the virtues that are quite necessary to nonviolent campaigns, interactions, and lifestyles.

We then go on to the practical applications: a chapter on conflict resolution or transformation of conflicts in which people are talking to each other and willing to listen; the next chapter on when one side is not willing to talk, since it understands it has power and does not wish to "give it up"; a chapter on coping and healing; and finally a chapter with notes on positive proactive ways of building a more nonviolent society.

NOTES ON STYLE

The author having a PhD in psychology and normally writing on that topic, the style for references in this book does not use footnotes or endnotes but instead the APA (American Psychological Association) style. This means that the citations in the text are by last name and year, and the reader who wants to find them goes to the References section at the back and finds the first author's last name alphabetically, where it is followed by the year. If there is no year, which happens frequently on web page sources, it is designated "n.d."—no date. The one exception to APA style is that the reference list also gives full first names instead of initials, so that information is not lost.

The current common worldwide calendar is used for historical years. This is derived from the Christian calendar, where "BC" means "Before Christ" and "AD" means Anno Domini, Latin for "Year of Our Lord," the number of years after the birth of Jesus. Because this is not meaningful in other religions, for them the notation of "BCE" means "Before the Current Era," and "CE" means "Current Era." The year numbers are the same.

Even in Christian terms, the years are inaccurate; they were set by a monk named Dionysius the Short, and he miscalculated. King Herod is important to the story of the birth of Jesus, yet Herod died in 4 BC, four years before the year Jesus was set to be born in this calendar.

Jesus would also have had to have been born in the year zero, being one year old in the year 1 AD, and yet there is no year zero. The calendar goes from 1 BC to 1 AD.

Nevertheless, the "BC" and "AD" notation will be used in chapter 6 on Christianity as being the Christian years, while all other chapters use BCE and CE. Chapter 1 on Judaism will also add the Jewish years for historical dates, which are based on the time the world was to have been created. Chapter 7 on Islam will add the Muslim years, on a calendar that starts with the all-important Hijra, escape from Mecca to Medina.

In Part I, when scriptures are cited in a specific religion's chapter, they come from that religion unless noted otherwise. In Part II, since the reader may not know from which scripture a citation comes, this is normally designated. Because the Bible for Jews is part of the Bible for Christians, citations from those books will be designated as coming from the Bible. For Christians, the Bible includes the New Testament, but this is not so for Jews, so when citing from those books, they will be designated as coming from the New Testament or as being a Gospel.

DELVING DEEPER

History and Effectiveness of Nonviolence

Waging Nonviolent Struggle: 20th Century Practice and 21st Century Potential
Gene Sharp
Boston: Extending Horizons Books, 2005
Web page: www.aeinstein.org

A Force More Powerful: A Century of Nonviolent Conflict
Peter Ackerman and Jack Duvall
New York: St. Martin's Press, 2000
Web page: www.aforcemorepowerful.org
Includes documentary series of same name, broadcast by PBS in the United States

Why Civil Resistance Works: The Strategic Logic of Nonviolent Conflict
Erica Chenowith and Maria Stephan
New York: Columbia University Press, 2012

Nonviolence: The History of a Dangerous Idea
Mark Kurlansky
New York: Random House/Modern Library, 2006

Recovering Nonviolent History: Civil Resistance in Liberation Struggles
Macie J. Barkowski, Editor
Boulder, CO: Lynne Rienner Publishers, 2013

Several Religions Consider Peace

Subverting Hatred: The Challenge of Nonviolence in Religious Traditions
Daniel L. Smith-Christopher, Editor
Maryknoll, NY: Orbis Books, 1998

Religion and Peacebuilding
Harold Coward and Gordon S. Smith, Editors
New York: State University of New York Press, 2004

Interfaith Just Peacemaking: Jewish, Christian, and Muslim Perspectives on the New Paradigm of Peace and War
Susan Brooks Thistlethwaite, Editor
New York: Palgrave MacMillan, 2012

Understanding World Religions: A Road Map for Justice and Peace
David Whitten Smith and Elizabeth Geraldine Burr
Lanham, MD: Rowman & Littlefield, 2015

PART I
Nonviolence in Religious Traditions

1

Judaism: Shalom

Major contributions of Judaism to nonviolence: a history and scriptures that highlight the needs of the oppressed and marginalized; a form of monotheism with equality of all human beings as a consequence; a peaceful creation story which, in contrast to contemporary tales, posits peace rather than violence as foundational to the world; a prophetic tradition in which people speak truth to power no matter the consequences to themselves; and a long history of remaining a coherent faith group under a series of empires and as a marginalized minority group in a variety of countries, thereby showing creativity, endurance, and firmness.

JEWISH HISTORY AND SCRIPTURES

Historically, Judaism introduced monotheism to the world in a long-lasting way, and this is a major feature of the religion. The first recorded stirrings of monotheism were with Pharaoh Akhenaten of Egypt, who reigned for 17 years in the mid-1300s BCE, but this was imposed from on top by a hierarchy and did not survive his death. Given the timing and vicinity, this may have been one of the many Egyptian influences on Judaism. Zoroastrianism was also a form of monotheism arising in the area of Persia, allowing for interaction with Judaism.

According to the Jews' historical scriptures and archeological evidence, the concept of monotheism grew among the population slowly before it took firm hold. This is how religious innovations normally work when they lead to long-lasting religions—grassroots rather than imposed from on top and taking time to develop as sincere adherents start small and become more numerous. Sociologist Rodney Stark develops this point in several of his books on history of religions.

The primary Jewish scripture is the Torah, also called the Pentateuch, the first five books of the Bible. These are the most important and set the foundation for all that follows. They start with the creation of the world, cover formational events for the human community, and then cover formational events for the Jewish community. The formational events start with the tales of Abraham, his son Isaac, and his son Jacob. Jacob in adulthood gained the name of Israel, which is where the term "children of Israel" for the Jews comes from. The story is that a large group of their descendants were enslaved in the land of Egypt, and as a group they managed to escape under the leadership of Moses, along with his brother Aaron and his sister Miriam. Thus, the very foundation of the religion involves sympathy with the oppressed and lack of sympathy for those who oppress them. In their scriptures, admonishments to avoid oppressing others will commonly make reference to their own history of being the oppressed (for example, see Deuteronomy 5:14–15, 15:14–15, 16:11–12, 24:17–22). So their concept of the one God is of one who always takes the side of and occasionally frees the oppressed.

Several other books of the Bible then cover subsequent history. Jews remained a loose group of tribes until at one point they developed into a kingdom. During the fourth king's reign, King Rehoboam, in around 931 BCE (about AM 2830, Hebrew calendar), they split into two, Israel and Judah, over an argument that said king was overly oppressive (1 Kings 12:1–16). While the historical books constantly refer to chronicles in which other acts of the rulers were written, these have not survived. The books that became scriptures were primarily interested in the moral components of their reigns.

This included whether they worshiped idols and other gods and whether they were just in their dealings. The two were seen as being connected; other gods were an excuse for misbehavior, as a way of legitimizing injustices that the one God of Israel would not tolerate. Other gods could also demand appalling blood sacrifices (see, for example, Leviticus 18:21; Deuteronomy 18:10; 2 Kings 16:3, 17:17, 21:6, 23:10; Jeremiah 7:31, 19:3).

Additional books, called the Writings, include a large book of poetry called Psalms, a book mainly involving proverbs, and books offering essays on the topic of wisdom. These are essentially ahistorical and timeless in a Wisdom tradition that is found in several different religions.

The set of scriptural books called The Prophets are mainly historical writings from the prophets or their sympathizers. These decry injustices of the monarchs, predict disasters that will arise as a result of those injustices, and deal with the aftermath when those disasters do occur. They can be remarkably harsh in some places and admirably hopeful in others.

The two major disasters were that the Assyrian empire conquered the northern kingdom of Israel, and centuries later the Babylonian empire conquered the southern kingdom of Judah. With the Assyrian invasion, some people fled down to Judah and others were dispersed. That was the end of Israel and of those tribes. In the case of the Babylonian conquest, the Jewish elite were taken off to live in exile in Babylonia, where they festered for about 70 years. The Persian king then conquered Babylon and liberated them to go back to Israel. Their scriptures and practices had kept them coherent as a group during the time of the exile, and continued to develop once several of them returned to Judea and kept contact with those who remained in Persia.

Jews were then ruled by a succession of empires. They never fully accommodated themselves to any of them, but kept their religion in protest of them all. They did manage to throw off the Greek empire and have their own line of kings for about a century (164–63 BCE). What was scripture became fairly solidified over time, and a Greek translation called the Septuagint became available as a service to the wide number of Jews who were living around the empire and did not know the original Hebrew (and some Aramaic) in which most of the scriptures were written.

Once the Roman Empire took over in 63 BCE and appointed the kings and high priests, events intensified. Messianic fever was high, and several people laid claim to being the Messiah who would deliver Israel. All were killed by the Romans, and all but one had essentially no more influence once that occurred. That one exception, however, did not immediately get Israel out from under the violence of the Romans, so he was not recognized in Judaism as being the Messiah. Those who did accept him as such launched another religion with Judaism at its root, to be covered in chapter 6.

War broke out against the Roman Empire in 66 CE (AM 3827), and lasted four years until the Romans invaded the capital city Jerusalem and destroyed the huge and magnificent Temple. That Temple had served for some time as the central focal point for the ceremonies involving forgiveness and the place where the Holy One dwelt. Its destruction was a huge blow to the religion, an event still mourned by Jews to this day.

The aristocratic elite (Sadducees) and the priests were no longer organized entities and became entirely uninfluential in further developments. The Pharisees were more in touch with common people, and because their focus had been on everyone living pure and ethical lives according to the scriptural law, which can be done anywhere and without worship at the Temple, they were the group that best survived and kept the religion robust from then on. They were no longer called Pharisees, but rabbis. The recent development of synagogues had served those Jews who lived outside Israel, and now that almost all Jews did, they had the synagogue tradition to serve as a foundation for the needed transition. The religion stayed strong despite the horrific slaughter and political collapse they had just endured. Rabbinic Judaism is the form that survived and is still practiced these two thousand years later.

Rabbinic writings are quite extensive in the Talmud, a 64-tractate collection of writings that interpret and expand upon the original scriptures. In standard print, it is over 6,200 pages long, and offers the teachings and opinions of thousands of rabbis. Topics range from law and ethics and customs to history and stories. It is the basis for the codes of Jewish Law, based on the laws in the Bible but going into more detail.

The dispersion of Jews all over the world is called the Diaspora. Many went to Europe, some went to Africa, and many stayed in many parts of the Middle East. When the Muslims took over in Spain in the 700s, many Jews flocked there, because their talents were welcome. When they were expelled by Catholics in 1492, the Ottoman emperor was astonished at the foolishness of sending talented people away and was delighted to take many in.

Throughout the centuries, Jews have been a minority group in a large number of countries, and in numerous areas where they have been badly mistreated. They have been limited in what occupations they could have and where they could live. They endured insults during mild times, and when events became extreme, they were victims of large massacres. While it is unsurprising that some Jews left the religion and went to live their lives outside the community, the perseverance and endurance of a community through all this treatment for such a long time is itself an admirably remarkable nonviolent achievement.

This came to a head, however, with the most horrific massacre of all, most commonly referred to as the *Holocaust*, also called by Jews the *Shoah*. Germany, Eastern Europe, and surrounding areas had attracted

Judaism: Shalom

a large Jewish population in previous centuries, and that population was now at the mercy of Nazi ideology, which was genocidal. Nazis were racists who used the concept that Jews were a race, as opposed to a religion. They made use of centuries of bigotry and contemporary technology to kill around 6 million Jews and millions of others, primarily in concentration camps. Survivors and the children and grandchildren of survivors are still recuperating from this major trauma, as is the entire community, and the entire world.

The reestablishment of the state of Israel occurred as a direct result of this, and serves as a focal point to many but not all current Jews. Many Jews still live elsewhere, as has been true since the Babylonian exile around 2,500 years ago. There are currently around 14 million Jews in the world today.

Jews who have won the Nobel Peace Prize as nonviolent activists (not as deal-making politicians) are:

- Cowinner Tobias Michel Karel Asser, 1911 (AM 5672), for his work in forming the Permanent Court of Arbitration at the first Hague Peace Conference of 1899
- Cowinner Alfred Hermann Friedd, 1911 (AM 5672), an Austrian Jewish pacifist, journalist, and cofounder of the German Peace Society in 1892
- René Cassin, 1968 (AM 5729), for his work on helping to draft the Universal Declaration of Human Rights adopted by the United Nations in 1948
- Elie Wiesel, 1986 (AM 5747), for his work on Holocaust remembrance
- Joseph Rotblat, 1995 (AM 5756), shared with the Pugwash Conferences in which he was a leader. Rotblat was the only physicist to leave the Manhattan Project (the U.S. team that invented nuclear weapons), doing so on grounds of conscience, and continued contributing his expertise and advocacy against nuclear weapons

JEWISH BELIEFS AND PRACTICES SERVING AS FOUNDATIONS FOR NONVIOLENCE

In the Beginning

The first chapter of the book of Genesis is widely known for its beautiful poetry and images of the creation of the world. Day by day, the one God creates specific things, and then affirms their goodness.

At the time it was written, it was actually an assertive advocacy of nonviolence. It will startle many to think of it that way, but the key to doing so can be found by comparing it to the context out of which it came.

Scholars who are familiar with the Babylonian creation myths in the *Enuma Elish* can see that the Hebrew story used the same stages of creation. Yet the original Babylonian story was full of horrific violence: the god Marduk slew the dragon Tianmut (who was his own mother or grandmother). Her body was divided and one half became the earth and the other became the sky. In other words, conquest and violence were at the very foundation of the creation of the universe. The emperors and members of the elite and the conquering army wanted to see it that way.

Jews were at this point a minority group among the dominating Babylonians. They were a conquered people keeping a firm grasp on their identity as a group and on their religion, which already included stories of successful rebellion against a previous empire.

So they recast the story entirely. Not gods, but one God. The stars were made by that God for a practical purpose, and were not gods themselves. The one God created everything in an orderly and logical way—and most of all, *peacefully*. Then, at each stage, God saw that it was good.

This was a basis that aided the later development of science, which would be impossible under the arbitrary rules of the original myth. It was a basis that helped the development of democracy since the religious validation for violent conquest and admiration for tyranny was undone. And it set peace and nonviolence at the foundation of the world, giving a perspective far different from those who wanted to use violence to dominate others.

As Anthony Prete put it:

> Something inside me clicked into place when I learned that the seven-day creation account took shape during or after the Babylonian Exile (587–538 B.C.E.). Of course! What else would you do after a conquering army had laid siege to your city, savagely killed your people or drove them into exile, and reduced to rubble the temple where you communed with your God? . . . This poem [Genesis 1:1–2:4] affirms their God as the power and the genius that called

into existence, part by part, the entire world as they knew it.... Had I not known this exilic background—which the text presumes but does not reveal—I would not have recognized this text as a bold and defiant manifesto by a defeated and dislocated people. (Prete, 2006, pp. 31–32)

The original violent myths are known mainly to scholars and others interested in that area. The nonviolent alternative is one that far more people, including children, are familiar with. Its influence has now lasted millennia.

Monotheism

Nonviolence does not require monotheism, since polytheists, pantheists, and atheists have all been active in nonviolent campaigns and lifestyles. Nevertheless, it is a perspective that can be helpful. This is explained in Malachi 2:10: "Are we not all children of the same Father? Are we not all created by the same God? Then why do we betray each other, violating the covenant of our ancestors?" The founder of Hasidism, Rabbi Yisroel Ben Eliezer, also called Baal Shem Tov (1698–1760), explained it this way: "'Thou shalt love thy neighbor as thyself.' Why? Because every human being has a root in the Unity, and to reject the minutest particle of the Unity is to reject it all."

As Thomas Cahill put it in *The Gifts of the Jews*:

The Jews gave us a whole new vocabulary, a whole new Temple of the Spirit, an inner landscape of ideas and feelings that had never been known before. Over many centuries of trauma and suffering they came to believe in one God, the Creator of the universe, whose meaning underlies all his creation and who enters human history to bring his purposes to pass. Because of their unique belief—monotheism— the Jews were able to give us the Great Whole, a unified universe that makes sense and that, because of its evident superiority as a worldview, completely overwhelms the warring and contradictory phenomena of polytheism. They gave us the Conscience of the West, the belief that this God who is One is not the God of outward show but the "still, small voice" of conscience, the God of compassion, the God who "will be there," the God who cares about each of his creatures, especially the human being he created "in his own image," and that he insists we do the same. (Cahill, 1998, pp. 239–40)

Prophets

Truth is what it is, not what the king decides he wants it to be. The just and merciful and compassionate way to behave is the behavior to be expected, even from—especially from—rulers who are inclined to be arrogant about their power and commit all kinds of violence for their own material benefit. While many ancient rulers used worship of many gods to find a god who would approve the dictatorial behavior they wanted to do, those rulers throughout the ages who claimed monotheism also managed to rationalize engaging in grotesque injustices. They would often draft the one God to endorse their own agenda (traditionally called "taking the Lord's name in vain").

Thus arose in Israel and Judah (as their contribution to the Axial Age, see Chapter 5) a group of prophets who spoke out against the status quo in no uncertain terms. They used eloquent words as well as symbolic actions to make their points and appeal to consciences.

Jeremiah, for example, was frequently jailed for speaking out, but persisted. He took a clay jar and gathered elders and priests, who had been making fiery human sacrifices of children to the gods Baal and Molech. Jeremiah then denounced them and dashed the jar down, shattering it to pieces, to show how dangerous their behavior was (Jeremiah 19). Yet when his prediction of disaster came true and the Babylonians were about to conquer Judah and carry people off to exile, he deliberately bought a farm as a sign of hope that they would be returning (Jeremiah 32:6–15). His symbols were not just protests, but proclaimed an expectation for future peace.

These were the nonviolence campaigns of the day, rebellion that was absent in other contemporary cultures in the vicinity. The rulers against whom the prophets inveighed are only remembered now because of being part of the prophet's story. These nonviolence campaigns have an endurance that has now lasted millennia. They were so foundational to concepts needed to nonviolence that people who engage in nonviolent campaigns nowadays will often be referred to as *prophetic*.

Philip Yancey comments on this:

> God granted them (and, through them, us) the extraordinary vision to see past this world, dominated as it is by great powers and larger-than-life tyrants, to a different level of reality. . . . Who is really running the world? the Hebrew prophets asked. King Ahab or God? The Assyrian empire or God? (Or, we might add, the U.S. Congress or God?) With no weapon other than the sheer moral force of the

spoken word, they stood against the powers of their day. One of the great vindications of the prophets is that their predictions, which seemed preposterous at the time, proved true. What did pipsqueak Hebrews know about the intricacies of power politics? A lot, as it turned out: Assyria fell, as did Babylon, mighty Babylon, and eventually Persia, Greece, and ultimately even Rome. Today, archeologists in Iraq must dig through layers of dirt to find any remnants of Babylonian culture. Nebuchadnezzar is a mere footnote of history. Yet the prophecies of Jeremiah and Daniel have been preserved and are still studied by millions around the world. (Yancey, 1999, pp. 188, 190)

For the most part, the prophets did not make the changes they were hoping for in their own time. But their writings and stories are still read every day by millions of people.

An End to War

The prophets also gave us a lot of images that we still use today for ideals about peace. One common image comes from two different prophets, and so was probably a common idea in Jerusalem at the time: "They will beat their swords into plowshares and their spears into pruning hooks. Nation will not take up sword against nation, nor will they train for war anymore" (Micah 4:3; Isaiah 2:4). "The Peaceable Kingdom," with the lion lying down with the lamb, is based on the vision of Isaiah 11:6–9. These are the most well-known of many examples throughout the prophets; another example is that Hosea also has God putting an end to war: "I will break bow and sword and weapon of war and sweep them off the earth, so that all living creatures may lie down without fear" (Hosea 2:18).

The Psalms also take up this theme in places:

Some boast of chariots and some of horses
but our boast is in the name of the Lord our God.
They totter and fall,
but we rise up and are full of courage. (Psalms 20:7–8)

A king is not saved by a great army,
nor a warrior delivered by great strength.
A man cannot trust his horse to save him,
nor can it deliver him for all its strength.
The Lord's eyes are turned towards those who are in awe of him.
  (Psalms 33:16–19)

The Lord sets no store by the strength of horse
and takes no pleasure in runner's legs;
his pleasure is in those who are in awe of him,
who wait for his true love. (Psalms 147:10–11)

From end to end of the earth he stamps out war:
he breaks the bow, he snaps the spear
and burns the shield in the fire. (Psalms 42:9)

Let me hear the words of the Lord:
are they not words of peace,
peace to his people and his loyal servants
and to all who turn and trust in him?
Deliverance is near to those who worship him,
so that glory may dwell in our land.
Love and fidelity have come together;
justice and peace join hands. (Psalms 85:8–10)

This theme is carried on also in the Talmud. For example, "Great is peace, because peace is to the earth what yeast is to dough. If the Holy One, blessed be He, had not given peace to the earth, the sword and wild beasts would desolate the world" (*Baraita de Perek ha-shalom*). Peace is even more important than the most basic commandment: "Great is peace, because if the Jews were to practice idolatry, and peace prevailed among them at the same time, God would say, 'I cannot punish them, because peace prevails among them'" (Gen. Rabbah 38:6).

Protest

The Jewish tradition is full of positive attitudes toward protest. At the very foundation, Genesis chapter 18 has a classic story where Abraham politely protests the very plans of God. God was going to wipe out Sodom due to its great sin, and Abraham proposes this is unjust if there are righteous people there. He talks him down from 50 to 40 to 30 to 20 to 10 righteous people, that the whole city would be spared. Similarly, Moses and Aaron protest when God wants to strike a whole community on the grounds that only the sinful ones should be struck (Numbers 16:20–22). In the book of Job, Job protested against being treated unfairly himself. His three friends scolded him that he must have done something wrong or else the calamities would not have happened to him. Yet when God appeared in the whirlwind, he declared Job to be right and the friends to be wrong (Job 42:7). God likes protest.

The Talmud makes a quite explicit case:

> Whoever can protest against the injustices of his [or her] family but refrains from doing so, is accountable for the crimes of his [or her] family. Whoever can protest against the injustices of the people of his [or her] community, but refrains from doing so, is accountable for the crimes of his [or her] community. Whoever is able to protest against the injustices of the entire world, but refrains from doing so, is accountable for the crimes of the whole world. (Shabbat 54b)

Another Talmudic passage (Gittin 55b–56a) explains why Jerusalem was destroyed by the Romans. There was a man in Jerusalem who loved Kamtza and hated Bar-Kamtza. He intended to invite Kamtza to a feast but his servant mistakenly invited Bar-Kamtza instead. The man threw Bar-Kamtza out, even after Bar-Kamtza offered to pay for the entire feast if allowed to stay. Bar-Kamtza said: "Since the Sages sat here and did not protest. . . . I will go slander the Jews to [Caesar]." According to this story, Jerusalem was destroyed because the Sages witnessed an injustice and did not protest. While this may be historically dubious, the existence of the story itself says much about the requirement to protest.

Another Talmudic passage says: "If the man of learning participates in public affairs and serves as judge or arbitrator, he gives stability to the land. But if he sits in his home and says to himself, 'what have the affairs of society to do with me? . . . Why should I trouble myself with the people's voices of protest? Let my soul dwell in peace!' If he does this, he overthrows the world" (Sanhedrin 54b). Note the theme here that those who protest disturb the peace, so that the people who are actually building peace are accused of doing the opposite because they raise tensions with those who would rather ignore what is being protested. This is addressed again: "If the community is in trouble, a person must not say, 'I will go to my house and eat and drink, and peace shall be with thee, O my soul.' But a person must share in the trouble of the community even as Moses did. He [or she] who shares in its troubles is worthy to see its consolation" (Taanit 11a).

The importance of protest is also shown by Rabbi Judah Loew, a medieval philosopher, also called Maharal of Prague (ca. 1525–1609), who explained: "While a person may be individually pious, such good will pale in the face of the sin of not protesting against an emerging communal evil . . . such a pious person will be accountable for having been able to prevent it and did not" (Kimelman, 1970, p. 41).

Enemies as Friends

The concept of treating even enemies well is one theme through Jewish history. Biblically, there are such admonitions as "Do not rejoice when your enemy falls, and let not your heart be glad when he stumbles" (Proverbs 24:17) and "If your enemy is hungry, give him bread to eat; and if he is thirsty, give him water to drink; for you will heap coals of fire on his head, and the Lord will reward you" (Proverbs 25:21).

In the midrash of the Talmud there is a story of Rabbi Meir praying for the death of some robbers on the highways who were terrorizing the neighborhood. His wife Beruriah protested such a prayer as illegitimate. She expounded Scripture, saying it is written "Let sins cease." Is it written "Let sinners cease?" No. The word is "sins." This is in Psalms 104:35, and it goes on "and let the wicked be no more." She pointed out that once the sins have ceased, there will be no more wicked men. She asserted that he should rather pray that they will repent. Then there will be no more wicked people. So he changed his prayer—and they did repent.

A Jew in Spain at the time of Muslim rule, Samuel ibn Nagrela (993–1056) rose to prominent positions in the king's court. An enemy spoke to him harshly in the king's presence. The king gave orders for Samuel to tear out the offender's foul tongue. Instead, Samuel treated him with kindness and won his friendship. He explained to the king: "I have torn out his angry tongue and given him a gentle one instead" (*Avot De-Rabbi Natan* 23).

HISTORICAL NONVIOLENT ACTIONS

Biblical Noncooperation

When the Hebrews were enslaved in Egypt, the story goes, the Pharaoh feared that they were becoming too numerous and decided to dispense with neonates who were most likely to grow up to take up arms—the males. He ordered two Hebrew midwives, Shiphrah and Puah, to kill male children as they were born. The two women told him that the Hebrew mothers were already delivered of the children before they showed up. The Pharaoh at first apparently accepted the idea that once the children were entirely born, it was too late—only at birth was the proper time for killing. The boys were saved for the time being, and the scriptures comment that God was pleased with the midwives and blessed them (Exodus 1: 15–21).

This form of noncooperation is not using truth to stand up to power, but rather using deception. Such trickery is commonly found among all oppressed people as they deal with their oppressors, and so many tales of admired trickery are found throughout the Bible as well as throughout the stories of oppressed peoples around the world and throughout history.

Such deceptions, which are not violent, share with active nonviolence the basic feature of noncooperation with destructive authority. However, they share with violence the feature of not being long-lasting and only working in temporary emergencies. In this case, after all, Pharaoh finally decided to take more extreme action when he found this order did not work. The root of the problem was never addressed. Trickery can also make things worse in the long run by giving oppressed groups a reputation that feeds stereotypes.

The book of Daniel offers noncooperation more clearly done with honest truth-telling. In the third chapter, three young men—Shadrach, Meshach, and Abednego—refuse to bow to the king and so are thrown into a fiery furnace. In the sixth chapter, Daniel continues to pray to the Holy One after all have been ordered not to, and so is thrown into a den of hungry lions. In both cases, miraculous intervention causes the young men to survive their ordeals, and thereby be vindicated. They were all firm in their convictions, and remained polite to the kings who were ordering their problems—whether that was sincere or merely politic is not clear. While the deliverance was expected, it was not assured. The three young men told the king, "Our God is able to deliver us, *but if not*, we still will not bow" (Daniel 3:17–18).

In the third chapter of the book of Esther, the Persian government official Haman had arranged for a legal requirement that he be bowed down to, but the Jewish Mordechai refused despite threats of dire consequences. When these consequences turned out to be an order for the annihilation of all Jews on a certain day, Esther risked death by going to see the emperor without being invited, in a successful attempt to avert this (Esther 4 and 5).

Obadiah hid prophets in order to save their lives when Queen Jezebel was killing them (1 Kings 18:3–4). When King Saul ordered his soldiers to massacre some priests, they refused (1 Samuel 22:17).

Some take these stories literally, others believe them to be legends built upon actual events, and yet others think the stories were essentially made up. Which one is true is beside the point here: the point is, the point of view of the stories is sympathetic to those who refuse to cooperate with tyrants, and so the stories are part of the background of the Jewish tradition of nonviolence.

Maccabees

When Antiochus as a Greek ruler was trying to eliminate Judaism by decreeing the Jews were to act more like Greeks and ignore their own laws, there was a successful military response setting up a dynasty of Judean kings in 164 BCE (AM 3597). This is celebrated in the books of First and Second Maccabees found in the deuterocanonical section of the Catholic Bible, having come from the Greek Septuagint. But the books are not found in the Jewish list of the scriptures as set by the rabbis, and therefore are not in the Protestant Bible either. Judas Maccabaeus is never mentioned in the Talmud. In addition to the rabbis observing the Judean violence that followed that victory, by the time the rabbis were deciding which writings would be in the canon, the militaristic response to empire had recently proved disastrous with the destruction of the Temple by the Roman Empire in 70 CE (AM 3831) and the dispersion of people away from Judea. While the Jewish holiday of Hanukkah commemorates the victory, the passage for reading on the Sabbath of Hanukkah is from Zechariah: "Not by might and not by power but by my spirit, says the Lord of hosts" (Zechariah 4:6).

But there was also nonviolent resistance to Antiochus. People fled to the wilderness with their whole families and their possessions. This was an act of massive withdrawal that led to diminishing tax revenues. There was an active policy to bring them back, a search in 166 BCE (AM 3595), and punishment for fleeing gave way to an amnesty since punishment was not working (Bickerman, 1949, pp. 97–98).

First-Century Nonviolent Rebellions

Pontius Pilate was the Roman Empire's governor of Judea, from 25–36 CE. He is most famous for the sentencing of a well-known person a few years after this incident; the following event occurred around 26 or 27 CE (AM 3787 or 3788), right about the beginning of his term. As recounted by Josephus, a Jewish historian writing just a few decades later, about 75 CE (AM 3836):

> As procurator of Judea, Tiberius sent Pilate, by night and under cover, to bring into Jerusalem the images of Caesar known as standards. At daybreak, this caused an enormous disturbance among the Jews. Those nearby were alarmed at the sight since it meant that

their laws had been trampled on—for those laws do not permit any image to be set up in the city. The angry city mob was joined by a huge influx of people from the countryside. The Jews rushed off to Pilate in Caesarea and begged him to remove the standards from Jerusalem and to respect their ancestral laws. When Pilate refused, they threw themselves down on the ground around his house and stayed put for five days and nights.

The next day, Pilate took his seat on the tribunal in the great stadium and summoned the crowds, pretending to be ready to give them an answer. Instead he gave a pre-arranged signal to his armed soldiers to surround the Jews. Finding themselves in a ring of troops three deep, the Jews were dumbfounded. Then Pilate declared that he would cut them down unless they accepted the images of Caesar, and nodded to the soldiers to draw their swords. As if by arrangement, the Jews all fell to the ground, extended their necks, and proclaimed that they were ready to be killed rather than transgress the law. Astonished by the intensity of their religious fervor, Pilate ordered the immediate removal of the standards from Jerusalem. (Josephus, *Jewish Wars*, Book 2, Chapter 9, 2–3)

This is a classic pattern of nonviolent action: The sit-down was a confrontation. The response was a threat of violence. The protesters responded without showing fear and did not make any threats. They stuck to their demands with courage. In this case, it worked. A sympathetic dramatization based on this incident can be found near the beginning of the CBS mini-series called *Jesus*.

A similar incident occurred in the year 40 CE (AM 3801). The Roman Emperor Caligula, also called Gaius, decided to put up a statue of Jupiter, the chief Roman god, with features that remarkably resembled his own, in the Temple in Jerusalem. According to Josephus writing in about 93 CE (AM 3854):

> [Gaius sent Petronius] with orders to lead a large force into Judea and, if the Jews consented to receive him, to set up an image of Gaius in the Temple of God. If, however, they were obstinate, he was to subdue them by force of arms and to set it up. . . . Many tens of thousands of Jews came to Petronius at Ptolemais with petitions not to use force to make them transgress and violate their ancestral code. . . . Now Petronius saw from their words that their spirit was not easily to be put down and that it would be impossible for him without a battle to carry out Gaius's request and set up his image. Indeed, there would be great slaughter. Hence he gathered up his friends and attendants and hastened to Iberias, for he wished to

take note of the situation of the Jews there. As before, many tens of thousands faced Petronius on his arrival. . . . "Will you then go to war with Caesar?" said Petronius. "On no account would we fight," they said, "but we will die sooner than violate our laws." And falling on their faces and baring their throats, they declared that they were ready to be slain. They continued to make these supplications for forty days. Furthermore, they neglected their fields, and that, though it was time to sow the seed. . . .

At this juncture [several officials] appeared before Petronius and appealed to him . . . not to incite the people to desperation but to write to Gaius telling how incurable was their opposition to receiving the statue and how they had left their fields to sit protesting, and that they did not choose war, since they could not fight a war, but would be glad to die sooner than transgress their customs. Let him point out that, since the land was unsown, there would be a harvest of banditry, because the requirements of tribute could not be met. (Josephus, *Jewish Antiquities*, Book 18, Chapter 8, 2–4)

Petronius relented, deciding that he would rather die himself than kill several thousand unarmed people. He sent a letter to Gaius suggesting the statue was a bad idea. Gaius was furious and sent Petronius a letter ordering him to commit suicide. But that letter was on a slow-moving ship, and before it got to Petronius, word had already arrived that Gaius had been assassinated, in January of the year 41. So Petronius's life was spared.

The Jewish historian Philo also tells this story, but his version has the crops already harvested, with government officials fearing the crops would be sabotaged. Either way, there was a farmers' strike to go along with all the massive nonviolent demonstrations.

The Jews made a point of it that the crowds included women and children. Whole families came. The fact that the men were unarmed was shown especially well by the families being there.

FORMS OF VIOLENCE

This section will be included in each chapter, with generally the same list of forms of violence—those connected to religions and those that are common political issues. Since it is the same list, there will be times when it would be puzzling to bring up the topic, but comparisons and developments are more easily ascertained with a standardized list.

Blood Sacrifice

Ritual human sacrifice to please, placate, or bargain with divinity was frowned on in Jewish scriptures. There is a story that God commanded Abraham to sacrifice his beloved son Isaac, but the sacrifice was stopped by an angel (Genesis 22). There is another story about sacrifice of a grown daughter (Judges 11), but the moral of the story was how foolish it was to have made the offer. More commonly, the scriptures cite human sacrifice as an abomination practiced by other peoples that they were strictly prohibited from practicing themselves (Deuteronomy 12:31, 18:10; 2 Kings 17:17, 23:10; Psalms 106:37–38; Isaiah 57:5; Jeremiah 32:35; Ezekiel 16:20–21, 20:31, 23:37–39).

Ritual animal sacrifice, on the other hand, was practiced for the first several centuries of Judaism and had elaborate rules on how it should be done. Several of the prophets decried it as a poor substitute for justice or love (Hosea 6:6; Isaiah 1:11–17; Amos 5:21–24; Jeremiah 7:22–23). Because it was entirely restricted to being done in the Temple in Jerusalem, it ceased almost entirely with the Temple's destruction in 70 CE (AM 3831).

Currently there is a custom called "Kaporos" (atonements) before Yom Kippur (Jewish Day of Atonement) where some Orthodox Jews ritually sacrifice a chicken by chanting and transferring their sins symbolically onto the bird while swinging the bird around their heads, after which the chicken is slaughtered. Since this custom started in the Middle Ages and coins are another long-standing custom that can be used in this ceremony, many Jews advocate that nonviolent alternative. The mandate prohibiting cruelty to animals is called *tsa'ar ba'alei chaim*.

Slavery

Since the Hebrew nation's story began as God's help in escaping from slavery in Egypt, there is an antislavery theme in the religion. This has been used productively by later slaves in places such as the United States.

Still, slavery was practiced by the ancient Jews, a widespread custom in the ancient world. Rules about the treatment of slaves can be found in the very book describing the fleeing from slavery, Exodus 21:1–11. This includes a time limit on slavery for those slaves who want it, and is otherwise more humane than the slave laws of the surrounding cultures.

The presence of slavery in the Bible was used by later proslavery advocates as late as the 19th century. Current Jewish practice is as antislavery as the rest of modern society.

War

War was commonly practiced at times when Jews had a nation and were therefore in a position to engage in it. Later, Moses Maimonides (1138–1204) consolidated and expounded the "just war" laws and so is often referred to for what the rules are. The current state of Israel engages in war frequently. Conscientious objection is quite possible but not common, and Jews have been prominent in antiwar protests in Israel and elsewhere.

The Death Penalty

The death penalty was practiced for a wide number of crimes until the dispersion of the Jews in the Diaspora deprived them of authority to impose it. In modern Israel, it is allowed only in wartime and for genocide, crimes against humanity, war crimes, treason, and crimes against the Jewish People. The only person actually executed by Israel was the Nazi leader Adolph Eichmann in 1962 (AM 5722).

Infanticide and Feticide

Infanticide and feticide are not directly addressed in the scriptures, but observation in the Greco-Roman era indicates that at least by that time both were prohibited. Contemporary Jewish historian Josephus, writing probably in the early second century, reports that God "forbids women to cause abortion of what is begotten, or to destroy it afterward" (*Against Apion*, 2:25). This was an era when decisions about whether children lived or died were made by the patriarch of the family. In centuries since, infanticide has remained prohibited. Abortion has more variety of views in the modern world and is legal under some conditions in Israel.

Meat

Dietary restrictions, called *kosher*, do include being humane to animals slaughtered for food. A vegetarian diet is indicated as the first diet (Genesis 1:29) with meat-eating being a later concession (Genesis 9:3). A vegetarian diet would fill all the rules to be entirely kosher (except for rabbinical blessing). This is why Daniel and his friends wanted a fully vegetarian diet when in the emperor's court in Babylon (Daniel 1:8–15).

With the destruction of the Temple, the sacrificial system ended. Since the killing of animals outside of sacrifice was forbidden (Leviticus 17:3–4), many Jews gave up meat-eating. In the Talmud, Rabbi Yishmael is quoted as saying, "From the day that the holy Temple was destroyed, it would have been right to have imposed upon ourselves the law prohibiting the eating of flesh" (Tract Babba Bathra 60b).

There are many modern-day advocates of vegetarianism as most consistent with Jewish practice (Schwartz, 2001).

Poverty

The violence of poverty (structural violence) is a constant theme. Governmental officials and other rich people who caused it were excoriated by the scriptures and by the prophets, and actions for helping out the poor were regarded as required. See, for example, Ecclesiastes 5:8–10 and Ezekiel 45:9.

Violence in Scriptures

The Hebrew Bible (Tanakh) has a great deal of influence since it is also scriptural for Christians. There have been people who wish to use it to justify violence and can make it mean what they wish; for example, the idea that Noah's curse on his son Ham (Genesis 9:20–27) justifies Americans keeping Africans in slavery is quite a stretch.

Nevertheless, there are many passages that have God demanding or have humans with approval committing horrific violence; for example, genocide and scorched-earth conquest in Joshua 6–11 and Deuteronomy 7:1–2, 13:2–19, 20:16–17. This scratches the surface. There are a huge number of very troubling passages from the nonviolent point of view.

These passages are often dealt with by ignoring verses and sanitizing some of the stories. While this may be a suitable method for children, it is unhelpful for adults. Too many adults have used these passages as justification for their own horrific violence, and other adults have become disillusioned with the entire Bible upon contemplating them.

Eric A. Seibert in his book *The Violence of Scripture* (2012) proposes a nonviolent reading: rather than being "compliant" the reader should be "conversant" with the texts, giving them context and critique in light of the rest of the Bible. The Bible itself gives permission for arguments, after all; Abraham (Genesis 18) and Moses (Exodus 32) argued with God to defend people from violence. The Jewish tradition of Mishnah encourages several different interpretations and therefore much more insight.

Treatment of "Heretics"

While there was much more by way of enforcing orthodoxy in Biblical times, the concept of "heresy" is currently not widespread in Judaism. The practice of arguing different points is for the most part encouraged.

RELATIONS WITH OTHER RELIGIONS

Buddhism

There have been no historical conflicts with Buddhism, and there are several Jews that have taken an interest in Buddhist spirituality, mental discipline, and meditation techniques. The popular book *The Jew in the Lotus: A Poet's Rediscovery of Jewish Identity in Buddhist India* (Kamenetz, 1994) has two stories. One is historic dialogue between rabbis and the Dalai Lama, the first recorded major dialogue between experts in Judaism and Buddhism. The other is how Roger Kamenetz deepens his own understanding of Judaism by studying Buddhism.

Christianity

Attitudes about Jesus of Nazareth have ranged from the idea that he is the most influential and therefore most dangerous of the false messiahs to the idea that he was a perfectly good rabbi with some worthy things to say, along with many other rabbis, and at least achieved widespread monotheism in previously pagan people.

Christianity started out as a Jewish sect but so expanded to the non-Jews of the Roman Empire that after a time it got accounted as a separate religion. Once the Roman Emperor Constantine made Christianity the official religion of the empire, and for centuries afterward, Jews who lived in countries where Christians were dominant felt the need to assert their separate identity. Christians maintained bigotry and committed persecutions of Jews. Jewish-Christian relations took quite a bit of work to recuperate from these centuries of abuse.

Today, there are many Christian supporters of Israel and a concept of a *Judeo-Christian ethic*, a term which is intended to be inclusive, though many Jews see it more as an illegitimate taking over of their religion by a subsequent one. As with all things Jewish and Christian, views vary widely.

An organization called The Council of Christians and Jews was founded as one of the earliest interfaith efforts. Chief Rabbi Joseph H. Hertz and Archbishop William Temple formed it in 1942. As World War II raged and lethal anti-Semitism was at its peak, this was an assertive nonviolent response that has lasted over time.

Hinduism

There has never been any recorded persecution by either religion against the other. The world's first Jewish-Hindu interfaith leadership summit was held in New Delhi in February 2007 (AM 5767). Attenders dwelled on the similarities, including the importance of peace and nonviolence.

Islam

Jews under Muslim rule, while being treated as second-class citizens along with the Christians and being pressured to convert, generally fared better than they did under Christian rule.

In modern times, the establishment of the state of Israel in what had become a Muslim-dominated land has resulted in a great deal of animosity between Jews and Muslims in the vicinity of the Middle East.

The Foundation for Ethnic Understanding (http://www.ffeu.org) has held several projects for improving Jewish-Muslim relations, including an annual Weekend of Twinning in which synagogues and mosques pair up for one-on-one programs that focus on similarities in the traditions, rituals, and beliefs. This started in 2008 in North America, and by 2012, programs were held in 25 countries.

Zoroastrianism

Ancient relationships were quite positive, inasmuch as it was the Zoroastrian-influenced Persian government that liberated the Jews from their exile in Babylonia and allowed them to return to their homeland. The two monotheistic approaches influenced each other, and the Zoroastrian ideas of heaven and hell, and angels and the devil entered into Jewish thought.

Related Religions: Samaritans

There are still Samaritans. These were the group of ancient Israelites who remained in Israel when the rest were exiled to Babylonia. They believe they continued the true religion while the exiles had altered it. They numbered over a million in Roman times, but the centuries have been hard on them with deaths and with conversions to other religions. There are about 750 Samaritans left living in Israel.

2

Hinduism: Ahimsa

"Ahimsa" means nonviolence, and it has been a major tenet of Hinduism since ancient times. Hindus have a very pluralistic religion and a widespread understanding that all religions have merit and there should therefore be toleration among people of differing faiths. The campaign for independence in India, a multireligion campaign including Muslims, Sikhs, and Parsis (Zoroastrians), was one where the majority of people and leadership came from Hinduism. With the leadership and writings of Mohandas Gandhi, the successful campaign for Indian independence has become one of the major events people think of when they think of nonviolence. Among the many subsequent campaigns that have been inspired by this one, activists in the early years of the U.S. Civil Rights Movement traveled to India to see firsthand how it was done.

HINDU HISTORY AND SCRIPTURES

There are currently around 900 million Hindus, including the majority of people in India (about 80%) and Nepal, with many more scattered all over the world.

The Indian subcontinent has always had a large variety of related religious philosophies and practices flourishing; it is a family of different religions and traditions. It was not until the 19th century that the British classified them all together under the term *Hinduism*. Some have argued therefore that as a full-fledged religion it is actually fairly young. Others—and this is generally true of Hindus themselves—regard this as ridiculous and declare Hinduism to be an ancient Vedic culture. This refers to the scriptures of the Vedas, a set of four different kinds of scriptures from several sources, drafted about 900 to 1200 BCE. The oldest and most famous is the Rig Veda, which has 1,028 hymns praising gods. The Yajur Veda is a handbook for priests performing all-important rituals. The Sama Veda has chants for those rituals, and the Atharva Veda preserves many traditions and includes magic formulas.

This makes Hinduism one of the oldest living religions, and certainly the oldest of the four religions that number adherents in the hundreds of millions (the others being Buddhism, Christianity, and Islam). Hinduism has no single founder, but many voices throughout the centuries. It has several sets of scriptures set down throughout the ages.

The Vedas were transmitted orally for over three millennia, and it was forbidden to write them down. If heard by lower-caste men or any women, their ears were to be filled with molten lead. Finally, though, in recent times the British bribed a few Brahmins, so parts got written down. When others came forward, the other parts were all collected and are now available in writing and in translation to various languages. What was remarkable was that when the recitations of different people were compared, the versions were practically identical. These were transmitted for 3,000 years with hardly any error, even when in an archaic language not quite understood by those doing the memorizing.

The next set of scriptures that grew out of the Vedas were the Upanishads, a set of texts mainly composed by many people between 800 and 200 BCE. Part prose, part verse, many were dialogues that occurred between teachers and students or other audiences. They were also passed down orally at first, but did get written down over the centuries. They expanded to other castes besides the Brahmin priests. They were more opposed to animal sacrifice and moving more toward the understanding of nonviolence. The idea of karma ruling destinies became prominent, and death moved from a shadowy existence to the transmigration of souls in reincarnation.

Much of the tradition developed at the time when Buddhism and Jainism were becoming popular, so in some ways they were the Vedic answer to those anti-Vedic movements. This was a period of extensive pluralism, with different and contradictory schools of thought arising. From Brahmins who were a loose network of priests without temples and small political units, there was a rapid shift to a more urban society with kings who ruled larger areas with more diversity. Because there was no monopoly on religion, different religious ideas flourished. There was hardly any ruler with an interest in imposing orthodoxy. It was a remarkably free market of religious groups competing with each other for attention.

Firmly establishing karma and reincarnation meant that one's caste or status in society is a temporary material condition. The Gita has Krishna saying "the humble sages, by virtue of true knowledge, see with equal vision a learned and gentle Brahmin, a cow, an elephant, a dog and a dog-eater" (*Bhagavad Gita* 5:18). Vasu Murti comments: "Social ills such as racism, sexism, nationalism, casteism, and speciesism arise because souls falsely identify with their temporary bodies. On the spiritual platform, all are equal" (personal communication, November 14, 2014).

The doctrine of reincarnation and karma had another effect, as explained by sociologist Rodney Stark:

> Those on the bottom runs of the status pyramid could find considerable comfort in this doctrine, since they could strive to be reborn into far greater privilege by living righteously. However, it was much less appealing to the privileged, many of whom found far less satisfaction in their exalted status than those beneath them could imagine . . . there was no escape from life's many disappointments and sorrows and there was no more satisfying life to strive for.
>
> Thus, the goal of many Brahmans and other upper-caste Indians became release—an escape from the cycle of birth, death, and rebirth into an ultimate state of unconscious, everlasting bliss: Nirvana. (Stark, 2007, p. 228)

Another of the many scriptures is a long epic poem called the *Mahabharata*, composed between 500 BCE. and 100 CE. As with the *Iliad*, it recounted a lengthy war. Most famous is one of the most popular Hindu texts, its sixth book, the *Bhagavad Gita*, "Song of the Lord." The bulk of the book is a long dialogue between Krishna, an incarnation of God, and a human being named Arjuna (emphasis on first syllable).

There are a wide variety of beliefs, so that all of Hinduism cannot be pegged down as monotheist or not monotheist, polytheist (whether literal, or a good metaphor, or emanations from the one), pantheist (God is the universe, not apart from it), henotheist (many gods but only one of them really counts and is worshipped), or panentheist (God both outside and inside the creation). As with all large religions, there are those who are mystical and those who are strict rule-followers and others who are both or neither.

The tendency for what most Hindus believe is that there is one all-pervasive Supreme Being, both immanent and transcendent, creator and destroyer, manifested and unmanifested. Different aspects given different names; for example, the manifested is Krishna plus other names, and the unmanifested is Brahma. Divine beings also exist through which we can commune through temple worship, rituals, and devotionals. Hindus believe the four Vedas were divinely inspired and hold that these ancient and primordial hymns are the foundation of the eternal religion. God in the form of Krishna can also come in the body and does so when things have deteriorated badly enough that this is needed (*Bhagavad Gita* 4:7–8).

Hindus tend to believe that the universe goes through endless cycles of creation, preservation, and destruction and that the current one has been going for billions of years. There is a strict cause-and-effect karma whereby individuals create their own destinies. Reincarnation is where the karma works itself out over many deaths and rebirths. Yet this is not seen as a positive thing, as many Western believers of reincarnation see it, but rather something from which one wishes to be liberated. The liberation whereby reincarnation stops is called *moksha*, and many Hindus assert all souls will achieve this eventually.

Most religions have the idea of the benefits of having guidance from a spiritual director; in Hinduism (and Sikhism), these are gurus. The term *guru* has become so popular in the West to apply to people who have expertise, usually in spiritual matters.

As would be common in all religions, the practices of personal discipline, good conduct, purification, self-reflection, meditation, pilgrimage, and surrender to God are all expected. Devotional practice is called *bhakti*. The term *yoga* is an action form of bhakti; in the West, it has become identified as an excellent form of physical exercise, one that perhaps has spiritual components, but in Hinduism it means much more.

There are also many holy days specific to Hindus, the best known being Diwali or the Festival of Lights. The Ganges River is a holy site for pilgrimage and placement of ashes of the deceased. The Kumbh Mela Festival, which occurs every 12 years, attracts around 100 million people and so is the largest single peaceful gathering event of human beings on the planet (the Muslim annual hajj to Mecca comes in a distant second).

It is a widespread belief, to the point of being asserted as a necessary Hindu belief by many, that Hindus believe no one religion teaches the only way to salvation above all others. All paths to God are genuine; some are better than others, but those who take paths that are not quite as good as other paths are not to be criticized. Tolerance and understanding are expected toward all.

Hinduism: Ahimsa 43

While these beliefs were developing, a major historical event occurred during this period: the coming of the Muslims in the northern part of India, starting around the eighth century CE with traders. Political power was imposed by the Turkish sultanate around 1200 CE and Muslim power further rose with the Mughal empire starting in 1526 CE. Emperor Akbar (1542–1605) allowed Hindus to practice freely, but his great-grandson Aurangzeb (1618–1707) restricted Hindus and destroyed temples.

This begins the period of animosity between Hindus and Muslims, with Hindus seeing Muslims as conquerors who impose and Muslims seeing Hindus as pagans who require converting for their own good. The Sufi Muslims, however, got along much better with Hindus, as the mystics in both traditions found much in common (Pal, 2011, pp. 66–76).

Then came the British. At the Battle of Plassey in 1757 they defeated the Mughal Empire and started their own reign, giving their own Christian religion a poor image in India due to brutality and racism. While the British did at first allow free practice of Hinduism, the associated missionaries were badly hampered in being effective by being associated with conquerors, at a time when Hindus already had much practice in resisting the impositions of the Mughal empire. The missionaries also often had a bias toward "westernizing" on points that were irrelevant to sound religion.

This brought about many Hindu reformers in the 1800s who were quite conscious of Hinduism being a world religion with other religions and one with a rational, nonsuperstitious, and ethical basis. This solidified nationalism in India, and also Hindu missionary movements that journeyed around the world. One of the many reformers was Ramakrishna Paramahamsa (1836–1886), who declared the unity of all religions. This was developed by his disciple Vivekananda (1863–1902), especially noted for his rousing speech on the topic at the 1893 foundational Parliament of the World's Religions in Chicago, held in conjunction with the Chicago World's Fair, where he made quite an impression. His passion for ending religious bigotry and intolerance, which matched the whole point of the parliament, helped introduce Hinduism in the United States. He then traveled throughout the United States and Europe to spread the tenets of Hindu heritage. He started his own order of Hindu monks, which is still active in education and social services.

In the 1900s, the most famous Hindu contribution to nonviolence occurred with the massive and successful movement to have the

British leave the government of India and to do so willingly. This started in the 1920s with the work of the Indian National Congress, and after decades of struggle where most of the violence was done by the British, the British did indeed leave willingly in 1947. The most famous leader in this movement and one who wrote many books was Mohandas Gandhi. Gandhi's words and India's success, both based on previous developments, were instrumental in the history of nonviolence in establishing both the practical and principled aspects of nonviolence as a workable solution for countering massive governmental violence.

Unfortunately, this was followed by a bloody and violent partition of the country, much to Gandhi's chagrin. Such violence following nonviolent campaigns, of which there are other instances, occurs for two main reasons. One is that the nonviolent campaigns arouse people out of complacency or apathy or cowardice, all of which are every bit as contrary to nonviolence as violence is. The other is that so many people still have philosophies where violence is either understood as instrumentally necessary or as needed for revenge. Nonviolence is all they could do when they are weak, but once nonviolence itself makes them strong, they then deteriorate into doing what they understand the strong will do. This is one reason why Gandhi continually emphasized that nonviolence was best when done by the strong.

Many Hindu gurus and other adherents have sought influence in the West. One of the earliest was Vivekananda, as mentioned earlier, who starting in the 1890s traveled internationally.

Soon thereafter came Yogananda (1893–1952), who arrived in Boston in 1920 and then moved to Los Angeles in 1925 and established himself there for many years. With widespread speaking engagements, he offered concepts that science had only recently offered the vocabulary for and offered the practice of yoga and meditation in ways that led to widespread practice. When told his audience in Washington, D.C., was restricted to white people, he set up another session devoted to an audience of what was then politely called Negroes. He publically supported Mohandas Gandhi, which put him under suspicion in some quarters, and was able to meet with Gandhi on a return trip to India. He had a writing spurt in his last few years, including the book *Autobiography of a Yogi*. The former Beatle George Harrison distributed this to his guests, and it was passed out to attendees of Steve Jobs's funeral. It has had continued popularity.

Prabhavananda also did extensive writing and speaking in the United States, arriving in 1923 as a monk and disciple of Ramakrishna, following Vivekananda, and founded several Vedanta societies in California.

Another example comes from the late 1960s, when Transcendental Meditation achieved worldwide popularity, including among celebrities such as the Beatles. Its exponent, Maharishi Mahesh Yogi, also influenced a Hindu medical doctor to consider his Ayurveda roots and combine that with Western medicine; author Deepak Chopra has offered many books on achieving health and happiness with Hindu understandings. One book, addressing nonviolence directly, is entitled *Peace Is the Way* (Chopra, 2005).

Members of the International Society for Krishna Consciousness (ISKCON), more commonly known as Hare Krishna, are commonly seen in public offering literature such as the *Bhagavad Gita* and commentaries. This was founded in 1966 in New York City by Swami Prabhupada and comes from the Gaudiya Vaishnava tradition, which has had adherents in India since the late 1400s. It is now a worldwide confederation with more than 550 centers, including schools and vegetarian restaurants.

Currently, Hindus are grappling with the caste system, which is a more contentious issue than it used to be. Hindus are also grappling with the position of women, who have been held to be inferior to men in some parts of Hinduism; India has had a woman as prime minister, but it also has a horrific problem with female feticide and infanticide so severe as to cause a gender imbalance, along with bride burning and other problems. Hindu nonviolent activists have long been concerned, if not about the entire caste system, about avoiding unfair or cruel discrimination against those in the lowest caste and those who are below that without even having a caste, the so-called untouchables. These are now referred to by the government as "Scheduled Castes" and "Scheduled Tribes" and commonly call themselves Dalit, essentially meaning *the oppressed*.

Several successors to Gandhi, such as his own children and grandchildren and leaders such as Vinoba Bhave, have continued the nonviolence tradition in terms of campaigns, ashrams, and education. Kailash Satyarthi was one of two cowinners of the Nobel Peace Prize in 2014 for his educational and nonviolent action campaigns on behalf of children, getting them out of what amounts to slavery working conditions and into school.

HISTORICAL HIGHLIGHTS OF NONVIOLENCE

Throughout the history of Hinduism, there has been much advocacy for ahimsa in lifestyles and persuasion of others to do so. For example:

> Chaitanya Mahaprabhu (fifteenth to sixteenth centuries) . . . converted many cruel people who later became compassionate beings. The story is told that once Chaitanya Mahaprabhu heard that hundreds of cows and bulls were killed every year to feed the Muslim ruler of his area. He was saddened about the slaughter of innocent animals so he went to the court and met the Muslim ruler to explain the significance of nonviolence. He said that cows give us milk so they are like our mother. He said that bulls help to plow fields to produce food grains so they are like our father. Killing these cows and bulls to eat meat is like killing our mother and father and eating their meat. The Muslim ruler was convinced by Mahaprabhu's argument and ordered no more killing of cows and bulls and became an ardent practitioner of nonviolence. Mahaprabhu also converted many criminals and dangerous bandits of his time into great devotees of the Lord. They became compassionate beings. His way of nonviolence attracted thousands of followers. (Shastri & Shastri, 1998, p. 82)

Followers of Chaitanya Mahaprabhu are to follow his example and bring up the subject of vegetarianism with people of other faiths.

Note that this is the most basic and easiest form of nonviolence: persuading others to participate. This is always the first thing to try, and it serves as an ideal to aspire to. It solves all kinds of problems when it works, and it works quite a bit—there is more power in it than many people realize. Were it to become universal, peace would be achieved.

Nevertheless, many people refuse to be persuaded and react with violence to those making the pleas—at times, horrific violence. In some cases, of course, the pleas are being made not on behalf of others but by the victims themselves, so it is easily predicted that being assertive rather than acquiescing will bring on more violence against the victims.

Mass movements of confrontation for social justice were not a noteworthy part of the history of Hinduism until the first half of the 20th century. At that point, India provided such an overwhelmingly large and pioneering mass movement for its own independence that it often serves as the very first campaign people think of when nonviolence is mentioned.

As a young man, Mohandas Gandhi trained as a lawyer in London. Ireland was in turmoil at that time, but many effective nonviolent actions took place that Gandhi could observe relatively close at hand. Captain Charles Boycott, for example, much to his dismay, has permanently lent his name to a technique that was targeted at him by renters. Gandhi then went to South Africa, where he bore the brunt of the developing system of apartheid. He had an ongoing correspondence with Leo Tolstoy about nonviolence—Tolstoy had noted many effective instances of it in the 1905 Russian Revolution and then despaired when people dropped what was effective to take up counterproductive violence. In South Africa, Gandhi had some successes, many frustrations, and a lot of practice. By the time he got back home to India, he was well-seasoned.

In short, the campaign did not come full-blown out of the head of a genius with no prior experience. This was built up on a firm foundation of experience elsewhere. It then in turn served as another set of experience from which people have benefited ever since. The impact of this campaign on the U.S. Civil Rights Movement was direct and explicit and that movement has also provided more experience and inspiration from which people have drawn.

Features of the Indian campaign for independence will be covered throughout the book; Sikhs and Muslims were also prominent participants, after all. But the upshot is that the British did leave in 1947, have remained on friendly terms ever since, and have apologized for the violence they know they should have never inflicted.

Historical Quotations on Nonviolence

Rig Veda 10.191:2

> Come together, talk together,
> Let our minds be in harmony.
> Common be our prayer,
> Common be our purpose,
> Common be our deliberations,
> Common be our desires,
> United be our hearts,
> United be our intentions,
> Perfect be the union among us.

Rig Veda 10

> The peace in the sky,
> the peace in the mid-air,
> the peace on earth,

the peace in waters,
the peace in plants,
the peace in forest trees,
the peace in all Gods,
the peace in Brahman,
the peace in all things,
the peace in peace,
may that peace come to me.

Atharva Veda 7.52:1–2

Let us have concord with our own people,
and concord with people who are strangers to us;
Asvins,* create between us and the strangers a unity of hearts.
May we unite in our midst,
unite in our purposes,
and not fight against the divine spirit within us.
Let not the battle-cry rise amidst many slain,
nor the arrows of the War-God fall with the break of day.

*inseparable twin gods of medicine and healing

Atharva Veda 10.191:4

Peace be the earth,
peaceful the ether,
peaceful heaven,
peaceful the waters,
peaceful the herbs,
peaceful the trees.
May all gods bring me peace.
May there be peace through these invocations of peace.
With these invocations of peace which appease everything,
I render peaceful whatever here is terrible,
whatever here is cruel,
whatever here is sinful.
Let it become auspicious,
let everything be beneficial to us.

Dharma Shastras 6

[dates after the Vedas and before the current era]

The twice-born should endure high-handed criticism; he should insult none. While yet in his body, he should not pick enmity with

Hinduism: Ahimsa

anyone; he should not return anger with anger; decried, he should say a good word.

Dharma Shastras 10

Nonviolence, truthfulness, nonstealing, purity, sense control—this, in brief, says Manu, is the dharma of all the four castes.

Mahabharata 18.113:8

[epic poem which includes the *Bhagavad Gita*]

One should never do that to another which one regards as injurious to one's own self. This, in brief, is the rule of dharma. Yielding to desire and acting differently, one becomes guilty of adharma.

Mahabharata 18.115:8

Those high-souled persons who desire beauty, faultlessness of limbs, long life, understanding, mental and physical strength and memory should abstain from acts of injury.

Mahabharata 18.116:37–41

Ahimsa is the highest dharma. Ahimsa is the best tapas. Ahimsa is the greatest gift. Ahimsa is the highest self-control. Ahimsa is the highest sacrifice. Ahimsa is the highest power. Ahimsa is the highest friend. Ahimsa is the highest truth. Ahimsa is the highest teaching.

Sandilya Upanishad

[one of 108 Upanishads]

Ahimsa is not causing pain to any living being at any time through the actions of one's mind, speech or body.

Bhagavad Gita 10:20

God is seated in the hearts of all.

Bhagavad Gita 10:4–5

[*Krishna/God is speaking*]

> Discernment, knowledge, freedom from delusion, long-suffering, truth, self-restraint, inward calm, pleasure, pain, birth, death, fear and fearlessness, nonviolence, even-mindedness, contentment, austerity, beneficence, good and ill fame—all these various attributes of creatures proceed verily from Me.

Bhagavad Gita 16:1–3

> Fearlessness, purity of heart, steadfastness in *jnana* and *yoga*—knowledge and action—beneficence, self-restraint, sacrifice, spiritual study, austerity and uprightness, nonviolence, truth, slowness to wrath, the spirit of dedication, serenity, aversion to slander, tenderness to all that lives, freedom from greed, gentleness, modesty, freedom from levity, spiritedness, forgiveness, fortitude, purity, freedom from ill will and arrogance—these are to bound in one born with the divine heritage, O Bharata.

Yoga Sutras of Patañjali

[around 400 BCE]

> When one is established in non-injury, beings give up their mutual animosity in his presence.

Tiru Kural, Verse 312

[authored by poet Thiruvalluvar, traditionally around 30 BCE; written in Tamil]

> It is the principle of the pure in heart never to injure others, even when they themselves have been hatefully injured.

Tiru Kural, Verse 321

> What is virtuous conduct? It is never destroying life, for killing leads to every other sin.

Thirumanthiram, Verse 197

[authored by poet Thirumoolar, in the 400s CE; Thirumanthiram is the 10th of 12-volume Thirumurai, written in Tamil]

Many are the lovely flowers of worship offered to the Guru, but none lovelier than non-killing. Respect for life is the highest worship, the bright lamp, the sweet garland and unwavering devotion.

Ramana Maharishi, 1935 (1879–1950)

You do not like to suffer yourself. How can you inflict suffering on others? Every killing is a suicide. The eternal, blissful and natural state has been smothered by this life of ignorance. In this way the present life is due to the killing of the eternal, pristine Being. Is it not a case of suicide?

Swami Vivekananda (1863–1902)

[speech at the World's Parliament of Religions, September 11, 1893, held in Chicago]

I am proud to belong to a religion which has taught the world both tolerance and universal acceptance. We believe not only in universal toleration, but we accept all religions as true. I am proud to belong to a nation which has sheltered the persecuted and the refugees of all religions and all nations of the earth. I am proud to tell you that we have gathered in our bosom the purest remnant of the Israelites, who came to Southern India and took refuge with us in the very year in which their holy temple was shattered to pieces by Roman tyranny. I am proud to belong to the religion which has sheltered and is still fostering the remnant of the grand Zoroastrian nation.

Sectarianism, bigotry, and its horrible descendant, fanaticism, have long possessed this beautiful earth. They have filled the earth with violence, drenched it often and often with human blood, destroyed civilization and sent whole nations to despair. Had it not been for these horrible demons, human society would be far more advanced than it is now. But their time is come; and I fervently hope that the bell that tolled this morning in honor of this convention may be the death-knell of all fanaticism, of all persecutions with the sword or with the pen, and of all uncharitable feelings between persons wending their way to the same goal.

Siva Yogaswami (1872–1964)

If you plant eggplant, you can pluck eggplants. If you sow goodness, you can reap goodness. If you sow evil, you will reap evil. Do good to all. God is there, within you. Don't kill. Don't harbor anger.

Swami Sivananda Saraswati (1887–1963)

To be free from violence is the duty of every [person]. No thought of revenge, hatred or ill will should arise in our minds. Injuring others gives rise to hatred.

Mohandas Gandhi (1869–1948)

Truth is my religion and ahimsa is the only way of its realization. Search for truth is search for God. Truth is God. God is because truth is. The freedom from all attachment is the realization of God as truth.

Honest disagreement is often a good sign of progress.

I object to violence because when it appears to do good, the good is only temporary; the evil it does is permanent.

You must be the change you want to see in the world.

An eye for an eye makes the whole world blind.

The greatness of a nation and its moral progress can be judged by the way its animals are treated.

Peace will not come out of a clash of arms but out of justice lived and done by unarmed nations in the face of odds.

No power on earth can subjugate you when you are armed with the sword of ahimsa. It ennobles both the victor and the vanquished.

The votary of ahimsa has only one fear, that is, of God.

The power of unarmed nonviolence is any day far superior to that of armed force.

Vinoba Bhave, "The True Nature of Ahimsa and Our Duty," 1949

Ahimsa is not merely nonparticipation in destructive activities; it principally manifests itself in constructive activities . . . People say that the Goddess of Ahimsa has no weapons; I say that is wrong. The Goddess of Ahimsa has very powerful weapons at her command. They are the weapons of love and are, therefore, creative and not destructive. Yet they do destroy; they destroy hatred, inequity, hunger, and disease.

FORMS OF VIOLENCE

Blood Sacrifice

Ritual human sacrifice to please, placate, or bargain with divinity was practiced early on but stopped being prevalent millennia ago. As a fringe activity and primarily to the goddess Kali, individual instances in India are still making the news and are legally treated as murders.

Ritual animal sacrifice was found in the Vedas but disapproved in the Upanishads. It is currently not common and is especially frowned on by those with vegetarian practice, but does happen, primarily goats sacrificed to the goddess Kali.

Slavery

The Vedas declare liberation to be the universal ultimate goal, and slavery is contrary to this. A sutra from the Maha Nirvana Tantra (Method of Great Liberation) says: "the human body is the receptacle of piety, wealth, desires, and final liberation. It should therefore never be the subject of purchase; and such a purchase is by reason of my commands invalid."

However, using "debt bondage," indentured servitude, and similar mechanisms as a way of forcing labor or sex has occurred throughout Indian history, as elsewhere, and is currently an urgent problem for nonviolent activists to address (as it is worldwide).

War

In the wide range of Hindu thought, the teaching of ahimsa would preclude war, but those in the warrior caste, the Kshatriyas, were duty-bound to practice it as protection of others. Rules of war are set in the Rig Veda 6.75:15, with those breaking told they will go to hell. Several of the normal just-war rules are in place with the idea that sincere dialogue for peace should be practiced where it can be.

The Death Penalty

There is no hierarchy in Hinduism to decide the matter, and there are arguments about whether or not Hinduism supports the death penalty. Jagdish Muni summarized it this way:

> The scriptures speak both for and against the system of capital punishment. The scriptures give the ruler or the government the power to use capital punishment. However, the saints and mahatmas do

not believe in capital punishment. They believe in reforming people. There are a large number of instances in which saints have reformed criminals, in some cases so much so that the reformed people themselves became saints. (Muni, 2006)

India still has the death penalty, but the Indian Supreme Court has ruled it should be in only rare cases and there are few executions occurring.

Infanticide and Feticide

Infanticide and feticide have been practiced throughout the history of Hinduism. Targeted primarily against girl babies, both are still widespread in India today. Ultrasound technology allows for ascertaining gender before birth, and in the past advertisements for the technique advised it as a cost saving over paying a dowry later. Though sex-selection in abortions is illegal while abortion for other reasons is allowed, and infanticide is currently illegal, the practice of eliminating baby girls is widespread enough to cause a severe gender imbalance in the population. This happens despite the fact that several Hindu texts understand abortion as killing a human being, and Mohandas Gandhi said, "It seems to me clear as daylight that abortion would be a crime" (Gandhi, 1980, p. 150).

Hindu scriptures refer to abortion as *garha-batta* (womb killing) and *bhroona hathya* (killing the undeveloped soul). A hymn in the Rig Veda (7.36.9, RvP, 2469) begs for protection of fetuses. The Kaushitaki Upanishad (3.1 UpR, 774) draws a parallel between abortion and the killing of one's parents. The Atharva Veda (6.113.2 HE, 43) remarks that the fetus slayer, or *brunaghni*, is among the greatest of sinners (6.113.2).

Meat

Dietary restrictions are very strict about not eating cows. A strong tendency toward vegetarianism on grounds of compassion to animals is widespread, but not entirely consistent. Groups within Hinduism, such as the Hare Krishna, are strictly vegetarian.

Poverty

Involuntary poverty is often seen as resulting from bad karma from a previous life; still, offering help to the poor is a way of building up good karma.

Amassing too much wealth is at times frowned upon, as shown in this verse from the Vedas: "One may amass wealth with hundreds of hands but one should also distribute it with thousands of hands. If someone keeps all that he accumulates for himself and does not give it to others the hoarded wealth will eventually prove to be the cause of ruin" (Atharva Veda 3:24–25).

Violence in the Scriptures

While there are some notes of violence in the Vedas and Upanishads, the big concern is the war epic, the *Mahabharata*, and its very popular sixth book, the *Bhagavad Gita*. One way of dealing with this war epic happened in a later scripture, the *Bhagavata Purana*, written about the 10th century CE. It addresses the author of the *Mahabharata*, Vyasa: "It was a great error on your part to have enjoined terrible acts, acts involving destruction of life, in the name of religion on men who are naturally addicted to such acts. Misguided by these precepts of yours the ordinary man of the world would believe such acts to be pious and would refuse to honor the teachings that prohibit such action" (Bhagavata Purana 1.5.15). Mohandas Gandhi took an entirely different tack: "The author of the *Mahabharata* has not established the necessity of physical warfare; on the contrary he has proved its futility. He has made the victors shed tears of sorrow and repentance and has left them nothing but a legacy of miseries" (Gandhi, 1958, p. 140). In this respect, Gandhi does not have much support in the tradition; he intends to speak from experience, not to be a scholar (Sharma, 2011).

More problematic is the *Bhagavad Gita*. While most of it is a dialogue that could happen anywhere, in which Krishna does refer to nonviolence as one of many virtues (*Bhagavad Gita* 10:4–5), the story in which it does happen is that the incarnation of God, Krishna, is serving as charioteer. The warrior Arjuna is about to battle his own relatives and is recoiling at the horror of it. Yet Krishna urges him to do his duty and go forth; at the end, Arjuna does so. Most Hindus understand this as violence against criminals in defense of the innocent—war as a last resort when peace is not possible.

As with early Christians like Origen dealing with the violence of the Old Testament, Mohandas Gandhi saw allegory. The battlefield is actually the human body where the struggle over right and wrong continues, as we all experience daily. In this case, there are other instances of this interpretation. In classic times, Abhinavagupta was a well-known Indian scholar and scripture commentator, born around 950 CE. Both he and Gandhi interpret the first verse of the *Gita* to be setting up the battlefield as the human body, and Abhinavagupta indicates that this interpretation was one that other people understood as well (Sharma, 2011). This is also the understanding of Yogananda (1893–1952) in his two-volume commentary on the *Bhagavad Gita* for English-speaking audiences (Yogananda, 2013, Chapter 1).

Mohandas Gandhi's grandson Rajmohan Gandhi, in discussing this topic, points out that the scholar V. S. Sukthankar (1887–1943) has similarly said that the *Gita* hints at the psychological conflict within people of the good and evil propensities (Gandhi, 2004, p. 60). There is a one-page summary called the *Gita-Saar*, widely distributed in India, which never mentions war; it was the content of the dialogue that people find spiritual strength in. Rajmohan Gandhi summarizes:

> If the chariots steered by Rama or Krishna are available for carrying humans on the journey of life and not meant for fighting the other side with arrows and guns; if the body is the chariot, Arjuna stands for any individual, and Krishna and Rama are names for the Indwelling Guide exhorting us to fight the battle of life, against despair, against depression and fatalism, against evil, including hatred and fanaticism—if these things are true, then the epics . . . become the peacemaker's greatest allies. (Gandhi, 2004, p. 61)

Treatment of "Heretics"

The long-lasting pluralism of religious practice under Hinduism and the widespread assertion of the truth of various religions have meant there has been very little by way of imposing orthodoxy or opposing heretics throughout Indian history. One major exception has arisen recently, the Hindutva (Hindu-ness) movement, to unite Hindus against "threatening others"—including Muslims and Christians. Its political expression is in the BJP, the Bharatiya Janata Party, which has occasionally won elections. The Hindutva movement has been associated with riots and massacres and so is responsible for many deaths. The man who assassinated Mohandas Gandhi was a sympathizer of Hindutva who thought Gandhi was being too lenient with Muslims.

RELATIONS WITH OTHER RELIGIONS

Buddhism

Mohandas Gandhi is one of many Hindus who regard Buddhism as not being a different religion from Hinduism at all. Hinduism has many different groupings, after all. The reason Buddhism is generally regarded as a separate religion is that it explicitly rejected Vedic culture, while Hindus through the Upanishads and later developments retained the Vedas as also sacred. Nevertheless, Buddhism did arise in Hindu culture.

Christianity

Unlike Jews, Muslims, and Bahá'ís, Hindus are not troubled by the idea of God having an incarnation—being in a specific human body. The concept is that Krishna, as God incarnate says:

> When goodness grows weak
> When evil increases,
> I make myself a body.
> In every age I come back
> To deliver the holy,
> To destroy the sin of the sinner,
> To establish righteousness. (Bhagavad Gita 4:7–8)

Hence, while many Hindus ignore Jesus, there are other Hindus that accept Jesus as either a Hindu saint or good guru, and some—especially those with extensive contact with Christians—accept him as an incarnation of God. As Prabhavananda, founder of Vedanta societies in California, put it:

> A Hindu, then, would find it easy to accept Christ as a divine incarnation and to worship him unreservedly, exactly as he worships Sri Krishna or another avatar of his choice. But he cannot accept Christ as the *only* Son of God. Those who insist on regarding the life and teachings of Jesus as unique are bound to have great difficulty in understanding them. Any avatar can be far better understood in the light of other great lives and teachings. No divine incarnation ever came to refute the religion taught by another, but to fulfill all religions. (Prabhavananda, 1963, p. 45)

Yogananda put it this way:

> The saviors of the world do not come to foster inimical doctrinal divisions; their teachings should not be used toward that end. It is something of a misnomer even to refer to the New Testament as the "Christian" Bible, for it does not belong exclusively to any one sect. Truth is meant for the blessing and upliftment of the entire human

race. As the Christ Consciousness is universal, so does Jesus Christ belong to all. (Yogananda, 2004, p. xxiii)

Prabhavananda, a Hindu teaching in the United States for decades starting in the 1920s, wrote in 1963 a short book *The Sermon on the Mount According to Vedanta*. Yogananda wrote a massive two-volume, 1,642-page book covering all the gospels, called *The Second Coming of Christ: The Resurrection of the Christ within You*. Republished in 2004, its purpose in the dedication is "uniting the teachings of Jesus Christ and India's ancient science of religion."

In both books, each author has taken sections of the Bible, cited a passage, and given extensive commentary on it, then cited the following passage with more commentary, and so on, until he had completed the whole section. This is a form of religious devotion many Christians will be familiar with; the only difference is that the commentary is from a Hindu perspective.

Mohandas Gandhi had a highly favorable opinion of the Sermon on the Mount (found in the Gospel of Matthew, chapters 5–7) and a highly unfavorable opinion of racist behavior by people identifying themselves as Christians. For a book with Gandhi's speeches and writings with responses to his challenges, see *Gandhi on Christianity* (Ellsberg, 1991).

Islam

Islam is the second largest religion in India; because the partition of 1947 pulled out most Muslims from the new Indian borders, it is down to 14.6 percent of the population as of 2010. However, this is over 177 million people, only slightly less than Pakistan, and only Indonesia has a higher number of Muslims. India has almost 11 percent of the world's Muslim population (Pew Research Center, 2011).

Throughout the centuries, there has been a great deal of hostility and a great deal of neighborliness. Nonviolent Hindu activists do a lot of work on increasing the neighborliness and reducing the hostility. Sufis, as the Muslim mystics, have a long record of positive interaction with Hindu mystics (Pal, 2011, pp. 67–77).

Judaism

Vivekananda referred to Jews escaping to India from the destruction of the Temple, which occurred in 70 CE. The Cochin Jews (named after the Indian kingdom to which they fled) also have legends of a previous wave of Jews coming to India as traders as far back as the days of King Solomon, 500s BCE. Other small waves of immigrants came and settled in other areas. The Jewish community in India has been small, but all signs are that it has gotten along well with its neighbors and never suffered the anti-Semitism prevalent in other areas of the world.

Sikhism

Sikhism arose out of the two streams of Hinduism and Islam, having a series of gurus that took what they understood to be the best and most true during a historical period in an area when Hinduism and Islam were coexisting but frequently in conflict. They are currently concentrated in the Punjab district of India and actively participate in the life of the country.

Zoroastrianism

The Parsis are a long-lasting community of Zoroastrians in India, having fled from Persia/Iran soon after the Muslim conquest there and being welcomed in India. Parsis are active in Indian politics, including during the nonviolent campaigns for independence. Former prime minister Indira Gandhi's husband came from a Parsi family. Their influence far outweighs their numbers.

Smaller Related Religions: Jainism

Jainism is sometimes accounted as a separate religion and others account it as one of the many parts of the pluralistic Hinduism. Their numbers in the Indian census are not certain because some of them will list themselves as Hindu.

The Jain community was starting to take form in about eighth century BCE. Mahavira (traditional birth day, 599 BCE) is regarded as the man who gave Jainism its present-day form by reforming and popularizing an ancient religion (not the same as founding). In his times and following, Jains asserted that both those following the Vedic religion and Buddhists were not sufficiently implementing ahimsa. According to India's 2001 census, there are currently 4.2 million identifying as Jains living in India now, probably more who listed themselves as Hindu for census purposes, and a few thousand also scattered abroad.

Ahimsa paramo dharma is often inscribed on Jain temples, which means that nonviolence is the paramount duty for everyone. Ahimsa is central to the Jains, not allowing for killing even of insects. The overriding Jain founding principles are nonviolence, search for truth, forgiveness, and reform. The understanding of nonviolence as a matter of lifestyle is more scrupulous and comprehensive than in any other religion. The goal is to stop the accumulation of harmful karma involved in reincarnation and to achieve liberation of the soul. The basic ethical code for this is three jewels, the three guiding principles of Jainism: right belief (avoiding preconceptions and superstitions), right knowledge, and right conduct.

Vegetarianism or veganism is mandatory among Jains; vegans are vegetarians who in addition to meat also eschew dairy and eggs. The concept of ahimsa allows for neither ritual sacrifice nor hunting. Killing animals for food is prohibited, and while killing plants for food is inevitable, there are instructions for avoiding violence to plants. They tend to avoid going out at night for fear of stepping on insects.

Nevertheless, there is a hierarchy of life for practical reasons; those that can move are higher than those that cannot (animals vs. plants), and the more senses an animal has, the higher that animal is. Being rational (human) is highest of all.

Injury caused by carelessness is like injury caused by deliberate action. Harsh words are a form of violence, so a cloth ritually covering the mouth is a reminder not to allow violence in their speech.

However, as is common in religions, defensive violence is an exception. A soldier is expected to kill enemies in combat. According to Jain legal expert Lekh Raj Mehta, "Jain rulers, in fact, dealt with instances of crime as was done by any other ruler, including by capital punishment, though it was rare" (Muni, 2006). They maintained armies that fought and even eliminated opponents. Mehta says that issues of statecraft are not dealt with much in Jain scriptures; statecraft has always been the downfall of those religions who clearly advocate nonviolence.

There are five great vows, with nonviolence being one of them. The others are nonattachment to possessions, not lying, not stealing, and sexual restraint.

They do not believe in a God or gods. Yet there are beings worthy of devotion—Jinas, those who achieved the ideal state of an individual soul, that is, those who conquered temporal and material existence through self-discipline and attained a transcendent and external state of bliss—they are perfect examples for Jains to aspire to. Karma is a physical substance; karma particles attach to the soul by the actions of the soul, a mechanistic process, so no divinity deals with reward or punishment. They understand the existence of evil as evidence that a good creator does not exist.

Some people therefore regard Jainism as an atheistic religion, though others say it is more that Jains are not interested in the question of whether or not God exists. Yet others think the Jinas function as gods—pure souls who are omniscient, happy, and eternal. Each of us has the potential to become a Jina.

There are no priests, with the professional religious people being monks and nuns. Ethical standards are stricter for monks and nuns than for lay people. Prayers tend to be reminders of great people and great teachings; the beings they worship are beyond human contact and cannot intervene.

The scripture offers the teachings of Mahavira and are called the Agamas. Originally, the texts were memorized since monks and nuns could not possess books as part of their nonacquisition. Around 350 BCE a famine killed many monks and the memory of many texts went to the grave with them. Now there are two sects: the Digambara sect believes all the Agamas were lost in this famine, while the Svetambara sect believes the majority survived, since right after the famine they held several conferences to preserve the most important ones. There were, of course, arguments about which ones were authentic. The monks and nuns are now permitted to possess religious books, so the scriptures are not as vulnerable.

As a substantial part of the Indian population, some Jains were active in the nonviolent revolution to cast off British colonialism.

3

Buddhism: Metta

Buddhism was founded by a royal prince who renounced his worldly possessions for a spiritual journey. It was first popularized by converting a conquering emperor into essentially an advocate for nonviolence and nonviolent rule. It (along with Jainism) influenced Hinduism into more of a nonviolent direction, with "ahimsa" being the word for nonviolence used by both. Buddhism rejected Hindu castes and instead asserted human equality. The Mongols and the Tibetans were very war-oriented societies that became more nonviolence-oriented under Buddhist influence. Metta means loving-kindness, and meditations and actions on this are long-standing nonviolence training. The understanding of all things as interconnected, which modern science affirms, contributes to the foundation of nonviolent understanding of the world.

BUDDHIST HISTORY AND SCRIPTURES

In the 500s or 400s BCE, Prince Guatama or Siddhartha left behind the plush royal life, in which he was shielded from the sufferings of the world, because he was disconcerted when confronted with such suffering in the form of illness, old age, and death. After finding the deep asceticism common to religious seekers of that time to be unsatisfying, in deep meditation under a Bodhi tree he had a burst of insight, which Buddhists regard as *enlightenment*. It was a middle way, neither riches nor abject poverty. Becoming the Buddha, he then founded a spiritual tradition that has around 488 million followers worldwide as of 2010, 7 percent of the world's population. Most are Asians, with over 1 million in Europe and over 3 million in North America (Pew Research Center, 2012).

Just as Zoroaster and Moses had recruited from their immediate families, the family of Buddha that had been left behind years before were among his first converts: his wife, Yasodharā; his father, Suddhodana; his son, Rahula; and many others. They became nuns and monks.

As with the Hinduism from which it arose, Buddhists believe in reincarnation and karma. The state that adherents are trying to achieve is *Nirvana*, a state that transcends the self and means no more incarnations need to be endured. The cycle of death and rebirth is over. There is no personal God; some Buddhists still have several deities, others are more pantheist in orientation, but the deities are not the point. Beliefs about gods or God are not a focus, allowing for a multitude of views.

All teaching is based on the Four Noble Truths:

- Life is full of suffering.
- What causes the suffering is desire, grasping, and clinging.
- We can therefore be happy and free by dispensing with useless cravings.
- The Eightfold Path is what leads to the end of suffering.

That Eightfold Path is intended as a comprehensive set of ethical areas for making spiritual progress:

1. Right Understanding
2. Right Attitude, Thought, Emotion
3. Right Speech
4. Right Action
5. Right Livelihood
6. Right Effort
7. Right Mindfulness
8. Right Concentration

The Five Precepts are what the nuns and monks especially undertake to do, with lay people being influenced by these as well. Here we list the negative version, followed by positive wording:

- Abstain from killing living beings./Act with loving-kindness.
- Abstain from stealing./Be open-hearted and generous.
- Abstain from sexual misconduct./Practice stillness, simplicity, and contentment.
- Abstain from false speech./Speak truly, clearly, and with peace.
- Abstain from intoxicants./Live with mindfulness.

Buddha was opposed to the caste system and so admitted "untouchables." Women were active and encouraged in the Buddhist movement. Even a serial killer became a gentle disciple; no one was beyond redemption. All were equal.

Buddha also had an insight in where true power lies:

> *Brahmin Sela said to Buddha,*: You deserve to be a king, an emperor, the lord of chariots, whose conquests reach to the limits of the four seas ... Warriors and wealthy kings are devoted to you. O Gotama, exercise your royal power as king of kings, a chief of men!
>
> *The Buddha replied*: I am a king, O Sela, supreme king of the Teaching of Truth; but I turn the wheel by peaceful means—this wheel is irresistible. (*Sutta Nipata* 3.7.5–7)

In Buddha's time, the wheel was a symbol of the sun for the sky god Vishnu, and so the chariot wheels were the symbol of a universal conqueror or wheel-turner. Buddha declared himself King of Truth instead of being Lord of War and declared the peaceful version would be victorious. History bears this out, since statues of Buddha are multitudinous, while he would have been long forgotten had he remained a governmental prince-turned-king. Therefore, Buddha transformed the wheel from a military symbol to Peace Wheel, commonly portrayed in Buddhist art.

Buddhism spread for a couple of centuries and finally converted an emperor, Ashoka, covered in the following sections. Once time passed and royal patronage was not offered by successors, the Vedic priests came back and Buddhist missionaries went to other lands, especially in Asia and along trade routes.

It is not an exclusivist religion; that is, one can become Buddhist and still retain a previous religion or philosophy as well. People could be both Buddhist and Taoist or Confucian, they could be both Buddhist and Shinto, and so on. There were periods of persecution in some places, but in other places there was royal patronage and in others there was royal tolerance. So Buddhism has grown to be the fourth largest single religion in the world (after Christianity, Islam, and Hinduism).

As it developed, two major traditions came about: Theravada and Mahayana; there are also several smaller ones. Each of the two is more prominent in different areas, but they are two different schools with the same basic principles. They have no real animosity, only debates on certain points. "Theravada" means the teachings of the elders, and "Mahayana" means great or universal.

The Theravada Buddhists have a standard collection of scriptures called the Pali Canon (in the Pali language). This is the first known Buddhist scriptures, composed in northern India and passed down orally through the generations until finally put in writing on palm leaves at the Fourth Buddhist Council in Sri Lanka in 29 BCE. It is divided into the "Three Baskets":

- *Vinaya Pitaka*—"Discipline Basket"—rules for nuns and monks
- *Sutta Pitaka*—"Sutra/Sayings Basket"—mainly what Buddha said, occasionally other disciples
- *Abhidhamma Pitaka*—"Philosophy Basket"—also described as psychology or metaphysics

Beyond these, there is a vast collection of various kinds of texts that vary in popularity and authoritativeness from time to time and place to place.

The *Lotus Sutra* is in the form of a speech by Buddha toward the end of his life. Since it did not appear until around five centuries later, the story is that they were written down in his lifetime and stored in the realm of snake gods, then reintroduced into the human world at the time of the Fourth Buddhist Council of Kashmir (around 78 CE). Both the council and the Lotus Sutra are in the Mahayana tradition. (The sharp reader may have noticed that this differs from the "Fourth Buddhist Council" of Sri Lanka about a century earlier, as mentioned previously in this chapter; that was in the Theravada tradition). The idea behind why these teachings took so long to come to light even though they were better was that humanity was unable to understand them in Buddha's day and required more time to make them understandable. Both Nichiren Buddhism of Japan and Tiantai Buddhism of China, Japan, and Korea hold the Lotus Sutra to be the highest teaching, and it is generally held in high regard in Mahayana Buddhism.

Nuns and monks are prevalent in Buddhist countries, and they are organized in communities called *sanghas*. Historically they have also been well organized in ways that have made them very powerful.

Admired and enlightened people include *Bodhisattvas*, people who have achieved nirvana but nevertheless remain in this world in order to liberate others from suffering, and *cakravatrin* (wheel-turners) and *dhammaraja* (moral leaders), who conquer hearts and minds rather than enemies and territories using wisdom and kindness.

Buddhist Nobel Peace Prize awardees are the Dalai Lama in 1989 and Aung San Suu Kyi of Burma in 1991.

BUDDHIST BELIEFS AND PRACTICES SERVING AS FOUNDATIONS FOR NONVIOLENCE

Metta Mindfulness Meditation

Meditation of various kinds is a major practice in Buddhism. One is called *Metta Bhavana*—the loving-kindness meditation. That is, cultivating goodwill toward one's self and others, a root practice in Buddhist nonviolence.

The first exercise in a series of trainings called the "Divine Abodes" (*brahma vihara*), loving-kindness is complemented by practices of compassion (*karuna*, sympathy for those in pain), joy (*mudita*, appreciating the good fortune of others), and equanimity (*upekkha*, maintaining impartiality in times of gain and loss).

Starting with one's own state, the formula is:

May I be free from enmity.
May I be free from ill will.
May I be free from distress.
May I keep myself happy.

Then the meditation expands outward step-by-step to others. The person meditates on someone easy to love because they are already beloved—a parent or teacher. Next, think of a dear friend. The next round of meditation goes to a neutral or unknown person. Finally, the loving-kindness (or compassion, or joy, or equanimity) is extended to a person who is hostile or repellent.

Starting with the easy makes the mind more receptive before passing on to the next level, so that the feelings can build. See *Anguttaranikaya* 3:185, *Patisambhida* 2:130.

Other meditations that may help when feeling angry toward others include concentrating on the good qualities of the offender; realizing that it is not the person's actions but one's own resentment that will hurt the inner being; concentrating on the advantages of loving-kindness. A constructive act such as giving a gift to the offender may help calm the passions.

The Buddhists therefore have had millennia of nonviolence training for the emotions. The more people who practice this ancient art, the less violence there would be.

Pratitya Samutpada/Interconnectedness

Translated as dependent origination, codependent arising, interbeing, or interdependence, *Pratiya Samutpada* is a basic tenet of Buddhism. Thich Nhat Hanh explains its connection to nonviolence:

> Nonviolence can be born only from the insight of non-duality, of interbeing. This is the insight that everything is interconnected and nothing can exist by itself alone. Doing violence to others is doing violence to yourself. If you do not have the insight of non-duality, you will still be violent. You will still want to punish, to suppress, and to destroy, but once you have penetrated the reality of non-duality, you will smile at both the flower and garbage in you, you will embrace both. This insight is the ground for your non-violent action. (Hanh, 2002, pp. 65–70)

Modern physics confirms the interconnectedness of all things, so in addition to being a long-held religious view, it is the understanding of modern science. Biology has also understood the interconnectedness of our environment, that being basically what "ecology" means, and so it is also an important understanding for nonviolence with the planet.

One practical effect is that Chinese government officials, despite official secularism, are looking to Buddhism to encourage the deeper values needed to face their massive environmental crisis—more compassion to nature, an "ecological civilization" (*Religion & Ethics Newsweekly*, 2014).

A Sampling of Quotations

Since the scriptures are full of assertions of nonviolence, we offer just a few here, including some of the most widely quoted ones.

> Hatred will not cease by hatred, but by love alone.
> This is the ancient law.
> All fear violence, all are afraid of death.
> Seeing the similarity to oneself,
> one should not use violence or have it used. (*Dhammapada* 1:5–6)

> Anger must be overcome by the absence of anger;
> Evil must be overcome by good;
> Greed must be overcome by generosity;
> Lies must be overcome by truth. (*Dhammapada* 17:3)

The one I call holy, though having committed no offence,
patiently bears reproach, ill-treatment and imprisonment,
has endurance for one's force and strength for one's army.
The one I call holy has let go of anger,
hatred, pride and hypocrisy . . .
who renounces violence toward all living beings, weak or strong,
who neither kills nor causes others to kill. (*Dhammapada* 26:399, 400, 405)

May all beings be filled with joy and peace.
May all be filled with lasting joy.
Let no one deceive another,
Let no one anywhere despise another,
Let no one out of anger or resentment
Wish suffering on anyone at all.
Just as a mother with her own life
Protects her child, her only child, from harm,
So within yourself let grow
A boundless love for all creatures.
Let your love flow outwards through the universe,
To its height, its depth, its broad extent,
A limitless love, without hatred or enmity.
Then as you stand or walk,
Sit or lie down,
As long as you are awake,
Strive for this with a one-pointed mind;
Your life will bring heaven to earth. (Sutta Nipata 1.8, Karaniya Metta Sutta)

This one is widely quoted and attributed to Buddha without citation:

If a person foolishly does me wrong, I will return to him the protection of my boundless love. The more evil that comes from him, the more good will go from me. I will always give off only the fragrance of goodness.

BUDDHIST HISTORICAL NONVIOLENT ACTIONS
King Ashoka

Ashoka (also spelled Asoka) was an emperor of ancient India, ruling around 273–232 BCE. After conquering the country of Kalinga, he was moved by such remorse when he saw the suffering he had inflicted that he renounced armed conquest. Legend has it that upon surveying the damage in 261 BCE he cried out:

> What have I done? If this is a victory, what is a defeat then? Is this a victory or a defeat? Is this justice or injustice? Is it gallantry or a rout? Is it valor to kill innocent children and women? Do I do it to widen the empire and for prosperity or to destroy the other's kingdom and splendor? One has lost her husband, someone else a father, someone a child, someone an unborn infant. (Nikam & McKeon, 1978)

He converted to Buddhism, saying conquest would instead be by dharma, or right thinking. One of the principles of dharma is nonviolence. He said he found it more successful to reason with people than to issue commands. He arranged for a series of Rock Edicts to be cared with his thoughts, and one of those is today a national symbol of India.

In spreading Buddhism, he spread vegetarianism. He also built up education, which included letting women into the academies. The arts of peace and service flourished during his reign. Missionaries of Buddhism led it to become one of the world's major religions, which it remains to this day. This is one of the cases where assertive nonviolence was promoted by the government.

Since the state had a vast stockpile of war chariots that would no longer be used, there was a need for economic conversion for another use. The elephants and fireworks are for patriotic holiday parades in an era of prosperity and peace:

> For many hundreds of years in the past, slaughter of animals, cruelty to living creatures, discourtesy to relatives, and disrespect for priests and ascetics have been increasing. But now . . . the sound of war drums has become the call to Dharma, summoning the people to exhibitions of the chariots of the gods, elephants, fireworks, and other divine displays. Now the inculcation of Dharma has increased . . . abstention from killing animals and from cruelty to living beings, kindliness in human and family relations. (Nikam & McKeon, 1978, p. 31)

While Buddhism did not maintain itself in its homeland once time passed and royal sponsorship was no longer available, it did spread throughout Asia through missionary efforts with this experience as a foundation. While doing so, several other countries with warring propensities, especially the Mongols and Tibetans, also moved to becoming more peaceful societies.

Engaged Buddhism

Engaged Buddhism was a term coined by Vietnamese monk Thich Nhat Hanh to describe activism by Vietnamese against their dictators and the American war. They walked between battle lines in an effort to stop bullets. They did not take sides but had allegiance to nonviolence and peace and wanted to call the attention of the world to the suffering of their people. Hanh mentioned the Buddha saying, "If someone is standing on one shore and wants to go to the other shore, he has to either use a boat or swim across. He cannot just pray, 'Oh, other shore, please come over here for me to step across!" Hanh comments, "To a Buddhist, praying without practicing is not real prayer" (Hanh, 1995, p. 79).

The idea spread, and in February 1989, The International Network of Engaged Buddhists was founded to connect engaged Buddhists around the world (web page: http://www.inebnetwork.org/) at a meeting in Thailand, organized by Sulak Sivaraksa and Maruyama Teruo. The organization maintains its office Bangkok. It has members in about 20 countries around the world, mostly in Asia, but also in the United States, Australia, and Europe.

> In facing history's report on the discord and warfare within Buddhist societies, we acknowledge that the Peace Chariot is only as reliable as its drivers and mechanics. On the other hand, Buddhism may take heart in the knowledge that their cherished vehicle of nonviolent peacemaking is still running, carrying new passengers and bringing relief and joy to those who suffer. (Queen, 1998, p. 44)

Engaged Buddhists have developed ideas of more nonviolent practice. The old Buddhist idea was that suffering is caused by the ignorance and cravings of the sufferers. The new insight is that much suffering is caused by ignorance and cravings of persons *other* than the sufferer. The practice of loving-kindness and all the other virtues is no longer to transcend this world, but to relate to it. There is an obligation to relieve suffering. There is a belief in the usefulness of the *collective* practice of the dharma—that is, social movements and all their activities. Engaged Buddhism is egalitarian, nonhierarchical, and encourages equal leadership for women.

We now cover some examples of current Engaged Buddhism, along with historical cases and backgrounds before the concept recently arose.

Burma

Britain had fought wars in the 1800s to take over Burma just as it had India, and from 1910 to 1940, being a neighbor of India, Burma was participating in much of the same techniques being used in India. The Buddhist monk U Ottama was especially eager after visiting India in 1920 to bring the techniques back home to Burma in 1920. Over the years, Mohandas Gandhi visited on three tours, and there was quite a bit of cooperation and communication between the Burmese independence movement and the Indian National Congress (Moser-Puangsuwan, 2013).

In 1906, the Young Men's Buddhist Association (YMBA, modeled after the Young Men's Christian Association [YMCA]) began with modest proposals about having the colonial government recognize Buddhist holidays on the official calendar, exempting Buddhist temples from colonial tax, and greater access to education. Once the massive barbarity of World War I came, however, the colonial justification on grounds of superior civilization being imparted was shown to be inaccurate. Therefore, more ambitious goals, for some people including ultimate independence, were sought.

There was a major student strike in 1920 against the Rangoon University Act, which was seen as limiting education, so students stayed outside and created their own classes. National schools as alternatives to colonial schools developed out of this.

In the 1930s arose the Thakin Movement. "Thakin" means "lord" and was what Burmese were required to call colonial officials, so they took the domineering nature out of the term by using it all the time with each other. These were the first to commit unreservedly to full-fledged independence, and sponsored student strikes, labor strikes, and a general strike.

The ending for Burma was, however, quite different from what it was in India. During World War II, leader Aung San was impatient with all the years that had been put in and believed that independence could be achieved more quickly with violence.

The Burmese not being able to muster effective violence themselves, asked the Japanese for help. This turned out to be a terrible mistake, in that the Japanese government of the time was not liberation-minded. It simply amounted to changing one colonial overlord with another.

Once the Japanese were gone, however, the armed violence that displaced nonviolent action meant that Burma was subjected to several decades of brutal dictatorship. Hence, what was supposed to be a shortcut to independence and democracy turned out to be a horrendous delay (Moser-Puangsuwan, 2013).

However, Aung San's daughter, Aung San Suu Kyi, was an effective advocate for democracy and nonviolence. She was so effective that the dictators put her under house arrest for many years rather than allow her to work freely. Yet they also put her under house arrest rather than prison or execution, out of respect for who her father was. She won the Nobel Peace Prize in 1991, so the world community was participating in her cause.

Then in August through October, 2007, came the Saffron Revolution. This was a massive nonviolent movement by Buddhist monks and nuns (saffron being the color of their robes). It was essentially crushed militarily. Yet this is another one of the many cases in which a goal was not achieved immediately but was closer to being achieved eventually. After enough time to save face so they could claim doing it on their own volition rather than at the bidding of monks and nuns, the government freed Aung San Suu Kyi and held elections in 2010.

Japan

Nichiren (1222–1282) was a Japanese reformer who regarded the Lotus Sutra as the highest teaching and founded a school of Buddhism based on this understanding. He saw it as the essence of the Buddha's enlightenment, that it held the key to transforming people's suffering, and that therefore it would enable society to flourish. His writings include "On Establishing the Correct Teaching for the Peace of the Land," written in 1260. It objected to aspects of the military and political leadership of Japan. Most of the current Engaged Buddhism of Japan comes out of this centuries-old school, since it includes a concern for society as a whole, the egalitarian approach empowering individuals to help transform society, and critiques of government.

This includes the practice of chanting what is called the daimoku: "Namu Myōhō Renge Kyō." Roughly translated, this is "devotion to the awesome principle of the lotus flower teaching." In 1976, several Japanese Buddhist monks headed the Continental March for Disarmament and Social Justice from the west coast all across the United States to the capital on the east coast beating drums and chanting this (I went from Oklahoma City to Kansas City, one month of the march, so saw it personally).

Japanese activists have a special concern about nuclear weapons, since Japan is the only country on which the nuclear bombs have been used with the intention of killing people, which was done twice—August 6, 1945, and three days later, on August 9, 1945. This left thousands dead and horrific aftermath. The survivors of the bombings of Hiroshima and Nagasaki are called *hibakusha*, and their educational activities about their own experience worldwide throughout the decades has been one of the things that has made further use of nuclear weapons in wartime more of a taboo.

The Nipponzan-Myōhōji-Daisanga was founded in 1917 by Nichidatsu Fujii, a small Nichiren Buddhist order of around 1,500 monastics and lay supporters. Actively engaged worldwide in the peace movement, they chant the daimoku at many peace walks. This includes in 1994–1995, The Interfaith Pilgrimage for Peace and Life from Auschwitz to Hiroshima by way of Bosnia, Iraq, Cambodia and other countries then experiencing the effects of war, and the 2010 Walk for a Nuclear Free Future, another walk across the United States.

Another worldwide Buddhist organization founded in Japan and based on the Lotus Sutra is called Rissho Kosei-kai (see http://www.rk-world.org). It was founded in 1938 by Nikkyo Niwano (he was president) and Myoko Naganuma (she was vice-president). Niwano also promoted interfaith activities and in 1970 helped to found the World Conference of Religions for Peace (http://www.religionsforpeace.org/).

Tsunesaburo Makiguchi (1871–1944) offered "value-creating education" theories and was a founder of Soka Gakkai (Society for the Creation of Value), one of Japan's most influential lay Buddhist movements. He resisted the government's demands of state-sponsored Shinto and emperor worship and so during World War II was imprisoned. He died in prison (see http://www.tmakiguchi.org).

Also imprisoned but surviving was Josei Toda (1900–1958), the second president of the organization. Based on Nichiren's teachings, Toda developed a methodology of personal transformation called "Human Revolution" that has become the foundation underlying the organization's work of engaged Buddhists promoting peace and personal empowerment (see http://www.joseitoda.org).

The third president of the organization, Daisaku Ikeda (born 1928), turned it into Soka Gakkai International in 1975. He also founded Soka University along with other cultural, educational, and peace research institutions. The organization claims to have more than 12 million members (Seager, 2006; see http://www.daisakuikeda.org).

Sri Lanka

The Sarvodaya movement, founded by A. T. Ariyaratne (born in 1931), started with 40 high school students and 12 teachers doing an "education experiment" of going to an "outcaste" village and helping villagers to fix it up. The success of this led to more such experiments, and the movement blossomed into a full movement. "Sarvodaya" means "the welfare of all," but Ariyaratne expanded it to mean "the awakening of all." This is a socially engaged Buddhist movement with three strands: Gandhian ideals, Buddhist philosophy, and ecumenical spirituality. Its purpose is to have a nonviolent spiritual revolution replace structural violence, starting at the village level. Millions of people have participated in the gatherings and meditations and work (Bond, 2003).

Vietnam

Buddist monk Thich Nhat Hanh said:

> When I was in Vietnam, so many of our villages were being bombed. Along with my monastic brothers and sisters, I had to decide what to do. Should we continue to practice in our monasteries, or should we leave the meditation halls in order to help the people who were suffering under the bombs? After careful reflection, we decided to do both—to go out and help people and to do it in mindfulness. We called it engaged Buddhism. Mindfulness must be engaged. Once there is seeing, there must be acting. (Rothberg, 1998, p. 268)

There was quite a campaign in which Buddhist monks and nuns were very active in opposition to the corruption of the regime of Ngo Dinh Diem, who was ousted as head of government in 1963. Writing of the struggle in a book called *Love in Action: Writings on Nonviolent Social Change*, Thich Nhat Hanh (1993) reports: "Political satirical songs are easy to learn by heart and can be circulated very quickly. They were widely used during the struggle against Ngo Dinh Diem. There were hundreds of them" (p. 11).

In February 1964, Hanh established the Tiep Hien Order—the Order of Interbeing, with a few dedicated followers devoted to Engaged Buddhism. The war with Americans was escalating. Buddhist teachings countered intense hatred and violence. The Order was founded on the Fourteen Precepts or Mindfulness Trainings. He and several university professors and students also founded the School of Youth for Social Service, which organized teams of young people to go into the countryside to establish schools and health clinics and to rebuild bombed villages.

In 1966, Hanh left Vietnam to call for peace but was not allowed to return. In 1967, Martin Luther King nominated him for the Nobel Peace Prize, saying "this gentle Buddhist monk from Vietnam is a scholar of immense intellectual capacity. His ideas for peace, if applied, would build a monument to ecumenism, to world brotherhood, to humanity."

In 1969, Hanh led the Buddhist Peace Delegation to the Paris Peace Talks, which were an attempt to negotiate an end to the American war in Vietnam.

By 1982, developments in France allowed Hanh to establish Plum Village, a meditation centre and home to the Order of Interbeing, where thousands of people from different faiths come from all over the world to attend retreats. A sangha (community of practice) of about 150 monks, nuns, and lay practitioners live there permanently.

FORMS OF VIOLENCE

Blood Sacrifice

Ritual human sacrifice to please, placate, or bargain with divinity was never originally contemplated under Buddhism. Ritual animal sacrifice was also rejected by Buddhism when rejecting the practice under the Vedas. Buddhism holds compassion to animals in strong regard.

The basic idea underlying much of blood sacrifice was that it was necessary to appease malicious spirits, but Buddhists understood that malicious spirits were to be tamed through the good will efforts from holy individuals. The theme of a holy person converting monstrous people was common as the way Buddhists interacted with the spirit cults in the lands to which it spread, thus undercutting the philosophy behind the animal sacrifices and making them cease.

Slavery

In the *Sigalovada Sutta*, "Discourse to Sigala," Buddha says, "In five ways should a master minister to his servants and employees: by assigning them work according to their ability; by supplying them with food and with wages; by tending them in sickness; by sharing with them any delicacies; by granting them leave at times." This does not allow for slavery. When discussing "right livelihood" on the eight-fold path, trade in human beings is excluded, so in theory Buddhists could not be slave-traders.

Slavery has nevertheless been practiced throughout history, sometimes with the logic that it was justified by reincarnation and the working out of karma. Even monasteries owned slaves. At the same time, escaped slaves have often used Buddhist temples as safe havens.

Slavery is not countenanced in contemporary times. Inasmuch as it exists as debt bondage or trafficking or similar forms, the mindfulness of Buddhism would suggest watching consumer choices to be sure not to participate.

War

Many Buddhists have refused to take up arms under any circumstances, and Buddhism in general has had a pacifying effect on war-like peoples. Buddhist countries have, however, engaged in wars and justifications of killing (Jerryson & Juergensmeyer, 2010) just as all the long-lasting religions with state power have.

The Death Penalty

Buddhist philosophy has advocated the rehabilitation of criminals, with a famous story of Buddha himself reforming the feared robber and murderer Angulimala, to the amazement of the king. Yet Ashoka, despite other moves to nonviolence, did show use of executions in his rock edicts. Chinese monk Fa-Hsien in the 300s CE wrote he met a king of India who "governed without capital punishment." Emperor Shomu of Japan eschewed the death penalty in the 700s CE. Otherwise, executions were commonly used by Buddhist rulers. Currently, the four countries that have Buddhism as their state religion are Bhutan, Cambodia, Sri Lanka, and Thailand. The status at the time this is written is that Cambodia eliminated the death penalty in 1993, Bhutan did so in 2004, Sri Lanka retains it legally and has many people on death row but had its last execution in 1976, and Thailand retains it.

Infanticide and Feticide

Buddhism has been forceful in its opposition to female infanticide, opposing it in the countries where it was practiced despite the teachings. There is no single Buddhist view on abortion, with varying laws in Buddhist-influenced countries, but it is most commonly regarded negatively as taking a life and therefore bad karma.

Meat

Dietary restrictions, similar to Hinduism, have a vegetarian foundation, which is widespread but not universal. The Mahayana Buddhist tradition is more strictly vegetarian, with monks and nuns entirely vegetarian and the laity encouraged to do so; it is less prominent in other traditions.

Poverty

Poverty is a form of ill-being and therefore one of the things the Buddhist path is to help avoid. Material wealth can make people miserable, while simple living can be done with contentment, but being deprived is another matter; it is violence and can lead to worse violence (Loy, 2003).

Violence in the Scriptures

The *Nirvana Sutra* (more formally, the *Mahayana Mahapari Nirvana Sutra*) in chapter 19 offers a story about one of Buddha's past lives; the Buddha said:

> When I recall the past, I remember that I was the king of a great state. . . . My name was Senyo, and I loved and venerated the *Mahayana sutras*. . . . When I heard the Brahmins slandering the *vaipulya sutras*, I put them to death on the spot . . . as a result of that action, I never thereafter fell into hell.

Chapter 19 goes on to praise a king who defended monks with weapons in battle and says, "A person who upholds the *Wonderful Dharma* should take the sword and staff and guard monks." In addition to protection of Buddhism, here we have "compassionate killing"—it was a favor to those killed to keep them from increasing their bad karma and to expend some of that bad karma. The idea is that killing done out of hatred or greed is wrong, but that done instead with compassion is different.

Chapter 5 of the same scriptural book has: "The [true] follower of the *Mahayana* is not the one who observes the five precepts, but the one who uses the sword, bow, arrow, and battle-ax to protect the monks who uphold the precepts and who are pure."

There is not a good way of turning these into allegories, and they are unsettling to many Buddhists who point out the preponderance of nonviolent scripture that overwhelms them. Nevertheless, they have been acted upon throughout Buddhist history. Those who were searching for a scriptural justification find it here. Buddhism has the same problem as all other ancient religions in this regard have.

Treatment of "Heretics"

Truth is important, but understanding and perspectives can be flexible, so persecution of heretics is not common in Buddhism.

The term for an incorrigible nonbeliever is *icchantika*. Some scriptures assert that even these can attain to Buddhahood eventually. However, there are several spots in the *Nirvana Sutra* that say that they must go to hell and that it is no sin to kill them (in chapters 22, 24, 34, 39, and 40). This is not the most widespread view, but it is an available one for those who want it.

RELATIONS WITH OTHER RELIGIONS

Christianity

Thich Nhat Hanh (1995) wrote a book considering Buddhism and Christianity together called *Living Buddha, Living Christ*. He emphasizes spiritual experience, mindfulness and aliveness as common to both: "We know that our body is the continuation of the Buddha's body and is a member of the mystical body of Christ. We have a wonderful opportunity to help the Buddha and Jesus Christ continue" (p. 58). He offers this comparison:

> The society of India at the time of the Buddha was less violent than the society into which Jesus was born, so you may think the Buddha was less extreme in his reactions, but that is only because another way was possible in his milieu. . . . If the Buddha had been born into the society in which Jesus was born, I think he, too, would have been crucified." (pp. 54–55)

On the negative side, Hanh does offer a common Buddhist view that any assertions that Jesus is unique are not helpful because *everyone* is unique and that Christian missionaries were encouraging rootlessness when roots are very important.

Hinduism

Once the royal sponsorship of Buddhism left Ashoka's empire, the Hindu traditionalists reestablished themselves. Missionary Buddhists then traveled to neighboring countries and spread out mainly unanchored from the India/Nepal roots.

Buddhism arose in a Hindu culture, but developed its own scripture and was explicitly uninterested in the caste system, giving an outlet to Hindus who oppose the caste system or other features to convert to a similar religion. Bhimrao Ramji Ambedkar (1891–1956), for example, was an Indian civil rights leader and a 1935 Buddhist convert. In October 14, 1956, the 2,500th anniversary year of Buddha's enlightenment and the traditional date of Ashoka's conversion, he and his wife and about half a million Dalit people ("untouchable" caste—Dalit means oppressed ones) officially publicly embraced Buddhism for this reason.

Islam

There are currently six countries where large populations of Buddhists and Muslims interact with each other: Tibet and Burma/Myanmar, where the Buddhists predominate over with Muslim minorities; Thailand, a Buddhist-majority country of which southern Thailand has majority Muslims; and Malaysia, Indonesia, and Bangladesh, Muslim-majority countries with Buddhist populations. Relations range from harmonious to problematic.

Judaism

Since Buddha is not worshiped as a divinity and practices of Buddhist forms of meditation can be appealing to some Jews, there has been some fruitful interchange. This includes a dialogue between rabbis and the Dalai Lama (Kamenetz, 1994).

The Japanese lay Buddhist group Soka Gakkai worked with the Simon Wiesenthal Center to combat anti-Semitism in Japan. Japan had been allies with Germany in World War II, and the rabbis at the Simon Wiesenthal Center expressed frustration about getting the Japanese media to understand about the Holocaust. The people from Soku University (founded by Soka Gakkai's president Daisaku Ikeda) developed a Japanese version of a traveling Holocaust exhibit, "The Courage to Remember," seen by over 2 million people (Seager, 2006).

Related Religion: Cao Dai

Cao Dai is a religion that began in Vietnam, officially founded on September 26, 1926, by 247 disciples following Ngô Văn Chiêu, who had several revelations during séances. It currently has around 2 to

6 million adherents and is the third largest religion in Vietnam (after Buddhism and Catholicism, not counting atheism). There are a few thousand adherents and some organized churches outside Vietnam.

It encountered violent prosecution from the French colonial government and organized an army in response, winning concessions. Once Vietnam was reunified in 1975, it was restricted by the Communist government, with a governing council under the direct control of the government. In 1997, it received official governmental approval.

It is a deliberately syncretic religion—that is, taking the best from various religions. It is organized with a hierarchy including a Pope at the top and has bishops and churches. Its holy texts include *The Collection of Divine Messages*, written by the founder. It is based on the principle that all religions have the same divine origin.

World history is divided into three periods of revelation. The first was when God inspired the founding of Judaism, Hinduism, and the Yi philosophy of transformation in China. A couple thousand years later, in the second period, God inspired Buddhism, Taoism, and Christianity. The third period is necessary now for the same reason the second period was: over time, the truth of the religions become distorted, and a fresh start was needed. While it was logical to having religions adapted to specific societies, now that we have a worldwide community, the multiplicity of religions is more of a problem. So it is time to unify on the same foundational ethic of love and justice.

Its web page statement of introduction is:

> The noble effort of Cao Dai is to unite all of humanity through a common vision of the Supreme Being, whatever our minor differences, in order to promote peace and understanding throughout the world. Cao Dai does not seek to create a gray world, where all religions are exactly the same, only to create a more tolerant world, where all can see each other as sisters and brothers from a common divine source reaching out to a common divine destiny realizing peace within and without.

4

Zoroastrianism: Good Conscience

While the current number of Zoroastrians is so low that it would not be enough to count as a world religion, perhaps around 200,000 worldwide according to the World Religion Database, its contribution to the development of nonviolence is substantial enough that it needs to be covered. Ideas that it established were highly influential on Judaism, Christianity, and Islam. It calls itself the Religion of Good Conscience; the concept of actually having a conscience, and practicing ethics as part of religion, countered the violent practices of the religions of the time.

ZOROASTRIAN HISTORY AND SCRIPTURES

Zoroastrianism was the official religion of Persia for over a millennium, from around 549 BCE until 651 CE, when Arabs conquered Persia and established Islam instead as Persia's official religion. It is one of the world's oldest monotheistic religions.

Depending on the dating for its founding prophet Zarathustra, also called by his Greek name Zoroaster, it may be the oldest by far. Linguistic language analysis of his writings and the language's similarities with the Hindu Rig Veda, as reported by Mary Boyce (1992), places him somewhere between 1200 and 1700 BCE. The traditional dating as told by the Zoroastrian Magi to the ancient Greek historians puts him at about a century before the Persian emperor Cyrus in the 600s BCE. There is other recent scholarship asserting this later period to be more likely to be accurate. Gherardo Gnoli (2000) is specific enough to make his years about 618–541 BCE.

This makes a difference in whether Zarathustra was in a stone-age nomad society or right before the start of the Persian empire. It makes a difference on whether there is a possibility of the historical stories being accurate about him being contemporary or recent to people such as the Judean prophet Ezekiel and the Greek Pythagoras. The latter date would also make him one of the sages of the Axial Age (see chapter 5).

Either way, Zoroastrianism clearly became much more prominent in that latter time period. For about a millennium it was one of the most powerful religions in the world. Though its influence is considerably diminished today, it does still have adherents. The majority of Zoroastrians are in Iran and in India; in India they are called Parsis due to their Persian heritage.

The one God who created the world was named Ahura Mazda, which means Wise Lord. Ahura Mazda was understood to have revealed the truth through the prophet Zarathustra. Ahura Mazda's qualities include being compassionate, just, all-knowing, all-powerful, unchanging, everywhere, and impossible for humans to understand fully. Ahura Mazda is the creator of life and source of all goodness and all happiness.

Zoroastrians traditionally pray five times a day. There is no tradition of monasticism or celibacy, and most worship happens in the family home rather than in congregations. They gather in communities during seven annual festivals. At their initiation ceremonies, the child is given a shirt and cord, which are considered sacred. They tie the cord around the shirt three times to remind themselves of the basic principles: Good Thoughts. Good Words. Good Deeds. This ritual is carried out with prayers several times a day and underscores what daily behavior is expected.

They also have Fire Temples, not because they worship fire but because fire symbolizes God's light and wisdom. Priests carry out rituals there.

Their primary holy scripture is called the *Avesta*. It contains two main sections. The older part contains the Gathas, 17 hymns understood to have been composed by Zarathustra himself. The Younger Avesta is composed of commentaries to the older Avesta, along with myths, stories, and details of ritual observances.

Zoroastrianism believes in dualism: good and evil are separate things, constantly opposing each other. They do so cosmically within the universe and morally within the mind.

Cosmically, there is an ongoing battle between Ahura Mazda and the evil Angra Mainyu. Angra Mainyu is not an equal opposite, but is the destructive energy opposing Ahura Mazda's creative energy.

Ahura Mazda created a pure world with creative energy, but Angra Mainyu continues to attack it. This is what causes disease, famine, natural disasters, and wars. Life is a mixture of these two opposing forces.

Moral dualism, then, involves these two opposing forces within the mind of individuals. Ahura Mazda gave humanity the gift of free will, so each individual has the choice to follow the path of truth or deceit. The path of evil leads to misery and hell, the path of righteousness leads to peace and everlasting happiness in heaven. The duality is the same as with cosmic dualism except for the emphasis on making choices. When all individuals choose Ahura Mazda and reject Angra Mainyu, evil will be defeated and we can have paradise on earth. There is a positive outlook, a belief that humanity is inherently good and that in the end good will triumph over evil. Human beings, rather than being the children or servants of God, are seen as God's helpers in this ultimate triumph through the making of positive choices.

This can also involve universalism in the idea that hell is not forever. Some Zoroastrians believe that once good overcomes all evil, the dead will rise, redeemed and purified. Even Angra Mainyu, the Spirit of the Lie, will repent in the end.

Action is important, as the "good deeds" principle would suggest. Zoroastrians are active in improving the local community with educational and other social initiatives and giving generously to charities. The Parsis in India are particularly well known for schools and hospitals and other benefits to the wider community in which they live.

Zarathustra is not worshiped, but revered as the bringer of the revelation. He worked as a priest, had a wife and three sons and three daughters. He was born into a culture where animal sacrifice was common. The ritual use of intoxicants was clearly linked to violent behavior. Religious rites also served to put young men into a frenzy to send them into battle or into raids.

The story is that when he was 30 years old, Zarathustra was bathing in a river during a purification rite and had a vision: on the bank of the river was a Shining Being made of light who stated his name was *Vohu Manah*, meaning Good Mind. Vohu Manah asked Zarathustra what he most wanted and, having got the reply of wisdom, led Zarathustra into the presence of Ahura Mazda and other radiant beings, the *Amesha Spentas*—Benevolent Spirits, emanating from God as light rays emanate from the sun. This was the first of seven visions, during which Zarathustra asked many questions; the answers he got were the foundations of Zoroastrianism.

The five Benevolent Spirits are understood as divine attributes of God, helping to fashion the world, each associated with a different aspect of creation. They represent spiritual attainments and it is through these Divine Attributes that we come to know God. These are:

1. *Vohu Mana*—Good Mind
2. *Asha Vahista*—Truth and Righteousness
3. *Spenta Armaity*—Love and Benevolence
4. *Kshathra Vairya*—Power and Just Rule
5. *Haurvatat*—Wholeness and Health
6. *Ameratat*—Immortality and Eternal Bliss

Zarathustra's assertions threatened the status quo and received animosity accordingly. After 12 years of trying, he did finally find a receptive audience outside his homeland: King Vishtaspa and Queen Hutosa of Bactria, an area now in northern Afghanistan. Unfortunately, this led other neighboring royalty to attack, and the king used defensive war to protect the new religion. Therefore, the "just war" concept, while not formalized, was present at the beginning, to allow the new religion protection from attacks. Zarathustra himself is said by legend to have died as an old man in one of these attacks when stabbed with a ritual dagger by a priest of the old religion.

Zoroastrianism was a well-established religion when the Archaemenian Empire started, that being the name of the family of pious Zoroastrians from which Cyrus came. Cyrus overthrew the Median court in western Iran and thereby founded the Persian Empire in 549 BCE. The fact that he and subsequent rulers conquered shows that Zoroastrianism is not sufficient to keep its adherents from warring—but then, no religion has achieved that when state power was at stake.

Cyrus understood himself as ruling according to Zoroastrian beliefs, which included not imposing the beliefs on subject territories. The act of kindness of letting the exiled Jews return to their homeland and rebuild their temple was a major event in the history of Judaism.

The defeat of Darius III by Alexander ("the Great") in 331 BCE dealt a major blow to Zoroastrianism, with many of the priests killed (thus losing oral traditions) and the major part of the scriptures destroyed, leaving only the core with the Gathas to survive. The Seleucids, who took over after Alexander (311 BCE–141 BCE), allowed the religion regional autonomy, then the Parthian Arcasids (141 BCE–224 CE) overthrew them. These Persians ruled for longer than the Archaemenians but were less centralized. They gathered back the scriptures that they could, were tolerant of various faiths, and tried to rule according to Zoroastrian principles. Then the Sasanians (224 CE until the 600s) took over, starting with Ardashir, who overcame the shock of the overthrow by arguing that the Arcasids were not orthodox Zoroastrians, whereas he was. His chief priest compiled the single canon of scriptures. In this period, a single church was developed under Persian's control; images in worship were banned; Fire Temples were promoted; and the traditional tolerance to other faiths was abandoned, as Jews and Christians among others were persecuted.

By the end of the period, the church-state was wealthy and authoritarian, keeping other religions out and becoming more oppressive by demanding time and money from ordinary people. It was ripe for reform. Therefore, the Arab conquest and rise of Islam were facilitated. As with the earlier invasion of Alexander, because of the conquest, libraries were burned and much heritage lost.

Islam did regard Zoroastrians, along with Jews and Christians, as People of the Book—they could retain religious practice while paying extra taxes. The new government offered many other inducements to convert to Islam, and over time the majority of the population did. Zoroastrianism became and remains a minority religion in Iran. Numbers currently in Iran are difficult to ascertain; since conversion away from Islam is considered a crime, conversions there (that is, converting back to what is known to be the previous religion) are often kept confidential.

In the 900s, however, there was a group who engaged in noncooperation by withdrawing to the Khorasan mountains. Being pursued there, they went to the port city of Hormuz, and being pursued there, sailed for India, another case of massive withdrawal to noncooperate with coercion. It also achieved the goal, since the Zoroastrians have been an active and sustained community in India to this day. There, they are called Parsis (Parsi being the Gujarati language word for Persian).

With the two major concentrations of Zoroastrians today being in Iran and India, there has been a global dispersion of others into various countries. Their sparse population spread out, and since everywhere it is a tiny minority, there have been struggles to keep the faith alive. But centuries of defying adversity and insisting on remaining true have kept the religion going this long despite all odds, and defying the odds (as with Judaism) lends itself to building good character—the kind of character quite necessary for any forms of nonviolent action.

ZOROASTRIAN BELIEFS AND ACTIONS ON NONVIOLENCE

The *Zend-Avesta* says: "The best way to worship God is to ease the distress of the times and to improve the condition of humanity." This is a general principle; the *Yacht* expands:

> We worship the Spirits of the Virtuous to withstand the wrong done by the oppressors who corrupt power and authority; to withstand the wrong done by the dead-in-conscience who forget the social good; and to withstand the wrong done by those yielding to passion, wrath, war, and violence.

Zarathustra was clearly rebelling against the religion of his culture. With many gods, the royalty and priesthood controlled ordinary people so there was an oppressive class structure.

He proposed instead that all human beings were equal. While the practice was that men dominated women and regarded them as inferior, Zarathustra insisted instead that men and women were equal (Gatha songs 3.2, 17.5, A Airyema Ishya, and Haptanghaiti songs 1.6, 5.3). Human equality is important in Zoroastrianism: male and female, rich and poor, young and old are all equal. The only way one human being surpasses another is through greater righteousness. The assertion of the equality of women is particularly notable for that time and subsequent time periods.

He opposed the animal sacrifices and the use of intoxicants in rituals. The gods of the old religion were pleased with strife and war and various other forms of violence, and Zarathustra said these were evil spirits. They were workers of Ahura Mazda's adversary, Angra Mainyu. Rather than religion being a set of rituals to placate angry gods, it was a motivation for ethical behavior.

Because Ahura Mazda created the world pure, all parts of creation should be treated with care and respect. The natural environment is thus not to be polluted, and so some have called Zoroastrianism "the first ecological religion." Zoroastrians are still especially active in the environmental movement today.

In short, Zoroastrianism was a religion founded in being opposed to violence—domination and inequality, aggressive war, and ecological damage.

By focusing on just and benevolent behavior toward other human beings, it laid a necessary foundation for nonviolence as a problem-solver. People have to actually care about what is and is not just or ethical or merciful before nonviolent action is even considered.

The appeals to conscience that make nonviolence so effective require that people be mindful that they have consciences.

The objective of the righteous is to win over the wrongful into the righteous camp. This establishes a good life for all (Songs 3, 4, 10, and many more references). It is also what nonviolent campaigns are organized to do.

The Parsis made generous contributions to Indian society. With a reputation for honesty and value of education; helping the poor; building schools, hospitals, and so on; and the ability for upward mobility unrestrained by the caste system of India, they have had an influence disproportionate to their numbers. Many of them did participate in the nonviolent campaigns for Indian independence, and they had accumulated enough wealth to be able to contribute economically and help social institutions for that cause.

FORMS OF VIOLENCE

Blood Sacrifice

Human sacrifice as a ceremony was never considered as a possibility in Zoroastrianism. Animal sacrifice was explicitly rejected by Zarathustra as contrary to the spirit of compassion or what God would want (see *Yasna* 32:3 and 32:8, for example). He expressed sympathy from the cow's point of view. Nevertheless, such sacrifice was reintroduced in later years. It is not practiced now and has not been for some time.

Slavery

Under the Persian empires, for the most part, a Zoroastrian was not to be held as a slave, and a non-Zoroastrian was not allowed to own slaves. Slavery did exist, but not the kind of mass slavery that contemporary cultures practiced. It is long gone among adherents now.

War

The religious foundations for raids and battles were undercut by Zoroastrian practice, and the end of wars was one of the expectations for the spreading of goodness. Their presence is the work of Angra Mainyu. However, defensive war was practiced on Zarathustra's behalf in his lifetime, and of course the Persian empires that embraced the religion practiced war as part of their conquering practice.

The Death Penalty

Though a case could be made against capital punishment from the Zoroastrian scriptures from those who wish to do so, executions were practiced when it was a state religion.

Infanticide and Feticide

Zoroastrian scripture understands abortion as an unjust taking of the child's life and reassures a pregnant, unmarried woman that she need not feel shame and thus resort to it. The father and the community also have obligations toward sustaining the child's life, prenatally and postnatally (Vendidad 15:9–16).

Meat

There has been vegetarian sentiment historically. A few scattered verses of scripture have been read that way, though others have read the same verses differently.

In the *Sayings of Adarbad Mahraspandan*, who was the high priest and prime minster under King Shapur II (309–379 CE), we find:

> Abstain rigorously from eating the flesh of cows and all beneficent animals, lest you be made to face a strict reckoning in this world and the next; for by eating the flesh of cows and other domestic animals, you involve your hand in sin, and thereby think, speak, and do what is sinful; for though you may eat but a mouthful, you involve your hand in sin, and though a camel be slain by another person in another place, it is as if you who eat its flesh had slain it with your own hand. (Adapted from Zaehner, 1956, p. 110)

This edict comes from High Priest Atrupat-e Emetan in *Dinkard, Book 6* written in the 11th century CE: "Be plant-eaters (*urwar khwarishn*, i.e., vegetarian), O you people, so that you may live long. And stay away from the body of useful animals. As well, deeply reckon that Ohrmazd [Ahura Mazda] the Lord, has for the sake of benefiting useful animals created many plants" (Eduljee, 2014).

The poet Ferdowsi's epic, the *Shahnameh*, written around 977–1010 CE, has an early legend of a king being seduced into eating meat by the devil in the form of a cook. This suggests vegetarianism was understood as being practiced before that time.

There have been proposals that early Zoroastrian vegetarianism influenced Hinduism, Buddhism, and Jainism to the east of Persia, but this is difficult to verify. Today, there is a Parsee Vegetarian and Temperance Society that actively promotes vegetarianism, but the diet is not common in Iranian Zoroastrians.

Poverty

Zoroastrians regard involuntary poverty as one of the afflictions that they want to work to remove from the world, a product of Angra Mainyu and destructive energies. As Parsis, they have been active in poverty-prevention programs (such as schools) in India.

Violence in the Scriptures

A web search found neither discussion nor references to writings on violence in the Zoroastrian scriptures.

Treatment of "Heretics"

Zoroastrianism has primarily been in harmony with other religions and is currently for the most part not seeking converts (with some exceptions), holding that people should remain in whatever religions God guided them into. There have of course been historical periods when rulers used imposition of orthodoxy as a way of consolidating their own power. However, suppression of heresies has not been a major theme.

RELATIONS WITH OTHER RELIGIONS

Judaism

Whichever dates for Zarathustra are correct, it clearly predates the Jewish exile in Babylon. Therefore, the ideas were prominent when the Jews were forced to live there. The influence became more prominent when the Persians overthrew the Babylonians, and it made a positive impression on Jews when a royal adherent of Zoroastrianism allowed them to return home from exile.

Parallels with the Hebrew prophet Ezekiel have been noted. For example, Ezekiel's vision of the dry bones lying exposed (in chapter 37 of his Biblical book) would be horrifying to Jews, who buried their dead, but expected in Zoroastrianism, where the dead are deliberately exposed to the air to be made into bones. That this becomes the scene of general resurrection—when resurrection was not previously a theme of Jewish scripture—suggests Zoroastrian influence.

Before the exile, death was seen as going to the shadowy realm of *Sheol*; afterward, the concept of heaven and hell were more pronounced (see the Biblical Daniel 12:2). Before the exile, Satan was simply an accusing angel who showed up infrequently, but afterward, the role of an evil angel as a dualistic opponent of God who causes calamities—the Jewish version of Angra Mainyu—became more common. The concept of a last judgment day when all are bodily resurrected appears first in Zoroastrianism, and then appears in Judaism timed with the exile.

There is a logic to all this, after all; both religions are strongly monotheistic in highly polytheistic environments. Judaism had trouble maintaining this and many accounted their Babylonian exile as being a result of that fact. Zoroastrianism offered some monotheistic concepts that helped solve some of the conundrums that Judaism had experienced. This is said from a sociological point of view; from the point of view of divine revelation, it can be said that God deliberately exposed the Jews to these ideas in order to help in their spiritual development.

Hinduism

When Muslims took over in Persia and persecution of Zoroastrians was strong, a large group fled to India; tradition mainly ascribes this to the year 936 CE, though likely many waves went since other years are also given. They asked for asylum from the local Hindu ruler, Jadi Rana, who granted it on five conditions: that they educate him about their religion; give up speaking Persian and only speak the local Gujarati; women would dress in saris like Indian women; men would give up their weapons; and they must hold weddings only in the evening to keep from interfering with Hindu ceremonies.

This was after some persuasion. Rana held up a pitcher with milk overflowing to show his area was already full, but the Zoroastrians added some sugar to the milk to show that they could add something without making things overflow. They were given a small amount of land, and since Parsi is the Gujarati word for Persian, they have been called Parsis (or Parsees) ever since.

The Parsi community has remained in India for over a millennium, active in helping the entire community with establishing schools, hospitals, libraries, and so on. Since they were not bound by the Hindu caste system, which impeded social mobility for Hindus, they were also successful in business and banking. They are a very small minority in India, but India currently has the highest concentration of Zoroastrians in the world.

Christianity

All that is said previously about the relationship of Zoroastrianism to Judaism would also apply to Christianity, where the concepts of heaven and hell, the devil, and a physical resurrection with judgment have been prominent from the start. Yet there is more that is specific to Christianity.

As Zoroastrianism was moving westward, one of the groups that decided to join was a priestly tribe of Medes who were keepers of medical lore and astronomy, called Magi. Anyone familiar with the Gospel of Matthew's story of Jesus's birth will recognize that group as having members who came from their homeland to see the newborn baby. Tradition has three wise men and even gives their names, but Matthew only says that there was a group of them. The number three may have arisen later from the three gifts they brought of gold, frankincense, and myrrh.

However, Zoroastrians were not only monotheists with ideas of religion being about ethical behavior but they also anticipated a savior to come, the Saoshyant. Since Matthew mentions them and Luke does not (and only these two of the four Gospels have birth stories), some have understood that Matthew selected that detail to make an appeal to Gentiles in general. But it would clearly make an appeal specifically to Zoroastrians. It has them be active in the unfolding of the Christian story.

We do not know how successful this was, though there are many stories of early Persian converts. However, non-Christian Zoroastrianism continued to be very strong for centuries afterward. At the time of the beginning of Christianity, Zoroastrianism was among the most powerful religions and one of only two prominent monotheistic ones (Judaism being the other, and Christianity was not yet regarded as a separate religion from Judaism). So an appeal by a Christian evangelizer that directly included Zoroastrian participation made a great deal of sense.

Islam

Since Zoroastrians were concentrated in Persia, now Iran, when Arabs and later Turks and Mongols conquered Persia, the conquerors spent the first few years in a majority Zoroastrian country. Gradually many converted to Islam. The two religions shared belief in one God, heaven and hell, angels, a final judgment day, and even a practice of praying at specified times five times a day. Islam also recognized earlier prophets sent to all nations, so Zarathustra could still be given respect. Converting to Islam was updating to the final prophet, rather than rejecting the previous one.

Nevertheless, many Zoroastrians did not convert, and in the 900s CE, some fled to India in order to preserve their religion. However, many remained in Iran and are there to this day. There are some Iranian Muslims who take pride in the native group's perseverance.

Some of the Parsis—Indian Zoroastrians—ended up in Pakistan when India was partitioned, and they are mostly concentrated around Karachi. One was a mayor there for 12 years and there are streets named after Parsi individuals.

Bahá'ís

The Bahá'ís believe their founder, Bahá'u'lláh, was a direct descendent of Zoroaster, and that Bahá'u'lláh is the predicted coming saviour. Zoroastrianism is one of the nine religions recognized as having been founded by divine revelations to a divine messenger.

Related Religions: Yazidis

Yazidis live mainly in Iraq in the Kurdish area, with communities in Armenia, Georgia, and Syria who have large portions migrating to Europe. Estimates of how many there are range from 70,000 to half a million. They are monotheists whose religion is related to Zoroastrianism and other ancient Mesopotamian religions with some Sufi Muslim influence.

The creator God placed the care of the world under seven angels, and the chief archangel, Melek Taus (Peacock Angel), caused both good and bad to befall. Thus he fell out of God's favor, but his remorseful tears extinguished the fires of his hellish prison, and he was reconciled to God. Due to misunderstanding the story, some have equated Melek Taus with the devil and called the Yazidis devil worshippers. The charge is offensive to the Yazidis, but has been associated with much historic persecution.

Yazidis became newsworthy in 2014 when the Islamic State in Iraq and Syria (ISIS) targeted them for forced conversion or annihilation. In response to all of what ISIS was doing, many Muslim scholars signed an Open Letter to al-Baghdadi (2014) calling on ISIS to repent, and point 11 said: "It is obligatory to consider Yazidis as People of the Scripture." This gives the Yazidis the same status as other monotheists like Zoroastrians, Jews, and Christians; their right to practice their religion should be respected by Muslims.

5

Ancient Times and Religious Revolutions

ANCIENT ACTION

The first recorded labor strike occurred in ancient Egypt, around 1155 or 1170 BCE, in the 29th year of Pharaoh Ramses III. The government owed rations to the artisans building the necropolis (pyramids where the dead were laid to rest). When those rations did not come, there were several strikes, using the temples as a base, until they finally succeeded (Edgerton, 1951; Frandsen, 1990).

As another example, Roman workers got the power of the Veto in 494 BCE with the nonviolent action of the walkout. The ancient Roman historian Livy gives the following account about the first time the plebeians (the lower-class workers) held a walkout against the patricians (the rich upper class). As he begins, consuls are giving trials to debtors who were unable to handle the high interest changes. Livy starts with one man about to be tried:

> As he stood silent, and a number of men had closed round him to prevent his being seized, the consuls sent a lictor [police officer] to him. The lictor was pushed away, and those senators who were with the consuls exclaimed that it was an outrageous insult and rushed down from the tribunal to assist the lictor. The hostility of the crowd was diverted from the lictor, who had simply been prevented from making the arrest, to the senators. The interposition of the consuls finally allayed the conflict. There had, however, been no stones thrown or weapons used. It had resulted in more noise and angry words than personal injury . . .
>
> [*After much debate in the Senate, the plebeians*] decided, at the instigation of a certain Sicinius, to ignore the consuls and withdraw to the Sacred Mount, which lay on the other side of the Anio, three

miles from the City. . . . There, without any commander in a regularly entrenched camp, taking nothing with them but the necessaries of life, they quietly maintained themselves for some days, neither receiving nor giving any provocation. A great panic seized the City. Mutual distrust led to a state of universal suspense. Those plebeians who had been left by their comrades in the City feared violence from the patricians; the patricians feared the plebeians who still remained in the City, and could not make up their minds whether they would rather have them go or stay. "How long," it was asked, "would the multitude who had seceded remain quiet? What would happen if a foreign war broke out in the meantime?" They felt that all their hopes rested on concord amongst the citizens, and that this must be restored at any cost. . . . Negotiations were then entered upon for a reconciliation. An agreement was arrived at, the terms being that the plebs should have its own magistrates, whose persons were to be inviolable, and who should have the right of affording protection against the consuls. And further, no patrician should be allowed to hold that office. (*Livy's History of Rome* 2.29–2.33)

This was called the *first secession*. There was another one 50 years later, and a third one in 297 BCE. Rights that were established and reestablished included the right to have a Tribune that could say, "Veto," which is Latin for "I forbid," so patricians could not pass laws the plebeians could not tolerate. They also got to pass resolutions called "plebiscitas," from which we got our modern word *plebiscite*.

Livy wrote more than four centuries after the event he recounts, and he has a patrician bias, so some scholars have skepticism accordingly. Nevertheless, the story did last all that time.

These are two fairly prominent examples from the ancient times, when the polytheistic indigenous religions held sway. So there were appeals to the gods for help, just as there were for all kinds of other endeavors. In each case, the appeal of nonviolence was not a universal principle, since these were struggles between people of the same society, who might have been willing to be violent to those outside the society, but not to those within it. Primarily, nonviolent tactics were used here because of their effectiveness. Noncooperation was in the hands of the initially powerless. Those powerless people came to understand that because of their ability to cooperate or not, they had more power than had originally been thought.

In the theoretical discussions of nonviolence, there are those who hold to it as a matter of principle, even in circumstances where it might not be practical. There are others (notably, Gene Sharp) who argue that it is the very practicality of nonviolence that recommends it and that we need not convince people to be pacifists in order to see the value of it. Religious people, of whatever religion, often take the principled view because having principles is a major thing that religion is all about. Still, there are religious people who follow various "just war" traditions who will indeed be more influenced by practicality.

THE AXIAL AGE

The concept of an age being an axis, a pivot, commonly called the Axial Age, first arose with Karl Jaspers (1953) who noticed that the period mainly around the sixth century BCE saw the rise of individual thinkers, and "the spiritual foundations of humanity were laid simultaneously and independently in China, India, Persia, Judea, and Greece. And these are the foundations upon which humanity still subsists today" (Jaspers, 2003, p. 98). He saw some striking parallel developments. Sages arose during periods of similar political situations: smaller states with many internal and external wars. Old certainties were crumbling so that new ideas were needed. The Axial Age idea has its critics, but it has led to a lot of scholarly discussion. Included in the Axial Age are:

- China had its Warring States period. The most famous sages are Confucius/K'ung Fu Tze for Confucianism, and Lao-Tsu for Taoism (covered later in this chapter). Mo Tse is of special interest for the history of nonviolence and is covered more extensively later in this chapter.
- For India, the rise of the "sramana" traditions that include Buddhism, which we covered in chapter 3, and Jainism, which we covered as a religion related to Hinduism in chapter 2. Both of these religions were assertively nonviolent in their origin. The Upanishads were also written in this period as a major advance in Hinduism.
- Judea had the prophets, such as Isaiah, Jeremiah, Ezekiel, and Elijah. We covered in chapter 1 the crucial role these figures played in the development of nonviolence philosophy.
- Greece had the era of classic philosophy, which included Socrates, Plato, and Aristotle, along with several other Greek thinkers. For establishment of nonviolence, Pythagoras will be of most interest and is covered later in this chapter.
- Persia may well contribute the rise of Zoroastrianism to this era; Jasper thought so and included Zoroaster in his Axial Age list, due to the traditional dating of when Zoroaster lived. There are scholars that date Zoroaster as much earlier, but in any event,

the religion became more widespread and official during this time period. For our purposes, being more interested in religious innovation than in the theory of the Axial Age, the exact dating is not as important as noting the religion's role in abhorrence of violence and advocacy of nonviolence over the previous religion of its area.

Karen Armstrong (2006) did an extensive history of this era, calling it *The Great Transformation: The Beginning of our Religious Traditions*. Her book expands the period and covers from around 900 BCE to around 200 BCE. She noted features the sages of this era had in common, including most especially compassion for others and the various versions of the Golden Rule. She comments:

> Some people have concluded either that religion itself is inescapably violent or that violence and intolerance are endemic to a particular tradition. But the story of the Axial Age shows that in fact the opposite is the case. Every single one of these faiths began in principled and visceral recoil from the unprecedented violence of their time. (Armstrong, 2006, p. 393)

ANCIENT CHINA

Ancient Philosophers and War

Mo Ti (480–390 BCE), more commonly called by the title of Mo Tse (which means Teacher Mo), lived in the small state of Sung during China's Warring States period. He was a governmental minister in one of the states and a respected philosopher. He taught the importance of universal love (*chien ai*). In contrast to Confucius, who had a hierarchy of love with family first, Mo Tse taught love of everyone. He saw this as essential:

> Whence come disorders? They arise from lack of mutual love ... robbers and brigands who likewise love their own households, but not the homes of others and so rob others' homes for the benefit of their own. Like unto those, too, are state officers and princes who make war on other countries—because they love their own country but not other countries, and to seek to profit their own country at the expense of others. The ultimate cause of all disorders in the world is the lack of mutual love.

He especially detested offensive war. His opposition was a passionate one, as can be seen by a story that is told about him in numerous sources. Kung-Shu Pan was the state engineer of the state of Chu and had just completed a new intention—a "cloud ladder"—for use in besieging walled cities. Because of this, the king of Chu was planning an invasion into the state of Sung. As soon as Mo Tse learned about this, he started out from his native state and traveled 10 days and 10 nights all on foot. He arrived at the capital city of Chu with sunburnt face and battered feet and secured an interview with Kung-Shu Pan. He then proceeded to convince the state engineer that his cause was to be condemned. Kung-Shu Pan is reported to have said, "Before I met you, I had wanted to conquer the state of Sung. But since I have seen you, I would not have it even if it were given to me without resistance but with no just cause" (Shih, 1963, p. 58). Being then presented to the king, Mo Tse succeeded finally in convincing him not to wage an offensive campaign.

He was taken seriously, because he lived in an age when philosophers were highly respected. Several times he succeeded in stopping attacks. His basic argument was:

> To kill one man is to be guilty of a capital crime, to kill ten men is to increase the guilt ten-fold, to kill a hundred men is to increase it a hundred-fold. This the rulers of the earth all recognize and yet when it comes to the greatest crime—waging war on another state—they praise it!
>
> It is clear they do not know it is wrong, for they record such deeds to be handed down to posterity; if they knew they were wrong, why should they wish to record them and have them handed down to posterity?
>
> If a man on seeing a little black were to say it is black, but on seeing a lot of black were to say it is white, it would be clear that such a man could not distinguish black and white. Or if he were to taste a few bitter things and were to pronounce them sweet, clearly he would be incapable of distinguishing between sweetness and bitterness. So those who recognize a small crime as such, but do not recognize the wickedness of the greatest crime of all—the waging of war on another state—but actually praise it—cannot distinguish right and wrong. So as to right or wrong, the rulers of the world are in confusion.

Much of his case against war was utilitarian, a case that is easily made. To the counter-argument that four of the states had grown powerful by war, he pointed out that there were 10,000 that had gone under. How useful is a medicine that cures 4 patients out of 10,000?

War destroys, and conquerors are no better than kleptomaniacs. It would not be the sword, but justice and virtue that would be able to conquer the world.

Both Mo Tse and his followers, like Sung Keng, engaged in trying to talk kings out of waging war quite often. Other than the preceding story, it is not widely reported how often they succeeded, if ever, in convincing the rulers.

His followers kept up his ideas for a few centuries. In many places during that time, Moism was a vigorous rival to Confucianism. K'ung Fu Tzu (Confucius) did not disapprove of all war, but did offer a critique that limited its practice, which would have been distressing enough to the warriors of the time. For an exposition of peacebuilding resources in Confucianism, see Berling (2004).

The Taoist *Chuang-Tzu* book does record philosophers following the example of Mo Tse in nonviolent campaigns against war:

> They sought to unite men through an ardent love in universal brotherhood. To fight against lusts and evil desires was their chief endeavor. When they were reviled, they did not consider it a shame; they were intent on nothing but the redemption of men from quarrelling. They forbade aggression, and preached disarmament in order to redeem mankind from war. This teaching they carried throughout the world. They admonished princes and instructed subjects. The world was not ready to accept their teaching, but they held to it all the more firmly. It was said that high and low tried to avoid meeting them, that they forced themselves on people.

Since Mo-ism is no longer a living religion, it is not available for interaction and does not have adherents for modern-day nonviolent action. Its value is in knowing what has happened in human history. Much of history focuses on the violence as part of the apologetics for violence, giving a false impression of violence as endemic to the human race.

Other philosophers, while not as active in confrontations, did advocate against massive violence. Meng Tzu (372–298 BCE), also known as Mencius, did not follow the utilitarian concepts of Mo Tse, but did base appeals against war on love and righteousness. He criticized successful generals as criminals:

> When land is the cause of contention, corpses fill the field; when a city is the cause of contention, corpses fill the circuit of the walls. This is teaching the very soil beneath us to devour human flesh—a crime for which death cannot atone.

Probably living in the 300s BCE was Hui Shih, like Mo Tse from the state of Sung but not being a follower of Mo. His school was the School of Forms and Names, or Dialecticians. In a period of war he preached universal love and pacifism: "Love all things equally; the universe is one" (Chuang Tzu 33). In the next century lived another Dialectician, Kung-sun Lung, from the state of Chao, advocated pacifism on the rulers of Chao and Yen: "The idea in ending war springs out of a mind holding universal love towards the world" (Lu-shih Ch'un Ch'iu 18.1).

Taoism

Taoism, beginning probably around the fourth century BCE, is about the Tao, usually translated as *the Way*. The World Religion Database estimates around 8 million Taoists currently.

It is the ultimate creative principle of the universe. All things are unified and connected in the Tao, which cannot be described in words but only hinted at. It is not God and is not worshiped; the deities must follow it like everyone else. It promotes achieving harmony with nature, being virtuous but not ostentatiously so, improving self-development, and pursuing spiritual immortality. The method of following the Tao is called *Wu Wei*—letting things take their course, as a river does in the countryside, not interfering when things are working properly. One can be proactive, but not ego-driven. People live in detachment and calm.

It is a religion of unity and opposites at the same time, worded as Yin and Yang, complementary forces—action and nonaction, light and dark, hot and cold, and so on. Things depend upon one another rather than making any sense on their own. Opposites are in harmony. The Tao is gender-neutral and the role of women is more equal since masculine and feminine are equal and complementary. Female imagery such as the mother of all things is used for the Tao in the *Tao Te Ching*, the main scripture. Women took priestly roles from the earliest days of the organization.

Taoism emphasizes characteristics such as softness and yielding, modesty and nonaggression—that the weak overcome the strong as water overcomes a rock. Practices include meditation, *feng shui* (a way of ordering material things in a household or other building), fortune telling, and reading and chanting of scriptures.

Before the Communist revolution of 1949, Taoism was one of the strongest religions in China. Because postrevolution activity included campaigns to destroy all non-Communist religion, the numbers reduced and a survey to ascertain how much it remains is difficult to conduct.

Taoist ethics focuses more on being a good person who lives in harmony rather than specific good deeds, but the normal ethical prohibitions of killing, stealing, lying, and so on are present. Altruistic behavior is encouraged. The way to live well is to try to see what fits best in the natural order. In theory, then, Taoists tend not to initiate action, but wait for events that make action necessary. That action would then be based on harmony with nature rather than their own compulsions. This benefits others as well.

As with other long-lasting religions, there have been outbursts of violence in its name; for Taoism especially, the Yellow Turban Rebellion against corrupt authorities starting in 184 CE, suppressed with thousands dead. Throughout Chinese history, however, it has had a more peaceful influence.

As a historical note connecting religions, there is a story traceable back to the second century CE that once Lao-Tzu finished writing the *Tao Te Ching* and was done with his work in China, he travelled to India and either consulted with or appeared as the Buddha (Morgan, 2001, pp. 224–225). While the story is historically implausible, its existence as a story that long ago is interesting; Buddhism did, of course, gain quite a foothold in China.

Peaceful Quotations from the Tao Te Ching

Tao Te Ching: 30

> He who by Tao purposes to help the ruler of men
> Will oppose all conquest by force of arms.
> For such things are wont to rebound.
> Where armies are, thorns and brambles grow.
> The raising of a great host
> Is followed by a year of dearth.
> Therefore a good general effects his purpose and stops.
> He dares not rely upon the strength of arms;
> Effects his purpose and does not glory in it;
> Effects his purpose and does not boast of it;
> Effects his purpose and does not take pride in it;
> Effects his purpose as a regrettable necessity;
> Effects his purpose but does not love violence.
> For things age after reaching their prime.
> That violence would be against the Tao.
> And he who is against the Tao perishes young.

Tao Te Ching: 31

>Of all things, soldiers are instruments of evil,
>Hated by men.
>Therefore the religious man (possessed of Tao) avoids them.
>The gentleman favors the left in civilian life,
>But on military occasions favors the right.
>Soldiers are weapons of evil.
>They are not the weapons of the gentleman.
>When the use of soldiers cannot be helped,
>The best policy is calm restraint.
>Even in victory, there is no beauty
>And who calls it beautiful
>Is one who delights in slaughter.
>He who delights in slaughter
>Will not succeed in his ambition to rule the world.

Tao Te Ching: 37

>The Tao never does,
>Yet through it everything is done.
>If princes and dukes can keep the Tao,
>the world will of its own accord be reformed.
>When reformed and rising to action,
>Let it be restrained by the Nameless pristine simplicity.
>The Nameless pristine simplicity
>Is stripped of desire (for contention).
>By stripping of desire quiescence is achieved,
>And the world arrives at peace of its own accord.

Tao Te Ching: 67

>The best captain does not plunge headlong
>Nor is the best soldier a fellow hot to fight
>The greatest victor wins without a battle:
>He who overcomes people understands them.
>There is a quality of quietness
>Which quickens people by no stress:
>"Fellowship with heaven," as of old,
>Is fellowship with people and keeps its hold.

Tao Te Ching: 78

>There is nothing weaker than water
>But none is superior to it in overcoming the hard,

For which there is no substitute.
That weakness overcomes strength
And gentleness overcomes rigidity.

ANCIENT GREECE

Pythagoras, an ancient Greek philosopher, was most famous for his contributions to geometry. He was also a musician, vegetarian, and spiritual teacher. He taught a nonviolence ethic and lifestyle rooted in the kinship of all living beings. He and his disciples ate no meat, and up until the word "vegetarian" was coined in the 1800s, Western people who ate no meat were often called Pythagoreans (though the school of thought had long since died out as a coherent organized entity). He also broke with the custom of his times by equally allowing women into his academies.

Empedocles, a later follower of Pythagoras, said that the Pythagorean idea of a Golden Age would be under the rule of a Goddess when

> every animal was tame and familiar with people—both mammals and birds; and mutual love prevailed . . . nor had these happy people any War-God, nor had they any mad violence for their divinity. Nor was their monarch Zeus or Kronos or Poseidon, but Queen Kypris (the divinity of Love).

Most of what we know about his movement is in fragments. One direct contribution of the Pythagorean ethic remains to this day: the Hippocratic Oath. Some life-respecting provisions of the Oath are still widely held up as integral values of medical practice—the commitments to "do no harm," to observe confidentiality, and to refrain from sexual abuse of patients, even one's social "inferiors." It also says, "I will not give a lethal drug to anyone if I am asked, nor will I advise such a plan; and similarly I will not give a woman a drug to cause an abortion." This is why physicians to this day (even those no longer taking the Oath) are professionally forbidden from participating in executions for capital punishment. Since abortion, infanticide, and euthanasia were commonplace at the time, this Oath of nonviolence for physicians was countercultural—yet it has survived for centuries. Christians adopted it.

There were at least three principles upon which the Pythagorean school of wisdom based its teaching of nonviolence:

1. They believed in the kinship of all living things, based in part on the idea that all souls reincarnate after physical death. Therefore,

no animal is soulless and so are not to be killed or eaten. Pythagoras is reported to have said: "Do not defile your bodies with sinful foods. The earth affords you a lavish supply of riches, of innocent foods, and offers you banquets that involve no bloodshed or slaughter." He is also reported to have said: "Alas, what wickedness to swallow flesh into our own flesh, to fatten our greedy bodies by cramming in other bodies, to have one living creature fed by the death of another!" And again, "For as long as humanity continues to be the ruthless destroyer of lower living beings, we will never know health or peace. For as long as people massacre animals, they will kill each other. Indeed those who sow the seeds of murder and pain cannot reap joy and love."
2. They had the conviction that force of arms or any other form of coercion was impractical. They might appear to work for resolving conflict in the short run, but they necessarily add the fuel of resentment to fires of conflict to happen in the future. This metaphor of flames was used to make the point in a saying attributed to Pythagoras: "Don't stir the fire with a knife." This makes the flame burn more fiercely and makes the knife too hot to handle.
3. They understood a life of virtue was the goal everyone should strive for. Virtue is cultivated by simplicity, inner harmony, and just treatment of others. If the laws of the land were unjust or tyrannical, then this was contrary to the just treatment of others and the nonviolent lifestyle being recommended.

As for other ancient Greeks, Aristophanes was a famous ancient Greek playwright. In 411 BCE, he wrote a play called "Lysistrata." The name of the title character means "releaser of war." It was a bawdy play about the women of Athens and Sparta getting disgusted with the men fighting a war. They organized to refuse to make love to their husbands until the war stopped. This is a fictitious case of nonviolent action, but it shows ideas that ancient people had. It was also a protest of war, making it an indirect action for peace.

Aristophanes also wrote a play called *Peace*, which includes these lines:

> Oh! Zeus, what are you going to do for our people? Do you not see that our cities will soon be empty husks?
> Now, oh Greeks! is the moment when freed of quarrels and fighting, we should rescue sweet Peace and draw her out of this pit.
> Come, laborers, merchants, workmen, artisans, strangers, whether you be domiciled or not, islanders, come here, people of all

countries, come hurrying here with picks and levers and ropes! This is the moment to drain a cup in honor of Peace and set her free.
Yes, let us pray.
Oh! Peace, mighty queen, venerated goddess, thou, who presides over choruses and at nuptials, to accept the sacrifices we offer thee.
We will take the knife and sacrifice the sheep
No, we cannot, the goddess does not wish it.
Blood cannot please Peace, so let us spill none upon her altar.

Socrates (469–399 BCE) was a famous Greek philosopher whose philosophizing was sufficiently countercultural to get him sentenced to execution by drinking hemlock on a charge of corrupting the youth, turning them against the gods. He was exploring concepts of justice and beauty and similar virtues; he never was specific on the topic of nonviolence and had been a soldier in one of Athens's wars. Yet much of what he had to say could apply. His student Plato wrote down Plato's version of what Socrates said, and in the Dialog called *Gorgias*, Socrates says:

> You deemed Archelaus happy, because he was a very great criminal and unpunished. I, on the other hand, maintained that he or any other who like him has done wrong and has not been punished, is, and ought to be, the most miserable of all men; and that the doer of injustice is more miserable that the sufferer.

This is a sentiment that could very effectively be used in nonviolent campaigns.

6

Christianity: Blessed Are the Peacemakers

Christianity built on its roots in Judaism and benefited from all Judaism's foundations in nonviolence. It focused on the nonviolent parts of the Jewish tradition for its early centuries. It was a movement for various kinds of social justice that became more universal, deliberately bringing in different nationalities, races, classes, ages, and both genders. It grew in numbers and is now the world's largest religion, with about a third of the world's population identifying themselves with it. It therefore has the largest network of people and resources available.

HISTORY AND SCRIPTURE

In first-century Judea, Jews were afflicted by the Roman Empire and longed for relief. As is frequent in such situations, the hope for someone to deliver them was high. The concept of a Messiah was normally majestic and militaristic, a king to drive out the Romans. A few men with this concept announced themselves to be the Messiah, mounted a military campaign, and were crushed.

One man from the small village of Nazareth, off in the hinterlands in the province of Galilee—Jesus of Nazareth—offered a startling innovation: instead of military imagery, the imagery of the Suffering Servant (Isaiah 53). Conquerors would not be overcome by violence, a counterproductive technique leading to foreseeable calamity when the Temple was destroyed in October of 70 AD. Jesus is reported to have forecast this (Matthew 24:1–32, Mark 13:1–30, Luke 21:5–32). This took no magic; it was obvious to anyone who understood the social dynamics of the time. Instead, Jesus used an assertively nonviolent approach.

After much healing and itinerate preaching with nonviolence constantly featured, he was arrested and brutally executed (traditionally, 33 AD; due to the year when weekdays fell at the right time to fit, many scholars think it was 30 AD). Pictures of crucifixes are much less bloody than the reality. He would have had no loincloth to cover his private parts; this was intended to be humiliating. The serene expression on his face in most pictures belies the incredible pain involved.

The Christian story is that on Friday he was placed in a tomb sealed by a rock, and on Sunday morning he was alive again. This is called the Resurrection. Though the interpretations of it are many, understanding it as a real historical event is central to Christianity.

Filled with joy, his disciples spread the news. They used the Roman imperial word "Gospel"—good news—as the word for biographies. Later generations decided on four Gospels, along with various letters and a biting apocalyptic satire, as their scriptures. They called Jewish scriptures the Old Testament. The new scriptures, theirs alone, were the New Testament.

In addition to proclaiming Jesus rising from the dead, the idea was proclaimed that he was the Son of God. In one sense, this means simply that he was very much like God—he had said, after all, that peacemakers were children of God (Matthew 5:9).

However, much more was meant. He was an incarnation of God—God in a human body. Jews and Muslims are aghast. Hindus say this is fine, but why limit it to only one incarnation? This is due to different concepts. Hindus see God as needing to come to help when things are getting out of hand (Bhagavad Gita 4:7–8), while Christians leave that task to divinely inspired people. Christians see the one and only incarnation as a fulfillment of God acting in history through the long story of Israel. Further, it achieved reconciliation between divine and human that needed to be done only once; the reconciliation happened for all time. As for the idea that God can be incarnated at all, Christians understand that it is in the nature of God to have experienced what it is like to be stuck inside human skin, in poverty, and facing injustice. God therefore has not mere intellectual sympathy, but heartfelt empathy with the downtrodden. God has faced what we face, and God is present in the suffering.

The idea of a Trinity developed: God in three personas or roles—later translated as persons—much to the confusion of other monotheists like Jews and Muslims who did not understand a three-in-one concept. Again, Hindus do, with a different trinity. For Christians, the three were the Father, the Son, and the Holy Spirit.

The trinity has been explained as a matter of how creativity functions—first the idea, then the physical expression of the idea, then the reception by observers or hearers or readers (Sayers, 1941). It has been explained in many other ways as well. At the time, it was making the concepts intelligible to the Greek mind; other minds have had more trouble with it. But the concept has endured.

Christians suffered waves of persecution in the first three centuries, yet their numbers grew steadily. The works of charity and their steadfastness when suffering martyrdom impressed many. They offered an appealing innovation: salvation was available to everyone, not just to an elite. The afterlife offered was far more attractive than the prevailing ideas.

Christians also had a higher quality of life—physical health and communities helping each other. The prominent role of women and the rights they had by comparison with women in contemporary societies attracted more women. Christianity also appealed to philosophers dissatisfied with the immoral antics of the pagan pantheon, finding monotheism and its appeal to ethics and compassion more logical.

If there were roughly a thousand Christians in the year 40 AD, it would take only a 3.4 percent growth rate to be almost 15 percent of the population in the year 312 AD, and since that is exponential, Christians could have been half the population by the year 350 AD. This matches various methods of estimating how many there were at different points in this time period. Many modern religious movements have been observed sustaining such growth rates for decades, so this is sociologically quite plausible (Stark, 2007, pp. 312–315).

Finally, with their numbers, events occurred so that Constantine, in his successful struggle to become Roman emperor, converted to Christianity and made it the official religion. This led to official councils that set up official creeds. Before Constantine, Christians were mainly opposed to all violence. After Constantine, the requirements of pleasing the government and the ability to impose one view over another led to much violence. The change from persecuted to favored meant those whose motivation was not religious but promotion would use Christianity to get government posts.

This had two effects. It eviscerated the nonviolent stand of primitive Christianity. Yet it also turned governments into vehicles to carry nonviolent advocacy on to future generations. Appealing to the origins of the religion has historically been a strong authority for Christian activists.

Unlike Judaism, Christianity was and still is a strongly missionary religion. Jesus told his followers to spread the good news to all nations (Matthew 24:14, Mark 13:10, Luke 24:27). During the first three centuries, doing this by convincing people and providing good role models were the only methods possible.

After Constantine, converting the royal household and thus in theory converting the whole nation became more common. Christianity spread through Europe with this as a common technique. Yet when people are told by their kings and queens what religion to have, even those happy to comply may not have as clear an understanding as those who chose to convert from direct persuasion.

So violence was committed not only in spite of Christianity, but in its name. In 1054, the Bishop of Rome (now called the Pope) and the Patriarch of Constantinople excommunicated one another. Thus was Christendom split into the Roman Catholic and Eastern Orthodox. In the 16th century, people mainly in northern Europe split from the Catholic Church to form various Protestant denominations.

However, wars and persecutions over finer points of doctrine left a bad taste for many Europeans, along with laws requiring their participation in church services. Christianity has subsided somewhat in Europe, but is still growing in many parts of the world.

Violence on its behalf has amounted to recrucifying Jesus yet again. Appealing to the nonviolence of Christianity's origins is more likely to have the same appeal that those origins had to the original converts two millennia ago.

JESUS AND HIS FIRST FOLLOWERS: FOUNDATIONS FOR NONVIOLENCE

Jesus: Symbolic Actions

"Palm Sunday" can be seen as an ancient peace demonstration. The symbol had the king riding into the capital city of Jerusalem, but not on a valiant steed with swords blazing—rather, on a humble donkey. Palm branches rather than swords were in the hands of the crowd. This was a different idea of what a leader was supposed to look like.

In the "cleansing of the Temple," Jesus drove out those trying to sell animals to be killed as blood sacrifice and freed the animals. This can be seen as an early act of civil disobedience. It was against the rules, it was done out in the open with honesty, and the legal consequence came down hard (within days, according to the first three Gospels).

The legal consequence was due to more than that one action, since witnesses recorded that rulers had much lethal ill will toward Jesus before this. This was a campaign rather than a single event, and the campaign continued. It could not be squelched by the violence aimed at it.

Jesus: Tortured and Humiliated, then Resurrected

There is not much more thorough a method of communicating that a military messiah is not the program than for the proposed messiah to be executed in a horrific way rather than triumphing by killing others. There were several men claiming the title of messiah in that era, and they were all executed as well; they used military strategies, and the Romans crushed them. It was because the resurrection was seen as God vindicating Jesus as right that the nonviolent revolution that Jesus started continued.

Jesus was also seen as the "first fruit." There had in recent centuries arisen the idea that rather than remaining dead, everyone would in the end be resurrected, with the righteous having everlasting life (Daniel 12:2). People who had been killed for persevering in their principles would therefore get justice in the end; otherwise, the injustice would remain permanent. This had been a mere assertion up until then. Early Christians asserted the understanding that once it actually happened once, then the idea that it was true for everyone was more than hopeful fantasy. It was evidence.

There are arguments over exactly what actually literally happened, what we would have seen had there been a camera videotaping the events. The fact that the stories in the four different Gospels contradict each other in specific literal details is to be expected from a crowd of different eyewitnesses.

What is unambiguous is that the *belief* that the event had actually occurred had a socially explosive effect starting then and throughout the ages. The afterglow of the event is still with us. Anglican bishop Tom Wright (also called N. T. Wright) discusses the implications for nonviolent movements:

> No wonder the Herods, the Caesars and the Sadducees of this world, ancient and modern, were and are eager to rule out all possibility of actual resurrection. They are, after all, staking a counter-claim on the real world. It is the real world that the tyrants and bullies . . . try to rule by force, only to discover that in order to do so they have to quash all rumours of resurrection, rumours that would imply that their greatest weapons, death and deconstruction, are not after all omnipotent. (Wright, 2003, p. 737)

Love of Enemies, Love of the Poor and Marginalized

The idea that everyone is to be treated with love and to be prayed for, and that includes people who are acting as enemies, is found in the Gospels (Matthew 21:24, 5:43–44; Luke 5: 27–36, 22:49–51, 23:24). The theme is also common in the rest of the New Testament (for example, Romans 12:14–18, Colossians 3:2–13, Hebrews 10:32–34, James 1:19–20). This is not some esoteric point that comes from digging around to find what one wants to find. This point is so basic that no one can claim to be familiar with the teachings of Jesus without being aware of this.

As for how near and dear those in poverty are to God's heart, a list here must be too skimpy; see http://www.compassion.com/poverty/what-the-bible-says-about-poverty.htm for a list. Jesus is strong enough on the point to say that whatever is done to help "the least of these, my brothers and sisters" amounts to the same thing as doing the compassionate act for God (Matthew 25:40). It is no mere nice thing, but something with cosmic meaning.

The theme continues and gets applied in the early centuries:

> Regarding the rest of humanity, you should pray for them unceasingly ... Meet their animosity with mildness, their high words with humility, and their abuse with your prayers. But stand firm against their errors, and if they grow violent, be gentle instead of wanting to pay them back in their own coin. (Saint Ignatius of Antioch, *Epistle to the Ephesians*, 10)
>
> Since they know we cannot endure to see a man being put to death even justly, who of them would charge us with murder or cannibalism? Who among our accusers is not eager to witness contests of gladiators and wild beasts? ... But we see little difference between watching a man being put to death and killing him. So we have given up [gladiator games] ... the same person would not regard the fetus in the womb as a living thing and therefore an object of God's care, and at the same time slay it. ... Nor would someone refuse to expose infants, on the ground that those who expose them are murderers of children, and at the same time do away with the child he [or she] has reared ... But we are altogether consistent in our conduct. We obey reason and do not override it. (Athenagorus, "A Plea Regarding Christians," Section 35s)
>
> The question is now whether a member of the faithful can become a soldier and whether a soldier can be admitted to the Faith ... how will a Christian do so? ... the Lord, by taking away Peter's sword, disarmed every soldier thereafter ... What kind of war would we, who willingly submit to the sword, not be ready or eager for ... if it were not for the fact that according to our doctrine it is more

permissible to be killed than to kill. For us, we may not destroy even the fetus in the womb. (Tertullian, *On Idolatry*, 9.1, 9.6)

For more documents from the prominent names in Christian peacemaking throughout the ages, see *Christian Peace and Nonviolence: A Documentary History* (Long, 2011).

Women's Rights

Jesus let a Gentile woman win an argument with him (Mark 7:25–30) and speaks with the Samaritan woman, something a self-respecting Jewish man would normally avoid doing (John 4:7–27). He justifies Mary for being "at his feet," the position of the student to a rabbi, not one that women were normally allowed to take (Luke 10:38–42). When a hemorrhaging woman touched him (Mark 5:25–34), the issue of blood was a contaminating impurity, which would make touching others prohibited (Leviticus 15:19). He was kind and healed her.

The Gospels indicate active female participation in leadership traveling with Jesus. Luke 8:1–3 lists women financing the ministry; see also Matthew 27:55 and Mark 15:40.

In the crucial role of witnessing the resurrection, the fact that women were prominent is not especially noteworthy to the modern mind, but was startling in that era (Matthew 28:1–10, Luke 24:1–11, John 20:1–18). That women were relied on as witnesses is one of the arguments for why the story was not simply made up. If it were, they would not have used such a lame detail as having *women* as witnesses.

The New Testament covering the early church also shows women in prominent leadership roles (see, for example, Acts 17:4, Romans 16:1–3, 1 Corinthians 1:11). In Paul's letter to the Romans, he greets 18 men and 15 women by name. Paul has received a worse reputation than he deserves; some of the translations reflect more the translator's views than Paul's (Bristow, 1988; Gaventa, 2010).

In the Roman Empire, the advantage for Christian females began at birth. They were allowed to live, not victims of female infanticide. As sociologist Rodney Stark reports:

> A study of inscriptions at Delphi made it possible to reconstruct six hundred families. Of these, only six had raised more than one daughter. As would be expected, the bias against female infants showed up dramatically in the sex ratios of the imperial population. It is estimated that there were 131 males per 100 females in the city

of Rome, and 140 males per 100 females elsewhere in the Empire. (Stark, 2007, pp. 320–321)

Unlike pagan women, Christian wives did not have abortions inflicted on them by domineering husbands. These were dangerous enough to help account for pagan women's lower life expectancy.

Christian girls were far less likely to be subjected to marriage in their early teens to older men. There was no double standard of chastity for women; men were expected to hold the same standard. Within marriage, both partners were equal in terms of having conjugal rights to each other (1 Corinthians 7:3–5).

THE EARLY CENTURIES

Stories abound of persecuted Christians, hurt or killed because of perseverance in the face of demands to deny their beliefs. These were martyrs, admired by other Christians. Brutal repression was counterproductive.

Christian beliefs included many forms of nonviolence. Refusing to participate in any war was common. Some were killed or imprisoned for refusing to join the army. The killing of newborn babies was opposed by taking care of those who could be rescued, which was easily done since the usual method of killing the infants was to leave them outside exposed. A large number of Christians refused to eat meat to avoid killing animals (Akers, 2000).

The gladiator games in Rome, called spectacles, were an especially cruel form of "entertainment." Christians were often targets, killed by lions, and the imagery of this has remained as a symbol of persecution to this day. After the Roman Emperor Constantine converted, Christians were no longer victims, but the "spectacles" continued.

In the early 400s, a monk named Telemachus traveled quite a distance from the east to the Coliseum in Rome. Seeing crowds cheering murder, he jumped into the arena and stood between the gladiators, shouting about how wrong this was. The crowd of around 8,000 was outraged—as their fun had been spoiled—and stoned Telemachus to death. Then a hush fell over the crowd. Silently, the Coliseum emptied. When Emperor Honorius heard about the monk being killed, he banned the gladiator games. They petered out rather quickly. The nonviolent intervention of Telemachus not only stopped the fighting that day but it was also the final step in taking out the popularity of the games.

Another permanent reform was the end of crucifixions. The artwork portraying Jesus during crucifixion did not appear until the fourth century, after actual crucifixions stopped. By that time, few living people had seen a real-life crucifixion, and so depictions in art became something people could bear looking at.

The writings of those early centuries show that opposition to all violence was widespread and understood to be universal. As Rob Arner puts it:

> I have traced the ethic of the pre-Constantinian church through a series of individual moral issues related to the taking of human life, and have found that, without exception, the church strongly condemned the taking of human life in any form whatsoever. Neither homicide, nor feticide, nor infanticide, nor suicide, nor capital punishment, nor killing in war were considered acceptable. (Arner, 2010, p. 1)

SUBSEQUENT CENTURIES: A SAMPLING

Francis and Clare of Assisi

Francis of Assisi (1182–1226) was born into a wealthy family, but renounced military glory to instead serve the sick and poor. He founded a monks' order, and within 11 years there were over 5,000 Franciscan Friars. Clare of Assisi (1194–1253) founded a similar group for women. In 1210, his preaching led to an agreement between the lower and upper classes of Assisi. This foreshadowed the soon-to-come Magna Carta, since it gave bondsmen the right to free themselves from their lords.

In 1219, he traveled to Egypt and Saracen territory to preach nonviolently, in contrast to others who were at that time carrying out Crusades. Since he and a friend went unarmed, he was the guest of the Sultan. The Crusades themselves were one of the violent episodes most commonly used in arguments against Christianity, especially by Muslims and atheists, but nonviolent activism occurred at the same time.

Pacifist Churches Arising

In 1440, Peter Chelcisky, a Czech reformer, published *The Net of Faith*, which argued Jesus should be taken at his word: no oaths, no living by the sword. The book influenced several decades of nonviolent witness in the Bohemian Brethren, which later evolved into the Moravian Church. When Czechoslovakia in 1968 had one of the largest nonviolent resistances to the Soviet Union up to that point, and less than two

Christianity: Blessed Are the Peacemakers

decades later won its independence from the Soviets in the nonviolent revolutions that freed several Eastern European countries, it had this heritage to draw on.

Also in the Czech heritage was Jan Amos Comenius (1592–1670), a teacher and a bishop of the Moravian Church. Starting in 1628, he published several popular books on reforming education. His idea, new at the time, was that education should be for everyone and the same for all regardless of class or gender. He thought if people were educated about different religions, languages, and ways of life, this would help develop peace. Some of the books were translated into various European languages, Arabic, and Persian. He was invited to help reform schools in several European countries.

As part of the Reformation, several denominations started with pacifist ideals, hearkening back to Christian origins. They eagerly searched for nonviolent ways to solve problems. They also had chances to practice their nonviolence—courage to stand up to persecution against them but not respond in kind. They were often put in jail for their beliefs, their practices, or for not cooperating with the military draft.

Different groups called "Brethren" held pacifist principles, as does the Church of the Brethren today. Anabaptists, starting in the mid-1500s, were another group of pacifists; Menno Simons organized many together, and the Mennonite Church is still active in nonviolence. In the mid-1600s in England, the Religious Society of Friends (Quakers) started, and it also has contributed a great deal of thought and active participation in the growth of nonviolence, especially in the Holy Experiment of Pennsylvania and later in slavery abolitionism, among many other pursuits.

The Holy Experiment

The Holy Experiment of 1682–1756 is among the most long-lasting of experiments in nonviolence. Because William Penn inherited a debt to his father from the king, in 1680 he got a grant of land in America. He wanted to name it Sylvania for its forests, but the king insisted on adding the Penn name, making it Pennsylvania. Having become a Quaker, Penn wanted to set this up as a pacifist experiment. This included religious tolerance, so that people of all types were welcome, but it was especially a shelter for Quakers.

Unlike other colonies, William Penn made a treaty with the native peoples and treating them fairly. All land bought from him, as owner according to the king, also had to be bought from local tribes. Any disputes and the undoing of past injustices could be done by "an equal number of honest men on both sides." He wanted to live as neighbors and friends, and the Indians responded accordingly. There were practically none of the kind of Indian attacks plaguing other colonies.

Unfortunately, Penn's sons did not remain Quakers. Thomas Penn gave a "Walking Purchase" land deal with a deed to take an amount of land that could be walked in a certain amount of time, but then had professional runners to mark it out. This kind of cheating was followed by more people who were not Quakers getting elected to the legislature. Finally, on June 7, 1756, Quakers resigned from the assembly. This ended the 74 years of an experiment with a pacifist government.

Quaker Jonathan Dymond wrote of this in 1824:

> The reader of American history will recollect that in the beginning of the last century, a . . . most dreadful warfare was carried on by the natives against the European settlers. . . . But amidst this dreadful desolation and universal terror, the Society of Friends, who were a considerable proportion of the whole population, were steadfast to their principles. They would neither retire to garrisons, nor provide themselves with arms. They remained openly in the country, whilst the rest were flying to the forts. They still pursued their occupations in the fields or at their homes, without a weapon . . . And what was their fate? They lived in security and quiet. The habitation, which, to his armed neighbor, was the scene of murder and of the scalping knife, was to the unarmed Quaker a place of safety and of peace. (Dymond, 1824)

Though it did not endure, it did three things:

- It showed such a government could last decades, in a frontier, alongside a markedly different culture, and with constant pressures for violence from its own culture.
- It influenced the ideals on which the later U.S. government was based, including religious tolerance.
- Finally, Quakers no longer in government had a burst of energy for doing other things to fit their principles—most especially, the movement to abolish slavery.

NINETEENTH CENTURY: UPSURGE OF ACTIVISM

Foreshadowing the later Civil Rights movement a century later, there was a boycott of public transportation in the U.S. city of Boston,

Massachusetts, from 1841 to 1843. It succeeded, permanently making transportation available to people of all races.

Of course, the greatest infliction of harm to people of African descent in Europe and the Americas was slavery. While there were those identifying as Christians who supported slavery and cited Old Testament scriptures for the institution (though none could be cited for allowing abuse of slaves, which was rampant), most of the people who made great sacrifices of time and energy and occasional danger did so with explicitly Christian motivation.

William Wilberforce, for example, whose story is told in the movie *Amazing Grace*, was a British parliamentarian who over many years sought and finally succeeded in ending the slave trade from Africa in Great Britain. This was a step to abolishing slavery itself. He was aided by around 300,000 Britons stopping the use of slave-produced sugar. Later, around 800,000 Englishwomen signed a pledge to boycott the sugar, producing a drop of a penny per pound—serious money in those days.

The method of massive withdrawal happened when around 6,000 people left the Methodist Church because of the church's squelching of their antislavery actions. They founded a new denomination, which quickly grew to 15,000 people. The Methodist Church in the northern states did then give its abolitionist members more freedom in order to avoid more walkouts.

Slavery was abolished fairly peacefully in the British West Indies on July 31, 1834, freeing around 776,000 slaves. This gave a model abolitionists elsewhere hoped to follow. When American abolitionists organized, large numbers signed a pledge of "nonresistance" in 1833. Since our current understanding of "resistance" was exactly what they were doing, we need to understand this was what they called "nonviolence" at that time.

The largest and most sophisticated action by far in the United States was the Underground Railroad. At great personal risk, its agents helped enslaved people escape to freedom from the 1830s to the 1860s. This helped individuals immediately, and it put a major strain on the system of slavery. Estimates are that around 100,000 slaves escaped.

Nonviolent rescues included finding out when slave-catchers were in town and having people follow them around announcing these were slave-catchers. They shouted about how they should be ashamed of themselves. Several slave-catchers left because of this pressure, which was usually but not always entirely nonviolent.

Technically, the Emancipation Proclamation that took effect in 1863, and the Civil War victory by the North in 1865, brought an end to legalized chattel slavery in the United States. This further impacted other countries.

Yet the treatment of former slaves, with segregation and humiliation, continued for another century, especially in the South. By 1904, abolitionist Moncure Conway wondered if abolitionists who died in the war to free the slaves might wonder, "Was it well then to shed our blood in order that the Negro might be freely lynched?" (Conway, 1904, p. 195).

It took another major nonviolent campaign to put a major dent in that problem. Fortunately, the movement that helped in starting to heal the South and the rest of the United States of its racism would become one of the major inspirations in the history of nonviolent action.

Meanwhile, many other social justice movements arose in the 19th century. Abolitionists' biographies show they tended to be involved in several issues.

Many women abolitionists noticed they were suffering from a lack of rights themselves. They pushed for laws banning men from legally beating their wives and laws allowing married women to own property. Women's rights advocates saw Iroquois women taking these rights for granted, and this inspired them to demand the same (see chapter 8). They also pushed for the rights of children, both born and unborn (Derr, MacNair, & Naranjo-Huebl, 2005). Women went to jail, went on hunger strikes, did massive marches and rallies, and perfected a lot of the techniques that have been used by social movements ever since.

In the 1840s, the word "vegetarian" was coined. The Graham cracker was invented by Sylvester Graham, and whole-grain flaked breakfast cereal by John Harvey Kellogg, both vegetarians, to substitute for meat with healthy alternatives. Many people saw this as a nonviolent diet, since animals must be killed to make meat.

RECENT

Since the 20th century saw the rise of so many movements, we will mention just a few here.

From 1931 to 1961, several Latin American countries had "huelgas de brazos caídos," meaning a strike of "fallen arms," which is to say, nonviolent. A general strike—all workers, societywide—brought down dictatorships: in Chile, July 21–26, 1931; Cuba, July 27–August 11, 1931 and again July 27–August 11, 1933; El Salvador, April 26–March 11, 1944; Guatemala, June 23–July 1, 1944; Haiti, May 17–December 14, 1956; Colombia, May 2–May 10, 1957; and the Dominican Republic, November 28–December 7, 1961.

In 1956, Italians in Sicily added a twist: a strike in reverse. Unemployed men worked on a road in desperate need of repair, without charge. That got them arrested. Word spread, and the Italian government was furious. It drew attention to how little they had done. So several men were sent to trial on what amounted to a charge of obeying the law. This drew more attention in a successful campaign.

A quite famous nonviolent movement among Christians is the U.S. Civil Rights movement of the 1950s and 1960s. As with Gandhi, the Rev. Martin Luther King is among the most well-known and quoted apostles of nonviolence. He wrote a book in 1958 about the first campaign called *Stride toward Freedom: The Montgomery Story*. His 1963 *Letter from a Birmingham Jail* is a classic, an open letter responding to clergy who counseled against civil disobedience, explaining patiently why the techniques of nonviolent struggle were necessary rather than lobbying and gradual change. He was famous for the eloquence of his sermons and other writings (Washington, 1986).

Another round of nonviolent actions happened in Latin America as Argentina from 1977 to 1983 and Chile from 1983 to 1988 nonviolently threw off their dictatorships. The Philippines had a nonviolent revolution after a stolen election in 1986, in which the Catholic Church was quite active, and this is the campaign that gave the word People Power its name. The series of revolutions in Eastern Europe in 1989 had the participation of many different groups, but Christians were active there as well, especially Catholics in Poland, where the recently elected Pope John Paul II came from.

Andrea Bartoli sums up the point about where Christianity stands now:

> It is impossible to find a single conflict in the world in which there is no Christian serving victims, defending human right, educating children and adults, and defending the space of civil society from oppression of violence. Christianity offers a remarkable network of people across the world, which is transnational and constantly moves people, goods, services, information, and ideas, making much of today's peacebuilding possible. (Bartoli, 2004, p. 159)

FORMS OF VIOLENCE

Blood Sacrifice

Ritual human sacrifice to please, placate, or bargain with divinity was entirely out of the question from the beginning of Christianity.

Some interpretations of the crucifixion hold it to be such a sacrifice. Yet as a human sacrifice, it was the sacrifice to end all sacrifices. It has been used in missionary work to stop human sacrifice in other cultures, not by explaining such blood ceremonies as wrong, but that the purpose has been done for all time and need not be done again.

Other Christians do not subscribe to this interpretation and simply hold human sacrifice to be wrong. In any event, the crucifixion was clearly not performed by Christians for ritual purposes. The Eucharist or Communion is sometimes seen as such a ritual in imitation, but if so, it is a nonviolent form, in sympathy with the victim.

Ritual animal sacrifice was always out of the question in Christian practice, as they objected to the Temple practice (Akers, 2000). Baptism (using water) was a nonviolent alternative for forgiveness of sins. Jesus cited Hosea 6:6, that God desires mercy and not sacrifice (Matthew 9:13 and 12:7).

Slavery

In Biblical times and throughout contemporary societies, slavery was a common practice and accepted as a crucial part of the economy. Slavery varied in how brutal or kind it could be, and often words from scripture or early writings that used to be translated as "slave" are translated as "servant" now. An example of how such slavery differed from later practice: if a slave could read, this was an added benefit in being able to teach the children. This was in stark contrast to the reading prohibition of slavery as practiced in the United States.

There were opponents of slavery, such as Saint Patrick of Ireland, who had been a slave himself and escaped.

Once the African slave trade became prominent, and a racial component entered the concept of slavery, more opposition arose. Both those who wanted to abolish slavery entirely, called abolitionists, and those who insisted on keeping slavery as part of the natural order of things appealed to scripture and principle.

The Christian abolitionist movement is one of Christianity's major contributions to nonviolence. Christians can currently be counted on to oppose slavery just about unanimously.

War

In the first three centuries, war was something that Christians were only allowed to engage in metaphorically. Early Christians were not allowed to be soldiers, and soldiers who became Christians were to remain only if they never killed; soldiers could be engaged in construction projects.

Later, Augustine (354–430) developed the Just War Theory, further expanded by Thomas Aquinas (1225–1274), which put strict rules on war and did still discourage it. This was based on Greco-Roman ideas with no basis in early Christian writings.

Most denominations accept something similar to the just war concept, though many are quite aware that very few wars come anywhere near the needed criteria. There are also pacifist denominations that follow the early teachings.

More recently, a "Just Peacemaking" model has been proposed to transcend arguments about just war and pacifism by proposals to be proactive in peacemaking (see http://justpeacemaking.org).

The Death Penalty

The death penalty was entirely forbidden in early Christianity but was reintroduced in later practice. Current opinion varies widely.

Infanticide and Feticide

Infanticide and feticide were strictly prohibited in early Christian writings and practice. Christians would often rescue infants exposed to die. Abortions in the Greco-Roman world were dangerous to women and were often imposed by dominating fathers or husbands, so Christian prohibition was quite countercultural and helpful to women. Female infanticide was common enough to cause gender imbalance, so the advantage of Christian females began at birth when they were allowed to live (Stark, 2007, pp. 320–321). There is currently a much wider variety of views on feticide, though infanticide is usually still frowned upon.

Meat

Vegetarianism was prominent among early Christians (Akers, 2000), but the abandonment of the kosher regulations of Judaism led to a variety of practices on what to eat. Romans chapter 14, if read with this in mind, does indicate avoiding meat was a common practice among the Christian community and that Paul would abstain as well when he was among those doing so. There has been a vegetarian strain throughout Christian history (see, for example, Roberts, 2004). Most Christians today do not understand vegetarianism as expected, but there are many Christians who advocate and educate about the practice.

Poverty

The violence of poverty has always been a major concern of Christian scriptures and countering it is a constant theme of Christian practice.

Violence in Scriptures

The Jewish Bible is called the Old Testament by Christians, so what is said on this topic in chapter 1 will also apply here. The book cited there as *The Violence of Scripture* (Seibert, 2012) is written by a Christian and subtitled *Overcoming the Old Testament's Troubling Legacy*.

In the early centuries, a common method of dealing with these violent passages was to treat them as allegories. They saw the destruction of destructive ideas or institutions, rather than of actual people. Many stories are enriched with varying allegorical interpretations. These became less common as historicity was more emphasized.

It is worth noting how Jesus quoted: he never recites the troubling passages of violence in all his many times of citing scripture. In one case, the omission is abrupt. He read from a scroll at a synagogue, with Luke 4:18 reporting the same passage as Isaiah 61:1, which contained inspiring wording about healing and liberating. The next verse of Luke is the same as the first part of the next verse of Isaiah: "To proclaim the acceptable year of the Lord." In Luke, this is it. Luke 4:20 says Jesus closed the scroll, gave it back, and sat down. He deliberately left out the next part of the verse in Isaiah 61:2: "and the day of vengeance of our God." Jesus did selective reading to stress the points of nonviolence and avoid contrary points.

There are two areas where violence as being approved by God in the New Testament is understood by some: hell, and startling and extreme imagery of the book of Revelation.

In the Old Testament, what is sometimes translated "hell" is usually Sheol, a shadowy realm of the dead—not torment. The idea of a pleasanter afterlife came later. It is often used this way also in the New Testament; Revelation 20:14 has both Death and Hell being cast into the fire. Many mentions are simply warnings about hell as a spiritual danger (Matthew 5: 29–30, 10:28, 18:9; Mark 9:45–47; Luke 12:5; James 3:6).

Other instances are more graphic. There are the major motifs of darkness and of fire: outer darkness with gnashing of teeth (Matthew 8:12, 22:13, 25:30); dark pits without the teeth-gnashing (2 Peter 2:4); a fiery furnace (Matthew 13:41–43), and fiery torment (Luke 16:19–31). If taken literally, the contrast of darkness and fire would contradict. Metaphors, however, by their nature do not contradict, but only illuminate different aspects.

The story of Luke 16:19–31 gives the perspective that in the spiritual world the fate of the rich man and the poor beggar are reversed. That point appeals to nonviolent advocates; the beggar Lazarus is after death in the bosom of Abraham, while the rich man suffers fiery torments. There is a great gulf between them, and the rich man has still not gotten the point: he asks Abraham to have Lazarus come give him water. He does not ask Lazarus. He is still thinking of Lazarus as someone who is supposed to serve him and still has not humanized the poor man. He is still in a hellish state of mind.

People thinking vengefully are sometimes gleeful about describing the torments of hell. This is not the nonviolent approach. The idea of the judgment of God to sentence people to a place is different from the idea that the judgment of God means discernment—God being able to see which people are already stuck in a hellish state of mind.

The poetic metaphors are important for getting across that this state of mind is not a minor thing. They hold up a mirror so that complacent people can see what that hellish state of mind looks like spiritually. This is all the more reason to have worry and concern for people who are in it.

On the New Testament book of Revelation, many read it as a literal rendition of the coming end of the world. They use clues to figure out when. The dates seem to always be soon, within their lifetimes. If an exact date or year comes and goes with no end of the world having happened, they recalculate. This literal-prophecy approach, reminiscent of soothsaying, has not proven terribly workable. It also crashes against the very first verse: Revelation 1:1 says that all these events are to happen very soon, and 1:3 repeats that the time is near.

The book is mainly a series of visions, where author John, exiled on the island of Patmos, sees things not how they are presented on earth, but the way God sees them—God's nightmare. The horrific violence in the book castigates the horrific violence of the contemporary society, where glories of empire turn out to be no glories at all. As Janet Ross put it:

> John reveals the hypocrisy of the Roman Empire; namely, that it has used its wealth to seduce the kings of the earth (see Revelation 17:2, 18:3) and has used its armies to force its inhabitants to participate in their own and others' religious and economic oppression (see Revelation 15:8, 17:18, 19:19). . . . Drawing on scriptural texts and images (primarily from Ezekiel, Jeremiah, and Isaiah, who also condemned exploitative trade and economic domination), Revelation contains a scathing visual condemnation of Rome's entire exploitative system, one that drained the lifeblood from the majority to enable an affluent, small minority. (Ross, 2006, p. 284)

The book was written to churches full of members justifiably terrified of what may happen to them just for being Christians. John is bolstering the case for taking nonviolent stands, despite horrific personal consequences. Anglican Bishop Tom (N. T.) Wright comments:

> Does it count as a compromise if I use Caesar's coinage, even though it has words like "son of god" stamped on it? Is it a compromise if I put my stall out by the side of the road during one of the great imperial festivals, to catch the crowds as they are going to the temple, even if I don't go myself? . . . For us, does it matter if . . . I work for a company that, through one of its other offshoots, is cheerfully polluting lakes and rivers and destroying their wildlife? Should I be worried that my bank is a major investor in companies that work in parts of Latin America where labour laws are practically non-existent, allowing them to get away with virtual enslavement of local populations? (Wright, 2011, pp. 121–122)

In the end, however, evil falls of its own weight. It self-destructs. A new heaven and new earth ensue.

For some of the writings with more extensive commentary on Revelation as being in the same assertive nonviolence mode as the rest of the New Testament, see Daniel Berrigan's book, *The Nightmare of God* (Berrigan, 1983); Bauckham, 1993; Ross, 2006; Tonstad, 2006; and Wright, 2011.

Treatment of "Heretics"

Around 180 AD, Irenaeus, the bishop of what is now Lyon in France, wrote a book called *Against Heresies*. He was trying to keep people straight on what Christianity is and is not. As an eventual martyr himself, one point he was keen to get across was that Christianity should not be watered down so that people could stay comfortable and avoid having to take a public stand.

Since then, however, the term *heresy* has been liberally applied to opposing parties in theological disputes. Irenaeus simply offered an argument; had exertion against "heresies" remained in the realm of vigorous reasoning, it might have had the desired impact of being persuasive.

However, since Constantine and centuries of state power established one view at the expense of another, people who were understood to be heretics have been a major source of killing and other horrific violence committed under the label of Christianity. Violence against heretics has accounted for a horrendous number of deaths and a major amount of disillusionment.

RELATIONS WITH OTHER RELIGIONS

Buddhism

Buddhism began centuries before Christianity and had an active missionary movement. Buddhists were a small presence in the Roman Empire's grand mixture of religions. Any influence on Judaism or Christianity has been conjecture only. Early Christians mentioning an awareness of the Buddha include Clement of Alexandria from the late first century and Saint Jerome in the fourth century. Eastern Christians in Asia (from a schismatic group sometimes called Nestorians), especially in China, seem to have some syncretic mixing with Buddhism in the early centuries. Later on, however, Christianity diminished in those areas and there was not much contact between the two religions until the 13th century, when European missionaries sent back reports. By the 16th century, there was more contact, and by the 18th century, Buddhist documents were more commonly available in Europe. Modern times have seen more exchanges between the two.

Since both religions began with a charismatic founder who taught nonviolence and all the virtues that accompany it, such as compassion and warnings against excessive materialism, many of their ways of putting the points are similar; see, for example, the book *Jesus and Buddha: The Parallel Sayings* (Borg, 1997). Even some of the legends are similar, such as how they faced the devil right before the beginnings of their ministries.

Hinduism

The Jesuit Roberto de Nobili (1577–1656) traveled to India to do missionary work. He was the first recorded outsider to study the Vedas,

Upanishads, and Bhagavad Gita and spent years in dialogue between Christian and Hindu traditions. This was approved by the Vatican (the city where the Roman Catholic Church is headquartered), but not by everyone there. Not much more happened until the 1800s, when there was much more interchange, where commonalities were noted especially in monasticism and mysticism. Since mysticism involves direct contact and experience with the divine, it is often a core on which to base commonalities among different religions (Teasdall, 1999).

Howard Thurman (Dixie & Eisenstadt, 2011) and Martin Luther King Jr. (1959) were among those African Americans that made a trip to India to learn more about Gandhian nonviolence for their own practical use back home.

Islam

When Islam first began, John of Damascus (675–749) assailed it as the "heresy of the Ishmaelites." Ishmael was the older son of Abraham; Isaac was understood as progenitor of the Jews, and Ishmael of the Arabs. To this day, there are a scattering of Christians who regard Islam as a Christian heresy. In most cases, however, it is understood as a separate religion.

Islam holds Jesus in high regard as the penultimate prophet, Mohammad being the ultimate one. Since Islam is explicit that the crucifixion and resurrection did not occur, that God cannot have a son, and that there is no Trinity, the views about Jesus differ sharply.

Christianity and Islam have much in common. They can for the most part be accepting of each other's worship styles, and can easily work together on issues of peace and social justice and toppling dictatorships. Yet they disagree about the founders of each. Ideally, for interfaith dialogue, they can at least understand the others' viewpoints.

Judaism

Christianity began as a sect of Judaism and still uses its scriptures as its own. The history of Israel up to the time of Jesus is crucial to understanding Jesus as final fulfillment. While some early Christians (notably, Marcion) wanted to jettison the Jewish past, the Church was quite emphatic about keeping it.

Nevertheless, there was hostility between Jews and Christians in early centuries. This intensified when Christianity became the state religion. Centuries of horrific abuse followed. Anti-Semitism is a word often used of anti-Jewish bigotry (although the Arabs are also Semites), ranging from mere discrimination to outright violence. It has been a major embarrassment for Christendom.

The horror of the Holocaust shook the foundations of this attitude within Christianity. Christians knew that even if the Nazis were outside of Christianity, for which a strong case can be made, they relied on centuries of hatred and stereotypes. They got acquiescence, if not participation, by many church-goers. Conversely, there were many Christians active in the Underground Railroad and other attempts to save Jews. As mentioned in chapter 1, the Council of Christians and Jews was founded in 1942, and attempts to have warmer relationships have succeeded and grown.

Zoroastrianism

Currently, there is not much discussion of Zoroastrianism in Christian circles, but knowledge of this ancient faith would be enriching—including the knowledge that the Magi of the Christmas story were Zoroastrians.

7

Islam: Salaam

Islam boasts the world's first (and so far, only) nonviolent army, the Khudai Khidmatgars, meaning the Servants of God. This was part of the struggle of India for independence, in the north of India (now Pakistan). Beginning in Arabia at a time when female infanticide, revenge feuds, and tribal warfare were rampant, Islam set up nonviolent ways of worship and emphasized community. Recent practice has shown widespread use of nonviolent campaigns for toppling dictators and otherwise establishing justice.

HISTORY AND SCRIPTURES

Into an Arab society of high violence was born a man who would assert monotheism, ethics, and community harmony. The connection of monotheism to ethics is explained: "There is no god along with Allah; else would each god have assuredly championed that which he created, and some of them would assuredly have overcome others" (Qur'an 23:91).

Muhammad was understood to be the last in a large group of prophets that God had sent to all peoples, including the Jewish prophets and as the penultimate prophet, Jesus. Muhammad was to give the final message. "Allah" is the Arabic word for God, used by Arabic Christians as well.

He was an orphan under the protection of his uncle, struggling in the caravan trade. Khadija was a rich caravan owner and proposed marriage to him. When he started having visions, she encouraged him. For several years, he worked in the Arabian city of Mecca, gained converts and was highly patient as they were constantly persecuted. This "early Meccan period" is especially held up as a model by many

Muslim nonviolent activists; Badshah Khan said, "There is nothing surprising in a Muslim or a Pathan like me subscribing to the creed of nonviolence. It is not a new creed. It was followed fourteen hundred years ago by the Prophet at the time he was in Mecca" (Easwaran, 1984, p. 183).

Once conditions became untenable, however, Muhammad and his loyal followers needed to leave to avoid assassination attempts. Opportunity presented itself when he was invited to the city later called Medina to come help them mediate their disputes, since he had a reputation for integrity. Muslims slipped out of Mecca and trekked up to Medina. This event changed them from a scattered set of converts into a community with a government and is called the *Hijra*. It is such a major event in Muslim history that it is when the calendar starts. The Islamic calendar (Hijri calendar) is a lunar calendar of 12 months in a year of 354 days, which is why the month of Ramadan happens at different times of year as time passes. The first year was 622 CE, that being 1 AH (Anno Hegirae, The Year of the Hijra).

Because Medina had Muslims in charge of government, the violence that often comes with state/religion mixtures occurred, with executions and battles. There are controversies as to how much and the meaning. We are deliberately not covering those here, as they are more appropriate to a different book.

Finally, Muslims were able to maneuver their way into taking over back in Mecca. Muhammad granted a general amnesty. He set up the Ka'aba as a place for pilgrimage for Muslims, as it remains to this day. The annual event is called the *Hajj*, the largest annual gathering of people on the planet.

The visions that Muhammad had were ones that he recited; the understanding was that the angel Jibril/Gabriel had given him the words, and the words came from God. After Muhammad died, these were collected and edited into the Qur'an. This is the most sacred scripture, accounted as the final and complete word of God, correcting previous corruptions, and to be studied and treated with great reverence. It is divided into 14 *surahs*, further divided into *ayat*. These are the same as chapters and verses and numerically cited the same way. A sample verse: "The servants of the Compassionate are those who walk upon the earth in humility and when the ignorant address them, answer 'Peace'" (Qur'an 25:63).

There were also several collections of *hadith*, which were other people's recollections of what the Prophet said, taught, and did. The authoritativeness of a hadith is measured by the chain of narrators called *isnad*, which links the hadiths to the prophet. They are not themselves scriptures, but a living expression of the Qur'an.

One well-known hadith deals directly with nonviolence: "[Muhammad said] 'Help your brother, whether he is an oppressor or he is an oppressed one.' People asked: 'O, Allah's Apostle! It is all right to help him if he is oppressed, but how should we help him if he is an oppressor?' The prophet said: 'By preventing him from oppressing others'" (Sahih al-Bukhari 1992, vol. 3, bk 43, no. 623). Another one is especially well-known and often hung in calligraphic adornment in Muslim homes:

> Whenever violence enters into something, it disgraces it, and whenever gentle-civility enters into something it graces it. Truly, God bestows on account of gentle conduct what he does not bestow on account of violent conduct. (Abu-Nimer, 2003, p. 43)

Islam then experienced the Shia/Sunni split but nevertheless spread into other countries and continued spreading especially into Asia and Africa. One image has been that Muslims conquered various countries and got mass conversions by force, but this is sociologically implausible and not borne out by history. Population studies show in most places it took around 250 years for Muslim conversions to reach being half of the population. By comparison, Christianity took around 310 years to become half of the Roman Empire. There is a difference in governments promoting conversions compared to governments providing draconian punishments, perhaps accounting for the greater length of time for Christianity. Still, both cases work with a conversion rate of 2–4 percent per year sustained over time. This has been observed in contemporary movements and is quite workable through social networks (Stark, 2007, pp. 374–376).

In ensuing centuries, Muslim scholars made great strides and also preserved much of the scholarship from Greco-Roman empire times. This had fallen by the wayside in Europe, but was available for the Renaissance in large part due to Europeans getting the literature from the Muslims.

Rabia Terri Harris, with Muslim Peace Fellowship, sums up the case for nonviolence from the origins of Islam from her perspective:

> In the world, Muhammad was the civilizer of the Arab tribes, and his heart was with all oppressed people everywhere. His historical mission was no more, and no less, than the establishment of peace and justice where cruel custom and tyranny had reigned. He worked

Islam: Salaam 131

in, and with, the substance of his times, toward a goal far beyond the horizons of his times. He used extraordinary spiritual means toward equally extraordinary political ends. Through his labor and insight, a great world culture emerged out of a fractured landscape of petty tribal wars. If we trouble to look, we easily find in Muhammad a master strategist of nonviolence. (Harris, n.d.)

Muslim Nobel Peace Prize winners as nonviolent activists (not peace-deal politicians) are:

- Shirin Ebadi of Iran, 2003 (1424 AH), human rights activist, especially for women and children
- Mohamed ElBaradei of Egypt, 2005 (1426 AH), for his work against nuclear weapons
- Muhammad Yunus of Bangladesh, 2006 (1427 AH), for founding the microfinance movement for the poor
- Tawakkol Karman of Yemen, 2011 (1432 AH), for nonviolent struggle for women's safety and rights
- Malala Yousafzai of Pakistan, 2014 (1436 AH), for her struggle for the rights of all children, especially girls, to education.

MUSLIM BELIEFS AND ACTIONS ON NONVIOLENCE

The Five Pillars and the Hijra

Chaiwat Satha-Anand (1993) expounds on how the values underlying the Five Pillars are core values for nonviolent action:

1. Reciting the *Shahadah*, "There is no God but God, and Muhammad is His Messenger": obeying only God and the Prophet means disobeying others if those are contradictory. In practice, this should mean those who go against the basics of compassion and justice.
2. The daily practice of five prayers (*salat*) is developing the practice of patience and self-discipline. Rabia Terri Harris says:

"Our God," we Muslims are asked to recite, at the end of every formal episode of prayer, "You are peace, and peace is from You." Peace is an intrinsic attribute of the Ultimately Real. *Whoever* serves peace, serves God, and will enter the infinite among the servants of God. (Harris, n.d.)

3. Supporting the poor through the *Zakat* contributions, 2.5 percent of savings, expresses concern and helps the downtrodden directly and is a form of self-discipline.

4. The fast of Ramadan—*Sawm*—develops patience and empathy, as well as being another form of self-discipline.
5. The pilgrimage to Mecca, the *Hajj*, develops unity and brother/sisterhood of those going. Rabia Terri Harris comments:

> The great counterbalance to Dr. King—the "bad cop" to Dr. King's "good cop" in the interrogation of racial injustice in the United States—was Malcolm X. And Malcolm X famously affirmed the potentials of unarmed struggle for the first time as a *result of the hajj*. That al-Hajj Malik al-Shabazz was martyred soon after this affirmation has only increased its power. (Harris, n.d.)

Some see the Prophet's migration to Medina as a strategic act of nonviolence (Abu-Nimer, 2003), a massive withdrawal from the violent situation. This took away the power of violence and enabled the Prophet to construct a powerful center of Islam, a "constructive program" that served as an alternative institution, still a model for a Muslim community.

Women's Lives and Rights

This will seem odd to many when rigid rules restrict women in many modern-day Muslim countries, but the coming of Islam in its seventh-century Arabian context was an advance in protecting women. This is why so many women joined the new movement.

Lethal violence came with the news that the baby just born was female. Warrior societies value males and therefore female infanticide has been a common practice. In pre-Islamic Arabia, newborn girls were buried alive:

> When one of them is given news of the birth of a baby girl, his face darkens and he is filled with gloom. In his shame he hides himself away from his people because of the bad news he has been given. Should he keep her and suffer contempt or bury her in the dust? "How ill they judge!" (Qur'an 16:58–59)

This is in a set of things, including the idolatrous worship, that are illustrating how ill they judge.

Another castigation of the practice is in Qur'an 81:8–9, dealing with the Day of Judgment, "when the baby girl buried alive is asked for what sin she was killed." One commentary says:

> The questioning refers to the time when, with the predominance of Islam in Arabia, the barbarous practice was to be abolished. But one

buried alive may stand generally for the female sex, and the reference here may, therefore, be to the general tyranny of the male over the female" (Ali, 1995, pp. 1148–1149).

The Qur'an frequently specifies that it is referring to both men and women equally ("whether male or female") when referring to ethical expectations; see, for example, 3:194, 4:124, 16:97, and 40:40. This may seem rather obvious to the modern mind, but it was an assertion of equality in the context of the times.

Even the veil, often seen as a way of putting women down, was at the time a way of saying women were not sex objects—a communication they were not sexually available as was expected of women. The veil is an example of how the attitude toward an item rather than the item itself can make a difference in violence or nonviolence.

Islam could never have gotten off the ground without active participation of strong-willed women. This is commonly true with new religions, but as with Christianity, the names of many are well recorded. Muhammad married his boss; Khadijah owned caravans and was 15 years older than him. She was the first to believe and promote his message, and she encouraged him when he himself was doubtful. His later wife Aisha was instrumental in the organization of the community and traditionally understood to have said 2,210 of the hadiths.

There are many Muslims who argue for the customs societies already had and give a Muslim justification for it, but nonviolence advocates are on firm ground in asserting a more egalitarian tradition. Both traditions are found in the religion, as is true of all long-lasting religions. Groups advocating for women's rights include the Women's Islamic Initiative on Spirituality and Equality (see http://www.wisemuslim women.org), which includes a project of a "Jihad Against Violence" against women. Books on this topic include *Believing Women in Islam: Unreading Patriarchal Interpretations of the Qur'an*, by Asma Barlas.

Three of the five Muslim nonviolence activists who have been awarded the Nobel Peace Prize, mentioned earlier in this chapter, are women who have been active in helping to secure the rights of women and girls—Shirin Ebadi of Iran, Tawakkol Karman of Yemen, and Malala Yousafzai of Pakistan.

Justice, Concern for the Poor, Racial Equality, and Social Empowerment

There is a strong duty in Islam to uphold justice and oppose injustice. See, for example, Qur'an 16:90, 42:15, and 42:42. Quoting 5:8, "You who believe, be steadfast in your devotion to God and bear witness impartially: do not let hatred of others lead you away from justice, but adhere to Justice, for that is closer in awareness of God."

Scholar Mohammed Abu-Nimer says:

> Islam's rapid growth was in large measure a response to its deep commitment to empower the weak, and it remains a religion of dynamic social activism in terms of individual duties and sense of social responsibility. Struggling against oppression (*zulm*), assisting the poor, and pursuing equality among all humans are core religious values throughout the Qur'an and Hadith. (Abu-Nimer, 2003, p. 55)

Sheheryar Ahmad similarly comments:

> A white has no superiority over a black nor does a black have any superiority over a white except by piety and good action. These were the words of Prophet Muhammad during his farewell address.
>
> He not only taught Muslims to not discriminate based on race but also showed it from his own example by assigning Bilal, an ex-slave, the critical duty of making the daily call for prayers.
>
> Fourteen centuries later, Malcolm X, one of the greatest leaders of the civil rights movement, stated, "America needs to understand Islam because this is the one religion that erases from its society the race problem." (Ahmad, 2014)

Sufis and Peace Branches

Sufis are often described as the mystical branch of Islam, present since soon after the beginning. As such, they are regarded as heretical by some legalistically minded branches. This is common in other religions, having a mystical group treated with hostility by those not mystically minded.

However, they were among the most active in spreading Islam, especially in Asia. They focus on love and peace and have an interest in religious harmony with other religious groups (Pal, 2011, pp. 59–77). It is in the nature of mysticism—direct communion with God—to search for expansion and to avoid rigid boundaries. This makes them ideal for spreading the religion. They make it attractive to newcomers.

Commonly, the more legalistically minded come later, after the religion has become large enough to allow for it, because of the activities of people like Sufis. This explains in part why we find the most rigidly legalistically oriented in the centers of origin and more tolerating and interested in principles in areas further away. Those interested in guarding the boundaries are not the ones who expand them. Islam could not be a major world religion today without the missionary work of the Sufis (see Pal, 2011, 81–82 for more details).

Sufis still provide many of the nonviolence activists in Islam today, and Muslim nonviolent activists that originated elsewhere tend to find Sufi writings and practice attractive.

There are other pacifist movements within Islam, such as the Ahmadiyya, which has been a vibrant reform movement in various countries (Pal, 2011, 77–81).

Books

In 1964 (1384 AH), Syrian-born Sheik Jawdat Sa'id wrote a book called *The Doctrine of the First Son of Adam*, articulating Muslim nonviolence. The title refers to the Qur'anic story of Cain and Able, found in 5:27–29, in which the un-named Abel as the first son says to Cain (paraphrased) "if you stretch out your hand against me to kill me, I will not stretch out my hand against you to kill you, for I fear God." Sa'id used this as a springboard into discussing nonviolence.

Books on the theme have flowered in recent years and include *Islam and Nonviolence* (Paige, Satha-Anand, & Gilliatt, 2001), which is based on a conference held on the theme; *Islam Means Peace: Understanding the Muslim Principle of Nonviolence Today* (Pal, 2011), written in journalistic style; *Nonviolence and Peace Building in Islam: Theory and Practice* (Abu-Nimer, 2003), a scholarly study; *Islam and Peace* (Khanneh & Salameh, 2006), which covers important concepts; and *Islamic Pacifism: Global Muslims in the Post-Osama Era* (Iftikhar, 2011), which addresses the post–September 11 attacks situation.

MUSLIM HISTORICAL NONVIOLENT ACTIONS

The World's First Nonviolent Army (1929–1947 [1348–1366 AH])

The Frontier was a northern district of what was then India, occupied by the Pathan, also called Pashtun. They had a code called "badal"— blood revenge for the slightest insult. Once a man (and it would be a man) does get revenge, the family of the other man must get revenge on him. There were times when over a hundred people were killed in a long-lasting feud, yet no one remembered how it started.

During the Indian struggle for independence from Britain, a Pathan man named Abdul-Ghaffar Khan (1890–1988 [1307–1408 AH]), a devout Muslim, developed his own theory of nonviolence while reading the

Qur'an in jail and was also impressed with Mohandas Gandhi's work. Khan wanted to get his people out of the cycle of violence that kept them in poverty.

He organized the world's first large, professional, nonviolent army. They were called the Khudai Khidmatgars, the Servants of God. They were also called the Red Shirts; the original white shirts got dirty too quickly, so they found a cheap brick-red-colored dye. There were over 100,000 of them, very well organized and very disciplined.

They all took a strict oath of nonviolence. Almost all kept it, even while some very nasty things were inflicted on them. The British were startled. They tried to provoke the Pathans to violence, so the British could respond with familiar violent techniques.

Gandhi did not share the common puzzlement as to how people with such a tradition of violence could organize a nonviolent army. As he put it, "There is hope for a violent man to be some day nonviolent, but there is none for a coward." Gandhi was pleased because he had been worried people would see nonviolence as something used only by the weak. People might think it would only be used by those who did not have the ability or the will to use violence.

Khan's achievement does not get as much attention as it deserves because he opposed the partition of India after independence, and this brought animosity from the government in what became Pakistan. While the same group from which he drew—the Pashtun—supplies much of the people who join the Taliban, the numbers that joined the Khudai Khidmatgars was far greater. This supplies Pakistan with a solid nonviolence tradition of its own.

Khan was nominated for the Nobel Peace Prize in 1985.

Books on Khan's work include *A Man to Match His Mountains: Badshah Khan, Nonviolent Soldier of Islam* (Easwaran, 1984); *Abdul Ghaffar Khan: Faith Is a Battle* (Tendulkar, 1967); *Thrown to the Wolves: Abdul Ghaffar Khan* (Pyarelal, 1966); and *The Frontier Gandhi: His Place in History* (Korejo, 1993).

Egypt

Egypt is well-known recently for its part in the Arab Spring of 2010–2011 (1432 AH); it had a nonviolent revolution following the inspiration of nearby Tunisia, which succeeded in toppling a dictator. The aftermath had an election with so many people running that the two that made the run-off were both uninteresting to the people most active in carrying out the revolution. This shows the importance of strategizing politically as well as in nonviolent campaigns. A free society takes more work than one successful toppling of a dictator. Rabia Terri Harris of the Muslim Peace Fellowship points out what more was achieved:

> Two more remarkable things about this movement were the religious cooperation and the increased status of women. The push for national unity brought cooperation between the Muslim majority of the country and the Coptic Christian minority. Women participated in women's demonstrations and other parts of the revolution. Their increased visibility and leadership made the uprising much larger and more effective, and they gained improvements with the changes. Benefits of nonviolent action can often be more than just the immediate goal at hand. (Harris, n.d.)

There was a long-standing tradition of nonviolent action in Egypt. A similar uprising occurred in 1805 (1220 AH). Egypt was under the Ottoman Empire, and their governor set oppressively high taxes and otherwise lost the consent of the governed. Egyptians petitioned him for redress and were turned down, so turned to religious scholars for a ruling. The ruling was that people had a right to remove rulers who deviated from the path of justice. Large demonstrations ensued, beating drums and shouting, with women putting mud on hands and hair as a visible form of dismay. Soldiers were shaken and assured the crowds they empathized with their grievances. People proposed an alternative ruler, one more popular, and then thousands surrounded the unpopular one's palace and kept surrounding it for four months. Finally, the sultan of the Ottomans relented and withdrew the unpopular ruler and replaced him with the popular one (Abdalla & Arafa, 2013, pp. 126–128).

Another successful revolution started after World War I. The British had Egypt under their "protection" since 1882. The campaign started with a 2-million-signature petition which was rejected, leading to mass protests. The Empire set up a British Inquiry Commission to reassert control in December 1919. Until its end in April 1920, it was almost unanimously boycotted by Egyptians in what was called the Sea of Silence. Seven British experts found blank faces and people refusing to talk, often turning and leaving when they approached. Meanwhile, Egyptians made good use of broadcasting their plight abroad, through the press and with diplomacy, and especially using peace proposals from the end of the war. Finally, Britain did recognize Egypt's independence and sovereignty (with caveats) on February 22, 1922.

A constitution was promulgated in 1923, and elections were held in January 1924. This was the first victory over 19th-century imperialism, the first withdrawal of expansionist Europe (Lacouture & Lacouture, 1958; Pal, 2011, pp. 174–176; Abdalla & Arafa, 2013, pp.131–138).

Iran

In 1891 / 1308 A.H., the shah of Iran gave a monopoly on tobacco to a British company. This appeared to many to be the sale of Iran to Europeans. Before the time of knowing tobacco's health hazards, this was a product Iranian businessmen had had control over. When the company's agents arrived and tried to set deadlines, there were massive demonstrations. In December 1891 (1309 AH), a nationwide boycott on tobacco started, observed even by the shah's wives.

The government tried giving in partway by stopping the monopoly inside the country, but leaving the company with an export monopoly. This was not found suitable, with more mass demonstration in the capital city of Tehran. Government forces shot into the unarmed crowd, killing several people. This led to even larger protest rallies. The government canceled the entire grant in early 1892 (1309 AH).

The Iranian constitutional revolution is usually thought to have started in December, 1905 (1323 AH), when the governor of Tehran beat the feet of sugar merchants for not lowering prices as ordered. The merchants took sanctuary in the royal mosque. They were dispersed by the police. This made a large crowd of influential religious scholars gather at a shrine and make demands on the shah. They wanted a "house of justice" to make decisions. In January, 1906 (1323 AH), the shah agreed to this, so the people left the shrine and came back to the city.

Yet the shah did not keep the promise and kept up violence. With no press in opposition, preaching was a main way of getting opposition across. Finally, in July 1906 (1324 AH), a great mass of clerics and others left Tehran to take sanctuary in the city of Qom. Even more people, around 12,000–14,000 merchants, took sanctuary with the British embassy. The withdrawal of all these crucial people brought the city's business to a standstill.

People began talking about having a representative assembly and constitution—a constitutional monarchy, not an absolute monarchy. In July, the shah agreed to the assembly, and it opened in October. The assembly drafted a document based largely on the Belgian constitution. This formed most of the Iranian constitution that lasted until it was replaced in 1979 (1399 AH), when the shah was completely overthrown.

Throughout the years, the constitution was better observed at some times than others, and times when opposition to the shah was violent, giving him an excuse to put it down. But this constitution also allowed for freedom of the press and of assembly. This meant a flourishing of new newspapers with political comments, poems, and satire (Keddie, 2013).

The revolution against the shah in 1979 was also mainly a nonviolent revolution—it happened because massive numbers of people withdrew cooperation and got the shah out of office. Yet there were also some riots involved. Most tragically, once the revolution had succeeded, there were students who took Americans hostage in a crisis that lasted well over a year. This did much to make people forget the mostly nonviolent character of the previous revolution.

In June 2009 (1430 AH), there were massive protests again when many were convinced the election had been stolen. This was called the Green Movement (Pal, pp. 164–173). The movement did not achieve its stated goals of an immediate toppling of the candidate, or securing a recount. But it is one of those campaigns that may have had a delayed impact, a deterrent effect on similar cheating in future elections. The following election did seem to most observers to be far cleaner with a legitimate outcome.

Maldives

The Republic of the Maldives is a small island nation in the area of the Indian Ocean and Arabian Sea. It suffered a 30-year-long rule by Maumoon Abdul Gayoom, starting in 1978 (1398 AH) and ended by nonviolent revolution that led to elections; he lost the election in 2008 (1429 AH).

Journalist Mohamed Nasheed was imprisoned and severely tortured in the early 1990s because of publishing critiques of the government. In 2003 (1424 AH) massive public protests started as a teenager was found to have been tortured to death. Continued pressure showing Gayoom's unpopularity brought problems from other countries and resignations from government officials, until finally Gayoom allowed elections in 2008 (1429 AH). He and Nasheed were the top in the first round, so opposition votes coalesced around Nasheed, who then won the election. Gayoom actually conceded defeat. This is unusual for a dictator, but by this time the reaction of massive nonviolent noncooperation after stolen elections in the Philippines, Serbia, Georgia, and Ukraine may have had a deterrent effect. He knew this was the plan for his country as well. Nasheed was sworn in as president. Other democratic reforms also happened (Pal, 2011, pp. 221–224).

Having come from prison and therefore being empathetic with those suffering, Nasheed started off his term with positive nonviolence:

> During his first post-election press conference, Nasheed called on Maldivians to 'be humble in victory and courageous in defeat.' These words marked a significant change in mood, and radio stations across the Maldives soon began talking about the benevolence and peaceful style of president-elect Nasheed. Some religious speakers even equated his words to the traditions of the Prophet Muhammad. (Shareef, 2008)

Nasheed told an interviewer, when asked how the ousted dictator would be treated, "Islam teaches you there is no future if we hate. The embittered and revengeful cannot become agents of change" (Pal, 2011, p. 224).

Many More

This is not a comprehensive list by any means, and descriptions are skimpy. The list is to demonstrate that nonviolent action and advocacy are widespread in the Muslim world and that a large number of cases would be expected since Muslims comprise about a fifth of the world's population. In alphabetical order these are:

Algeria

The violent 1955 (1374 AH) war for independence from France finally succeeded. Previous violent attempts had failed, but the standards for what "works" with violence are different from those for nonviolence. Algerian history has since extolled the glories of that achievement, but there were effective nonviolent actions occurring from the 1830s on which the final success was made possible. This included, at the time of conquest, a massive withdrawal with a major economic impact, plus social boycotts and continuing agitation (Rahal, 2013).

Bangladesh

When Muslim separatists achieved partition of India, they were in two areas: Pakistan, and what was then East Pakistan, now Bangladesh. It became its own country through nonviolent action. It started with a Bangla Language Movement in 1948 (1367 AH) and again in 1952 (1371 AH). Pakistan tried to impose one national language, but strikes, demonstrations, and civil disobedience said otherwise. Bangladeshis built alternative institutions and eventually had de facto independence. Yet Pakistan invaded and India intervened, so the dramatic violent end is what is often remembered. Bangladeshis had of course been witnesses to and participants in the movement for independence of India from Great Britain, so techniques were familiar (Hossain, 2013).

Chechnya

Kunta-haji Kishiev (1828–1867 [1243 AH–1284 AH]) has the nickname of the "Chechen Mahatma Gandhi," which is rather odd since he died about two years before Gandhi was born. He founded a Sufi branch called Zikrism, which became a majority religion in Chechnya with people tired of the bloody wars and is still popular in Chechnya today. He became a strong supporter of nonviolence and peace. While on his hajj in Mecca, and with wars raging he wrote back home:

> War—it is savagery. Remove yourself from anything that hints of [reminds you of] war if the enemy hasn't come to take away your faith and honor. Your strength is wisdom, patience, fairness. The enemy will not withstand this strength and sooner or later will admit his defeat. No one will have the strength to defeat you and your truth if you don't turn away from the path of your faith. (Schaefer, 2008, p. 69)

He was seen as a threat to Russian imperial teachings and died in prison.

Kosovo

Slobodon Milosevic, leader of Serbia, who was to have problems in his own Serbian people in a later nonviolent revolution, deliberately removed the autonomy of Kosovo in 1989. Noncooperation ensued during the 1990s under the leadership of Ibrahim Rugova. This included cultivating alternative institutions, especially schools, and intervening to stop their own internal blood feuds. Though not unmarred by violence, the goal was finally achieved (Pal, 2011, 141–161; Clark, 2013, pp. 279–296).

India

Muslims remain a large portion of the Indian population and were even more so before partition. Accordingly, there was much Muslim participation and leadership in the Indian movement for independence. Mohandas Gandhi, in his work on Hindu-Muslim harmony, commented, "My reading of the Qur'an has convinced me that the basis of Islam is not violence but is unadulterated peace. It regards forbearance as superior to vengeance. The very word 'Islam' means peace, which is nonviolence." One of the Muslims active in the movement was Abul Kalam Azad, renowned theologian, who served as president of the Congress Party (the main organization working on Indian independence) and after independence served as education minister. Another was Zakir Husain, who ran Jamia Milia University for many years and worked hard on educational progress and religious harmony (Pal, 2011, pp. 125–139).

Iraq

In January of 1948 (1367 AH), and on into the spring, there was a nonviolent uprising called the Al-Wathbah (The Leap). Sparked by a treaty for British "protection," it achieved some successes before being stopped by martial law and war in Palestine. It did pave the way for future events including overthrowing the monarchy and establishing an elections system.

More recently, Muslim Peacemaker Teams (http://reconciliation project.org/2012/muslim-peacemaker-teams) began in January of 2005 (1425 AH), responding to erupting violence since the U.S.-led invasion in 2003 (1424 AH). It was inspired by Christian Peacemaker Teams, which have been active in Iraq since 2002 (1423 AH). Another group is called La'Onf, which means "no violence" in Arabic. It pushes for nonviolent solutions to problems of terrorism, occupation, and governmental corruption (Pal, 2011, pp. 173–174).

Pakistan

In Pakistan in 2007, lawyers and others waged a nonviolent successful campaign to topple dictator Pervez Musharraf and restore an independent judiciary. In the elections that followed, the Awami National Party made an admirable comeback in the border regions—this was the party formed by the successors of Ghaffar Khan (Pal, 2011, pp. 213–221).

Tunisia

It was in the small North African county of Tunisia, that the massive demonstrations toppled their own dictator and sparked the same in Egypt, an event called the Arab Spring, 2010–2011 (1432 AH).

FORMS OF VIOLENCE

Blood Sacrifice

Ritual human sacrifice to please, placate, or bargain with divinity has always been out of the question in Islam. The near-sacrifice of Abraham's son Isaac in Jewish scriptures was changed to a near-sacrifice of his older brother Ishmael and is a major theme, but Islamic practice is for five times of prayer per day and other nonviolent requirements for the purpose of worship.

Ritual animal sacrifice occurs only during the Hajj and during Eid al-Adha, symbolizing the substitution of the ram for the human sacrifice in Abraham's story. However, it is transformed into a provision of meat for the poor. Thus, the meaning is charity, not placating or bargaining.

Slavery

Islam began when slavery was a common institution. The Qur'an neither forbids it, nor indicates it is an institution that should continue. That setting slaves free is a virtue or a method of making up for wrongdoing is mentioned in verses 2:177, 4:92, 5:89, 24:33, 58:3, and 90:13. The one verse that allows capture of prisoners of war explicitly does not permit them to be held in slavery (47:4). When discussing the *Zakat*, "charitable contributions," which is one of the five pillars of Islam, verse 9:60 lists one good use of the money as freeing slaves.

Nevertheless, slavery was practiced by those identifying themselves as Muslims throughout Muslim history. The capture of Africans for the purpose was happening at the same time as those identifying themselves as Christians and was also a vast brutality.

The recent Islamic State of Iraq and Syria (ISIS) claimed that abolishing slavery was going against Sharia law, but in an Open Letter to Baghdadi signed by dozens of Islamic scholars, point 12 refutes this:

> No scholar of Islam disputes that one of Islam's aims is to abolish slavery [citing Qur'an 90:12–14 and 58:3] . . . The Prophet

Muhammad's Sunnah is that he freed all male and female slaves who were in his possession or whom had been given to him. For over a century, Muslims, and indeed the entire world, have been united in the prohibition and criminalization of slavery, which was a milestone in human history when it was finally achieved.... After a century of Muslim consensus on the prohibition of slavery, you have violated this.... You have resuscitated something that the *Shari'ah* has worked tirelessly to undo and has been considered forbidden by consensus for over a century. Indeed all the Muslim countries in the world are signatories of anti-slavery conventions. (Open Letter, 2014, p. 12)

War

War is to be practiced within strict guidelines similar to other just-war traditions; actual practice has had similar results to other just-war traditions.

The Death Penalty

The death penalty is practiced.

Infanticide and Feticide

Infanticide is strictly prohibited, and feticide is prohibited once ensoulment occurs. The gestational point of when ensoulment is thought to occur varies. Female infanticide was common in the Arabic world of Muhammad's time and is opposed in the Qur'an 16:58–59 and 81:8–9. Infanticide for either gender is opposed in the Qur'an 17:31: "And kill not your children for fear of poverty—We provide for them and for you. Surely the killing of them is a great wrong."

Meat

Dietary restrictions are called halal and are similar to kosher except for an additional prohibition of alcohol. Animals may be killed for food but should not be killed without justifiable reason, and maltreatment such as branding or starving or blood sports is something several hadiths show Mohammad regarding with horror (http://www.islamicconcern.com/islamicteachings.pdf). The slaughter of animals for meat should be done with a sharp knife so that death is mercifully instant, and there should be no other animals slaughtered in the vicinity to terrify the animals. Current groups encouraging vegetarianism and animal welfare from an Islamic perspective, citing especially Qur'an 6:38 and 24:41 about high regard for animals, include Islamic Concern (http://www.islamicconcern.com).

Poverty

Poverty has always been a major concern in Islam, and all Muslims who can afford to are expected to contribute the mandatory annual *Zakat* for its alleviation, and *Sadaqa* is encouragement for further charity giving. Qur'anic verses stressing the importance of giving to the needy include 2:177, 2:215, 5:89, and 59:7. The fast of Ramadan is in part a way of empathizing with the poor, and social systems that perpetuate poverty are unjust.

Violence in the Scriptures

The most commonly cited verse advocating massive violence is the Sword Verse, *ayat as-sayf*, Qur'an 9:5. It says to slay the idolaters wherever found, unless they repent. Scholars have found 113 (or maybe 124) verses that are cancelled out—"abrogated"—by this one. The idea of "abrogation" is that later verses superseded earlier ones, and the ninth surah was either the last or next to last written. When Muslims were weak in the beginning years in Mecca, they had to be patient; when they got stronger in Medina, defensive war was allowed and the previous commands were cancelled; when they became stronger yet back in Mecca, conditions were set for more aggressive warfare on behalf of Islam, thus cancelling out previous directives. This is how this verse, and also 9:29, is read by violent jihadists. While the verses that contradict these two are far more numerous, they were also earlier revelations.

Others argue that the violent jihadists' interpretation of these verses are ripped out of context; reading the whole of Surah 9 and knowing the historical context renders these two verses more defensive in nature and reticent about using violence. The idolaters referred to were constantly attacking at the time. When scholars offer instead of abrogation a "context of revelation" method of interpretation, this commonly results in a more inclusivist reading of the Qur'an.

Abrogation has commonly been applied when two verses on a specific rule contradict each other. The method of selecting which one applies is to take the later one. The Qur'an itself, uniquely among world scriptures, provides for abrogation (2:106 and 17:86). Jewish rabbis tended to solve this problem of contradiction in their laws by creative reinterpretations to keep the two verses from contradicting, but abrogation when choosing between one verse and another is a clear-cut and long-standing resolution within Islam.

Yet if the understanding is that 1 or 2 verses cancel out around 113 verses and their contexts, so much of what went before, this essentially says there is neither much point in taking the full Qur'an into account, nor in studying or citing a large portion of it.

The Open Letter to Baghdadi proposed that the entire Qur'an must be taken into account when ascertaining what verses mean, and this will apply to all the verses cited for justifying violence:

> It is also forbidden to cite a portion of a verse from the Qur'an—or part of a verse—to derive a ruling without looking at everything that the Qur'an and *Hadith* teach related to that matter. In other words, there are strict subjective and objective prerequisites for *fatwas*, and one cannot "cherry-pick" Qur'anic verses for legal arguments without considering the entire Qur'an and *Hadith*. (Open Letter, 2014, p. 1)

In another violent verse, Qur'an 4:34 in some of the translations says that men may beat or scourge their wives. The verse basically starts by saying (depending on the translation and the translators' assumptions) that since men are stronger and provide for wives financially, wives should obey, and a virtuous wife will. If disobedient, however, he starts by reasoning with her, escalates to staying away from bed, and then may beat her. Yet Muhammad commented that this means a "light tap that leaves no mark" and was not on the face. In short, it was meant to indicate the seriousness of an extreme situation symbolically.

Nevertheless, this verse has been used by men who wish to justify domestic violence, given the common translation of "beat"—and also ignoring the following verse, which refers to appointing arbitrators equally for husband and wife in case of conflict. Also, the end of 4:19 admonishes husbands to be kind to wives, suggesting that if there is something they hate in them, it may be that God put that there for their own good. Fatwas (rulings by religious scholars) against domestic violence, and therefore against reading this verse to allow it, have been issued by the Islamic Supreme Council of Canada (2012), and by Kabbani and Ziad (2011).

Verse 5:38 directs cutting off the hands of thieves as an exemplary punishment. Those inclined to high punitiveness take it literally; those not so inclined understand the wording of "cut off" as metaphorical, cutting off their ability to do it further, as with imprisonment. They point to other uses of the verb meaning "cut off" in other places in the Qur'an to justify this interpretation.

Verse 5:33 is a horrifying verse when taken out of context, saying that the recompense for those who fight against Muslims is cutting off of hands or feet on alternative sides, or crucifixion. But these peculiar specifics are put in the mouth of Pharaoh, threatening Moses and his people, in 20:71 and 7:123–124. The previous verse, 5:32, mentions directly the Children of Israel and forbids killing: whoever kills one person (without cause—capital punishment is allowed), it is as if that person killed everyone. Therefore, many understand this verse not to be a command of what believers should do to those who fight them, but rather as a statement that what Pharaoh threatened is instead what Pharaoh himself deserves, along with others who are similar (see http://www.quranicpath.com/finerpoints_cut_hands_feet.html).

This does still leave many verses that threaten hellfire and harsh punishments that God sends, as with the Christian scripture, with similar thoughts and controversies about what they mean.

After pointing out that such problematic passages are found in holy books from all the major religions, authors of a Qur'anic commentary say:

> The Qur'an does have difficult and awkward verses whose meaning depends on the interpreter's state of consciousness and intention. In the imagery of the Sufi poet Rumi, both bee and wasp drink from the same flower, but one produces nectar and the other, a sting. (Rahman, Elias, & Redding, 2009, p. xiv)

Treatment of "Heretics"

Charges of heresy can be lethal and have been throughout Muslim history. Christianity and Islam share this as a major problem of violence inflicted in their names.

RELATIONS WITH OTHER RELIGIONS

Buddhism

Buddhist scriptures prophesy the coming of another Buddha, Maitreya, when humans have forgotten the dharma. There are Muslim scholars who argue how this fits the description of Muhammad, making this tradition one of many that pointed to the Final Messenger. This is not the most common view, however, among Muslims and even less so among Buddhists. Buddha is certainly not mentioned in early Muslim literature as one of the preceding prophets—but then, there were thousands, and most of them were unnamed. Still, the differences about strict monotheism, what happens in the afterlife, and various other ideas are in stark contrast.

Christianity

The Jesus of Christianity is regarded as the next-to-last prophet in Islam, paving the way for Muhammad, predicting him as the final Prophet. Jesus, named Isa Ibn Maryam, is covered in 93 verses in the Qur'an. His mother Mary, understood to be a virgin when he was born, is the only woman mentioned by name in the Qur'an, is mentioned there in more verses than she is in the New Testament, and is one of only eight people to have an entire chapter named after her, Surah 19. Many parts of their stories are changed in ways that would be startling to Christians.

Jesus is unique among the prophets for his miraculous birth and healings; he is the word and spirit of God and prophet of peace, though the idea of him being an incarnation or son of God is denied as impossible, given the nature of God. There is a long tradition of Jesus with images of healing. During the 200-year Crusades war, a major low point in Muslim-Christian relations, Muslims pointed to the glaring disparity between the prophet of peace and the brutal behavior of people claiming to be his followers.

Currently, the Church of the Holy Sepulcher, erected in 325 CE (306 BH) over the site where Jesus was believed to have been crucified and buried, is opened and closed every day by the Muslim Joudeh and Nuseibeh families. They have the keys and have been doing this task since 1187 (583 AH). It was as early as 637 CE (16 AH), when Muslims took over Jerusalem, that the guarantee of protection of Christian holy sites was made.

Hinduism

Hindus and Muslims live together in India, sometimes amicably, often with great animosity. Pakistan was originally part of India and partitioned off specifically to make a Muslim-majority country. Even so, India has the fourth largest population of Muslims in the world in absolute numbers. Interaction is frequent, and work on Hindu-Muslim harmony is a major theme of nonviolent activists in that area.

Judaism

Many of the Jewish stories, both from the Hebrew Bible and from the Mishnah (stories related to the scriptural stories) are found in the Qur'an. Adam, Noah, and Moses are especially prominent. Some of the Qur'anic stories are quite different; Muslims understand that their religion corrected texts that had become corrupted by human hands. Jews do not believe that these constituted corrections, but distortions.

Jews are People of the Book and Muslims have had interactions with them since early days. The Qur'an says:

> Those who keep faith (with this revelation), and those who follow the Jewish way, and the Christians, and the Sabeans [from Sheba/Yemen]—any who have faith in God and the Last Day, and perform righteous works—shall have their reward with their Sustainer. On them shall be no fear, neither shall they grieve. (Qur'an 2:62)

The state of Israel became a Jewish homeland over the objections of Muslims, many of whom were living in the area as Palestinians. This has resulted in much animosity and outright violence, in both directions, as well as some nonviolent campaigns.

The Foundation for Ethnic Understanding is one group that works directly on improving Jewish-Muslim relations, as covered in chapter 1.

Sikhism

Sikhism began with both Muslim ideas and Hindu ideas. Muslims interact well with Sikhs in Punjab, in the area of India where Sikhism is most concentrated.

Zoroastrianism

Zoroastrians are regarded as People of the Book and so are treated the same way as Jews, Christians, and other monotheists.

Related Religions: Bahá'ís and Druze

Religions that came from Islam and were originally treated as heresies include the Bahá'ís and the Druze, both of which regard Muhammad as one of many good messengers from God. The Bahá'ís number around 6 million worldwide and are covered in chapter 10.

The Druze number around a million and are mainly concentrated in the Levant, in Syria and Lebanon with many in Israel and some in Jordan, with about 2 percent or so scattered around the world. The Druze, started in the 11th century, is a hereditary religion not seeking converts and has a syncretic set of beliefs from Islam, Christianity, Hellenism, and other influences. Having been underground much of their existence to avoid persecution, many of their tenets are secret.

The main claim to fame for a Druze nonviolent campaign started in 1981 in the Golan Heights, which Israel had recently taken over. Israel wanted the Druze to accept Israeli citizenship and the Druze declined. In addition to the normal strikes and demonstrations, the Druze did a reverse strike in which they worked for free on a sewer system the Israeli government was not working on. Israeli identification papers when forced upon people were strewn in the streets. When Israeli soldiers surrounded villages and cut off food supplies, the Druze used entirely unarmed people in sheer numbers to go through the blockades. An order of fire on crowds was refused by Israeli soldiers, who understood themselves as defending Israel, not as attacking unarmed people. There were some initial successes in this campaign (Kennedy, 1984; Zunes, 1999, p. 46).

8

First Nations of North America

A league of nations with a participatory democracy over a thousand years old profoundly influenced practices in the United States and Canada, and from there spread throughout the world. A sense of human equality in stark contrast to Europe and Asia's autocratic regimes and an understanding of women's rights that disproved arguments for natural inferiority also provided crucial foundations to worldwide activists who oppose the violence of dictatorships and social inequalities. Though adherents of original religions north of the Rio Grande in North America are now much fewer in number, the impact on worldwide nonviolence theory and action has been enormous.

BASIC BACKGROUND

North and South America had been essentially divided from the rest of the world (as has Australia) for thousands of years before the last five centuries. The millennia of separate development has allowed for some differing perspectives that have vastly enriched the world community, especially in the areas of freedom and human equality.

Most reporting of world religions does not cover the First Nations' religions on their list. One reason is that there is no *one* religion. Different nations had different approaches, with groups of nations in different areas sharing common features but not regarding themselves as having the same religion. Another is that the category of "religion" does not fit as well, with no boundaries set on beliefs to be defended against other beliefs. Many of the categories that other religions address are not regarded as relevant in many of the Native American traditions.

Still, there are features that are important to understanding the human condition as it relates to nonviolence. The contribution of First Nations to the worldwide practice of nonviolence is actually quite substantial, as will be covered in the following, and so it must be included in any book whose topic includes the historical development of nonviolence and religion.

Yet another reason that there is not much coverage is that the number of people practicing these traditions has gotten so low as to keep these, even if accounted together as one category of religion, from being one of the major ones in the world. They are fewer than 0.3 percent of the U.S. population, which would be around 675,000 people (Pew Research Center, 2008); add to that the unknown number of Canadians, and it is not likely to be much more than a million and may be less. Yet, as with Zoroastrianism, which used to be one of the major world religions in its heyday and is now practiced by only around 200,000 people according to the World Religion Database, these traditions as a whole were once practiced by many millions of people in a major land area of the world—much larger than ancient Persia. As with Zoroastrianism, they have also had a major influence on worldwide developments.

There is an image of the American continents being scantily populated before the arrival of Europeans and Africans, but the tragic truth is that the continents were instead heavily *de*-populated. Early accounts said that the coastline of what later became New England was thick with villages; de Soto reported heavy populations when he explored Florida; an early boat-traveler along the Amazon River reported villages so thick as to go past 20 in one day. These were all early reports. Villages became deserted in the northeast. Travelers a century and a half after de Soto found hardly any people where they went. The Amazon River basin has been regarded as a place of low population for a long time, and the man who wrote otherwise early was discounted as unreliable (Mann, 2005).

The problem was that epidemics raged, mainly small pox but also others, and the results were truly devastating. The world has known many pandemics; in the mid-1300s, somewhere from a quarter to a third of the European population fell to the bubonic plague. But the plagues in the Americas killed probably over 90 percent of the population.

There were several reasons for this. The new diseases were suddenly introduced to people who had never had a chance to build up any kind of biological resistance to them. Europeans of that time, after all, were all people who had descended from those who survived the bubonic plague, along with previous outbreaks of small pox and other diseases. There was nothing sudden about it for the Europeans.

Because of the separation from other continents, Indians had much more homogenous DNA. This was marvelously practical in terms of avoiding many of the genetic diseases common across the oceans, but it meant that there was not enough variation to come up with more resistant groups of people.

The Indians did very little by way of domesticating animals—some farmed with very little meat, and others had a system of managing animals to be away from the village, and then would go hunt them. This gave them a huge advantage in never having had the epidemics that Europeans, Asians, and Africans had acquired from their own domesticated animals. But this meant the Indians had not built up any immunity to those. It also meant that the domestic animals themselves, when introduced, were a major source of contagion; de Soto's men brought pigs along, and those that escaped to the woods may well have been responsible for the depopulation there.

Since the people indigenous to the Americas had never faced epidemics of this kind before, this millennia-long superiority became a sudden disadvantage in that they did not have the foggiest idea of how to handle the novel situation. Europeans could be quite brutal in their use of quarantines, boarding people up in their houses, because even without the germ theory they had ascertained that the problem was contagion and contagion needed to be stopped. Indians had no concept of quarantine. Often, the diseases were passed to them by other Indians long before the first European even showed up in their area.

Had the Europeans been kind-hearted souls who wanted to minimize the damage, there actually was very little they could have done to prevent this monumental tragedy with the level of knowledge available at the time. They could have at least taken the edge off, made it a little less cruel. However, many were astonishingly hard-hearted, interpreting the massive deaths as God's way of clearing the continent for their benefit. So they added to the death toll. They added even more to the death toll by being shockingly cruel and lethal, directly and in a large number of ways.

Both Europeans and Indians shared the common human trait of regarding their own group as the normal one and the other as strange and not as good. The North American Indians had several details on which to base a negative assessment of the Europeans. The Europeans were shorter due to being less well-nourished, had unsightly marks left from diseases, and did not bathe as much as later custom and contemporary Indian custom expected. They were startling in how badly women were treated, with battering and rape of wives being entirely legal, and such treatment of women other than wives being practiced enough to keep women from being able to walk about safely. Indians were also baffled at social classes where people were supposed to be deferential to their "betters."

Europeans had a sense of their own superiority. They thought there were no farms because plants were not in neat rows, but indigenous agriculture used a "Three Sisters" system where corn, beans, and squash were all grown together. Because these plants complemented each other in their growing needs, this system was superior in terms of the amount of food grown in the allotted space. It was also a well-rounded nutrition. Europeans noted that there was little by way of domesticated animals but were not aware that Indians were managing the land by carefully setting fires in such a way as to clear out dead growth and encourage new growth and that they actually wanted the animals at a distance, with the expectation of hunting. North of the Rio Grande, Europeans would perceive leaders in terms of kings and queens, princesses and princes, but these categories did not quite fit, and the lack of fit was seen as backwardness. In actuality, it was a more democratic form of government, as would become more obvious later.

Being the people with ships who were arriving in many places during those centuries, Europeans held the same high view of themselves as being "above" the Chinese and Asian Indians as well. The difference was that the Oriental nations managed to stay well populated and thereby maintain their cultures more robustly. Much of what Europeans viewed as "backward" in the Americas was actually a result of depopulation. Once farms and managed animals were abandoned because the people managing them had died from rampant disease, the environment reverted to wilderness.

Details of this are found in the book *1491: New Revelations of the Americas before Columbus* (Mann, 2005). Another example he gives is that in the Amazon, what was once understood to be jungles admirably high in fruits were actually ancient orchards; the trees were deliberately planted in the area where the soil was poor for annual farming but worked well for trees. Trading networks were clearly quite extensive throughout the Americas, as can be seen by items from one place appearing a thousand miles away. The similarities between the complicated Maya calendar and the Tsigali/Cherokee calendar are great enough to posit some communication across great distances.

South America did have empires, and as with the strike in ancient Egypt (see chapter 5), they may well have had nonviolent rebellions as a normal part of the human condition. Inca records were in thread rather than paper and so it took a while to understand they were complicated writings and to start reading them. Maya and Aztec records were deliberately destroyed by Spaniards. We know quite a bit through stone records, but the people carving in stone were doing so to glorify the royalty, and royalty can be expected not to make detailed records of any successful nonviolent rebellions against it in the format of stone monuments.

In the case of America north of the Rio Grande, however, empires and large cities did not arise. The large number of languages attests to this—no hegemonic power consolidated which language would be used.

The one exception is a city-state of about 15,000 people, currently called Cahokia, from around 600 to around 1350 CE. Located near where the Mississippi and Missouri Rivers meet (currently in Illinois across from St. Louis, Missouri), it was part of the Mississippian mound-building cultures with some especially large mounds. It had many of the features common to cities, including evidence of violence, and it fell due to environmental mismanagement. Such mismanagement has been common elsewhere in the world and people restarted cities elsewhere. The North American Indians did not find it a model worthy of trying to emulate further.

All in all, the concept of "backwardness" was an ethnocentric concept on the part of Europeans. It has no objective basis. The indigenous peoples of the Americas have had as long to develop as other people have and that they have sometimes done so in different ways has been enriching for us all—especially in the areas involving nonviolence.

BELIEFS AND HISTORICAL INFLUENCE FOR NONVIOLENCE

Human Equality

When discussing the "Jesus is Lord" concept, a book called *Native American Theology* notes:

> There is no analogue in North American indigenous societies for the relationship of power and disparity which is usually signified by the word "lord." To the contrary, North American cultures and social structures were fundamentally marked by their egalitarian nature. Even a so-called "chief" had typically very limited authority which even then depended much on the person's charismatic stature within the community and skill at achieving consensus. (Kidwell, Noley, & Tinker, 2001, p. 67–68)

Jesus never referred to himself as lord. When other people in the New Testament did, it was for the purpose of establishing that it was the humiliated and executed man who was lord—*and not Caesar*. It was actually an assertion against the cruel and violent having lordship and proposing that the gentle and loving did instead.

But there must be an original "lord" to contrast to, to make the alternative "lord" make any sense. Any culture that has no lords to begin with will naturally be unable to make sense of the concept.

Just as loving one's enemies means one does not actually have enemies at all, having a "lord" who is a friendly guide means not actually having a "lord" at all. However, hierarchical societies have had trouble grasping this point. They are therefore using language that makes sense to them. Yet it is at best puzzling to many Native Americans.

The book further comments on the widespread nonhierarchical nature of indigenous spirituality:

> The circle is a key symbol for self-understanding in these tribes, representing the whole of the universe and our part in it. We see ourselves as co-equal participants in the circle standing neither above nor below anything else in God's Creation. There is no hierarchy in our cultural context, even of species, because the circle has no beginning or ending. . . . When a group of Indians forms a circle to pray, all know that the prayers have already begun with the representation of a circle . . . the intentional physicality of our formation has already expressed our prayer and deep concern for the wholeness of all of God's Creation. (Kidwell et al., 2001, p. 50)

This sense of human equality is not merely a feature of one set of religions to find interesting. Historically, it has been crucial to the worldwide development of widespread nonviolent action.

Charles C. Mann, in his book *1491: New Revelations of the Americas before Columbus*, devotes an appendix to "The Great Law of Peace," covered more later in the chapter, in which he gives a most eloquent rendition of the original North Americans' enormous contribution to the practice of nonviolent action in modern times:

> The sense that anyone is as good as anyone else . . . is widely identified as one of the Americas' great gifts to the world. When rich stockbrokers in London and Paris proudly retain their working-class accents, when audiences show up at La Scala in track suits and sneakers, when South Africans and Thais complain that the police don't read suspects their rights as they do on *Starsky & Hutch* reruns, when anti-government protesters in Beirut sing "We Shall Overcome" in Lebanese accents—all these raspberries in the face of social and legal authority have a distinctly American tone, no matter

where they take place. To be sure, apostles of freedom have risen in many places. But an overwhelming number have been inspired by the American example—or, as it should perhaps be called, the *Native American* example, for among its fonts is Native American culture. (Mann, 2005, pp. 357–358)

Mann asked seven experts—anthropologists and historians—whether in the year 1491 (right before first contact) they would rather have been typical European citizens or Haudenosaunee/Iroquois. All seven selected the Indians as more appealing (p. 364). This was a point that was not lost on European immigrants of the time—while efforts to "civilize" Indians into European ways were repeated failures, it was a common thing for colonists to go join with the Indians.

This meant that the colonial governments had to avoid being too oppressive, or people would vote with their feet. Partial withdrawals of a few people happened all the time; larger withdrawal was a real possibility, because the escape hatch was readily available.

Therefore, in addition to the Native peoples being good role models on human equality in regard to class distinctions, over about a century and a half—many generations—the colonies sustained practices that would keep people from fleeing to Indian Territory (Mann, 2005, 364–365). There were of course many other influences as well, but this was good training for the government that would be decided upon after independence from Britain.

Even as late as a classic 1884 novel set in the 1830s, *The Adventures of Huckleberry Finn*, Mark Twain has Huckleberry say in the last paragraph: "But I reckon I got to light out for the [Indian] Territory ahead of the rest, because Aunt Sally, she's going to adopt me and civilize me, and I can't stand it." The escape hatch was well known about and entrenched through colonial times and thereafter.

Haudenausee/Iroquois: The Law of Peace

Deganawidah lives in oral history as The Peacemaker. He probably lived around 1000 CE. Legend has him born of a virgin, a shamanistic outsider who floated from his home village in a canoe made of white stone to wander among the tribes in the area mainly now encompassed by northern New York that were then fighting each other constantly. Bloody wars were frequent. He was believed to be sent by the Creator to teach a message of peace, helped by people's amazement that stone could float.

Stories vary, but as he set about the long and hard work of persuasion and found a speech impediment as an obstacle, he met Ayonwatha (the same as Hiawatha of the history-garbled Longfellow poem) whose daughters had been killed by Tadodaho, head of the Onondaga. Rather than swear revenge, Ayonwatha wanted to see to it that no other parent had to go through that kind of pain, and so he worked with The Peacemaker and the two of them persuaded other tribes to accept The Law of Peace, until Tadodaho was the only holdout.

Deganawidah gave Tadodaho a single arrow and asked him to break it, which was easily done. Then he gave him five tied together, which would not break. Deganawidah prophesied in the same way that the Five Nations would fall into darkness if left separate, but would be strengthened if together. Soon thereafter, a solar eclipse occurred, and the shaken Tadodaho agreed to have the Onondaga join the confederacy on condition that he be the main speaker, and his name has been the title of the main speaker ever since.

In a different version of the story, after many attempts to convince Tadodaho had failed, 49 men sang the Great Song of Peace, focused on the purpose of winning over his evil mind. This finally worked, and The Peacemaker offered him a position of watching the fire on behalf of the alliance.

The Peacemaker then saw that men still carried weapons and decided they needed a symbol that would remind them of their promises to each other. A very tall tree had clusters of five needles, symbolizing the five nations, and so was called the Tree of Peace. He uprooted it and instructed the men to cast their weapons in, to bury their greed and hatred. The tree was re-placed on top. The Great Peace was established.

The Five Nations were then the Mohawk, Onondaga, Oneida, Cayuga, and Seneca; later it became Six Nations as the Tuscarora joined. There were 117 codicils to the Law of Peace, which do as much to limit the government's powers as to delineate them. Jurisdiction was strictly for relations among the nations, not within. There was a council of sachems, who were expected to submit important matters to be decided by their people—in short, the consent of the governed.

There were no exact dates in the oral history, but there was a record of 145 lifetime appointments of Tadodaho. Mann and Fields (1997) calculated roughly how much time that would take, using the average of other lifetime positions—popes, kings, queens, and judges—and arrived at an estimate of around the 12th century. The calculations in astronomy are more precise: if the pivotal role of the solar eclipse is correct, the one in that time frame that would have been observable from that area was on August 31, 1142, fitting very well with the Mann and Fields estimate. Scholars still debate this, of course. But whatever the precise figure, it is the second-oldest continuous parliamentary-type body in the world (the first being Iceland's in 930 CE).

In the 1700s and 1800s, interaction between Indians and people of European descent was extensive. For example, John Adams reported that as a boy he would frequently visit a wigwam a mile from his house and always be given fruit and that Indians were also frequent visitors at his house (Mann, 2005, p. 362).

Many aspects of the Haudenosaunee legal codes, especially the check-on-power provisions, did have a deep influence on the U.S. Constitution. Had there been more influence yet, such matters as allowing slavery and enfranchising only men would not have been there. Nevertheless, the influence of the Haudenosaunee Confederacy and its Law of Peace on the U.S. Constitution was profound (Schaaf, 1988). This was recognized by the U.S. Congress with the passage if the Iroquois Recognition Bill of 1987.

Haudenosaunee/Iroquois and Others: Women's Rights

In upstate New York Haudenosaunee territory lived several stalwarts of the beginning feminist movement—Elizabeth Cady Stanton, Lucretia Mott, and Matilda Joslyn Gage. Gage was adopted by the Wolf Clan of the Mohawk nation and given the name "Ka-ron-ien-ha-wi" ("Sky Carrier").

An argument of the time was that women held an inferior position in society on grounds that this is what God and nature intended. These women were able to point to the model of the Haudenosaunee they knew well as disproving the point. This case was bolstered throughout U.S. lands by various groups of its indigenous peoples (Wagner, 1996).

The Law of Peace explicitly orders the Council to "heed the warnings of your female relatives," with failure to do so meaning removal. (This was not a system of equal participation in all institutions—roles were still quite separate. Women were clan heads and appointed the men to the Council and could remove them; men were the chiefs and were on the Council.) Additionally, Indian women owned their own property and could sell or give it without it even occurring to them that they needed to consult their husbands (Wagner, 1996). On direct violence, Europeans were legally allowed to beat their wives, while Indians found this appalling.

Early feminists of European descent were impressed. Their agitation for women to have the vote, participate in the government, have property rights, and have legal protection from violence gathered steam in a nonviolent movement that is still making progress today.

There was clear nonviolent action by the women that got them more power to veto unregulated war, happening in the 1600s. As with the ancient but fictitious Greek play *Lysistrata*, they refused all lovemaking and child-bearing while the men were engaged in warfare. They also withheld supplies, which they had control over. This worked, becoming a classic case of nonviolent action (Sharp, 1973, p. 191), and they still had this power when offering models to the 19th-century European American observers.

The Hopis

Thomas Banyacya (1910–1999) said: "The true Hopi people know how to fight without killing or hurting." He was one of many Hopis who went to prison rather than cooperate with the military draft, spending seven years there. Only 10 percent of those drafted complied, so 90 percent held on to the peace tradition—some signed up to help in other ways, and others were imprisoned as Banyacya was.

The Hopis organized and lobbied to argue they should have conscientious objector status due to religions principles forbidding the bearing of arms. Finally, in 1953, the Hopis were granted the right to claim official conscientious objector status due to religious beliefs.

The Hopis have a 900-year-old religious tradition that Maasau'u, Great Spirit and Guardian of the Earth, assigned them the duty of taking care of the world's natural balance and gave them ominous prophecies with guidance on how to avoid specific threats. These were a secret oral tradition until 1948. Hopi religious leaders were alarmed about the use of the atomic bomb and its mushroom cloud, which they saw as the highly destructive "gourd of ashes," which had been foretold.

They appointed four messengers to warn the world about these prophecies and the guidance on how to avoid them. Thomas Banyacya was one of those, and among his many activities he had the opportunity to speak to the United Nations Assembly in 1992.

Since the prophecies include not just the threats but guidance on solutions, there is this prediction on the rise of nonviolent-action movements: "When the earth is dying there shall arise a new tribe of all colors and all creeds. This tribe shall be called The Warriors of the Rainbow and it will put its faith in actions not words."

First Nations of North America 161

The Miwok

Despite what Gandhi said about nonviolence being a tool of the strong, it is still true that the weak who really do have no other option do in fact have that option. One tale from California illustrates this:

> As settlers spread out across the continent, traditional lands were claimed. . . . As a result, many Indigenous peoples were brought to the point of extinction. In the case of the Miwoks things were made even worse by the fact that they were hunted with guns.
> So it was that the last group of survivors was tracked down and surrounded. As the Miwok people faced their executioners they made a last request: Before they died they wished to sing their sacred healing song . . . while the song was being sung the guns were lowered and the posse turned away and rode off, leaving the Miwoks to survive and carry their songs into the future. (Peat, 1994, p. 142).

Persistence

Religions in general have rituals and symbols that have deep meaning for those participating, and these are potent enough to those who have those emotional and spiritual connections that they are not to be toyed with by others. The specific clothing that a priest wears, for example, is not meant to be copied by people who like the idea of being a priest but have not made the serious preparations and group approval needed for it. Even Quakers (members of a Christian Protestant denomination), who lack hierarchy and have very simple and unprepared worship meetings in silence broken only by short messages any participant is free to give (and anyone is welcome to be a participant), do not have in mind that anyone unfamiliar with the spiritual practices can come and playact. On one occasion, due to protests for an oncoming war, a TV reporter wanted to videotape the worship, and there has not been a single fellow Quaker that I have related this story to that has not been aghast at the idea—it showed a complete misunderstanding of the free and unposed moving of the Spirit.

In the same way, Native Americans have their own spirituality that is theirs, and it is their decision what makes sense to share and what remains their own possession and their own spiritual journey. As one put it:

> Spiritual traditions cannot be used as some sort of Whitman's Sampler of ceremonial form, mixed and matched—here a little Druid, there a touch of Nordic mythology followed by a regimen of Hindu

vegetarianism, a mishmash of American Indian rituals somewhere else—at the whim of people who are part of none of them . . . to play at ritual potluck is to debase all spiritual traditions, voiding their internal coherence and leaving nothing usably sacrosanct as a cultural anchor for the peoples who conceived and developed them, and who have consequently organized their societies around them. (Churchill, 1993, p. 213)

Yet it is far deeper than a mere fear of being shallow:

The non-Indian appropriator conveys the message that Indians are indeed a conquered people and that there is nothing that Indians possess, *absolutely nothing*—pipes, dances, land, water, feathers, drums, and even prayers—that non-Indians cannot take whenever and wherever they wish. (Deloria, 1992, p. 37)

This is crucial to the persistence of the religions:

Traditional ceremonies and spiritual practices . . . are precious gifts given to the Indian people by our Creator. These sacred ways have enabled us as Indian people to survive—miraculously—the onslaught of five centuries of continuous effort by non-Indians and their government to exterminate us by extinguishing all traces of our traditional ways of life. . . . Because our sacred traditions are so precious to us, we cannot allow them to be desecrated and abused. (Churchill, 1993, pp. 279–280)

As with other religions that have received astonishingly intense persecutions and massacres (Jews, Samaritans, Zoroastrians, etc.), the very fact that the practices continue is in and of itself an admirable achievement in assertive nonviolence.

Other Peace Practices

Christopher Ronwanièn:te Jocks, in discussing the feelings about non-Indian appropriate of Indian religions, recounts this tale of what a Mohawk woman answered when she was asked by some New Age non-Indians how to do an Indian ceremony:

First, you prepare the feast. Cook up lots and lots of food. We Mohawks make corn soup, but you can substitute tofu stir-fry if you like. As you're cooking it, think about the people you'll be inviting, about their lives, and about your own. Think about the ingredients too, where they come from, and who helped bring them to you. Then invite everyone you know to come over. Make sure you have enough food. Everybody that comes, you feed them. And you listen to them, pay attention to their advice, their problems. Hold their hands, if that's what they need. If any of them needs to stay over, make a place for them. Then, next month, you do the same thing again. And again, four times, the same way. That's it! You've done an Indian ceremony! (Jocks, 1997, p. 61)

Jocks indicates there was no sarcasm in this at all; she was gently letting them know the importance of community, what parts can be shared with others, and what is useful or accessible or teachable to others. The specific kind of food, after all, is not an important point except to the extent of being meaningful to the guests, and different foods have different emotional associations for different cultures. The features that are important to building up a peaceful community are what are important in this religious ceremony, and all the incidentals can be changed.

In another peace practice, the Tsilagi, more commonly known as Cherokee, had what they called Peace Villages. These were cities set aside where people could flee for sanctuary. These are similar to the "cities of refuge" of ancient Israel (Bible, Numbers 35:11–14, Joshua 20:2) except that they lasted into recent times and were going strong well after contact with Europeans began. The Peace Villages were places where no blood was shed and where communities consecrated the ground for holy living.

The Cheyenne especially, and to a certain extent other western tribes, had an institution called Peace Chiefs (Hoig, 1980). The Cheyenne had a Council of 44 such chiefs instituted by a man named Sweet Medicine. They concentrated on being peacemakers, sometimes opposed the warriors, and could not do violence to anyone themselves, no matter how bad the provocation. Rituals included ways of getting everybody to discuss an issue through.

FORMS OF VIOLENCE

Blood Sacrifice

Ritual human sacrifice was common in the empires south of the Rio Grande as it has been in ancient empires around the world, but much less common in the north. Evidence of human sacrifice just north of the Rio Grande appears to be from immigrating Mesoamericans who practiced on the Anasazi in Chaco Canyon. The Timucua people of northeastern Florida practiced sacrifice of babies and occasionally adults, but they were immigrants from the Orinoco River basin in South America, not indigenous.

The primary indigenous instance found by archaeologists has been servants of the king buried alive in his tomb at the city of Cahokia.

For the most part, the foundational concept for blood sacrifice, that divine beings might be angry or needed to be placated, is not present in First Nations religions in the north. The idea that such sacrifices were necessary to increase fertility was also not present, with the exception of the Pawnee, who sacrificed one adult per year. Treatment of war captives in revenge has sometimes been said to be human sacrifice because of its ceremonial nature.

Ritual animal sacrifice for the purpose of placating divine beings is also primarily absent. Hunting for food and other uses is common, and there are ceremonies involving being grateful to the animals for providing food.

Slavery

With the possible exception of the city of Cahokia and those influenced by it, slavery was not practiced as an institution before European arrivals. Captives were taken in war and held prisoner, but this was never intended to be a permanent status and no buying or selling was involved.

War

War was widely practiced and warriors were admired. These were primarily not wars of conquest, since empires did not develop, and common defenses such as walls or moats did not develop—Cahokia again being the main exception with its high walls and guard towers. Limitations on war were based on cultural assumption rather than stated laws.

Meat

When eating animals or eating plants, both deserve respect and gratitude for giving their lives to help feed people. That plant foods were plentiful is shown by the fact that about half of the plants farmed today were first cultivated by inhabitants of the Americas and were unknown until the time of contact between peoples.

There's an image of the Great Plains Indians as having the hunting of buffalo as their primary source of food, clothing, and other materials—but this occurred after the arrival of Europeans. It was fostered by the introduction of the horse and gun. Indians as a whole were such good farmers on such fertile land that the new inhabitants coveted their land and took it away; the Cherokee and Choctaw sent to Oklahoma found ways to make the farming there quite productive as well (Laws, 1994).

Rita Laws, a Choctaw and vegetarian activist, makes this case:

> Without realizing it, the Indian warriors and hunters of ages past played right into the hands of the white men who coveted their lands and their buffalo. When the lands were taken from them, and the buffalo herds decimated, there was nothing to fall back on. But the Indians who chose the peaceful path and relied on diversity and the abundance of plants for their survival were able to save their lifestyles. Even after being moved to new lands they could hang on, re-plant, and go forward. (Laws, 1994)

Violence in the Scriptures

Since there were no set scriptures, violence in them was not an issue. Violence in the stories told varied greatly. The creation stories mainly did not have much violence in them and often had cooperation and friendliness in them, in contrast to the stories that empires told.

RELATIONS WITH OTHER RELIGIONS

With a continent full of nations whose wars were over something other than religious beliefs or practices and a fairly common understanding of pluralism in respecting other people's beliefs, First Nations find it easy to accept worldwide religions and many do participate in interfaith events such as the Parliament of the World's Religions.

The religion of greatest contact is Christianity, and historically it was not well introduced. With the exception of Quakers in the northeastern United States for a few decades in the 1700s, it was the religion of hard-hearted and arrogant conquerors, or of missionaries many of whom thought they were doing the Indians a favor by trying to eliminate their religious traditions. For the most part this did not go over well.

A large portion of current Indians are Christians and attend church regularly. A large portion retains an animosity toward Christianity and holds to traditional spirituality. A large portion has a syncretic religion, taking elements of both their traditions and of Christianity. This is easily done, since elements of universal love, community, vicarious suffering as service to others, concern for the oppressed, and so on are common to both. Christianity has a long-standing practice of blending with local customs.

An Oconoluftee Cherokee chief named Yonaguska (1759–1839) insisted he needed to hear the Cherokee-language gospel of Matthew read to him before allowing its circulation. He reportedly said about the gospel: "Well, it seems a good book—strange that the white people are no better, after having had it so long" (Kephart, 1936, p. 31).

Nonviolent adherents in the Christian tradition are among those most likely to enjoy and appreciate that story.

Related Religions

One feature that many of the world's indigenous religions have is that they have refused to be conquered by larger entities. This occasionally involved violent resistance, but it very often involved assertive nonviolence.

The Australian aborigines, for example, did not offer large-scale violence to Europeans because it was against their understanding of how the world ran. In the last century, they have deliberately used nonviolent campaigns to achieve various rights. As a major event on February 13, 2008, an official Australian government apology for past wrongs was broadcast.

The use of songs was common as a way of assertive nonviolence in several indigenous religions, allowing for expression of spirituality and public practicing of that, which had been banned by would-be conquerors (Walker, 2009). One nonviolent technique of dealing with rapists was the "shaming song" from Africa:

> When a man has raped or violated a woman, the women from the surrounding area, carrying their children, gather around this man's hut to sing their shaming song. There is no need to punish the offender, to have him arrested or put on trial; the women simply sing throughout the day and into the night until the man leaves the village and is never heard of again. (Peat, 1994, p. 142)

Another common feature in indigenous religions, what gives them an appeal to remain in the face of contrary forces, is a deep rootedness. Often tied to the land, to ancestors, and to tradition, this shows the importance of keeping an anchor in the natural world and not becoming rootless. In addition to having its own merits, this is environmentally sound. Much of the violence being done to the environment now is being done by people who feel disconnected from it.

African indigenous religions have had a profound influence in the diaspora of African peoples in the Americas who have become Christians. The enthusiasm in the worship style, with joy in the communion with the divine, is widespread. The influence on Gospel singing has deeply enriched American cultures.

The popularity of the Kwanzaa religious ritual during the last week of the calendar year developed explicitly from African religions. Its seven principles, one each focused on daily, are: *Umoja* (unity); *Kujichagulia* (self-determination); *Ujima* (collective work and responsibility); *Ujamaa* (cooperative economics); *Nia* (purpose); *Kuumba* (creativity); and *Imani* (faith). It is intended to give rootedness to the uprooted community of people of African descent—whether Christian, Muslim, or other. It is to give voice to the vulnerable and to the moral obligation to care for the natural world and for each other.

9

The Sikhs

Most world religions fall into one of two categories: the "Abrahamic" and those derived from Hinduism. The Sikhs practice the largest religion that comes from both. They arose in the 1500s in India between Hindu and Muslim populations and took elements from each. They are monotheistic and see humanity as equal, and so do without the castes of the Hindus. With the Hindus they share the belief in reincarnation, yoga, and ashrams. Their major nonviolent campaign activism has been in the Indian movement for independence, where they had a major impact far outweighing their numbers. They focus on a nonviolent lifestyle and community service.

HISTORY AND SCRIPTURES

Most Sikhs, around 90 percent, live in the Punjab district of India and Pakistan, where the religion was founded in the 1500s by Guru Nanak. Many live all over the world. There are about 25 million according to the World Religion Database, with about 90 percent living in India.

The Sikh religion is based on Guru Nanak's teachings and those of the nine gurus that followed him in succession. Hinduism and Islam were the major religions in the Punjab area around 1500; Guru Nanak taught a faith that was quite distinct from both and yet clearly took elements from both.

The Sikh religion was well established when the fifth in the line of gurus, Guru Arjan, finished establishing Amritsar as the Sikh capital. By this time the community had become a threat to the state and Guru Arjan was executed in 1606. This led the sixth guru, Guru Hargobind, to start defensive military posturing and battles. After this, it was relatively peaceful until the Mughal emperor Aurangzeb tried to force conversions to Islam. He executed the ninth guru, Guru Tegh Bahadur, in 1675. This led the 10th guru, Guru Gobind Singh, to establish the Khalsa in 1699 as a clear community with boundaries to be militarily defended. He established the *khandev di pahul*, the right of initiation. He was the last human guru.

In 1799, when the Khalsa community was a century old, Ranjit Singh captured Lahore and established Punjab as an independent state with himself as ruler. Sikhs were still in the minority and he took part in religious ceremonies with both Muslims and Hindus. No executions occurred. When he died in 1839, the state crumbled and was taken over by the British in 1846.

To Sikhs, the most important thing is the religious state of the individual. They are monotheistic and stress the importance of actions over rituals. The way to a good life is to keep God in heart and mind all the time, to live honestly, to work hard, to treat everyone equally, to be generous to those less fortunate, and to serve others.

The place of worship is called a *Gurdwara*. The scripture is the *Guru Granth Sahib*; the book is considered a living guru. The 10th of the line of 10 Sikh gurus decreed this book as the spiritual guide for Sikhs after his death, so the book has the status of a guru. Sikhs show it the respect they would give a human guru.

The Sikh community is the Khalsa, founded by that 10th and final human guru. The Khalsa celebrated its 300th anniversary in 1999. Whenever the *Guru Granth Sahib* does not have answers, Sikhs decide issues as a community based on the scriptural principles.

Beliefs about God are: there is only one, without form or gender. Everyone has direct access to God and is equal before God. Empty religious rituals and superstitions are without value; it does not please God to ignore others while being devoted to rituals. God cannot be understood by humans, but can be experienced through love, worship, and contemplation. God is both inside and out in the surrounding world which God created.

Understanding the divine order helps to understand the nature of God; the creation is the visible message of God. We misunderstand the universe if we think it exists on its own. It exists because God wills it, as a portrait of God's own nature.

Life is focused around the community and the relationship with God. The ideal combines action and belief: do good deeds, meditate on God.

Sikhs share with other Indian religions the belief in reincarnation—a cycle of birth, death, and rebirth. With this goes a belief in karma, which sets the quality of life based on how well or badly a person behaved in previous lives. The only way out of the cycle—and rebirth is something one wishes to escape—is to achieve total knowledge of and union with God.

To meet this need of experiencing and becoming one with God, a person must change focus from themselves to God. This state is called *mukti*, meaning liberation (also coming from the Hindu), and it comes only through the grace of God—something God does for humans, not something earned. God does show people through holy books and examples of saints the best ways to get close. Most do not see God because of self-centered pride and overattachment to material things; these need to be overcome. Getting closer to God does not mean turning away from ordinary life, but using ordinary life as a way to get closer—hence, no monks or nuns, and no ascetics.

Ethics come from the *Guru Granth Sahib* scripture, from the *Rehat Maryada*, the Sikh Code of Conduct, from the examples set by the gurus, and from the 500-year experience of the Sikh community. These give general principles to apply.

There has been much postindependence violence and disgruntlement with the treatment by the Indian government. However, a Sikh man, Manmohan Singh, was elected Prime Minister of all of India for two terms, 2004–2014.

SIKH BELIEFS AND ACTIONS WITH NONVIOLENCE
Lifestyle

God is inside every person, and every person is therefore capable of change, no matter how wicked they appear. It says in the scripture *Guru Granth Sahib*: "Just as fragrance is in the flower, and reflection is in the mirror, in just the same way, God is within you." This belief is essential to that aspect of nonviolence that involves appealing to opponents as real people.

The way to serve God is to serve people; service gets rid of ego and pride. The *Langar* is a free food kitchen, and caring for the poor or sick is an important duty.

There are three duties: Pray, Work, and Give. The names are: *Nam Japna*, keeping God in mind at all times; *Kirt Karna*, earning an honest living (and avoiding gambling, begging, alcohol, tobacco, or working in any of those industries); and *Van Chhakna*, sharing one's earnings with others. There are five vices to avoid, since they build barriers against God: lust, greed, attachment to things of this world, anger, and pride. Overcoming these means being on the road to *mukti*.

Quotations from Scripture

Guru Nanak Hymn

No one is my enemy
No one is a foreigner
With all I am at peace
God within us renders us
Incapable of hate and prejudice.

Guru Arjun Dev Ji (ca. 1604)

I see no stranger, I see no enemy.
Wherever I look, God is all I see.
I don't think of us and them
No one do I hate or condemn
I see God's image—each one a friend.
Of any religion, caste or race
All I see is God's shining face
His smiling face, His gracious face.
Accept as beautiful all His design;
I learnt this truth in fellowship divine.
One Word resounds in me and you
The Word of God the Wonderful Teacher
In him, in her, in me and you
The Word of God the Wonderful Teacher
Beholding in every being His light
I bloom like a flower in joy and delight.

Indian Independence

As early as the mid-1800s, a Sikh named Ram Singh founded a movement to boycott the British overlords, the Namdhari Sect, on April 12, 1857. He encouraged people to boycott all British government services; schools, law courts, postal services, everything. They were asked to refer disputes to village councils rather than the British legal system. They were urged to boycott any purchase of British goods, so that the practice of wearing only homespun cotton cloth was established, to be reintroduced in the 1900s when the independence movement became more widespread throughout the country. Unfortunately, in this case, in 1872, some of the Namdharis committed violence called the Malerkotla massacre, and this gave the British colonial government its excuse for brutal suppression.

The major city for Sikhs is Amritsar. In 1919, around 10,000 people were holding a protest rally there. Given the location, a large portion would have been Sikhs. British General E.H. Dyer, thinking he was "teaching them a lesson," ordered his troops to open fire on them without warning, killing about 400 people and wounding around 1,000.

This incident is portrayed dramatically in the Hollywood movie *Gandhi*, because the Amritsar massacre was a major event in the campaign for independence. Some historians say this was the point where the decline of British rule started, since so many who might have been acquiescent to the status quo were aghast at this. Many of the British themselves were aghast. Accordingly, the fact that the response was nonviolent and strong made the event a major turning point. A violent response could have been suppressed with yet more violence and might have obscured the obvious injustice of the original massacre. In October 1997, Queen Elizabeth II laid a wreath at the site of the massacre, completing the understanding by all sides that this was a shocking injustice.

At the time, however, British attempts to break the spirit of resistance continued. In 1922, the Sikhs were refused permission to visit one of their temples. Every day, a hundred Sikhs marched up to the temple nonviolently to defy the ban. Every day they were viciously beaten, yet they kept coming. This campaign is called the *Guru Ka Bagh*. From the official British report of this incident:

> The use of force was persisted in again and again with the result that several cases of skull injuries resulting in concussion of the brain and unconsciousness occurred. The Akalis took all these beatings without any resistance or any attempt at retaliation. Divesting ourselves of all political bias we consider that the excesses committed reflect the greatest discredit on the Punjab Government ... we cannot help expressing our profound admiration for the spirit of martyrdom and orderliness which animated the Akalis and for their unflinching adherence to the Gospel of non-violence and for the noble way in which they have vindicated themselves under circumstances of prolonged and unusual exasperation.

Christian missionary C.F. Andrews, hearing of the events and going to witness what was happening to people who were unarmed and singing hymns, was more succinct: "I see hundreds of Christs being crucified every day by the Christians themselves" (Basarke, 2006).

In a related incident, on October 30, 1922, Sikh prisoners seized during this Guru Ka Bagh campaign were transported by train out of the area, but they were locked inside and kept without food. Since the train was to pass through the Sikh holy place Punja Sahib, the Sikhs requested the train stop there so they could feed the prisoners, at their own expense and with their own work. The British turned them down. Therefore, several sat peacefully on the tracks to stop the train. But according to government orders, the train did not stop immediately and therefore crushed and killed two people. The train did finally stop and the Sikhs fed the starving prisoners, but at a far greater cost than they had reason to anticipate.

During the time of the independence struggle, Sikhs comprised only 1.1 percent of the Indian population. Their participation in being the brunt of the brutal actions of the British was quite out of proportion to this: 2,125 Indians were sentenced to prison terms of one year or more due to participation, and 1,550, or 73 percent, were Sikhs; 2,646 Indians were deported, and of those, 2,147, or 81 percent, were Sikhs (Basarke, 2006). This is in addition to the beatings and killings outside of judicial proceedings. The incidents mentioned here are some of the major ones; there were many more.

The British did end up leaving India with a fair degree of good will. Some have argued that the reason nonviolence worked in India was that the British were more amenable to its influence than other nations, because they were more humane. The Amritsar massacre and the continual beatings of peaceful people wishing to attend their own temple, among other things, show otherwise.

FORMS OF VIOLENCE

Blood Sacrifice

Ritual human sacrifice was long gone by the time the Sikh religion arose, and animal sacrifice was not common. Blood sacrifices were a form of violence never considered.

Slavery

Slavery has always been forbidden; it does not cohere with the belief in human equality.

War

As with most religions, Sikhs have a "just war" concept; theirs is called *Dharam Yudh*—war in defense of righteousness. The war must be a last resort, with neither revenge nor enmity, there should be no mercenaries, the army must be well disciplined, only minimum force is used and civilians are not to be harmed, places of worship of any faith should not be damaged—similar requirements to other "just war" ideas.

Sikhs are expected to act against oppression, so when that is understood to require military action, they will readily engage in it. The principle would allow nonviolent action to be used for the purpose. Nonviolent action does, after all, require the same willingness to struggle and take risks against oppression as military action does.

The Death Penalty

Sikhs campaign against the death penalty (Dhar, 2007). Indian Professor Jagmohan Singh, a Sikh politician in the forefront of the campaign, makes these points:

> We wish to argue that our country can honour Mahatma Gandhi, the apostle of peace and non-violence and [Sikh] martyr Bhagat Singh by doing away with the death penalty altogether. A civil society should not descend to the status of murderers by preferring revenge over far better forms of justice. . . . If Afzal is a terrorist today, he was surely not born one. And he need not die one. Circumstances made him what he is. And circumstances may change him. The death penalty will change no one. Far from being a deterrent, martyrdom, as some will surely perceive his death, can only achieve the opposite effect. (Dhar, 2007)

The only time Sikhs were in a position to carry out a death penalty themselves was during the reign of Ranjit Singh in Punjab (1799–1839). Not one single execution occurred, even for people that physically attacked him.

Infanticide and Feticide

The *Guru Granth Sahib* on page 74 refers to life as beginning at conception, and in general deliberate miscarriage is regarded as destroying life as created by God and therefore a sin. The Sikh code of conduct, however, does not say anything about abortion.

Killing a daughter was specifically condemned by the 10th Guru, Shiri Guru Gobind Singh Ji, and is also condemned in the code of conduct. The term *Kuri-mars* translates into "daughter killers," and Sikhs are not only forbidden to be *Kuri-mars* but also to even associate with them.

However, the gender ratio in Punjab shows the actual practice of sex-selection abortion against female fetuses is currently a problem in the Sikh community of India just as it is in India as a whole. The Census of India showed it to be 880 girls to 1,000 boys in 2008. The practice is not matching the principles.

Meat

Only vegetarian food is served in the Gurdwaras, the Sikh temples, and many Sikhs follow a vegetarian diet. Several Sikh groups believe the Sikh diet should be entirely meat-free. Overall, they are allowed to eat meat as long as it is *Jhatka*, meaning the animal was quickly beheaded.

Poverty

"The poor and the rich are both brothers and sisters. This is Lord's immutable design" (Guru Granth Sahib, p.1159). The Sikhs dispensed with the caste system, regarded the poor who worked and treated others with respect as more worthy than the rich who were callous to others, and regarded charity works to alleviate or end poverty as a major part of the Sikh lifestyle.

Violence in the Scriptures

The movement toward *Dharam Yudh*, the "just war" concept, as a struggle against oppression, is reflected in the scriptures.

Treatment of "Heretics"

The official treatment of specified groups regarded as heretical according to the code of conduct is to forbid all associations with them—they are to be thoroughly shunned.

RELATIONS WITH OTHER RELIGIONS

From the Encyclopedia of the Sikhs, "We need to experience the fullness of humanity and the transcendence of the Divine. Together,

Christians, Sikhs, Hindus, Muslims, Jews, Buddhists, Jains, men and women, we should relish the plurality and diversity of our human culture" (Singh, 2009).

The Sikhs have historically had closest roots to Hinduism and Islam and during their interaction with the British rule had more contact with Christianity. They are currently interacting with local religions all over the world.

10

Bahá'ís: Unity

The Bahá'í religion arose as a matter of continuing revelation out of the Abrahamic traditions. Its hallmark is the unity of all humanity, so adherents are welcoming toward all religions, and world peace and human equality are major concerns.

HISTORY AND SCRIPTURE

The Bahá'í religion began to take form in 1844 in Iran, then called Persia, growing out of the Shi'a branch of Islam, when a man called The Báb announced that a messenger from God would soon arrive. This prophet would be the latest in a long line of prophets including Moses, Jesus Christ, and Muhammad. The theme of an announcer may remind Christians of John the Baptist; the Báb met a similar fate. He and his followers were persecuted by the Muslim hierarchy, and he was finally executed since he was contradicting the idea that Mohammed was the final prophet. This finality of Mohammad is universal in Islam, but Bahá'í scholars believe this is based on a particular interpretation of Qur'anic verses that allow for different interpretation.

One of the imprisoned followers in 1852, a man named Mirza Husayn Ali (1817–1892), had a revelation that he was the promised prophet. He named himself Bahá'u'lláh, which means "the Glory of God" in Arabic. He founded the Bahá'í religion in 1863, making it one of the youngest religions to have enough adherents to be regarded as a major world religion, with around 5 to 6 million adherents all over the world according to Bahá'í figures from various sources.

Among his extensive writings, he wrote the most important of Bahá'í scriptures, the Kitab-i-Aqdas, the "Most Holy Book," and the second most important scripture, the Kitab-i-Iqan, the "Book of Certitude."

He also wrote letters to many of his contemporary heads of state, such as Queen Victoria of Great Britain, the shah of Persia, the czar of Russia, and the Pope.

Bahá'u'lláh was succeeded by 'Abdu'l-Baha, who helped spread the faith and developed Bahá'í ideas of social reform and international justice. When 'Abdu'l-Baha died in 1921, he was succeeded by his eldest grandson, Shoghi Effendi, who furthered the missionary and philosophical development. Effendi also created or expanded the Bahá'í gardens in Israel. Once he died in 1957, the leadership passed to a group rather than an individual and now comes from the Universal House of Justice, a representative governing body with its seat located on Mount Carmel in the Holy Land, close to the shrine of the Báb.

The religious context involves the Shi'a Muslim belief that Mohammad's descendants were to be leaders of the faith. Called Imams, they were infallible, but not invulnerable. The Twelfth Imam went into hiding in 873 CE, hoping to avoid his predecessors' fate. He then communicated with the outside world through a series of four deputies with the title of "gate," or Báb; the last died in 941 CE. Shi'as believe the Twelfth Imam will appear again in the end times. God would appoint a successor to restore this channel of communication. This is the legend upon which the Báb of the Bahá'í faith was drawing. Báb is the word for someone who announces the coming of something portentous.

In the late 1700s, Shaykh Amad Al Ahsai searched for this Promised One and told his members to prepare for his coming, based on visionary experiences with the original 12 Imams. Siyyid Kazim-i-Rashti then continued the teaching after Al Ahsai's death in 1826, saying the Promised One was already on earth. Thus, there were many followers for whom the stage had been set once the Báb appeared.

For holy texts, writings of the Báb and Bahá'u'lláh are considered Divine Revelation, along with the scriptures of the earlier-stage religions. The Qur'an is fully authoritative, the Judeo-Christian Bible is mainly authentic, and the writings of 'Abdu'l-Baha are understood as sacred. The texts from other religions are read but not binding—the writings were appropriate to their own contexts, and we are living under different contexts.

The Qur'an had a special place as the most recent, and the original context was in a Muslim land, but Bahá'u'lláh interpreted this book and the Hadith in different ways from the orthodox Muslim understanding of the time. He also noted Persian mystical poetry, the New Testament, and ancient Greek philosophy, with some original ways of looking at them.

Bahá'ís believe Bahá'u'lláh is the most recent manifestation of God, but not the final one. The idea of progressive revelation is a major point for Bahá'ís. Bahá'u'lláh taught that Divine Messengers, or Manifestations of God, appear periodically throughout human history as God intervenes to reveal more.

The beliefs about God are similar to the family of religions in which Bahá'ís belong. God is transcendent, so cannot be directly known—is too great to be understood by the finite human mind. This is why the line of prophets is necessary for purposes of revelation. God created the universe, is omnipotent (has all powers), omniscient (has all knowledge), and perfect. Knowing God means knowing the attributes of God, though the only thing we can really know about God is that God exists. We can make imperfect analogies. The best way to comprehend is to consider the lives of the messengers and at the created world. The messengers are called Manifestations of God, but God cannot become incarnate in a human being (making this different from Christianity but not the other monotheistic faiths). God has no gender; the male pronoun is a matter of language.

There is no clergy; humanity has reached spiritual adulthood and each person is responsible for his or her own spiritual development. The practice is to have weekly programs called "Firesides," at someone's home or available facility, involving discussion and sometimes with a prepared talk on different topics. Non-Bahá'ís are welcome to these. Only Bahá'ís come to the monthly "Feasts," with prayers, reflections, and administrative business taken care of.

There are no dietary restrictions. A fast similar to that of Muslim Ramadan is observed from March 2 through March 20.

The life of the individual continues after death, in a realm more glorious but hidden from us in the same way that a child in the womb is surrounded by a glorious realm but unaware of its existence until birth. We do not have details on this realm because we could not bear to stay in this one if we did.

Heaven and hell are not places to which God assigns people, but nearness to God is heaven and remoteness from God is hell. All people will continue their spiritual journeys after death, no longer able to exercise free will to deny truths and disobey, and will start at the level of development at the time of death. This gives those who paid attention to their spiritual development during life a definite advantage.

There is no formal ceremony to become Bahá'í. A person simply declares belief in Baha'u'llah before Bahá'í witnesses.

BAHÁ'Í BELIEFS ON NONVIOLENCE

The core principle is *unity*. Everyone should work together for the good of all. How this can work for nonviolence is clear; any violence is, after all, a form of disunity.

The beliefs about human beings include that each individual has a soul that lives forever. All human beings are different, but equal—there is no inequality between sexes or races. All are members of one single human race and should be united in a single global community. Furthermore, due to greater development and maturity, we eventually will be united. Humans started in family groups, developed tribal groupings, then city-states, then nations. Now is the time to move forward to global maturity, to one large human family.

Bahá'u'lláh said it succinctly: "The earth is but one country, and humanity its citizens." An official Bahá'í statement of August 2001 put it this way: 'The reality is that there is only the one human race. We are a single people, inhabiting the planet Earth, one human family bound together in a common destiny, a single entity created from one same substance, obligated to "be even as one soul."'

They wish to pursue peace by eliminating conflicts between religions and to encourage cooperation. Bahá'u'lláh said: "Consort with all religions with amity and accord." There really is only one religion, the religion of God; what we account as different religions are really just different approaches.

Bahá'ís do think, naturally, that their own faith is the most complete set of truths currently available, but this is not the final and complete truth for religion. Revelation continues. They study other religions as earlier chapters in the same changeless faith. They do not seek to convert people out of other faiths so much as to dialogue in the hopes of imparting insights that will aid in the final goal of global unity; they also accept that other faiths have insights to offer them.

Why do religions differ? Different societies at different times had different needs, and the religions therefore suited different contexts. The ones that were founded under different circumstances offered truth in the way that the people in that time and place could understand. Over time, we could come to understand more and more, and the greater spiritual awareness led to greater revelations of truth. These are all actually stages in one great religion.

Human equality is paramount. No group should regard itself as superior to any other. Any law or practice that disadvantages anyone as if they were inferior is immoral. Racial distinction and prejudice and bigotry are not a part of God's plan. They are unnatural. Women and men are equal, to be given equal education and opportunity. Bahá'ís are expected to work within their own communities to eliminate discrimination; doing so of course constitutes nonviolent action.

Quotations

'Abdu'l-Bahá, The Power of Unity, page 48, #4

> Indeed, the world of humanity is like one kindred and one family. Because of the climatic differences of the zones, through the passing of ages colors have become different. In the torrid zone, on account of the intensity of the effect of the sun throughout the ages the black race appeared. In the frigid zone, on account of the severity of the cold and the ineffectiveness of the heat of the sun throughout the ages the white race appeared. In the temperate zone, the yellow, brown and red race came into existence. But in reality mankind is one race. Because it is of one race unquestionably there must be unity and harmony and no separation or discord.
>
> Gracious God! The animal, notwithstanding, that it is a captive of nature and nature completely dominates it, attaches no importance to color. For instance, thou dost behold that the black, white, yellow, blue and other colored pigeons are in utmost harmony with one another. They never give importance to color. Likewise sheep and the beasts, despite differences in color, are in utmost love and unity. It is strange that humans have made color a means of strife.

From The Last Will and Testament of 'Abdu'l-Bahá

> O ye beloved of the Lord! In this Sacred Dispensation, conflict and contention are in no wise permitted. Every aggressor deprives himself of God's grace. It is incumbent on everyone to show the utmost love, rectitude of conduct, straightforwardness and sincere kindliness unto all the peoples and kindreds of the world, be they friends or strangers. So intense must be the spirit of love and loving-kindness, that the stranger may find himself a friend, the enemy a true brother, no difference whatsoever existing between them.

'Abdu'l-Bahá, Paris Talks, October 22, 1911

THE PITIFUL CAUSES OF WAR, AND THE DUTY OF EVERYONE
TO STRIVE FOR PEACE

> I wonder at the human savagery that still exists in the world! ... And for what object? To gain possession of a part of the earth! Even the

animals, when they fight, have an immediate and more reasonable cause for their attacks! . . . The highest of created beings fighting to obtain the lowest form of matter, earth! Land belongs not to one people, but to all people. This earth is not man's home, but his tomb. It is for their tombs these men are fighting. . . . However great the conqueror, however many countries he may reduce to slavery, he is unable to retain any part of these devastated lands but one tiny portion—his tomb! . . .

I charge you all that each one of you concentrate all the thoughts of your heart on love and unity. When a thought of war comes, oppose it by a stronger thought of peace. A thought of hatred must be destroyed by a more powerful thought of love. Thoughts of war bring destruction to all harmony, well-being, restfulness and content.

Thoughts of love are constructive of brotherhood, peace, friendship, and happiness. When soldiers of the world draw their swords to kill, soldiers of God clasp each other's hands! So may all the savagery of man disappear by the Mercy of God, working through the pure in heart and the sincere of soul. Do not think the peace of the world an ideal impossible to attain! Nothing is impossible to the Divine Benevolence of God.

If you desire with all your heart friendship with every race on earth, your thought, spiritual and positive, will spread; it will become the desire of others, growing stronger and stronger, until it reaches the minds of all. . . .

In this room today are members of many races, French, American, English, German, Italian, brothers and sisters meeting in friendship and harmony! Let this gathering be a foreshadowing of what will, in very truth, take place in this world, when every child of God realizes that they are leaves of one tree, flowers in one garden, drops in one ocean, and sons and daughters of one Father, whose name is love!

'Abdu'l-Bahá, "Star of the West," vol. 5, no. 8 (August 1914), 43, p.18

The ideals of Peace must be nurtured and spread among the inhabitants of the world; they must be instructed in the school of Peace and the evils of war. First: The financiers and bankers must desist from lending money to any government contemplating to wage an unjust war upon an innocent nation. Second: The presidents and managers of the railroads and steamship companies must refrain from transporting war ammunition, infernal engines, guns, cannons and powder from one country into another. . . . In short, every means that produces war must be checked and the causes that prevent the occurrence of war be advanced—so that physical conflict may become an impossibility.

Peace Statement, the Universal House of Justice, 1985

Banning nuclear weapons, prohibiting the use of poison gases, or outlawing germ warfare will not remove the root causes of war. However important such practical measures obviously are as elements of the peace process, they are in themselves too superficial to exert enduring influence. People are ingenious enough to invent yet other forms of warfare . . . a genuine universal framework must be adopted. . . .

Racism, one of the most baneful and persistent evils, is a major barrier to peace. Its practice perpetuates too outrageous a violation of dignity of human beings to be countenanced under any pretext. Racism retards the unfoldment of the boundless potentialities of its victims, corrupts its perpetrators, and blights human progress. . . .

The inordinate disparity between rich and poor, a source of acute suffering, keeps the world in a state of instability, virtually on the brink of war. . . .

Unbridled nationalism, as distinguished from a sane and legitimate patriotism, must give way to a wider loyalty, to the love of humanity as a whole. Baha'u'llah's statement is: "The earth is but one country, and mankind its citizens." . . .

Religious strife, throughout history, has been the cause of innumerable wars and conflicts, a major blight to progress, and is increasingly abhorrent to the people of all faiths and no faith. Followers of all religions must be willing to face the basic questions which this strife raises, and to arrive at clear answers. How are the differences between them to be resolved, both in theory and in practice? The challenge facing the religious leaders of mankind is to contemplate, with hearts filled with the spirit of compassion and a desire for truth, the plight of humanity, and to ask themselves whether they cannot, in humility before their Almighty Creator, submerge their theological differences in a great spirit of mutual forbearance that will enable them to work together for the advancement of human understanding and peace.

The emancipation of women, the achievement of full equality between the sexes, is one of the most important, though less acknowledged prerequisites of peace. The denial of such equality perpetrates an injustice against one half of the world's population and promotes in men harmful attitudes and habits that are carried from the family to the workplace, to political life, and ultimately to international relations. There are no grounds, moral, practical, or biological, upon which such denial can be justified. Only as women are welcomed into full partnership in all fields of human endeavor will the moral and psychological climate be created in which international peace can emerge.

The cause of universal education ... deserves the utmost support that the governments of the world can lend it. For ignorance is indisputably the principal reason for the decline and fall of peoples and the perpetuation of prejudice. ...

[I]n essence, peace stems from an inner state supported by a spiritual or moral attitude, and it is chiefly in evoking this attitude that the possibility of enduring solutions can be found.

FORMS OF VIOLENCE

Blood Sacrifice

Ritual human sacrifice and animal sacrifice were long gone by the time the Bahá'í religion arose and were never considered.

Slavery

Bahá'í arose in the era when slavery was a hotly contested issue, still legal in many places in the Middle East and the southern states of the United States, but abolished in Europe, South America, and the northern states of the United States. 'Baha'u'llah wrote in the Kitab-i-Aqdas, Paragraph 72: "It is forbidden you to trade in slaves, be they men or women. It is not for him who is himself a servant to buy another of God's servants, and this hath been prohibited in His Holy Tablet." He also wrote a letter to Queen Victoria sometime around 1868–1872 commending Great Britain for abolishing the slave trade.

War

Opposition to aggressive wars in Bahá'í is sharply worded. If a war is defensive to prevent further violence, it needs to be carefully explained to all involved. Attention must be paid to the roots of war—poverty, inequality, lack of education, and so on.

The Death Penalty

On the death penalty, 'Bahá'u'lláh states:

> Should anyone intentionally destroy a house by fire, him also shall ye burn; should anyone deliberately take another's life, him also shall ye put to death. . . . Should ye condemn the arsonist and the murderer to life imprisonment, it would be permissible according to the provisions of the Book. (Kitáb-i Aqdas, paragraph 62)

Further comment on this from a source that answers questions about the Bahá'í faith:

> Since Bahá'ís believe that everyone passes to the next world and will continue to progress spiritually in that realm, death is not the end, but the beginning, for criminals who cannot or will not obey the rules of God and society. (Tarbiyat Community, n.d.)

Infanticide and Feticide

The teachings are clear that the human life of an individual begins at conception. Shoghi Effendi said in a letter of August 25, 1939: "The practice of abortion—which is absolutely criminal as it involves the deliberate destruction of human life—is forbidden in the Cause." A letter written on behalf of the Universal House of Justice to the National Spiritual Assembly of Ireland, March 16, 1983, says:

> Abortion merely to prevent the birth of an unwanted child is strictly forbidden in the Cause. There may, however, be instances in which an abortion would be justified by medical reasons, and legislation on this matter has been left to the Universal House of Justice. At the present time, however, the House of Justice does not intend to legislate on this very delicate issue, and therefore it is left to the consciences of those concerned who must carefully weigh the medical advice in the light of the general guidance given in the teachings.

Meat

While Bahá'ís are permitted to eat meat, there are indications that the vegetarian diet is preferable. 'Abdu'l-Bahá said:

> Truly, the killing of animals and the eating of their meat is somewhat contrary to pity and compassion, and if one can content oneself with cereals, fruit, oil and nuts, such as pistachios, almonds and so on, it would undoubtedly be better and more pleasing. (Hornby, 1988, p. 295)

He predicted:

> What will be the food of the future? Fruit and grains. The time will come when meat will no longer be eaten. Medical science is only in its infancy, yet it has shown that our natural diet is that which will grow out of the ground. (Hornby, 1988, p. 295)

Similarly, Shoghi Effendi, while noting that eating meat is not forbidden, says: "It is certain, however, that if a [person] can live on a purely vegetarian diet and thus avoid killing animals, it would be much preferable" (Hornby, 1988, p. 295).

Poverty

The structural violence of poverty is understood as a form of inequality, which is entirely immoral. It needs to be reduced by charitable giving as well as by government programs.

Violence in the Scriptures

The primary role of violence in the scriptures is to be condemned, with the exception of the endorsement of the death penalty noted earlier.

Treatment of "Heretics"

There are Muslims who have considered Bahá'ís to be Muslim heretics and persecuted them accordingly, but Bahá'ís have not been in a position to persecute others as heretics. There would be no inclination to do so under current understandings.

RELATIONS WITH OTHER RELIGIONS

Bahá'ís recognize nine specific religions as having been revealed by God through one of the Manifestations of God (Divine Messengers): Hinduism, Jainism, Judaism, Zoroastrianism, Buddhism, Christianity, Islam, Babism (the immediate precursor to Bahá'í) and of course Bahá'í itself.

As described earlier in the chapter, the religion arose out of the context of Shi'a Islam. Bahá'ís also understand that 'Bahá'u'lláh was a direct descendant of Zoroaster and that he was the man who filled the Zoroastrian prophecy for a coming saviour.

11

Revived Paganism

As a reaction against the violence practiced by religions in their vicinity, many people have looked to earlier ancient religions for inspiration in the nonviolent, egalitarian, and ecological views.

HISTORY

The basic idea of revived paganism is to return to previous religions, primarily on the idea that what superseded them was patriarchal and harmful to the ecology. Yet because these follow rather than precede the other religions, Neopaganism has differences that make it a recent development.

The term *pagan* can be defined as an indigenous religion generally characterized by polytheism. That leads to a wide array of religions, of course; ancient Greece and Rome differed quite a bit from the Maya, who differed from the Chinese. Sometimes the word "pagan" has been used to cover anything out of the Judea-Christian-Islamic orbit, so that it would cover Hinduism and Buddhism. If we take the meaning of an indigenous religion rather than a reform religion, Buddhism was formed in reaction to a previous religion, and Hinduism has seen enough reforms, so these are a separate category rather than pagan.

Current pagans are for the most part not interested in previous practices of human and animal sacrifice, and certainly not in emperor worship. They draw their inspiration from the religions they understand to be previous to or at least separate from those problems. They draw on those aspects of worldwide indigenous religions dealing with reverence for nature. The concept of the feminine in the divine is also a major theme.

Contemporary pagans are a diverse group. They have organizations but no hierarchy to decide on positions about what they believe, and so any discussion of what they believe will not be definitional.

They respect nature as divine. This is at the heart. They see the power of the divine in the cycles of life and death. Being eco-friendly is paramount. There is no doctrine or liturgy, but ritual is designed to make for better communing with nature.

Women play a prominent role in the modern Pagan movement, and much of it is fueled by the idea that religions were originally pro-female and nonviolent and were later conquered by violent males. So the equality of the sexes is vital and is reflected in the imagery for the divine.

The restoration of indigenous religion applies primarily to European religions. Historically, the idea of reviving Druidry, the folk customs of Europe, and especially the gods and goddesses of ancient Greece and Rome, started with the outlook of the Renaissance in the 1500s. Being more aware of the art and philosophy and science of the ancient world is what "Renaissance" meant—a rebirth of what had gone before and had been dropped over time. The Muslim world kept many of the ancient documents, so they were available to see them again. Europeans started adding the pagan gods and goddesses in statues where only Christian saints had been.

Even solid Christians like Thomas Aquinas were using the thoughts of Aristotle to help interpret Christianity. Greek and Roman works were regarded as "classics" and part of any complete education. Europa was an ancient Greek goddess, and calling the continent "Europe" rather than "Christendom" started in about the 1700s.

Across Europe, people rediscovered their own ancient indigenous cultures. In the north, there were the Saxon and Norse traditions; the Norse had arranged for the twilight of their own gods on the way to converting to Christianity. Icelandic sagas were translated. The runes were studied in Germany. Folk traditions and folk tales and folk dances were revived in various places.

Still, these were all pagan thoughts integrated into a Christian framework. Revival of a tradition in which a religion had adherents came with the Druids in Great Britain. Scholars in the 1600s took an interest in their stone circles and monuments. Stonehenge is the most famous, but there were many. In 1717, one of the scholars, John Toland, became the first Chosen Chief of the Ancient Druid Order. This later became the British Circle of the Universal Bond.

In 1875, the Theosophical Society was founded by Helena Blavatsky, with an interest in Hinduism, Tibetan Buddhism, Neo-Platonic thought, and ancient Egyptian religion. Venerating nature with a polytheistic outlook was offered on the idea of being a sophisticated contribution to spirituality.

Interest in witchcraft developed in the 1800s, proposing that the supposed witches who had been burned at the stake in earlier European history were actually underground adherents of pagan religion. This was part of the idea that a nonviolent group of herbal healers and spell-casters were conquered by more bloody-minded and macho religion.

In 1951, modern-day practitioners surfaced as the antiwitchcraft laws were repealed in Great Britain because of a belief that witchcraft was unscientific and superstitious. This made the laws rather silly. A retired tea planter and amateur archaeologist, Gerald Broussaeu Gardner, then came out publicly with the announcement that he spoke for one of several covens of English witches who practiced a pagan religion dating back to the Stone Age. This was a fertility religion called Wicca.

"Wicca" is the most popular form of Pagan Witchcraft. It is a mystery religion venerating the divine in nature. It draws inspiration from pre-Christian religious traditions along with folklore and ritual magic. Gardner compiled *The Book of Shadows*, a book of spells, and wrote *Witchcraft Today* in 1954 and *The Meaning of Witchcraft* in 1959, thus launching the movement.

Four of the festivals follow the natural year: The Winter and the Summer Solstice, the shortest and longest days of the year, and the Spring and Fall Equinox, the two days when light and dark are equal in length of time. These four are in common with various other kinds of modern-day pagans, and indeed, there are nonpagans who are taking note of them as well, since what the natural world is doing can fit into any religion.

Magic, for Wiccans and other current pagans, involves an understanding that the human mind has power to effect change that science does not yet understand. In some cases, science does indeed understand. The placebo effect, for instance, is well established. People heal or avoid pain because they expect to, having been given a pill or otherwise been told in an authoritative way that this will happen. This is why placebos are generally used on the comparison group in experiments, to ascertain if improvement with the treatment goes beyond just the expectation. The voodoo effect is the opposite, where people suffer harm because they expect it. The voodoo effect would be "black" magic, however, and Wiccans are ethically bound to do only "white" magic.

The spells are for healing and otherwise helping people with their problems. It is unethical to harm people or to help some people in a way that would harm others or the environment. The understanding is that the energies we create influence what happens to us. Harmful magic will come back magnified threefold to the person trying it.

Wiccans believe in reincarnation. Yet this is quite different from the Hindu/Buddhist/Jain/Sikh concept of reincarnation as a burden from which humans are trying to escape. Instead, the reason we are reborn is to experience life again and again, often with the same people, until we learn all the lessons that need to be learned. Having more lives is thus seen positively. When the spirit ceases to reincarnate, it remains in a place of bliss.

Many of the Wiccan ideas have been taken up by the Goddess movement, appealing to both women and men who are distressed with male-dominated religions. They want to honor the divine in female form.

Glastonbury in southwest England has a Goddess Temple, opened in 2002, in the loft of an old house, with images of various worldwide goddesses. The figure of Mary, the virgin mother of Jesus, is regarded as one of the goddesses. This is not the view of her in her religion of origin, though venerating her did take the place of previous goddess worship in many locations.

Some understand that they are worshiping many goddesses, but there is also the idea that there is only one Goddess, with thousands of faces, so that a person could select the one she or he most resonates with. Some are particularly interested in the goddesses of several thousand years ago on the understanding that this was before patriarchy took over and so are the untainted images.

Are the Goddess or the goddesses understood to be conscious beings that have an independent existence, whether we recognize them or not, or are they poetic metaphors? Some will hold one or the other, and many will hold they are both.

They also hold the crones in high regard. The word "crone" has been used elsewhere as a pejorative word for old women, but disrespect for old women is rejected. It is a patriarchal view, that women who are no longer useful to men as lovers or for bearing more children are no longer of value. But they have life experience that the community needs, and so they are Wise Women, and the word "crone" is asserted as a positive.

BELIEFS AND ACTIONS FOR NONVIOLENCE

Starhawk's classic book on Wicca and ecofeminism is called *The Spiral Dance: A Rebirth of the Ancient Religion of the Great Goddess*. It was published in 1979, a second edition in 1989, a third in 1999. In the introduction to the second edition, Starhawk makes the connection of Goddess religion to nonviolent action:

> I saw *The Spiral Dance* as a political book, in the sense that it brought into question the underlying assumptions on which systems of domination were based . . . over the last decade, as the gap between rich and poor widened, as our nuclear arsenals were rebuilt, and the homeless began to die in our streets and the jobless to crowd the bread lines, as the United States moved into covert and overt wars in Latin America, and the AIDS virus spread, while legislators sat on funds for education and treatment, as the environment deteriorated, the national debt quadrupled, and the hole in the ozone layer grew ominously, a more active political engagement seemed called for.
>
> One of the core principles of theology presented here is that the earth is sacred. Believing that, I felt that action to preserve and protect the earth was called for. So our commitment to the Goddess led me and others in our community to take part in nonviolent direct actions to protest nuclear power, to interfere with the production and testing of nuclear weapons, to counter military interference in Central America, and to preserve the environment. It led me down to Nicaragua and into ongoing work to build alliances with . . . the native peoples whose own earth-based religions and traditional lands are being threatened or destroyed. (Starhawk, 1999, p. 18)

FORMS OF VIOLENCE

There is no hierarchy to proclaim positions, and no scripture to be consulted, so we will mention fewer items on the list of forms of violence here. Most Wiccans, Druids, and other contemporary pagan movements see themselves in reaction to violence, as is common to religious innovations.

Blood Sacrifice

Ritual human sacrifice is long in the past, and most pagans will insist they have nothing to do with it. It is often seen as part of the male-dominated violent religions that took over the more benign original earth-centered religions.

There are exceptions, however. In a book called *Pagan Meditations*, Ginette Paris says: "I believe it is time to sacrifice to Artemis the fetus to which we are not prepared to give the best" (Paris, 1986, p. 148). She is clear she is not speaking metaphorically. In a later book called *The Sacrament of Abortion*, she says:

> Men have the right to kill and destroy, and when the massacre is called a war they are paid to do it and honored for their actions. War is sanctified, even blessed by our religious leaders. But let a woman decide to abort a fetus . . . and people are shocked. What's really shocking is that a woman has the power to make a moral judgment that involves a choice of life or death. That power has been reserved for men . . . the ancient Goddess Artemis invites us to imagine a new allocation of life and death powers between men and women, an allocation that allows men to appreciate the cost of a life and women to make decisions based on their mother-knowledge. (Paris, 1992, pp. 25–27)

Some Neopagans may share this view, but many others would disagree. They did not have in mind having women becoming as lethal as men have been allowed to be, but rather to have the men be the ones who change and are no longer engaged in killing.

Animal sacrifice is generally not practiced; treating animals with kindness is part of the environmental concern as well as kindness in general.

War

War is devastating to the all-important environment and a result of patriarchy. Many Neopagans participate in antiwar demonstrations.

Meat

Many will be vegetarians due to environmental concerns as well as compassion for animals and make a point of eating local and organic for environmental reasons. This group may have a higher portion of vegetarians and vegans than the general population for that reason, but it is not a requirement, nor are there surveys to establish this.

RELATIONS WITH OTHER RELIGIONS

These pagan movements are, by definition, rebellions against previous official religions; if they are not, they are ancient rather than recent. Recent versions are all very small minorities wherever they are located, and so do tend to get along amicably with those of other views. Much of the emphasis on environmentalism is shared by other religions that take different approaches; monotheistic religions, which believe in one creator God, after all, can regard it as an affront to the host that the guests should sully the residence. See chapter 19 for more details on the ecological traditions within each religion.

Images of the divine feminine are also available in Judaism and Christianity. According to these religions, both women and men are created in God's image, so the femininity is within God's image (Genesis 1:27). Some examples in the Bible: God is described as relating like a mother (Hosea 11:3–4; Isaiah 66:13; Isaiah 49:15; Psalm 131:2); God's wrath is like that of a mother bear robbed of her cubs (Hosea 13:8); God is like a mother eagle (Deuteronomy 32:11–12); Jesus is like a mother hen (Matthew 23:37); and God gave us birth (Deuteronomy 32:18) and will cry out like a woman in labor (Isaiah 42:14).

A parallel image of God as female after a male image is given in Psalm 123:2–3, and the parable of God being like a woman searching for the one lost coin (Luke 15:8–10) follows a parable about a shepherd searching for the one lost sheep. These both use the common Hebrew literary device of parallelism, a thought following another to say the same thing in a different way—thus showing that the female image is, indeed, the same thing, all good metaphors for the actions of God.

Additionally, the figure of Wisdom is clearly a woman in proper translations of Proverbs 1:20–33, 3:13–18, 4:5–9, all of chapter 8, and 9:1–6. This means that when Jesus is called the "wisdom of God" in Corinthians 1:24, this is feminine imagery for Jesus. In the deuterocanonical Biblical books (Jewish books that were translated into Greek and included in the Septuagint as scripture, but not finally settled on by the rabbis as being in the canon, were kept as scripture by Orthodox, were second-listed by Catholics, but not considered scripture by Protestants), we have female imagery of Wisdom: The Book of Wisdom/Wisdom of Solomon 6:12–17, 7:7–14, 7:22–30, 8:1–18, 9:9–11, 10:1–21, 11:1–26; Ecclesiasticus/Sirach 4:12–18, 6:18–31, 14:20–27, 15:1–10, 24:1–29, 41:13–22; and Baruch 2:29–38, 4:1–4.

12

Tenrikyo: Joyous Life

Shinto practice in Japan has millions of adherents, primarily focused on nature worship at local shrines. Out of its tradition came a new monotheistic religion founded by a woman reporting revelations from God the Parent, a religion focused on joy, gratitude, and acts of kindness that bloom from them. Tenrikyo is active in peace conferences worldwide. Additionally, Konkokyo is a section of Shintoism that is focused on peace.

HISTORY AND SCRIPTURES

Tenrikyo means Teaching of Divine Reason in Japanese. It is a monotheistic religion that declares that the desire of God the Parent is that we should have a joyous life, so that God the Parent can share in that joy. When we are spirited, God the Parent is spirited, and vice versa. God being Parent of all, we are all brothers and sisters.

Tenrikyo has a founding date: October 26, 1838 (according to the Japanese lunar calendar). This was the date that a 41-year-old peasant Japanese woman named Nakayama Miki, despite family protest, accepted the invitation of God the Parent to be the Shrine of God. This meant that while She remained a woman in outward appearance, God the Parent used Her mouth to express thoughts. Therefore, what She said was coming from God the Parent, and when using "I" or "me" it is God the Parent who is speaking in the scriptures.

She was henceforth known as Oyasama (accent on second syllable, which has a long "a"). "Oya" means parent, and "sama" is an honorific title. She began to recruit Her first followers in 1854 by using the Grant of Safe Childbirth, a healing ceremony.

The followers of Tenrikyo believe that once She passed away in 1887, She went back to Jiba, a spot in Japan that is sacred to Tenrikyo as the place where the human race was conceived. There She remains. People can bow their heads and tell Her what is on their minds and confide anything to Her. She is always there to listen, to love, to be accepting, and to provide hope.

The Tenrikyo Church Headquarters is there at Jiba, in the city of Tenri, Japan. As worldwide headquarters, it has several educational and cultural institutions, a library, museum, orphanage, and hospital. Pilgrimages to this location are common and are done with joy to express gratitude.

Of all the religions discussed in this book, this is the only religion founded by a woman. The previous discussion, using the common terminology, is characteristically gender-neutral. The capitalization for "she" and "her" when referring to Oyasama is the common style. The Japanese for God the Parent is Tenri-O-no-Mikoto, also meaning The God of Origin and God in Truth. Tenri-O-no-Mikoto created humankind and the world. God is also called Tsukihi, meaning sun-moon—the all-encompassing giver of light and compassion.

Tenrikyo spread in Japan. During the period when being a Shinto religion was required in order to survive, they registered as Shinto in 1908. Once this restriction was removed after World War II, they became an independent religion. As would be expected from the time and place of origin, there is also some Buddhist influence. The institutions that adherents attend monthly are called churches, and the leaders include ministers and bishops.

They have become a worldwide religion, with branches in around 40 countries in Asia, North and South America, and Europe. This includes almost 17,000 locally managed churches. They may number about 2 million, with 1.5 to 1.75 million living in Japan.

The South Korea Mission Headquarters is of particular interest because of the historical period when Japan was controlling Korea as an imperial power and strongly resented as such. Other religions of Japanese origin did not fare well there once the Japanese left. Tenrikyo was an exception because of being considered a universal religion whose faith transcended nationalism. The missionaries were focused on the practices and were unconnected to the imperialism. The scriptures also show a dim view of those in "high places," as will be quoted later.

The human body is understood as something that God the Parent lends us and that we have borrowed. As with anything we borrow from others, we need to take especially good care of it. Only our minds belong to us, and proper usage of our minds leads to the joyous life. If we believe our bodies are ours and we therefore live by our own power, we get ill and anxious and otherwise have misfortunes. We need to acknowledge God the Parent and the divine providence that lets us live.

The joyous life is cultivated through mindfulness and through *hinokishin*, which means acts of kindness, great and small, from feeding large numbers of hungry people to picking up and handing back a pencil someone dropped. This is not a way of building up merit, but is rather an expression of joy and gratitude: "Only when your joy brings joy to others, can it be called true joy. If you enjoy yourselves while causing others to suffer, this cannot be called true joy" (Osashizu, December 11, 1897).

When we do otherwise and use our minds wrongly, God the Parent compares this to dust. This is seen as a fitting metaphor because a little dust can be expected to accumulate daily and can be swept away daily. Yet when it is not regularly swept away, it piles up mightily and becomes more of a problem.

It is not that the illness and misfortunes are *punishment* for wrong thinking or behaving, but are instead *manifestations* of the wrongdoing, just as dehydration is a sign of not drinking enough water. With divine guidance, we can sweep the dust and understand divine intention, which is the true path of salvation and joy.

The problems causing the wrongdoing are clearly defined. "Dust is: miserliness, covetousness, hatred, self-centeredness, grudge-bearing, anger, greed, and arrogance. Also watch out for falsehood and flattery" (Ofudesaki 4:104).

Since a build-up of excessive mental dust can be difficult for individuals to remove on their own, there is the Sazuke, a healing prayer service. This is administered by the Yoboku, which translates as "useful timber," referring to the timber from which a house is constructed. The construction of a world in which God the Parent and humanity live in joy is a major metaphor of Tenrikyo's mission. When people are trained and get the Divine Grant of Sazuke, they are qualified to administer the Sazuke prayer service to those suffering, asking for God the Parent's blessings for recovery. This does require sincerity from both the Yoboku and the sufferer, since the purpose is to clean the sufferer's mind of dust.

No matter how well we sweep, however, some will still have great misfortunes, called "knots." There are buds that can sprout from the knots—that is, there are blessings and chances for spiritual growth that can be found in them. They are opportunities for dialogue with God the Parent and discovery of meaning.

There are Three Scriptures, distributed as separate books.

- Ofudesaki translates as "The Tip of the Writing Brush" because it is what Oyasama Herself wrote, after She had been speaking for a long time and it was time to write things down. It is given in verses, and it is organized with part numbers similar to chapters, and then verses, so it can be cited in a manner similar to other scriptures.
- Osashizu, "The Divine Directions," is a more extended commentary and concrete precepts by people who followed Oyasama. Its passages are cited by date (as seen in the quote on joy earlier).
- The Mikagura-uta is "The Songs for the Service." This Service is the central focus of Tenrikyo.

Additional texts, not counted as scripture but as still being important, are a summary called The Doctrine of Tenrikyo, and the biographical books *The Life of Oyasama* and *Anecdotes of Oyasama*.

I attended the Service in the Los Angeles Mission headquarters in October, 2014. These are held monthly. The first few minutes were taken up with the congregation giving four claps in unison and then bowing their heads in prayer for a few moments, then doing so again. The helpful commentary provided through earphones to newcomers indicated that four claps was the way of establishing that what followed was a prayer to God the Parent.

The Service in full was then performed for an hour and a half, followed by a lengthy sermon in Japanese by the Tenrikyo bishop from Brazil, nicely translated into English through those earphones. It ended with the Sazuke prayers for specific individuals who went up front. The entire proceedings took two and a half hours.

The Service is a set of songs in Japanese. There were performers, three men and three women, along with those in charge of the drums and musical instruments. They went through the songs in more of a chant (similar to Gregorian chant, but Japanese) and mainly faced the altar filled with fruits with their backs to the congregation, occasionally turning around toward the congregation. The hand gestures that accompanied the songs were an important part of the ritual; one woman in the pew in front of me was reciting the songs and using the hand gestures while sitting. These gestures are understood as a dance and give a view of the joyous world that Tenrikyo is anticipating. The spiritual effect was quite impressive.

BELIEFS AND ACTIONS FOR NONVIOLENCE

The Service

The scripture that Oyasama wrote says:

> From now on, step by step, I shall teach you the Service unknown since this world began and train you in its hand movements.
>
> This Service is the path of salvation for the entire world.
> I shall enable even a mute to speak.
>
> Be firm day after day, you performers of the Service!
> Calm your minds and learn the hand movements quickly!
>
> What do you think this Service is about?
> It is solely to bring peace to the world and salvation to all.
> (Ofudesaki 4:90–93)

Thus, this highly scripted ritual is not merely a nice thing for the edification of attenders; it is far more important than that. It is the communication to God the Parent that we are listening. It thereby inspirits both God the Parent and us. It is not a minor matter to skip it.

But in the late 1800s, the Japanese state religion of Shinto was offended by it. The government of Japan at that time also did not permit women to be religious teachers.

They therefore arrested and imprisoned Oyasama on at least 17 occasions. Throughout, she remained cheerful, interacted in a friendly way with her jailers, and was steadfast in her determination that her followers should continue to perform the Service. In short, she had the response that nonviolent activists have when being persecuted—neither offering hostility nor acquiescence, but positive friendliness.

The followers were quite worried, both for the possibility of jail for themselves and for the physical toll this was taking on Oyasama herself. She was by now an old woman. From 1887, after a long detainment during the winter during which a follower and fellow detainee had died, Oyasama spent more time in bed. She urged her followers to understand this as a way to test their resolve to perform the Service at all cost. They finally did so on January 26 (lunar calendar) in fear of their lives, but no police officer came to interrupt.

During World War II, the Los Angeles headquarters was closed down as Japanese were sent to internment camps in the United States. The Service continued to be performed in those camps.

Quotations from Scripture

Here is a sampling of the verses that Oyasama wrote, ones especially useful for the nonviolence tradition. Through Oyasama God the Parent is speaking. Since this is understood as divine revelation, God is using Oyasama's mouth to speak God's own mind. Therefore, the "I," "me," and "my" are always God speaking. "Kara" is the metaphorical place of those whose minds are away from God. The "high places" and "people on high mountains" are metaphors referring to social status or governmental position. The "construction" is the task of Tenrikyo: constructing a more joyous world.

Ofudesaki 1:19–20

> Hereafter, I desire that those in high places
> gradually calm their minds and make peace.
>
> This peace may seem difficult to attain,
> but it will come step by step through God.

Ofudesaki 1:33–36

> My anger is not a small matter.
> It is the result of causes accumulated and piled up.
>
> To say why it is that I am angry:
> it is because the wrongdoing has not been removed.
>
> Unless this wrongdoing is completely removed,
> know that it will stand in the way of the construction.
>
> No matter how stubborn this wrongdoing may be,
> it will be removed by the admonition of God.

Ofudesaki 1:52–53

> Looking all over the world and through all ages
> I find no one who is evil.
>
> Among all humankind, there is no one who is evil.
> It is only a bit of dust stuck on.

Ofudesaki 3:57–58

> The central pillar of the high mountains is that of *Kara*.
> This is the prime cause of the anger of God.

Those in high places are doing as they please with the world.
What thought is given to God's regret?

Ofudesaki 3:120–125

Those in high places are doing as they please with all the world.
Do you not know the regret of God?

Until now, everything in the world has gone according to
those in high places. From now on, there will be changes.

Since the time I began this world,
I have not yet taught you everything.

Those in high places are thinking of the whole world
on their own terms, but their minds are wrong.

The trees which grow in the high mountains and
the trees which grow in the low valleys are all the same.

Ofudesaki 4:15–17

Day after day, I desire to make the mind of God quickly known
to the minds of the high places step by step.

Knowing nothing, those in high places obey those of *Kara*.
How pitiful are such minds.

Day after day, the mind of God impatiently awaits
those of *Kara* to replace their minds entirely.

Ofudesaki 8:43–50

All of you throughout the world are brothers and sisters.
There should be no one called an outsider.

That there is no one who knows the origin of this
is the very cause of the regret of Tsukihi [God]

Those living in the high mountains and those living in
the low valleys: their souls are all the same.

Furthermore, the instruments you use daily
are things lent by Tsukihi.

Unaware of this, the thought in the minds of all human beings
is that there are the high and the low.

By all means, Tsukihi desires to make the truth of this matter
clearly understood by the whole world.

If only this is clearly understood,
the root of rebellion will be cut off.

Tsukihi sincerely desires only to end the wars
among those in the high mountains.

International Prayers for Peace

Tenrikyo newsletters frequently have items about how they sent some of their leadership to international and interreligious peace conferences, so this is a major area of activity and of interaction with other religions. The importance is explained by Shinichiro Tsuji:

> The International Meetings of Prayer for Peace serve as venues where participants from various religious traditions overcome cultural and language barriers, build friendships, and deepen mutual understanding and respect through dialogue. Attending these meetings of prayer for peace over many years, the significance of Tenrikyo delegates building trust and relationships with religious leaders should be underscored. (Tenrikyo Online, 2014)

Leaders often speak in the meetings; here are a couple of quotations to give a flavor of what they say:

> We use the phrase "Joyous Life" to refer to a peaceful world that Tenrikyo is working toward. . . . At the individual level, it is also a way of living that entails moderating one's greed and freeing oneself from the selfish use of the mind. However, in the real world, greed knows no moderation and can, therefore, lead people astray, give rise to conflict, and even endanger the natural environment, the very sustainer of life, thus threatening humankind's survival itself. (Tenrikyo Online, 2013)

> The goal of human existence is to build a joyous and bright life in this world through mutual help. If we are to achieve this, it is necessary for religions, which are many, to promote dialogue and contribute to reducing conflict and antagonism and achieving world peace and humankind's happiness. (Tenrikyo Online, 2012)

FORMS OF VIOLENCE

Blood sacrifice and slavery were nonissues throughout the times and places that Tenrikyo flourished; there is essentially no violence in their scriptures except reports of what was inflicted upon them, and while there have been schisms as with all religions, there are no reports of physical violence resulting from these.

War

In Japan, The Russo-Japanese war of 1904–1905 and the Sino-Japanese war of 1937 were supported to prove they were good Japanese, to gain recognition as a religion and not be regarded as heretics.

Yet the practice of peace should bring about an end to wars. As mentioned before, leaders of Tenrikyo are quite active in peace forums.

Infanticide and Feticide

Tenrikyo churches participate in providing services to pregnant women, having many listed in directories under abortion alternatives as part of the *hinokishin* practice.

There is no explicit direction approving or disapproving of abortion. Oyasama is reported to have talked a woman out of an abortion on one occasion (in Anecdote 13), but did so by predicting that specific baby's accomplishments. She wrote in the scripture: "The conception of a baby is by Tsukihi [God]. Giving birth to it, also, is by the work of Tsukihi" (Ofudesaki 4:131). This is cited in support of a pro-life position, which is done gently through persuasion and providing needed services, consistent with Tenrikyo's not taking stands on social issues (which is why there is no position on the death penalty). Oyasama's interest in healthy childbirth in particular meant that she denied the then-prevalent idea of female pollution by childbirth.

Meat

There are no thoughts presented on meat-eating, and meat is offered at church meals.

Poverty

Deprivation-level poverty is contrary to the Joyous Life and results from the dust in the mind of people in high places. As equal children of God, those in low places are of equal value. Changes are coming.

RELATIONS WITH OTHER RELIGIONS

Tenrikyo was registered in 1908 as the last of the 13 sects of Shinto, but once that was no longer necessary for survival in Japan in 1945, they declared themselves a new religion. Jinja Honcho, the Association of Shinto Shrines, is mentioned as occasionally showing up at the same international peace prayer gatherings that Tenrikyo leaders attend; Jinja Honcho also shares the environmental concern since nature worship is part of the Shinto rituals.

Adherents of Tenrikyo make a point of interacting well with all religions and attending interfaith events, since religious harmony is one of the prerequisites of the joyous life.

Related Religion: Konkokyo

When Tenrikyo was no longer a Shinto sect, Konkokyo kept the status, though its doctrine is original and independent. Both Tenrikyo and Konkokyo looked for deliverance and salvation with a look to the future. Both were founded by charismatic people with humble origins who received revelations, thereby appealing to large numbers of people of humble origins. Both are monotheistic and reject the idea of karma.

Konkokyo may have up to half a million adherents, primarily living in Japan. It was founded by Konko Daijin in 1859. "Konko" means golden light, "kyo" as a suffix means religion, and in English it is therefore commonly called the Konko Faith.

The full name of God is Tenchi Kane No Kami, normally abbreviated as Kami. Kami is the parent of all humanity—the Principle Parent of the Universe—with love that envelopes and watches over all. Kami is not only the life and energy of the universe but also *is* the universe (pantheism) with a consciousness. Kami has no gender, though "he" is used for linguistic convenience.

All human beings, being children of Kami, are brothers and sisters and equal to each other. We exist in a relationship of interdependence with each other and the natural world. Avoiding rigid dogmas, there is a customized, personalized approach to ministering and advising individuals. The spiritual goal is to live in harmony with Kami and help others to do so.

In 1873, the Japanese government forbade Konko Daijin from having altars and offerings, holding prayers, and mediating for others, and so he went to a small room to think and meditate. Having nothing physical, he realized that was not what was important. This was when he received the words of the Divine Reminder from Kami. This is the core of the Konko Faith—it revealed people could pray directly and that individuals are responsible for their own relationship with Kami. A framed copy in Japanese is the centerpiece of the altar in Konko-kyo churches, and it is prominently displayed in facilities and homes. A small copy can be carried in a pocket. Here are the words in English:

The Divine Reminder

> Pray sincerely,
> With all your heart.
> Be one with Kami.
>
> Kami's blessings begin within
> Hearts grateful and caring,
> In harmony and joy.
>
> Look to Kami always,
> Now and forever.
> On this very day, pray.

Everyone is born with part of Kami's heart and spirit inside, so everyone has the latent ability to become an *ikigami*, embodying Kami's intentions to save people. The founder is naturally recognized as such, so will often be called Ikigami Konko Diajin.

Toritsugi is mediation, and while people can pray directly, they can ask for this from a minister if they feel the need for the help. It is performed one-to-one by the minister when a person visits the church. The person says the problem or concern or gratitude, the minister relays the words through Konko Daijin to Kami, who then speaks through the minister.

Upon death, each person rejoins Kami for eternity, and does so no matter what earthly behavior was. Therefore, there is no heaven or hell, except as it might apply to the mind currently during this lifetime. Since everyone is a part of Kami's body, is born a spirit and dies one, there is never any separation from Kami possible. There is also no reincarnation. The Universe is now and always has been our eternal home.

As for relations with other religions, this is how it is addressed on the website of Konko Churches of North America:

> Too many times, we get caught up in what we believe so thoroughly, that we become blind and cannot see that what is right for us may

not suit another. Medication curing cancer in one patient may actually harm another. It would be easy if one way worked for all, but just as one medication cannot suit all patients of an illness, one path to Kami will not suffice either. Not realizing the role of religion, people degrade each other, countless wars are fought, and countless lives suffer and are lost, because each of us insists that our religion is the only true one. It is hard to believe that this is what Kami wanted from religion. How can people re-bond to Kami with so much fear, hate, anger, and blind arrogance pushing them away from Kami? (Konko Churches of North America, n.d.))

The scripture is the *Kyoten-Gorikai*, Teachings of Konko Daijin, and comes in three parts. Citation starts with "G" and the Roman numeral for which of the three parts it is. One passage directly related to nonviolence is:

Though people say that they do not kill others, they do so with their hearts. This is a grave offense. They think killing someone means to shoot with a gun or to stab with a sword, but this is only physical, and the obvious. People often kill with their hearts, an offense invisible to the eye. Kami's heart cannot bear such offenses. When one kills physically, the government punishes. When one kills with his heart, Kami punishes. (GII: Sato Mitsujiro, 27:1–2)

Konkokyo followers hold annual Peace Gatherings throughout Japan and elsewhere, where participants offer prayers and discuss how to improve their surroundings before going out and implementing the ideas. With ambitions to do more, there is a Konkokyo Peace Activity Center that works with others in Cambodia, the Philippines, and Thailand to promote projects that focus on the well-being of children, including feeding the hungry, services for street children, scholarships, early child care, and many other helpful projects.

13

Ethical Atheism and Humanism

Ethical atheism arose in part because of a revulsion against use of religion for justifying and promoting massive violence, dictatorships, and social inequities. It contributes to nonviolence theory the point that ethical behavior should be seen as being worthy for its own sake, not requiring enforcement through mechanisms of divine judgment or karma. People motivated by an intense desire for social change and who act on this with great sacrifice of time and energy and property may be indifferent to religion as unhelpful, or disdainful of religion as a support of violent institutions they oppose. The actions and consciences of those unmotivated by explicitly religious concepts also provide further evidence that nonviolence is something more natural to the human condition than many defenders of violence have supposed.

BASIC BACKGROUND

Atheism is the assertion that there is no god, nor gods and goddesses. There are atheists who would object to being given a chapter in this book as if it were a religion, but there are probably many more atheists who would object to not be covered at all. Atheism has things to say about religion and nonviolence.

We designate "ethical atheism" to cover those whose atheism is based on moral principles, the atheists most likely to engage in public advocacy of atheism and to offer philosophical views. People who assert there is no god because they would like to believe there is no reason for behaving ethically do not have as much to offer the discussion.

There are related definitional groups. *Atheists* say there is no god; the prefix "a" means no, and "theism" is belief in God or gods and goddesses or any form of divinity. *Agnostics* say they do not know whether or not there is a god. *Nontheists* have a spirituality without including the existence of God; it is the presence of spirituality that makes the prefix "non" rather than "a," though these technically are the same. *Secular* people are those who believe that religion is irrelevant to the topic at hand, so this covers atheists, agnostics, nontheists, and religious adherents who leave a religion out of a particular area, such as government, or advocacy for a particular policy. *Secular humanism* is another term that has been used, where "humanism" adds the ethical dimension of bettering the human condition, with the idea that humans are responsible for doing so without divine assistance. While the term tends to be applied to atheists, there have been adherents of various religions who regard it as proper policy in a society where religion and state should be strictly separated. The term *humanist* by itself has also been used to designate atheism but indicates a more positive belief in humanity as opposed to a negative term about what one does not believe in.

There is a spectrum of opinions in relation to religion. At the milder end of the spectrum, some people identify themselves as atheists (or agnostics or nontheists) because they simply do not see that the divine or religions are necessary to explain things. They believe the natural laws of physics and biology are sufficient. They often see religion as a matter of superstition and magic, lacking evidence. They cannot make sense of it. Or perhaps religion does not seem relevant or interesting, especially if they were raised without it. They have no trouble living amicably with their religious family and neighbors and do not feel called upon to argue in any heated way.

On the other side of the spectrum are people who are positively hostile to religion and will make vociferous arguments against it. In some cases, they had been active with a religious group or were raised in a religious manner and found it abusive, or discovered grand hypocrisies.

Atheists often assert that ethics are to be followed for their own sake; human life is valuable because it is valuable. One can take that as premise and not require a religion to make it a conclusion instead. As one oft-quoted slogan goes, "If the only thing keeping you from being a horrible person is your religion, you're already a horrible person." Sharath Prabhu put it this way in several places on the web: "If the primary motivation for believing something is 'saving yourself,' then the belief is rooted in self-interest, not in love. Love is not compulsory and extracted through primitive threats of torture, but is what you feel of your own volition." There is nobility, after all, in doing the right thing because it is right and not for hope of reward or fear of punishment in an afterlife or due to karma.

In some cases, atheists are disillusioned from the idea that there is a God who is all-powerful, all-knowing, and all-loving when they observe the actual condition of the world in which so many innocent people suffer. This long-standing conundrum in theology has a name: theodicy. Since the observation of suffering is a given, and only the three characteristics of God can be at issue, they conclude that there is no God. Rather than concluding that God lacks a characteristic—is not all-powerful, all-knowing, or is not all-loving—they conclude that God does not exist at all.

The most vociferous arguments are made on the observation that various religions have done a tremendous amount of harm. They have had vast and long-lasting wars. They have had strict rules that suppress people's freedom and make them feel guilty over things that are trivial or, as with neglecting rituals, not wrong at all.

That religion has done a huge amount of harm is well known to devout religious people, especially the nonviolent activist ones, and is therefore not a point of disagreement in itself. The disagreement is over whether religion necessarily will lead to evil occurring, or instead that those who wish to do evil are inclined to use religion to justify themselves.

Either way, people who use religious reasoning for violence can do far more harm than people who are merely selfish can, because they will do it on a grander scale. Religions which began with clear nonviolent assertions are nevertheless drafted for war-making purposes by governments.

Religions are not always separate from atheism. Jainism is actually an atheistic religion—one that posits no God, gods, or goddesses. Jews who become atheist are still regarded by many as Jews, unlike Jews who become Christian; though Orthodox Jews especially tend to be unhappy about it, atheist and agnostic Jews number in the thousands. The reason the term *nontheism* was recently coined was to cover people who do not believe in God but do believe in spirituality.

Some atheists claim ancient roots by citing Greek and Roman philosophers. Epicurus offered a theory of materialism, that the material world is all that exists, bodies and the spaces between them. The soul is also material and so when the body dies the soul does as well. Lucretius thought the same and thought that human ideas about gods and fear of death make us unhappy—religion is "glowering on mortals with her hideous face."

Ethical Atheism and Humanism

Atheism started as a much more widespread phenomenon in Europe and in areas with European descendants when academic research started undermining the literal truths of the Bible. Thomas Hobbes made the case in his 1651 book *Leviathan* that Moses could not actually have written the first five books. In 1779, J.G. Eichhorn argued that the stories of Genesis were mythology akin to the Greek and Roman myths. Literary analysis began to cast doubts on the Bible as history.

In 1841, Ludwig Feuerbach proposed that God was merely a human invention to help us deal with our fears and hopes. This was not helpful, he said, because we project all the best qualities onto this fictional character, which made humans by contrast look pathetically inferior. So we are alienating ourselves from ourselves by doing this.

Later atheists developed this point: people believe in God because they want a father figure to protect them. They want meaning and purpose, they want death not to be the end of a life, and they want to believe they are important in the universe. If these are not true, but just psychological fantasies, then people are not dealing with the world as it is and can accordingly get themselves into trouble. They get in trouble even more quickly if what they want is a God who endorses their own prejudices.

Anthropological research compared religions and noted many similarities (a point often made in this book). The rituals and stories were similar, and tribal religions have many elements in common with Christianity (that being the major religion of the time in Europe). Some wondered how any religion could claim to be unique or the exclusive true faith under those circumstances.

The theory of evolution, as popularized by Charles Darwin, led many to understand that the material world was able to come about without an outside divine creator. As Richard Dawkins put it, "Darwin made it possible to be an intellectually fulfilled atheist" (Dawkins, 1986, p. 6).

Many religious people fought against it accordingly. To this day there are proponents of young-earth creationism who claim a scientific basis for their own understanding. This led to a perspective that religion and science were opposed to each other, and therefore, those who selected science understood themselves to be antireligion. They understood that selecting science meant choosing reason and evidence over superstition.

The theory of evolution brought three different kinds of reactions in the monotheist traditions. One was that staunchly religious people held tightly to their literal understanding and wrote volumes about why science and reason actually document their view. They are commonly called fundamentalists, with scriptural inerrancy being one of their fundamentals. Another reaction was to accept the science and have it inform the religion: God created the world, and God did so using evolution over the course of a great deal of time. This is the view of the Catholic Church, the Orthodox Church, "mainstream" Protestant denominations, the majority of Conservative and Reform Jews along with many Orthodox, and a large portion of Muslims, many Hindus and all Sikhs and Bahá'ís. The third reaction was the tack of accounting the scriptures as worthless or worse, and this is a common view among atheists.

Atheists and fundamentalists frequently set up debates between themselves because they make good counterpoints to each other. The debates can then be in more stark terms, since each position is more opposite the other one than either one is with the nonfundamentalist religious traditions. Atheists and fundamentalists both do at least agree on the absurdity of such ideas as astrology, and they both have an animosity to polytheistic religions.

In an additional argument, many atheists proposed that the form of Christianity that had been preached to them was immoral. The doctrine of Original Sin meant that God would punish people for a fault of distant ancestors, just because they were human. Why would we be spared from this unjust punishment because he punished his innocent son instead of us? John Stuart Mill said in *On the Philosophy of Sir William Hamilton* in 1865:

> I will call no being good, who is not what I mean when I apply that epithet to my fellow creatures, and if such a being can sentence me to hell for not so calling him, to hell I will go.

Furthermore, the Bible is full of violence and shockingly immoral behavior, making it unsuitable as a moral guidebook (see "Violence in Scriptures" in chapters 1 and 6). Atheists find the concept of everlasting damnation, especially with the lurid details offered with relish in art and literature, to be appalling.

The violent histories involved in major religions are also noted. The Bible reports the Jews as having scorched-earth and genocidal actions when conquering the Canaanites. Christians had the Inquisition and the Crusades. Islam has the current practice of terrorism fuelled by religious rhetoric. Every time a person yells in Arabic "God is great" at the very point of committing an act of violence against a large group of civilians, the case for atheism in bolstered.

There are counterarguments in all cases from nonviolent religionists, mainly having to do with suggesting that all human institutions, even those that are primarily good and essential to human happiness, have corruption. The atheist Soviets and Chinese, after all, did not have a good track record either. Yet the case that religion leads to violence is one that many atheists focus on. See, for example, the 2007 book, *God Is Not Great*, by Christopher Hitchens.

Atheists note (as do nonviolent religionists) that religion can be used to prop up unjust social hierarchies. When religion posits that God has organized the universe into a hierarchy, then asserts that the hierarchy of society is also well organized according to God's instructions, it follows that anyone who proposes a more fair and equal arrangement is going against the will of God. Not merely mistaken, not merely having a different point of view, but causing cosmic disruption. Hence is religion used at the service of tyrants and political bullies—and has been since ancient times and the days of emperor worship. Religion is used in the service of a nation that wishes to go to war, and in the service of a race that wants to declare itself superior to other races.

This was uppermost in the mind of Karl Marx. He understood religion as a tool by the capitalist class to keep the working class under control, calling religion, "the opiate of the masses." The workers would tolerate conditions that were intolerable because they believed they would be compensated for their patience in an afterlife, which Marx understood as an illusion. As the old union song puts it: "You'll get pie in the sky, by and by, when you die—*That's a lie!*" Marx saw religion as a distraction to keep workers from struggling for their rights in the here and now. It was like a drug, but what is needed is to cure the sickness, not to sedate the patients.

Marx's views had the greatest impact on the current numbers of atheists, inasmuch as Marxist takeovers in the Soviet Union, China, North Korea, Vietnam, and Cuba make atheism rank among the major world religions in terms of numbers, if it were a religion.

Meanwhile, in Europe especially, secular sentiment has grown exponentially. One major reason is that European history is replete with wars that were fought over different interpretations of Christianity, or which were fought for other reasons but used different interpretations of Christianity as their justification. A war-weary continent is bound to alienate peace-loving people away from dogmatic rhetoric.

Additionally, European countries had state-sponsored churches, whether Catholic or their own national churches (Anglican, Dutch Reformed, etc.). People were taxed to support the churches, holding any kind of public office was impossible without belonging to the church, and in some cases, attendance at Sunday services was required with draconian punishments imposed for noncompliance. This is all a recipe for lack of sincerity in religious practice. Ministers and others running the churches had no need to appeal to people in order to get their high incomes nor in some cases to get enough people to come in the door, so they paid little attention to the peoples' sincerity. Considering how high their incomes were, they did not always necessarily have sincerity of their own.

There have been atheists who have set up their own community groups, complete with weekly programs where they engage in discussion on specified topic or perhaps in service projects. Thus, they try to get the positive benefits of social support and intellectual stimulation that come with regular meetings by religious organizations, but without the religious component.

ATHEIST BELIEFS AND ACTIONS FOR NONVIOLENCE

In societies where principles of nonviolence, peace, and human equality are not the norm, then basing behavior on those principles can be unconventional. Atheists outside of Marxist-influenced countries are accustomed to being in the minority and unconventional. They do participate in nonviolent resistance against authorities that they regard as unjust just as their religious compatriots do. Atheists, both black and white, were active in the U.S. Civil Rights Movement of the 1960s. A famous example is A. Philip Randolph, a labor organizer who had the idea for the 1963 March on Washington and was standing right behind Martin Luther King Jr. as King gave his "I have a Dream" speech. In all other movements for justice, and all over the world, atheists and agnostics are active. It is very common that it is their social concern that leads to their atheism, since they offer a critique when religion is used for violence, inequality, or oppression.

Since atheism was the official stance of governments in the Soviet countries and in Communist countries of Eastern Europe, atheists would have made up a large portion of those participating in the nonviolent revolutions that led to the fall of the Berlin Wall, the move toward democracy, the undoing of the Soviet coup d'état against Gorbachev, and the fall of the Soviet Union. The same applies to the

Chinese student nonviolent uprising in Tiananmen Square in 1989 and some subsequent demonstrations. While it is true that religion was prominent in many of those movements, especially Catholicism in Poland, they were societywide movements that included people who kept the long-standing atheist views while otherwise critiquing the violence of the system.

As for the power of individual conscience, there is the little-known tale of the Soviet submarine navy officer whose conscience kept a nuclear missile from being launched during the Cuban missile crisis. It was told in full in the October 24, 2012 episode of *Secrets of the Dead* called "The Man Who Saved the World." Vasili Arkhipov was stuck in a submarine in international waters off Cuba on October 27, 1962. Moscow had been out of touch with them for weeks, their batteries were running low and air-conditioning had failed. The U.S. Navy was dropping explosives intended to force the submarine to the surface, unaware that it was armed with nuclear missiles. The explosions made the submarine stay too deep to hear any other radio broadcasts, including the communication that these were only depth charges to make them surface and not intended to be lethal. All this gave the submarine's captain, Valentin Grigorievitch Savitsky, the impression that war might have already started. He wanted to launch a nuclear torpedo.

The rules were that three officers had to agree unanimously. The two others agreed. Only Arkhipov was against the launch. Despite social pressure from the others, he steadfastly refused. He finally persuaded them to surface the submarine and await orders from Moscow. Thus, the one nuclear torpedo was never fired, which by itself could have done tremendous damage. Under the circumstances of the time, response and counterresponse could have led to an astonishingly catastrophic civilization-ending war.

We do not have a clear record that Arkhipov was an atheist, but it would have been expected of Soviet soldiers in that era and was necessary for achieving high rank. This is a tale that shows that, no matter how much some people are cynical about violence being intrinsic in the human condition, the power of one person's conscience can be found even amidst the most violent of situations.

FORMS OF VIOLENCE

There is nothing official to give positions on any of the forms of common secular socially approved violence, and so ethical atheists vary widely on all of the contemporary debated issues. On abortion, for example, polls in the United States consistently show the majority of atheists having a pro-choice position, but the group Secular Pro-life (www.secularprolife.org) points out that even if in the minority this still documents that several million atheists and agnostics take a pro-life position.

Positions on specifically religious violence such as human sacrifice, animal sacrifice, violence of scriptures, and prosecution of "heretics" and unbelievers will of course all be opposed by atheists, agnostics, nontheists, humanists, and secular humanists—practically by definition, unrelated to how they stand on other forms of violence such as war or the death penalty.

RELATIONS WITH OTHER RELIGIONS

Atheists have negative views of all religions, by definition. This varies in content and intensity and may involve more hostility to one religion than another, or to some sections within a religion rather than other sections. Agnostics have tentative views on all, by definition, with great variation. Spiritual-oriented nontheists vary in having been hurt by religious structures or merely lacking interest in them, with variations in views on other people participating in them and differing opinions on differing religions.

PART II

Religion in Nonviolence Traditions

14

Sins: Religious Critiques of Societal Injustices

There are a lot of religious thoughts on sin, ranging from individual acts being sins to anything causing bad karma being sinful to a state of alienation from God being a state of sin. Moving *all* violence into the category of sin is the view of pacifists. Most violence is in that category for everyone else, with the exceptions being carefully restricted, at least in theory.

The concept of sin became especially popularized in many places during the Axial Age, the set of religious revolutions in the era of around the sixth century BCE (see chapter 5). It allowed for more influence on social behavior at a time when the small village had no more influence and the larger city could not monitor individual actions as thoroughly.

Yet it also has this point for the rise of understanding nonviolence: it says that moral lapses *have transcendent consequences*. Religions vary in what those consequences are, but they all agree the consequences are undesirable.

At the very heart of all the forms of injustice that nonviolence is designed to counter are consequences that go far beyond the immediately visible. While theories of karma or heaven and hell or any other approach can vary widely and matter primarily to the individual, the historical consequences of sin to all of society are observable and constitute one form of consequence that transcends the original circumstances.

There is a strong tendency in the nonviolence traditions to frame the results of sinful or evil or unjust actions in terms of their spiritual natural consequences, rather than being punishments inflicted as a matter of sentencing. The punitive approach can come from a harsh mindset and is therefore more associated with violence in response to violence—a "fire-and-brimstone" form of preaching, which has historically been shown to be rather unpersuasive to those not already convinced. For an alternative approach, to use a metaphor, making people aware that jumping in a mud puddle leads to being muddy is gentler, more documentable, and shows concern for the person who is doing that metaphorical jumping.

One example of seeing it this way:

> Whereas [some] Islamic teachers might emphasize the importance of prayers . . . by telling practitioners that they will be punished in the hereafter if they neglect the five-times-a-day body prayer, Sufi teachers liken prayer to attendance at a celestial banquet. If you fail to pray, Sufis would say, you are missing out on the joy of the feast. That loss is your punishment. (Rahman, Elias, & Redding, 2009, p. 6)

As another example, Hindu guru Yogananda, writing before his death in 1952, is commenting on the Jewish and Christian Ten Commandments (with the quotation translated out of the non-gender-inclusive languages common to his era):

> The word "commandment," however, does not give the best connotation, for it is as if God is dictator and [the human is God's] servile attendant. These dictums should rather be regarded as a code of natural righteousness. If [humans do] not follow those laws which evince the divine image within [them, they] fall out of tune with God into delusive suffering of [their] own making.

As covered later in the section on Hatred and Anger, Buddhist monk Thich Nhat Hanh asserts that hell is not a place one is put because of being destructively angry, but rather that anger itself *is* hell (Hanh, 1995, p. 75). It is alienating one's self from other human beings as well as from divinity.

This applies to nonviolent approaches because it means having and showing concern for the spiritual well-being of the oppressors or other misbehavers. It is a common temptation to see those committing horrific injustices as suffering the torments of hell in a way that gives satisfaction in the ultimate triumph of justice as a tit-for-tat. But if those torments are asserted with any sense of gratification, then the targets of the vituperative language, no matter how much they might deserve it, are not being treated in the nonviolent manner that is most effective in causing changes in their behavior. Reaching their consciences will usually be far more effective by appealing to the idea that a disturbed conscience is in and of itself a grueling fate.

In this chapter, we will look at some of the characteristics that religions have weighed in on quite a bit, and which are helpful to understanding nonviolent action. There are, naturally, quite a few important ones that are not covered, as will always be true in any write-up of this kind. For example, we are not covering pride and arrogance, or fear and cowardice, or apathy, all of which are clearly held as immoral by religions and are traits that are to be opposed by nonviolent activism and lifestyles.

IDOLATRY

Many people, when thinking of idolatry, picture bowing to statues, and share the Biblical critique that this is silly, since statues are made by human hands (Psalms 115:4–5, 135:15–16; Isaiah 2:8, 31:7, 46:1–2; Hosea 13:2; Habakkuk 2:18). As such, it would be a minor irritation rather than a major sin. Yet Judaism, Christianity, and Islam all regard it as a primal sin underlying so many others. Since Hindus, Buddhists, and others do still bow to statues—as do Roman Catholics, and Eastern Orthodox have similar icons, both of which have caused controversy within Christianity—is it the use of statues in worship that is the problem?

No, the reason it is a primal sin is much deeper: it is taking that which is from the material world and treating it as if it were God. It is taking that which is not ultimate and treating it as if it were. Using statues or pictures as meditation devices still leaves the worshipper fully aware that these are only devices, not gods themselves. When the statues represent gods who tell the worshipper to go conquer the neighboring city and thereby give the worshippers their justification for doing so, this is when idolatry becomes a major foundation for violence. See, for example, the Bible's 2 Kings 17:15–17 and Jeremiah 19: 4–5; and the Qur'an 25:43 and 53:23.

Hindus and Buddhists do have a similar concept: nonattachment. This is one of their major goals; the Bhagavad Gita carries nonattachment as a major theme. Mohandas Gandhi expounds on this at length, asserting it as crucial to nonviolence. Buddhists regard as one of the Four Noble Truths excessive desire and craving—being overly attached to what is not worthy to be attached to—as the very source of suffering. This is a different approach, but the conclusion is the same: we are not to treat that which is not God, is not divine, as if it were.

A prime example is money. Money is a very fine tool, enabling us to do things that we could not do otherwise. If the second-grade teacher needs the services of a plumber, the plumber need not say, "Oh, I'm so sorry—my children are in the first and third grades. You have nothing to barter with me." The teacher is paid, the plumber is paid, and the exchange can go in wider circles and need not be direct. It can also be delayed—we can save for later. We can do sophisticated things with insurance and investments, and prosperity rises accordingly.

Money is, therefore, an excellent servant. It is a terrible master.

If it is treated as the tool it is, then it generally works well. When it is worshiped, when people will commit direct violence to gain more of it, when people will cause or tolerate structural violence to gain more of it, then it has become an idol, a material attachment. It is a cause of violence and intense suffering both to the victims of the violence and to the spiritual well-being of those doing the inflicting.

Former enslaved person Frederick Douglass commented on this in 1857. The Biblical reference is to Revelation 14:6:

> If such people as ours had heard the beloved disciple of the Lord, exclaiming in the rapture of the apocalyptic vision, "And I saw another angel fly in the midst of heaven, having the everlasting gospel to preach to them that dwell on the earth, and to every nation, kindred, tongue, and people;" they, instead of answering, Amen Glory to God in the Highest, would have responded,—but brother John, *will it pay?* Can money be made out of it? Will it make the rich richer, and the strong stronger? How will it affect property? In the eyes of such people, there is no God but wealth; no right and wrong but profit and loss. (Douglass, 1857/1985, p. 197)

That making an idol of money to the point of hurting other people is harmful to the money-makers follows from the point of idolatry or excessive material attachment and craving being harmful. Christian Quaker Thomas Kelly articulated this point: "The hard-lined face of a money-bitten financier is as deeply touching to the tender soul as are the burned-out eyes of miner's children, remote and unseen victims of his so-called success" (Kelly, 1941, p.41). Buddhist monk Thich Nhat Hanh also expounds on this:

> In Latin America, liberation theologians speak of God's preference, or "option," for the poor, the oppressed, and the marginalized. But I do not think God wants us to take sides, even with the poor. The rich also suffer, in many cases more than the poor! They may be rich

materially, but many are poor spiritually, and they suffer a lot. I have known rich and famous people who have ended up committing suicide. I am certain that those with the highest understanding will be able to see the suffering in both the poor and the rich. (Hanh, 1995, pp. 79–80)

Another example of treating something as God when it is not: power. Power simply means the ability to get things done. Getting power through nonviolence for the purpose of bettering people's lives is a good thing. Grabbing power for the sake of power, as is done by dictators and other bullies, means making a god out of power rather than using power as the tool that it is.

Sex is a third example. It can be among the most beautiful of experiences when done with love and to promote intimacy. It is also important for making new human beings, which is its irreplaceable biological function. When it is instead used as a means of power of one person over another—in extreme form, rape; in more mild form, exploitation—then it can be among the ugliest things that there is. It is because of sex's constant use as an idol or as material attachment that sexual restraint and outright celibacy have been common in religions concerned with ethics.

There are many other things that can be used as idols, attachments, or obsessions. These things are perfectly good when they are understood and treated as merely things, but can become vicious when miscategorized as if they were divine. If that which is merely a thing can bark orders to us, if we look for guidance for our behavior to things that should instead be merely tools, then we can get ourselves and our communities into deep spiritual trouble. The spirit of loving one another and wishing to do well to one another, after all, needs to override all else, if nonviolence is to prevail and that which is *actually* divine be the only entity worshipped.

CONSCRIPTING GOD FOR ONE'S OWN AGENDA

Comedian and atheist George Carlin once did a comic talk on the Ten Commandments of the Bible in which he ridiculed them one by one (see it on YouTube: https://www.youtube.com/watch?v=CE8ooMBIyC8). When he got to "not taking the Lord's name in vain," he used what has been a common interpretation—one should not use language in which the word "God" is used casually when God is not actually being thought of. He thought this entirely trivial, something easily dispensed with. Yet when he got to the commandment "thou shalt not kill," he was in full accord with the principle. He assailed Christians and Muslims for not having abided by the commandment, most especially with not merely killing—not merely doing so, but making it so much worse by doing so *in God's name*. With this point, he actually contradicted his earlier point. Taking the name of the Holy One "in vain" means using the name for nefarious purposes—as the New International Version translation puts it (Exodus 20:7), it is "misusing" the name of God. If George Carlin asserts that claiming religious justification for violence is more despicable than simply doing violence for admittedly selfish reasons, then the injunction against enscripting God by "taking the Lord's name in vain" is actually very serious indeed. It belongs in the top 10, as being in the Ten Commandments indicates.

Mohandas Gandhi put it bluntly: "I know of no greater sin than to oppress the innocent in the name of God" (Gandhi, 1980, p. 143).

The singer and songwriter Bob Dylan wrote a parody of the attitude with a song called "God on Our Side." Verse through verse, it goes through war after war with the final line of the verse indicating that all the death and destruction must be what is supposed to happen, because we always have "God on our side." The final verse ends: "The words fill my head/and they fall to the floor/If God is on our side/He'll stop the next war." This is one way of putting it; another way of saying it is that, inasmuch as "taking sides" is a relevant way of seeing a situation, we are supposed to inquire as to whether we are on God's side, not the other way around.

Religion has quite a reputation for violence. People who wish to do violence use religion to justify themselves rather than admitting to being selfish and brutal. When the selfishness and brutality are obvious to others, especially their victims, then this will give the claimed religion a tarnished reputation. This often keeps it from being available for when it is most desperately needed.

Nevertheless, we have the amazing phenomenon that people who are conquered or enslaved or exploited under dangerous conditions will embrace the same religion as their oppressors. In many cases, they embrace it more strongly than their oppressors do, albeit from a different perspective. Why would they do this?

Howard Thurman, an early civil rights activist who traveled to India to study the nonviolence approach there, put it this way:

> I have never quite understood why the Negro Freedman became a Christian unless it was due to the fact that he saw in the message of

Jesus Christ something which was deeper and more profound than what he was taught about the meaning of that message. (Dixie & Eisenstadt, 2011, p. xxii)

The enslaved people did not understand Christianity as the slave masters taught it, but rather understood the original story and the early meaning. They were undoing the misuse and going back to the roots.

DESTRUCTIVE OBEDIENCE AND CONFORMITY

Adolf Eichmann was in charge of making the Nazi death camps run—as a bureaucrat. When he actually visited one, it made him sick. So he no longer visited. Meanwhile, the people who put the gas into the gas chambers had no such escape, but they understood themselves as having no decision-making power. They were only following orders.

A couple of decades later, American psychologist Stanley Milgram wanted to understand how this could happen. He designed an experiment where people were ordered to give more and more severe electric shocks under the guise of a learning experiment. He expected Americans to rebel, Germans to comply, and this would help him find the cultural differences. What he found instead was that about two-thirds of Americans complied all the way to the top of the electric-shock scale. This experiment was replicated under various circumstances and different cultures. Essentially no differences between cultures were found.

Why do people obey? Most of the time, obeying is a good idea. People in authority usually do have the expertise they claim to have. If they have people's welfare in mind, it is best to follow the expert—doctor, plumber, or government official. Switching the mind to being aware that authority is asking for harm is not easy.

This would be especially true under real-life conditions. Emergency situations, which war regularly supplies, would make the sense of moral obligation even stronger than it would be for some mere experiment from a stranger.

Among the many reasons this result happened is that it was the authority that decided what the situation was. Participants saw the authority as having the responsibility, not they themselves.

Religions have long been sensitive to the point that people must obey God, and therefore the principles of justice and compassion, and must disobey the demands of authority that are violent or likely to lead to violence. For example, in the Biblical book of Daniel, chapter 3 has three young men thrown into a fiery furnace rather than bow down to the emperor, and chapter 6 has Daniel thrown into a den of lions for continuing to pray despite royal decree not to. In both cases, the persecuted were miraculously delivered, showing God's favor. The New Testament book of Acts has the apostles brought before the Sanhedrin accused of preaching in Jesus's name after being ordered not to and replying that they obey God rather than human beings (Acts 5:27–29). The very first pillar of being a Muslim—"There is no God but God, and Mohammad is his Prophet"—implies that disobedience is essential to that which is against God.

One innovative interpretation of the story of Adam and Eve and their temptation to eat the forbidden fruit (Genesis 3:1–13 in the Bible)—though certainly not a common interpretation—is that Eve and then Adam were obeying a face-to-face authority in a way that seemed innocent to them at the time but was actually quite destructive.

In Buddhism, since the disobeying of unjust authority is likely to invite suffering to be inflicted on the person disobeying, the act of disobeying constitutes engaging in suffering for the sake of making a statement against suffering in the hope of seeing that there is less of it. Thus, it is a Bodhisattva action, well in keeping with Buddhist practice.

In Hindu terms, of course, the voluminous writings of Mohandas Gandhi, among others, supply ample explanation for why noncooperation when authority misbehaves is essential.

GREED

Religions commonly decry greed as a sin that will put individuals into deep trouble and lead to devastating social consequences, and it is usually high on the list of the sins that will do so. For example, the Hindu Bhagavad Gita 16:21 says, "There are three gates to self-destructive hell: lust, anger, and greed." In the Christian New Testament: "The love of money is a root of all kinds of evil" (1 Timothy 6:10). In Buddhism, greed is one of the Three Poisons that lead to evil (hatred and ignorance being the other two). In Sikhism, greed is one of the Five Evils (along with lust, anger, temptation, and hubris). After commenting that with the Tao horses haul manure (fertilizer) but without it war horses are bred, the last half of chapter 46 of *Tao Te Ching* says, "There is no crime greater than having too many desires; There is no disaster greater than not being content; There is no misfortune greater than being covetous." Among the passages in the Qur'an that address this: "Let not those who hoard up that which

God has bestowed on them of His bounty think that it is good for them—nay, it will be worse for them" (3:180), and "God does not love such as are proud and boastful, who hoard their wealth and encourage greed in others, and hide that which God has bestowed on them of His bounty" (4:36).

Greed can lead directly to people being killed, as when merchants sell brutal arms to vicious dictators. This is direct violence. Yet it is far more complicit in what is called *structural violence*, where the society is set up to keep hard-working people in poverty or otherwise oppressed. When direct violence kills, it does so fairly quickly, dramatically, personally, and acutely. When structural violence kills, it does so indirectly, slowly, in a commonplace and impersonal way, and it is chronic. Getting rid of direct violence means keeping certain events from happening; without them, things remain as they were. This is guarding the status quo. Getting rid of structural violence means establishing social justice. Social institutions must improve or be replaced, changing the status quo.

Poverty has long been a concern of the scriptures from just about all religions. The Biblical book of Proverbs, for example, while still having plenty of sayings about avoiding poverty by not being lazy or drunk, also shows a keen awareness of poverty caused by the injustice of the way things are set up. Unused fields could yield plenty of food for the poor, but unjust people keep them from being farmed (13:23); a ruler who oppresses the poor is like a driving rain that leaves no crops (28:3); a good person knows the rights of the poor, but wicked people cannot understand such things (29:7); oppressing the poor shows contempt for their Maker (14:31). This was a constant outrage by the prophets of Judah and Israel (see, for example, Ezekiel 5:8–10, all of chapter 34, 45:9; Jeremiah 6:13–14; Micah 2:1–2; Amos 6:1–6). It is not a mere side issue in scriptures, but a major theme.

For Christians being quite vociferous in their denunciation of oppressing the poor, see especially the New Testament letter of James, 5:1–6. Upton Sinclair once pulled a trick on a group of pastors by reading them this passage and attributing it to his contemporary, the anarchist Emma Goldman. Instead of recognizing that he was reading scripture, the pastors declared she should be deported for saying such things (Sinclair, 1918, pp. 287–290).

Conditions that constitute structural violence appear to be peaceful to those in more powerful positions. If a nonviolent campaign of opposition arises, it is that campaign they see as "breaking the peace." Yet the assertion that the campaign is helping to establish peace rather than breaking it, by stopping structural violence, has ample support from practically all religious traditions. As the Biblical prophet Jeremiah says about greed leading to structural violence, "From the least to the greatest, all are greedy for gain; prophets and priests alike, all practice deceit. They dress the wound of my people as though it were not serious. 'Peace, peace,' they say, when there is no peace" (Jeremiah 6:13–14).

HATRED AND ANGER

Note that hatred or anger makes the list of top causes of evil (along with greed), mentioned before, for Hinduism, Buddhism, and Sikhism. Quite a bit of violence can be cold-blooded or can be structural violence or come from obedience to destructive authority as explained earlier and therefore can occur without hatred. Yet a large portion does come from hatred, and hatred is especially pernicious with sustaining cycles of violence. Hatred can be a reaction to violence from others, who then retaliate. Long-lasting feuds with strong hatred on all sides can be among the most intractable and difficult problems to solve.

Anger is related to hatred when anger clouds the judgment and when anger leads to actions that make anger and hatred hard to distinguish. However, anger is also a natural reaction to grave injustice, to the point that it would be strange not to feel it, and would amount to apathy or callousness. Anger, if handled well, can provide the energy to act.

The difference is between destructive anger handled poorly and constructive anger managed well. Whenever religions decry anger entirely, they are generally thinking of only the first kind. Mohandas Gandhi explained how to use anger constructively: "I have learnt through the bitter experience the one supreme lesson to conserve my anger, and as heat conserved is transmuted into energy, even so our anger controlled can be transmuted into a power which can move the world." Anger was at the heart of the energy, but only if it is well managed.

The Christian Gospel of Matthew deals with anger in the Sermon on the Mount, where Jesus is speaking:

> You have heard that it was said to the ancients, "You shall not murder, and anyone who murders will be subject to judgment." But I tell you that anyone who is angry with a brother or sister without cause will be subject to judgment. Anyone who says to a brother or sister, "you good-for-nothing" is answerable to the council. And anyone who says, "You fool!" will be in danger of the fire of hell.
>
> Therefore, if you are offering your gift at the altar and there remember that your brother or sister has something against you,

leave your gift there in front of the altar. First go and be reconciled to them; then come and offer your gift. (Matthew 5:21–24)

Buddhist Thich Nhat Hanh, comments on the first of the previous two verses: "Jesus did not say that if you are angry with your brother, you will be put in a place called hell. He said that if you are angry with your brother, you are already in hell. Anger is hell" (Hanh, 1995, p. 75). He is of course thinking of destructive anger poorly handled. Hanh has written a book on how to deal with anger constructively, including treating it as a baby to pay tender attention to and keep out of trouble (Hanh, 2002).

Notably, in the Gospel passage quoted before, though not in all versions, Jesus refers to the disapproved anger as "without cause." Having a legitimate cause for anger may be different, but it still needs to be channeled constructively and not cloud the judgment.

As for the second of the two verses quoted before, Prabhavananda offers a Hindu commentary:

> Suppose someone has wronged you, and you feel irritated. When you begin to meditate, what happens? Prayer and meditation concentrate the mind and intensify the emotions. Consequently, the molehill or irritation becomes a mountain of anger.... You find yourself unfit to pray and meditate, unable to come to God, until you are sincerely reconciled with your brother. (Prabhavananda, 1963, p. 49)

The point is made well in the Hadith from Islam: "The Messenger of God said: 'A strong person is not the person who throws his adversaries to the ground. A strong person is the one who contains himself when he is angry'" (Al-Muwatta 47.12).

STARTING SMALL AND GROWING

Buddhist scripture has a story that illustrates well the "slippery slope," where things start small and then add a little more and then more until the ending is something no one would have contemplated to start with (as with going up the scale of the electroshocks in the Milgram experiments discussed earlier). A king abandoned Buddhist teachings to rule with his own ideas, so did not arrange for the provision of the needed goods and services to the poor. Hence, poverty increased. Therefore, one man stole something. When the king asked why, the man said he had nothing to live on. The king thought that rather than being punitive he would do problem-solving and gave him enough to have a business and support his family. This then happened with a second man. Other people thought this sounded like a good deal, so they decided to steal in order to get those benefits. This got out of hand, so the king finally decided he needed to be punitive after all, in order to deter crime. He took a thief and beheaded him. Instead of deterring, it provided a model, and people took up arms to steal. Murderous assaults on whole villages resulted. "Thus, from the not giving of property to the needy, poverty became widespread, from the growth of poverty, the taking of what was not given increased, from the increase of theft, the use of weapons increased, from the increased use of weapons, the taking of life increased" (Digha-Nikaya [Lion's Roar Sutra], iii 65).

A little bit of destructive anger or hatred or greed can grow, and this is why religions are so concerned with stopping them when they are still minor and appear relatively innocent. Sometimes people think that religions are being overly harsh and judgmental about minor points. That may be so if they were to remain minor, but experience shows otherwise. The Bible says, "The start of an argument is like the first break in a dam; stop it before it goes any further" (Proverbs 17:14). The Buddhist Dhammapada says, "Even if the water falls drop by drop, it will fill the pot; and the fool will become full of evil, even though he gathers it little by little." The Jewish Talmud says, "Tremble before a minor sin, lest it lead you to a major one" (Derek Eretz 1.26).

The Hebrew Scriptures have a continual theme of not doing even a little bit of burning incense to an idol. It was not merely a puritanical strictness. If the first step is not taken, then the end product can be avoided. A common final product of the step-by-step descent into idolatry was child sacrifice (see, for example, Leviticus 18:21; Deuteronomy 18:10; 2 Kings 16:3, 17:17, 21:6, 23:10; Jeremiah 7:31, 19:3).

In 1811, Hannah Moore (a Christian Quaker) said in chapter 11 of a book called *Religion of the Heart*:

> Do small faults, continually repeated, always retain their original weakness? Is a bad temper which is never repressed not worse after years of indulgence than when we first gave the reins to it? . . . Does the habit of loose talking or allowed exaggeration never lead to falsehood, never move into deceit? Before we positively determine that small faults are innocent, we must try to prove that they shall never outgrow their primitive dimensions. We must make certain that the infant shall never become a giant.

This is of course not merely a danger for individuals, but for whole societies. This is important to nonviolence strategy because of the all-important point that it is so very much easier to be effective in opposing violence when it is still small, especially when it is in the realm of words and feelings, and also when the actions have not yet grown to unmanageable size. Paying attention to nipping problems in the bud, before a dictatorship or massacre or war or any other major killing occurs, will always be the most effective strategy when it can happen. While there are all kinds of things that can still be done when things have gotten out of hand, it is a fairly straightforward point that the most effective time to take action is as early in the slippery-slope process as is feasible.

JUST-WORLD VIEW

What happens if we think the world is already just—that good things happen only to good people, bad things happen only to bad people, rewards and punishments are divinely distributed properly right now, and everyone gets what they deserve, at least in the end? Then we have set up a belief that social psychology has identified as one of the causes of violence, or at least a cause of tolerating violence. It is commonly called the Just-World View—the view that the world *is now* divinely designed to follow the dictates of justice.

Working toward a more just world is exactly what nonviolence is for, so it may seem odd to regard something called the Just-World View as a problem. But the basic point is that we do indeed need to work for a more just world before we will have one.

Consider a woman who has been raped. Was her clothing suggestive? Did she come on to the man? Was she out at night? Rape is a draconian penalty for such minor matters, but that is not the point. The point is that as long as other women can find a way to make it her fault, those other women can feel safer. If they must admit there are completely innocent women who nevertheless are victimized, then they themselves can be victimized.

When observing people who live in poverty, the reasoning of the Just-World View is that they must be ignorant, have bad habits, or not have a good work ethic. Then people who are industrious and well-educated need not worry. If people are poor because even though they work hard they were cheated out of decent compensation, or if they are poor because they cannot find employment despite strenuous efforts to do so, then we are all less safe.

The Just-World View becomes a way of saying that victims are responsible for their own predicament. We do not need to feel outraged on behalf of those who are innocent, because none are innocent. If God were the Majestic Enforcer of the Just-World View, then it would actually be true that bad things happen only to bad people, and this would lower our sympathy for them.

The Just-World View reinforces arrogance of those with brutal power. If good things happen only to good people, then people who are rich and powerful deserve it. It would not be that they grabbed dictatorial power or sold vicious arms to others who did so, nor that they imposed or lobbied for unjust laws. They would be only virtuous people, by definition. We need to know what is wrong with the Just-World View in those cases where justice needs yet to be accomplished.

In the Biblical book of Job, Satan proposes that Job is only a good man because he is rewarded for it and would stop being so if he went through calamities (Job 1:8–11). Rabbi Harold Kushner wrote a well-known book in 1981, *When Bad Things Happen to Good People*, in which the book of Job figured prominently. He offered many more of the problems with this view:

> The idea that God gives people what they deserve, that our misdeeds cause our misfortune, is a neat and attractive solution to the problem of evil at several levels, but it has a number of serious limitations . . . it teaches people to blame themselves. It creates guilt even where there is no basis for guilt. It makes people hate God, even as it makes them hate themselves. And most disturbing of all, it does not even fit the facts. (Kushner, 1981, p. 10)

In the very same passage in which Jesus tells us to love our enemies (Matthew 5:43), he gives this reason: "for God makes the sun rise on the evil and on the good, and sends rain on the just and on the unjust" (Matthew 5:45). Charles Bowen (1835–1894) offered this reflection on the passage:

> The rain, it raineth on the just
> And also on the unjust fella.
> But chiefly on the just, because
> The unjust steals the just's umbrella.

Buddha made a similar observation:

> That great cloud rains down on all whether their nature is superior or inferior. The light of the sun and the moon illuminates the whole world, both those who do well and those who do ill, both those

who stand high and those who stand low. (Sadharmapundarika Sutra 5)

Early Muslim Sufi saint Rabia al-'Adawiyya, (ca. 717–801; Islamic years 99–185 AH) points out how being good only for the sake of reward or avoiding punishment detracts from true devotion:

> O God, if I worship you for fear of hell, burn me in hell, and if I worship you in hope of paradise, exclude me from paradise; but if I worship you for your own sake, deny me not your eternal beauty. . . . I want to throw fire into Paradise and pour water into Hell so that these two veils disappear, and it becomes clear who worships God out of love, not out of fear of hell or hope for Paradise.

Applying to nonviolent action, the Just-World View might make people fatalistic about accepting injustices inflicted upon them, or accept injustices inflicted on others, rather than joining nonviolent campaigns to resist the injustices. The Just-World View is a way of saying that God is supposed to work some magic so that we do not have to do hard work and make sacrifices. It is saying that God already does do such magic, so what we see in the world is interpreted through that lens. We would be less likely to feel responsible to help the unfortunate, whether in charity work or in work to make the social system more just so that they are more fortunate. God would be a dictator taking care of it for us.

Yet the Just-World View is not entirely incorrect, not something to dispense with entirely the way hatred and greed are. The very fact that nonviolent uprisings have been shown to be more effective than violent uprisings (Chenowith & Stephan, 2012) indicates that there have been so many of them that the world is capable of moving toward justice in the end. An "unjust-world view," after all, is no more warranted.

15

Virtues: Religious Character-Building for Nonviolent Discipline

THE LISTS

Religions have a tendency to do lists of what virtues are to be commended. Here are some examples.

Hinduism

> Discernment, knowledge, freedom from delusion, long-suffering, truth, self-restraint, inward calm, pleasure, pain, birth, death, fear and fearlessness, nonviolence, even-mindedness, contentment, austerity, beneficence, good and ill fame—all these various attributes of creatures proceed verily from Me. (Bhagavad-Gita 10:4–5; Krishna/God is speaking)
>
> Fearlessness, purity of heart, steadfastness in *jnana* and *yoga*—knowledge and action—beneficence, self-restraint, sacrifice, spiritual study, austerity and uprightness, nonviolence, truth, slowness to wrath, the spirit of dedication, serenity, aversion to slander, tenderness to all that lives, freedom from greed, gentleness, modesty, freedom from levity, spiritedness, forgiveness, fortitude, purity, freedom from ill will and arrogance—these are to bound in one born with the divine heritage, O Bharata. (Bhagavad-Gita 16:1–3)

Buddhism

> Peace and calm come from living wisely. The one who is skilled in goodness, and who wishes to attain that state of calm should act thus: He or she should be able, upright, perfectly upright, obedient, gentle and humble; contented, easily supportable, with few duties,

of right livelihood, with senses controlled, discreet, not impudent, not greedily attached to families. He or she should not commit any slight wrong on account of which otherwise people might censure him or her. May all beings be happy and secure, may their hearts be wholesome! (Karaniya Metta Sutta: Loving-Kindness, Sn. 1.8)

Christianity

But the fruit of the Spirit is love, joy, peace, forbearance, kindness, goodness, faithfulness, gentleness and self-control. Against such things there is no law. (Galatians 5:22–23)

Finally, brothers and sisters, whatever is true, whatever is noble, whatever is right, whatever is pure, whatever is lovely, whatever is admirable—if anything is excellent or praiseworthy—think about such things. Whatever you have learned or received or heard from me, or seen in me—put it into practice. And the God of peace will be with you. (Philippians 4: 8–9)

Islam

Goodness does not consist in turning your face towards East or West. The truly good are those who believe in God and the Last Day, in the angels, the Scripture, and the prophets; who give away some of their wealth, however much they cherish it, to their relatives, to orphans, the needy, travelers and beggars, and to liberate those in bondage; those who keep up the prayer and pay the prescribed alms; who keep pledges whenever they make them; who are steadfast in misfortune, adversity, and times of danger. These are the ones who are true, and it is they who are aware of God. (Qur'an 2: 177)

Commenting on the angels in this passage, Maulana Muhammad Ali says:

The belief in angels may not be as universal as a belief in the Divine Being, but it is accepted generally in all monotheistic religions.... Just as our physical faculties are not by themselves sufficient to enable us to attain any object in the physical world without the assistance of other agents—as, for instance, the eye cannot see unless there is light—so our spiritual powers cannot by themselves lead us to good or evil deeds, but here, too, intermediaries which have an existence independent of our internal spiritual powers are necessary to enable us to do good or evil deeds . . . to bring these [good or evil] attractions into operation, external agencies are needed, as they are needed in the case of physical powers. . . . If we respond to the attraction for good we are following the angel or the Holy Spirit, and if we respond to the attraction for evil we are following Satan. Our belief in angels carries, therefore, the significance that whenever we feel a tendency to do good we should at once obey that call and follow the inviter to good. . . . As a disbelief in the devil [2:256] means that we should repel the attraction for evil, so a belief in angels means we should follow the inviter to good. (Ali, 1995, p. 72)

HOPE

Hope is both a cause and an effect of nonviolence. The absence of hope—that is, despair—can be a cause of violence, or can be another of its effects. When people are feeling the effects of violence, hope is what can call them to action and have the fortitude to continue, even when the evidence in front of the eyes makes it appear unrealistic. Over and over, people in conditions that appeared hopeless nevertheless prevailed over time because their religions taught them that what was in front of their eyes was not the final word.

Martin Luther King addressed this directly: "We must accept finite disappointment, but we must never lose infinite hope." Doctor of the Church Teresa of Avila (1515–1582) advised: "Let nothing disturb thee; Let nothing dismay thee; All Things pass; God never changes." In her book *Interior Castle* she said: "If you should at times fall, don't become discouraged and stop striving to advance. For even from this fall, God will draw out good." Rabindranath Tagore said, "Within us we have a hope which always walks in front of our present narrow experience; it is the undying faith in the infinite in us; it will never accept any of our disabilities as a permanent fact" (Tagore, 1916, p. 42). Dorothy Day, cofounder of the Catholic Worker Movement, was blunter: "No one has a right to sit down and feel hopeless. There's too much work to do."

The Biblical Psalms, known for the exploration of human emotions, give a couple of instances showing how this works:

> How long must I endure trouble? How long will sorrow fill my heart day and night? How long will my enemies triumph over me? . . . I rely on your constant love; I will be glad, because you will rescue me. I will sing to you, O Lord, because you have been good to me. (Bible, Psalms 13:2, 5, 6)
>
> I have set the Lord always before me. Because he is at my right hand, I will not be shaken. Therefore my heart is glad and my tongue

rejoices; my body also will rest secure, because you will not abandon me to the grave, nor will you let your faithful one see decay. (Bible, Psalms 16:8–10)

The New Testament frequently addresses hope as a common theme and related to peace. For example, "May the God of hope fill you with all joy and peace as you trust in him, so that you may overflow with hope by the power of the Holy Spirit" (Romans 15:13).

Muslim Sufi saint Rabia al-'Adawiyya, (717–801; Islamic years 95–179 AH), who had lived the life of an enslaved person before being freed and therefore knew what a hard life could be, heard that Salih of Qazwin was teaching by the phrase, "Knock at the Door and it will be opened to you." She responded: "How long will you persist in saying this, O Salih—when that Door has never been shut?" (Shah, 1996, p. 75).

In her writings about the Christian life, Quaker Hannah Whitall Smith (1832–1911) said:

What else can the Lord, who is our Shepherd, do with His sheep, but just this? He has no folds that are not good folds, no pastures that are not green pastures, and no waters but still waters. They may not look so outwardly; but we who have tried them can testify that, let the outward seeming be what it may, His fold and His pastures are always places of peace and comfort to the inward life of the soul. (Smith, 1906, p. 28)

Episcopalian bishop Desmond Tutu of South Africa, deeply involved in the ending of apartheid there and then in the recuperation from it in the South Africa Truth and Reconciliation Commission, added to the theme:

After the grueling work of the Commission I came away with a deep sense—indeed an exhilarating realization—that though there is undoubtedly much evil about, we human beings have a wonderful capacity for good. We can be very good. That is what fills me with hope for even the most intractable situations. (Tutu, 1999, p. 205)

Since history has shown over and over again that even situations that seemed intractable at the time have indeed come to an end, the hope that is recommended by religions is not merely a pie-in-the-sky-when-you-die kind of magic. When taking the long view over the centuries, we see that violent institutions have fallen and nonviolence has prevailed over and over again.

HUMOR AND JOY

Humor's place in active nonviolence comes from several features. It can be used as a prophetic instrument in nonviolent campaigns, cutting the pretensions of the powerful; the powerful seem much less powerful when aspects of their foibles are found amusing. Joking reframes issues or episodes, transforming passive suffering thrust upon people into an active response.

Yet, conversely, forms of humor that a campaign's opponents are able to share can lead to communication breakthroughs, or at least to greater friendliness with all that entails for the likely success of the campaign.

For activists, humor can help them avoid burnout. It can also deflate their own pretensions, thereby keeping them from descending into an arrogance that can lead cause-oriented people to violent thoughts. The humility that goes with such deflated pretensions also puts the activists more in line with reality, makes them more appealing to onlookers, and allows for new ideas that can be breakthroughs in resolving conflicts. Humor can make it easier to understand differing points of view, differing sides of an issue.

Nonviolent campaigns by their very nature involve clear-eyed views of human foibles. Without the kind of haughtiness and disdain for the enemy generally required for violence, humor comes naturally as a side effect.

Quaker Tom Mullen explains part of the dynamics of how humor relates to nonviolent action:

> Those able to see the humor of a situation are usually more understanding of the human condition than those who can't. Seeing the funny or ironic side of events is a way of seeing the truth they contain. An inability to laugh at human foibles is blasphemy. It treats human beings as if they were godlike, and they aren't. I foul up. You foul up. All God's children foul up, and laughing about our foibles is a form of confession. . . .
>
> Relief results both from formal confession . . . and informal confession—poking fun at our pretensions. Those able to laugh at themselves find relief, and they release others around them to do the same . . . an inability to laugh about our concerns too often results in idolatry of the cause. . . .

> If Karl Marx's revolution had had a healthy dose of Groucho Marx's comedy, lives would have been saved—and the resulting regime would probably have been more humane. . . .
> Cheerful crusaders are cheerful lovers of humanity—sinners and saints alike. They relate to the human race as if they were part of it. (Mullen, 1989, pp. 49–52)

Humor also helps calm us in uncomfortable or terrifying situations. Psychologist Victor Frankl, survivor of a Nazi concentration camp, in discussing his observations of fellow Jewish inmates there, said:

> Humor is another of the soul's weapons in the fight for self-preservation. It is well known that humor, more than anything else in the human make-up, can afford an aloofness and an ability to rise above any situation, even if only for a few seconds. (Frankl, 1984, p. 63)

In religion, a frequent related term is "joy." Joy can help religious goals in many ways, but when religion is done well, joy is also a major effect of religion and spirituality on the human community.

This is a major theme in religious literature; to offer some examples, "A cheerful heart is good medicine, but a crushed spirit dries up the bones" (Bible, Proverbs 17:22). Christian saint Teresa of Avila said: "A sad nun is a bad nun. I am more afraid of one unhappy sister than a crowd of evil spirits. . . . What would happen if we hid what little sense of humor we had? Let each of us humbly use this to cheer others" (Martin, 2013).

Muslim Indries Shah put it this way:

> Not only do humorous tales contain valuable structures for understanding. Their use also helps to weed out people who lack a sense of humor. Sufis hold that people who have not developed or who have suppressed their capacity to enjoy humor are, in this deprived state, also without learning capacity in the Sufi sphere. (Shah, 1996, p. 21)

Hindu Mohandas Gandhi, as a major pioneer in nonviolent techniques, said in 1928: "If I had no sense of humor, I would long ago have committed suicide." He found humor to have healing power on the many occasions when events did not go as he would have wished.

FORGIVENESS

There is a paradox in forgiveness, shown by the two components necessary:

1. An event or condition is very, very wrong, unjust, and intolerable, which would justifiably lead to anger and resentment in response.
2. We will not respond with the anger and resentment it deserves.

Much of the time, there are people who are committing injustices but who nevertheless will not accept the first component and are offended by it. When that is the case, forgiveness in public amounts to letting them get away with something they never admitted to be wrong. A person being forgiving in private can mean only that the person does not wish to let anyone they dislike inflict extra emotional distress by way of festering resentment, even when—especially when—the people continue doing the wrong. Yet any public pronouncements or interactions that offer forgiveness can be seen as not really believing the first point. Justice and forgiveness, both strongly recommended in practically all religions, are in conflict.

This mixture is shown in this passage of the Qur'an:

> Far better and more lasting is what God will give to those who believe and trust in their Lord . . . and defend themselves when they are oppressed. Let harm be requited by an equal harm, though anyone who forgives and puts things right will have his reward from God Himself—He does not like those who do wrong. There is no cause to act against anyone who defends himself after being wronged, but there is cause to act against those who oppress people and transgress in the land against all justice—they will have an agonizing torment—though if a person is patient and forgives, this is one of the greatest things. (Qur'an 42:36, 39–43)

The same mixture is shown from the Bible's Micah 6:8: "What does the Lord require of you? To act justly, and to love mercy, and to walk humbly with your God." Justice in the positive sense of giving people the good things they deserve fits well with mercy, but justice in the sense of giving people the comeuppance they deserve is contrary to mercy. One way to define mercy is deciding to abandon the giving of deserved punishment.

Therefore, the ideal time when forgiveness works well is when it is used for reconciliation—either one party agrees that what it did was wrong, or all parties agree that what they both did was at least wrong enough to not do it anymore.

A prime example is the Truth and Reconciliation Commission of South Africa, a model that has been followed elsewhere. When Bishop

Tutu (1999) wrote about this experience, the title of the book was *No Future without Forgiveness*. Yet the country did not deal with the post-apartheid situation by simply forgiving all those who had committed horrific brutality under the previous regime, as if it were a matter of forgetting what happened. There were requirements of confession before amnesty could be granted for crimes that occurred during apartheid. There was giving of information so families could know what happened to their loved ones. There was interaction between victimizers and surviving victims. It was hard and gut-wrenching work, not simply wiping the slate clean—amnesia was not part of forgiveness.

It was also difficult to convince all of the victims that this was the best road to take, but what Tutu meant by "no future" was that the country could never heal and progress if it were instead mired in festering albeit justified resentments. Tempering anger and resentment, as well as dispelling anxiety and depression, is important to the success of a nonviolent campaign, just as in individual therapy.

When the brutality is still ongoing, however, forgiveness cannot be given with the kind of formal finality that a Truth and Reconciliation Commission can offer when done well. When convincing a group or government that what it is doing is wrong, it would appear odd to say this is not resented. Therefore, forgiveness is more an attitude of the nonviolent—as Christian Quaker Hannah Moore (1745–1833) put it: "Forgiveness is the economy of the heart . . . forgiveness saves the expense of anger, the cost of hatred, the waste of spirits."

It goes with continued firmness about the truth of that first component, that something is very wrong. As Barbara Deming put it, nonviolence gives us two hands upon the oppressor: "one hand taking from him what is not his due, the other slowly calming him as we do this" (Linn, Linn, & Linn, 1997, p. 9).

HUMILITY

Some have said that humility is a virtue people can have only if they are unaware of it; any people who understand themselves as having humility have lost it. That would make it a virtue that requires mindlessness, and one that cannot be cultivated.

Humility can instead be seen as a form of wisdom that requires great mindfulness—one that is straightforwardly aware of reality. Each one of us is only one person among several billion and the universe is not centered around us. Our knowledge is overwhelmingly limited and only scratches the surface of what can be known. These things are simply true and bring with them the relief of knowing we are not alone responsible for managing the world. Nor do they involve putting ourselves down—after all, these things are true of everyone else as well.

We each have our own flaws and weaknesses, and we are wiser if we are familiar with what they are. This does not mean we must castigate ourselves unduly, since that is no more accurate; we can, for example, admit to not having the skills needed to be a good carpenter without saying we have no skills at all. Along with our flaws, we can be aware of our strengths, which is the same form of wisdom.

Yet it also follows that because everyone else also has their flaws and their strengths, we can be more tolerant of flaws and more admiring of strengths in other people. This improves interaction.

At any given time, the point of view or facts we are asserting may be found to have weaknesses in them, and it is a matter of wisdom to accept that this is so. It also makes it easier to interact with nonviolence, allowing for flexibility in thinking.

The idea of having this awareness is frequently found in practically all religions—it is, after all, a stand against arrogance. Confucius (551–479 BCE) said: "Real knowledge is to know the extent of one's own ignorance." The Jewish Talmud asserts: "Every debate that is for the sake of heaven will make a lasting contribution" (Avot 5:20). Early Christian Augustine of Hippo (354–430) declared: "If you should say, 'It is enough, I have reached perfection,' all is lost. For it is the function of perfection to make one know one's imperfection." Swami Turiyananda said: "Stubbornness is not strength. Stubbornness merely hides one's weakness. Strong is he [or she] who is flexible like steel and does not break. Strong is he [or she] who can live in harmony with many people and heed opinions others than his [or her] own" (Prabhavananda, 1963, p. 50).

Some sections of most religions have rigid requirements and authoritarian orientations. There have been outright wars claimed to be fought over small points in creeds. Heated controversies split up religious bodies. Harsh laws and cruel customs have resulted from this perspective.

Yet the sections of each religion with a nonviolent orientation are more inclined to celebrations of diversity in insights. There have been various nonviolent and charitable campaigns for human betterment where different people from different religions and no religion cooperated. They required the creativity that goes with understanding complexities.

They have an ability to see others with whom they are in conflict as people deserving of respect. People following each religion have had trouble with this when they get overly dogmatic and demonize their "enemies" or those with other religious points of view. They have been at their best when they recognize that we are all children of God, and therefore all are entitled to respect—or, even better, love.

There is a Buddhist saying that you should always act as if every single small action you take has great, cosmic significance. Then you must laugh at yourself for thinking that anything you can possibly do might have any impact whatsoever.

Some religious groups, such as the Quakers, deliberately do without creeds on the idea that truth does not fit into a box. Other religions, whose creeds provide definitions and structure rather than fighting points, commonly tolerate ambiguity by referring to the concept of mystery. Mystery, humility, and the delight of caring for others with all our differing ideas are some of the ways religion counters rigid intolerance, thereby offering peacemaking institutions and support for nonviolent approaches.

PATIENCE AND ENDURANCE

The founder of the nonviolent army, as covered in chapter 7, Abdul Gaffar Khan, explains the importance of patience to nonviolent action:

> I am going to give you such a weapon that the police and the army will not be able to stand against. It is the weapon of the Prophet. . . . That weapon is patience and righteousness. No power on earth can stand against it. . . . When you go back to your villages, tell your brethren that there is an army of God and its weapon is patience. . . . Endure hardship. If you exercise patience, victory will be yours. (Tendulkar, 1967, p. 129)

Mohammed Abu-Nimer in his book *Nonviolence and Peace Building in Islam* also points out the necessity: "Patience is a key virtue in peacebuilding and socioeconomic development projects, whose benefits are often more apparent in the long term than in the short term" (Abu-Nimer, 2003, p. 71). He expounds that the Arabic word used by Muslims for patience is *Sabr,* a major virtue with many shades of meaning: (1) thorough, not hasty; (2) perseverance, steadfastness; (3) systematic rather than chaotic; and (4) a cheerful attitude when faced with sorrow or defeat. He suggests that the Qur'anic verses that especially promote patience are 2:45, 2:153, 3:186, 3:200, and especially 16:126–127. Additionally, verses that advice patience and steadfastness to The Prophet are 10:109, 11: 115, 20:130–132, 40:55, 77, and 50:39.

Hindu Mohandas Gandhi put it succinctly with the pairs of opposites: "Overcome hatred by love, lies with truth, and violence with patience."

Some insights on this point are also found in the Christian literature:

> Be patient, then, brothers and sisters, until the Lord's coming. See how the farmer waits for the land to yield its valuable crop, patiently waiting for the autumn and spring rains. You too, be patient and stand firm, because the Lord's coming is near . . . Brothers and sisters, as an example of patience in the face of suffering, take the prophets who spoke in the name of the Lord. As you know, we count as blessed those who have persevered. (New Testament, Letter of James 5:7–8, 10–12)

> Not only so, but we also glory in our sufferings, because we know that suffering produces perseverance; perseverance, character; and character, hope. (New Testament, Letter to the Romans 5:3–4)

Cyprian (ca. 200–258) wrote an entire treatise entitled "On the Advantage of Patience." Paraphrased from a translation of section 15:

> Charity is the bond of brotherhood, the foundation of peace, the holdfast and security of unity, which is greater than both hope and faith, which excels both good works and martyrdoms, which will abide with us always. . . . Take patience away from charity; and deprived of patience, charity does not endure. Take from charity the substance of bearing and of enduring, and it continues with no roots nor strength.

Both Jews and Christians share some insights from the scripture they have in common; for example, "An ill-tempered person stirs up strife, but a patient person allays discord" (Proverbs 15:18).

The virtue of patience directly on countering violence comes from this quote from Buddhist scriptures:

> The fool thinks he has won a battle when he bullies with harsh speech,
> But knowing how to be forbearing—that makes one victorious.
> The worse of the two is he who, when abused, retaliates.

Virtues: Religious Character-Building for Nonviolent Discipline   243

> One who does not retaliate wins a battle hard to win.
> Knowing that the other person is angry, one who remains mindful and calm
> Acts for his own best interest and for the other's interest, too.
> He is a healer of both himself and the other person also.
> He is thought a fool only by those who do not understand the Dharma.
> The greatest prayer is patience. (Dhammapada, Samyutta Nikaya I, 163)

All this is understood to apply to patience while taking action, not to counseling inaction and waiting. When clergy who were sympathetic to the cause of the U.S. Civil Rights Movement of the 1960s nevertheless suggested that a gradual approach through legislation would be better than the tactics of civil disobedience being used, Martin Luther King wrote his powerful *Letter from a Birmingham Jail* (1963), which argued that the situation was far too dire to wait; the people making the suggestion were not the ones suffering the injustice. This may sound like impatience, but actually King was patiently sitting in jail and patiently reasoning with his critics, and remarkably patient in discerning the strategies and tactics that would be most effective. Proposed legislation itself came about more quickly because of the civil disobedience campaigns; the Voting Rights Act, for example, was stalled until the brutal events at Selma, Alabama, in 1965 showed the country that the matter was urgent.

Urgency is not the opposite of patience; both can be done at the same time, and in well-done nonviolent campaigns, they will be. The opposite of patience is impatience, and the danger of impatience is that it will cloud the judgment. This is especially so when there is some sense that violence is a shortcut to the goal and that the use of nonviolence as a principled matter is not so principled because it is delaying the use of violence, which is a shortcut to actually achieving the goal.

Yet history shows many examples when violence was no shortcut at all. The nonviolent uprising of several decades in Burma, for example, switched to the "shortcut" of violence and ended up with several decades of brutal dictatorship, which took more movements of nonviolence to dislodge, a process still ongoing at this writing (see chapter 3). The U.S. Civil War, which went from 1861 to 1865, was reported to have ended slavery with the Emancipation Proclamation of 1863 and the Constitution amended in 1865. Yet some in the South used such systems as debt peonage and loitering laws with the prison system;

loitering laws meant that people were essentially arrested for not having jobs, and put to slave-labor work on chain gangs and plantations. Segregation laws and brutal attacks and lynchings were rampant. This went on for a century, and it took a major set of nonviolent campaigns to dislodge those—in a process that is still ongoing, especially with the structural violence of major economic inequalities and poverty still needing addressing. The U.S. Civil War turned out to be no shortcut at all for the real needs of African Americans, since it embittered rather than reaching the hearts and consciences of those perpetrating the violence and inspired them to find ways to circumvent genuine emancipation.

SHORT COMMENTS ON MORE VIRTUES

- Cooperation—Bruce Banta (1997) discusses the difference between violent and nonviolent societies and draws the conclusion that the biggest predictor for is the difference how much they engage in competition versus cooperation, with cooperation predicting more nonviolence. Of course, nonviolence by definition can involve a great deal of noncooperation, but it still requires that the people within the nonviolent community cooperate with each other. Competition is more of an opposite of cooperation than noncooperation on principle is.
- Service— Rabindranath Tagore (1861–1941) said, "I slept and dreamt that life was joy. I awoke and saw that life was service. I acted and behold, service was joy."
- Self-control—Hindu Yogananda comments on how self-control directly applies to nonviolent action in a commentary on the New Testament Gospels verses of Matthew 5:38–40 and Luke 6:29, with the famous phrase "turn the other cheek":

The ideal of nonretaliation does not justify supine surrender to wrongdoing or tacit approval of evil. To turn the other cheek is not calculated to make a person into a mental or moral weakling, or to suggest enduring an abusive or violent personal relationship, but to instill the strength of self-control gained by overcoming the impulse to act under the influence of revenge. It is an easy reflex to retaliate, but it requires great mental strength not to strike back (Yogananda, 2004, p. 475).

- Courage—as covered in the Introduction, being apathetic or afraid are obstacles to nonviolent action, so courage is required as one of the virtues of nonviolent discipline.

- Providing positive alternatives—This will mainly be covered in chapter 19 on building a nonviolent society.
- Compassion—Clearly needed for principled nonviolence and advocated in all major and most minor religions. Compassion as an attribute of God begins all but one surah in the Qur'an and is called the Bismallah, common in prayers and in Arabic calligraphy artwork. Christian Catholic nun Mother Teresa of Calcutta said in 1985: "Kindness has converted more people than zeal, science or eloquence." The Dalai Lama said: "This is my simple religion. There is no need for temples; no need for complicated philosophy. Our own brain, our own heart is our temple; the philosophy is kindness."
- The Golden Rule—Variations on the ethical principle that one should do to others the way one would like them to do, or the negative version of not doing to others what one finds hateful, are found in practically all religions. It is a rather basic ethical principle and serves as a major foundation for all nonviolence. One delightful tale about this comes from the first century CE in Judaism, when a gentile went to two different well-known rabbis and said he would convert if the rabbi could recite the Torah while he (the gentile) stood on one foot. Rabbi Shammai, known for a tendency to strict legalistic interpretation, chased him away with a stick. But Rabbi Hillel took the challenge. He said "Whatever is hateful to you, do not do to your neighbor. That is the whole of the Torah; all else is commentary. Now go and study."

16

Conflict Transformation

PRINCIPLES OF DEALING WITH CONFLICT

Win or Lose?

Conflicts can be "won" by having one side dominating and the other side losing. They can be resolved by coming to a compromise or the similar idea of making a trade whereby each side gets the thing most important to it by sacrificing something they care about less.

But conflicts can also be a creative time. They can be transformed by coming up with a solution that satisfies everyone. This cannot always be done, but people do well to have the skills needed to know when it can be. With enough creativity, wisdom is built and people may be better off than they were even when there had been no conflict at all. It is the difference between a destructive approach and a constructive approach.

The most basic point of how to transform a conflict is to note the difference between *positions* and *interests*. Positions tend to be more rigid, but when looking at the interests instead, the possibility of finding a solution that can satisfy those becomes more likely. The classic example is a brother and sister who both take the position that they want the one remaining orange. Upon further discussion, they find that the interest of the brother is in eating the inside, while the interest of the sister is having the rind to make marmalade. Once this bit of analysis is clear, the solution is obvious. The interests of both can be satisfied. Because they went beyond positions to actual interests, they were able to find a solution.

A problem comes when conflicts are settled by one side winning or a compromise happening: the material is rearranged, but the underlying interests have not been addressed. The likelihood is high that a rematch will be sought, which means the conflict was never finally resolved at all. It remains ongoing.

As the Taoist scripture puts it:

> If terms to end a quarrel leave a bad feeling, what good are they? Therefore the Sage holds the left tally, and does not put the guilt on the other party. The virtuous person is for patching up; the vicious is for fixing guilt. But the way of Heaven is impartial; it sides only with the good person. (Tao Te Ching, 79: Peace Settlements)

Another translation of the first two lines that also gets the point across well is: "Patching up a great hatred is sure to leave some hatred behind. How can this be regarded as satisfactory?"

In a 1924 book called *Creative Experience*, social psychologist Mary Parker Follett offered the idea that rather than domination or compromise, when the situation allows for it, "integration" means analyzing the desires or intentions of the parties and thereby working out a new solution, with the idea that the new solution will satisfy all. This concept of *integrative solutions* is still a major foundation of current thought on effective conflict resolution.

When it comes to win-or-lose, there are three major types of conflicts. One is "zero-sum": the win achieved by one party is matched by the loss suffered by the other, so that the positive for one is canceled out by the negative for the other and the final score for all involved therefore adds up to zero. This would be true of an election, a lawsuit, or a sports game. The second type is a "mixed motive" conflict, in which both sides could win, or both could lose, or one wins and the other loses. In a pure cooperative, either both win or both lose, so naturally they both take steps to see to it that they both win.

The reason this matters is that strategies and tactics differ. People who believe they are in a zero-sum conflict when they are not can behave in ways contrary to their own interests. Zero-sum conflicts are a lot rarer than many people realize. So, for example, if a brother and sister inherit an acre of land, they can deal with it by having a lawsuit or a coin toss to see who will get the whole thing. They could have a compromise and split it so each gets half. Yet they could also share it as joint owners. There are times when that sharing would never work, but if a brother and sister would have been able to share it, it would be a shame for the two of them to think in zero-sum terms so that one of them must lose or so that both of them end up with less than they could have had if only they had been thinking about the best interests of both.

There are times when a zero-sum approach is needed because one side is unjust and therefore has no legitimate interests to be addressed. If a conflict arises because a bully has been stealing lunch money and the other people do not want their lunch money stolen, the bully could announce as a solution to the problem that people just give him or her the lunch money, and then he or she would not be stealing it any more. Despite the creativity of the proposal, the bully's interest in having other people's lunch money is not legitimate, and therefore resolving the conflict in a nonviolent way involves instead a method of helping the bully to understand that he or she does not have this right and that this is why he or she will not be allowed to exercise it. Yet there may also be deeper issues underlying why the bully wishes to do so that can be addressed, if there is enough communication. "Interests," after all, are not merely about material things; emotions can involve some very deep needs.

On a wider scale, a nonviolent campaign that arises to confront injustices is designed to establish justice and so does not need to consider the other parties' "interest" in domination and illegitimate power. This is not the same as the many conflicts in which both sides (or all sides—there is often more than just two) do have legitimate concerns to be addressed. Still, the campaigners will do well to consider the interests of the parties on the other side; for example, the interest of the police or soldiers when they are afraid of what happens to them and their families if a campaign involving a change in regime is successful.

Conflicts of this kind, which necessarily involve confrontation, will be covered more extensively in chapter 17. Conflicts in which individuals must deal with people who are bullying will be covered later in this chapter. We will now continue with conflicts in which both sides, or all sides, are willing to come to some kind of accommodation with each other, so that having the skills to calmly reason with one another is workable.

Communication and Consultation

In addition to creativity, conflict transformation needs gentleness, consideration, and listening to what the others say. When people listen attentively, understand the others' perspective, and continually check that they are succeeding in doing so, then creative solution becomes more likely. People need to communicate in a way that makes it clear they do understand the others' perspectives—and also that they regard understanding someone else's perspective as important, since we are all worthy of respect. Such skills have been strongly recommended in by most religions for a long time.

This point is among the hardest to remember in the heat of emotional debates. This is why the Quakers have a practice of calling for a moment of silence for reflection when discussions get too heated in their meetings. Any form of prayer or meditation can perform the same function.

The Biblical book of Proverbs addresses the gentle approach to conflicts: "Thoughtless words can wound as deeply as any sword, but wisely spoken words can heal" (Proverbs 12:18); "A gentle answer turns away wrath, but a harsh word stirs up anger" (Proverbs 15:1); "The start of an argument is like the first break in a dam; stop it before it goes any further" (Proverbs 17:14).

A similar point is made in the Christian scripture: "My dear brothers and sisters, take note of this: Everyone should be quick to listen, slow to speak and slow to become angry, because our anger does not produce the righteousness that God desires" (New Testament, James 1:19–20).

In the Qur'an, Surah 42 is called by the Arabic term for "Consultation" or "Deliberation" or "Counsel" after the recommendation to engage in this was made in its verse 38. Qur'anic verses that assert the oneness of humanity and advise seeking harmony among those who differ include 2:213 and 10:19. Another passage that speaks to the Islamic community:

> You who believe! Stand out firmly for God, as witnesses to fair dealing, and let not the hatred of others to you make you swerve to wrong and depart from justice. Be just: that is next to piety. And fear God. For God is well-acquainted with all you do. (Qur'an 5:8)

In a 1996 conflict resolution workshop in the city of Gaza, some the trainers found that a professor from the Islamic university there was among the most enthusiastic participants. The professor articulated his support this way: "those values are often repeated in the weekly preaching in the mosque. Your training workshop is only a way of systematically operationalizing those skills, so they become accessible to all segments of the society" (Abu-Nimer, 2003, p. 87).

While it is certainly possible for atheists and agnostics to participate in dialogue to find creative solutions to problems, as can be seen by the fact that they do so quite a bit, the point that there is a foundation in doing so because of the oneness of humanity that derives from being created from the same divine source is one that is found throughout religions. Czech Christian bishop Jan Amos Comenius (1592–1670) expounds on this point:

> Strife—in philosophy, religion, and politics—has certainly gained so much ground that it is impossible for us to reconcile with one another. But it is possible to find reconciliation . . . by means of the foundation of all things, which is God. For God does not cease to be the same for all people, irrespective of our differences. His earth bears us all, even if we preferred to see that the ground would cleave asunder beneath our enemies.
>
> The sun sends his rays upon us directly, paying no heed that we look askance at one another. The rose smells sweetly to both the Jew and the Christian, and to the Muslim too. And so God is God of all, and whatever he says, he says in the same manner to all that are ready to listen. If then we look to our own rules, books, and works, which we have made ourselves and which differ in many thousands of ways, we are irreconcilable. But if with due attention and honor we accept God's ideas regarding our lives . . . reconciliation is easy.

Nonviolent Communication

Marshall B. Rosenberg (1999) developed what he calls "Nonviolent Communication," and training sessions are offered worldwide (see http://www.cnvc.org). The communication skills involve "power with" rather than "power over," and are intended not merely for confrontational situations but for everyday life and interactions with family, friends, and colleagues. Features include:

- Seeing the difference between observation and evaluation, being able to observe without yet evaluating, and to specify what behaviors and conditions are impacting us;
- Seeing the difference between feeling and thinking, identifying and expressing feelings without implying judgment or blame;
- Ascertaining the universal needs and values that are being met or not met; and
- Putting a request in specific terms about what we do want (rather than what is not wanted), that is, a request rather than a demand, which is done in a compassionate way, taking into account other persons' understandings.

Rosenberg (2004) reflects on the spiritual aspects of the practice by saying that the technique evolved out of spiritual concerns to be practical about love with one another and practical about bringing the social changes we need to see. He has learned from the similar messages in all the major religions that this is "a natural language. Do that which contributes to life" (p. 4).

RESPONDING TO THREATS: CONNECTING AND CHANGING THE SCRIPT

Nonviolence is a third way, because it is neither violence nor cowardice or apathy. In terms of immediately facing dangerous circumstances from individuals who are not in authority (that is, criminals), the option of violence or cowardice is often framed as a "fight-or-flight" reaction. Flight can be a nonviolent reaction if it involves a deliberate strategy of withdrawal. When it is perceived as cowardice, however, then it can no longer be classified as a nonviolent reaction.

Nonviolent approaches include instead *connection* and *changing the script*. Any connecting done automatically changes the script, and if the script is changed, connecting is likely to be involved.

Connection means treating other people as people and reestablishing human interaction, not the kind of disconnection that leads to a violent confrontation—in short, the very essence of compassion and love as taught in all the nonviolence traditions of all the religions.

Changing the script is an assertive way of refusing to cooperate with the violent person's view of how the interaction is supposed to happen. An attacker generally has a script in mind that expects fight-or-flight, or perhaps posturing or submission. If the response is something else, the attacker is at least disconcerted.

A famous example in Buddhism is the Buddha's conversion of the fierce bandit and mass killer Angulimala, who ended up becoming a gentle disciple. Despite warnings of how fierce the bandit was, the Buddha walked into the forest anyway, and according to the *Angulimala Sutta*, he did connect with the bandit as a real person, and certainly changed the script of what the bandit expected.

Buddha speaks in one of the Buddhist texts:

> Phagguna, if anyone were to give you a blow with the hand, or hit you with a clod of earth, or with a stick, or with a sword, even then you should abandon those urges and thoughts which are worldly. There, Phagguna, you should train yourself thus: "Neither shall my mind be affected by this, nor shall I give vent to evil words; but I shall remain full of concern and pity, with a mind of love, and I shall not

give in to hatred." This is how, Phagguna, you should train yourself. (Kakacupama Sutta, Majjhima Nikaya 21)

Carleton Mabee (1970) offers several stories of times when American abolitionists had to deal with mobs. A couple of examples follow, illustrating different methods.

During a riot in New York City in 1834, when pro-slavery mobs were wrecking houses and churches, a friend warned Quaker bookseller Isaac Hopper to take away the display of antislavery books from his shop window. Saying he would not forsake his principles at the bidding of a mob, he walked out onto his steps when the mob came. He stood there calmly looking at the mob. The people in it finally became irresolute and moved on (Mabee, 1970, pp. 29–30).

Lucretia Mott was a petite woman, but she knew what to do when a mob broke up a meeting of the American Anti-Slavery Society in New York. In the confusion, she saw men were roughing up some women and asked the gentleman escorting her to go to their aid. He was worried—who would then take care of her? "This man," she answered. She quietly laid her hand on the arm of one of the rowdiest of the men who were breaking up the meeting. He was astonished, of course—this was way, way off script—but the man replied by conducting her through the mob to safety. The next day, Lucretia Mott returned and found the leader of the mob at a table at a restaurant and connected with him by sitting down to talk with him. She won his respect (Mabee, 1970, p. 31).

"Connection" is, of course, the same thing as is covered earlier in the section on "Communication and Consultation": the most basic point of the interactions needed to treat other human beings as human beings worthy of dignity and respect. Where the other human beings set up a situation to be a violent or potentially violent one, any form of connecting is also a form of changing the script. But "changing the script" also fits the section on "Win or Lose?" discussed earlier, because the original script that people who offer personal violence are following is the win-or-lose script in which they win and their victims lose. Anything that changes this script also changes the win/lose dynamic. In actuality, though it may take time for them to realize it and they may even never gain the insight, when done well, switching the script away from the win-lose and turning it into a win-win is a form of creativity that sees that their legitimate interests are met.

RESTORATIVE JUSTICE

The kind of grand-scale reconciliation efforts of societies recuperating from massive violence will often use the term *restorative justice*. These are covered in chapter 17 about healing. Here we will follow up the previous section on dealing with immediate individual violence to cover what can happen after such violence, mainly street crime, has occurred. This is smaller-scale restorative justice from smaller-scale violence. This form of violence is already against the law and therefore no advocacy for making such violence illegal is needed. Yet, one by one, these acts hurt, injure, and kill a large number of people worldwide, just as war does.

To have a nonviolent approach to violent crime as a social problem is worthy in itself, and transforms the conflict; additionally, any set of people who become skilled at a nonviolent approach here, or see that others are skilled at it, will help the practice of nonviolence grow.

"Retributive" justice, which contrasts with restorative justice, means that offenders get the punishment they are understood to deserve. It is more effective when those offenders are persuaded that they deserve the punishment, but efforts to persuade them of this are often not regarded as a necessary part of the procedure. The focus is on the offender, and the major benefit to the victim is merely to be satisfied that the offender was punished; if there are services for victims, these are added on rather than being an essential part of the process. Retributive justice is for the most part not a problem-solving approach that learns from experience or experiments about what is effective in preventing crime from happening in the future.

"Restorative" justice instead involves both victims and offenders in encounter programs, interactions designed to be a postcrime reconciliation program. Restorative justice emphasizes repairing the harm caused by crime. When victims, offenders and community members meet to decide how to do that, the results can be transformational" (http://www.restorativejustice.org).

Its core values are restitution, reconciliation, and reintegration for all concerned. Mediation, conflict resolution, and the offender engaging in community service projects are common. Victims, offenders, and members of the community take an active role in healing relationships broken by crime. Retribution is replaced by restoration. This benefits the victims and makes the offenders less likely to reoffend.

Juvenile programs are where the idea is most workable, and programs can be expanded to adults when more experience makes them workable. It becomes much more difficult when the charge is murder, and the retributive justice system will normally leave the murderer in jail accordingly, but principles can still apply when parties are willing. There are many such programs in localities around the world, and the United Nations (2006) offers guidelines to this problem-solving approach.

Related is a concept often paired with restorative justice: community policing, in which police take a more problem-solving approach with conflict resolution and prevention skills. It is a proactive rather than a punitive method that is becoming more widespread as empirical evaluation shows its effectiveness. It received more attention in the United States after the cases of police killing of unarmed Black men in 2014–2015 led to much publicity and massive protests; in addition to other merits, community policing may help prevent such lethal events from occurring.

As for the religious insights on this, a book entitled *The Spiritual Roots of Restorative Justice* (Hadley, 2001) has chapters from various religious traditions: aboriginal religion, Buddhism, Chinese philosophy and religion, Christianity, Hinduism, Islam, Judaism, and Sikhism. Buddhism has the tale of the Buddha's encounter with the bandit Angulimala in its origin stories, as mentioned in the previous section, but all of the religions with a nonviolence tradition have traditional beliefs and practices that fit well with programs for restorative justice.

There is quite a bit of literature dealing with specifically Muslim legal theory for restorative justice (Ammar, 2001; Qafisheh, 2012), especially the "qisas" category of crimes in which the victim is allowed to have a say in the sentence. It has therefore been practiced for centuries to have encounters between victims and perpetrators with forgiveness encouraged (Hascall, 2012). Specific countries that were analyzed include Saudi Arabia (Guoping & Garris, 2011), Iran (Rahami, 2007), and Morocco (Marder, 2014). Specific cases that were analyzed include a hate crime based on the September 11 attacks in the United States (Umbreit, Lewis, & Burns, 2003), and an Arab robbery of a Jew in Israel (Umbreit & Ritter, 2006).

17

Campaigns and Active Confrontations

It is clear that as a practical matter, religious facilities are among the most well-developed and therefore best situated to provide structural support for any nonviolent campaign. They provide large buildings that can serve as meeting places to consider tactics and strategy. They can serve as places to hold training sessions, places to have large numbers of people prepare for the bravery need to go out and face confrontations, and places for people to rest and heal after the confrontations. This is practical support.

They also provide good training in terms of the practices offered, and they can do this for years as a matter of ordinary life before any major social confrontation is in the planning stage. There are prayers, contemplation, and meditation and other ways of thinking things through calmly. There is self-discipline in habits and in getting along with others in a group. There are virtues such as compassion and patience. A great deal of successful nonviolent work involves remaining very calm, steady, and able to quickly think creatively. When dramatic circumstances arise, years of cultivating all of this will serve as crucial preparation. While such characteristics can be deliberately cultivated in the short term if need be, and training sessions are made available to do so, they will work in a more stable way if they are long-standing habits.

As we cover in more detail in the following, religions that are practicing their nonviolence traditions also provide the philosophical underpinnings that help make campaigns successful. When a religion is neither itself acting as an oppressive authority, nor being supportive of another oppressive authority, it can then be an *alternative* authority. This can have profound implications for the dynamics of the situation.

A religion can also provide support for smaller acts of witness when a large campaign is not in the offing.

In the final section of this chapter, we will offer insight on the historical case that most troubles people of good will when they are thinking about the effectiveness of using nonviolence: the intense brutality of the Nazis.

PHILOSOPHICAL FOUNDATIONS FOR THE POWER OF NONVIOLENCE

How Power Works

If power is something that only people with guns can have, then nonviolence would never work. But there are several conundrums with this. The people with the guns have to be willing to all cooperate with the entity giving them commands. The gun-holders cannot decide to change sides, and they cannot decide to simply put the guns down and go home. The people at whom the guns are pointed must remain cowed. Since keeping guns pointed at all people continually at all times is hardly practical, it becomes clear that true power relies on people cooperating with the government or other purveyors of violence.

Naturally, such cooperation is expected when the government is actually a good one doing its job well. Then that government is seen as legitimate and therefore people wish to cooperate. At other times, people may not feel so but nevertheless cooperate because they are afraid, or because they do not really care. Yet when an institution is corrupt and people are no longer willing to tolerate it, that is when People Power happens.

In 1548, at the age of 18, Etienne de la Boétie (1530–1563) wrote an essay in French called *Discourse de la Servitude Volontaire*, which means "Discussion of Voluntary Servitude." Three hundred years later, it greatly influenced Henry David Thoreau in America and Leo Tolstoy in Russia. Through them the idea spread to Gandhi and others. This quote shows the most basic understanding of why nonviolent action works:

> Obviously there is no need of fighting to overcome this single tyrant, for he is automatically defeated if the country refuses consent to its own enslavement. It is not necessary to deprive him of anything, but simply to give him nothing. . . . Everyone knows that the fire from a little spark will increase and blaze ever higher as long as it finds wood to burn; yet without being quenched by water, but merely by

finding no more fuel to feed on, it consumes itself, dies down, and is no longer in flame. Similarly, the more tyrants pillage, the more they crave, the more they ruin and destroy; the more one yields to them, and obeys them, by that much do they become mightier and more formidable, the readier to annihilate and destroy. But if not one thing is yielded to them, if without any violence they are simply not obeyed, they become naked and undone and as nothing, just as when the root receives no nourishment, the branch withers and dies . . . don't support the tyrant, and you will see him like a great colossus whose base has been stolen, of his own weight sink to the ground and shatter. (de la Boétie, 1548)

Quaker Jonathan Dymond in 1824 gave a clear exposition of noncooperation in a book entitled *An Inquiry into the Accordancy of War with the Principles of Christianity* (in which he concludes war is *not* in accordancy):

The public, therefore, whenever a war is designed, should diligently inquire into the motives of engaging in it . . . if they do not see it, should refuse to be led, blindfold, to murder their neighbors. . . . A people have the power of prevention, and they ought to exercise it. Let me not, however, be charged with recommending violence or resistance. The power of preventing war consists in the power of *refusing to take part in it* . . . as it is the most Christian method, so, as it respects war, it were certainly the most efficacious; for it is obvious that war cannot be carried on without the co-operation of the people. (Dymond, 1824, pp. 26–27)

This insight is also found in the *Tao Te Ching*, part of chapter 39:

Without the ennobling power, the princes and dukes would stumble. Therefore the nobility depend upon the common person for support, and the exalted ones depend upon the lowly for their base.
   That is why the princes and dukes call themselves "the orphaned," "the lonely one," "the unworthy." Is it not true then that they depend upon the common person for support? Truly, take down the parts of a chariot, and there is no chariot left.

This is not magic. Getting large numbers of people in agreement on how to go about noncooperating is difficult enough in free-speech democracies, and even more under conditions where such coordination is deliberately made difficult by the very oppression which is being opposed. Just as violence does not achieve its goals simply by being applied, but requires well-thought-out tactics and strategies suited to the specific circumstances, and a great deal of training, so do nonviolent campaigns.

Most importantly, knowing the truth about what is happening and enabling others to see it is crucial to the success of inducing large numbers of people to noncooperate. It is also indispensable in getting onlookers and people outside the conflict, including people from other nations, to be supportive. Documenting the case with integrity is usually the first step.

A Gentle Answer

If cooperation is required for power, and noncooperation takes it away, it is still true that noncooperation can be done with great animosity, sarcasm, and demonizing of opponents. This will still work on many occasions, but there will be many cases when this attitude badly interferes with the ability to be successful. It makes the opponents dig in their heels, depriving the campaign of one major road to success. It disenchants onlookers, whose reaction can be make-or-break for any campaign. Harsh rhetoric may be *not*-violent, but it does not fit the understanding of *non*violent, in that it is often less effective at actually *countering* violence.

"A gentle answer turns away wrath, but a harsh word stirs up anger" (Bible, Proverbs, 15:1). From the same book: "If your enemies are hungry, feed them; if they are thirsty, give them a drink. You will make them burn with shame, and the Lord will reward you" (Proverbs 25:21–22, Good News version). The power of persuasion, so foundational to nonviolent action, includes the use of kindness, listening to opponents, treating them as human beings and not demonizing them. "You have heard that it was said, 'Love your neighbor and hate your enemy.' But I tell you: Love your enemies and pray for those who persecute you" (New Testament, Matthew 5:43–44; see also Romans 12:14–21).

For a similar sentiment in Buddhism: "Hatreds do not cease in this world by hating, but by love, overcoming evil by good. Overcome the miser by giving, overcome the liar by truth" (Dhammapada 1.5, 17.3). Buddhist monk Thich Nhat Hanh, commenting on the New Testament passage from Matthew cited in the previous paragraph, in a way that sounds like he is contradicting the point but is actually supporting and expanding on it when he says, "To love our enemy is impossible. The moment we understand our enemy, we feel compassion towards him [or her], and he [or she] is no longer our enemy" (Hanh, 1995. p. 5).

The *Tao Te Ching* makes the point in part of Chapter 68:

The best warriors do not use violence
Nor is the best soldier a fellow hot to fight.
The greatest victor wins without a battle:
He who overcomes people understands them.
There is a quality of quietness
Which quickens people by no stress:
"Fellowship with heaven," as of old,
Is fellowship with people and keeps its hold.

This Qur'an verse is popular on protest signs of Muslim nonviolent campaigns: "Nor can goodness and Evil be equal. Repel evil with good and, lo, between whom and you there was enmity will become your warm friend (41:34).

Quaker founder George Fox said in 1625: "The peacemaker hath the Kingdom and is in it; and hath the dominion over the peace-breaker, to calm him in the power of God." Jonathan Dymond, quoted earlier, further explains the point:

There is, indeed, something in the calmness of reason—in an endeavor to convince rather than to intimidate—in an honest solicitude for friendliness and peace, which obtains, which commands, which extorts forbearance and esteem. This is the privilege of rectitude and truth. It is an inherent quality of their nature: an evidence of their identity with perfect wisdom. I believe, therefore, that even as it concerns our *interests*, moderation and forbearance would be the most politic. (Dymond, 1824, pp. 17–18)

Hindu Mohandas Gandhi, naturally, had quite a bit to say on this topic. A sample:

- "The hardest heart and the grossest ignorance must disappear before the rising sun of suffering without anger and without malice."
- "Democracy and violence can ill go together. Evolution of democracy is not possible if we are not prepared to hear the other side."
- "It is easy enough to be friendly to one's friends. But to befriend the one who regards himself as your enemy is the quintessence of true religion. The other is mere business."
- "What kind of victory is it when someone is left defeated?"

From Christian minister Martin Luther King Jr.:

> Compassion and nonviolence help us to see the enemy's point of view, to hear their questions, to know their assessment of ourselves. For from their point of view we may indeed see the basic weaknesses of our own condition, and if we are mature, we may learn and grow and profit from the wisdom of the brothers and sisters who are called the opposition.

Muslim Malala Yousafzai (who later won the Nobel Peace Prize in 2014) spoke at length on this point at her July 10, 2013, address to the United Nations General Assembly, in which she not only showed her personal experience and firm resolve but also connected it to many of the nonviolent religious traditions:

> Dear friends, on 9 October 2012, the Taliban shot me on the left side of my forehead. They shot my friends, too. They thought that the bullets would silence us, but they failed. And out of that silence came thousands of voices. The terrorists thought they would change my aims and stop my ambitions. But nothing changed in my life except this: weakness, fear and hopelessness died. Strength, power and courage was born. . . . I want education for the sons and daughters of the Taliban and all the terrorists and extremists. I do not even hate the Talib who shot me. Even if there was a gun in my hand and he was standing in front of me, I would not shoot him. This is the compassion I have learned from Mohamed, the prophet of mercy, Jesus Christ and Lord Buddha. This is the legacy of change I have inherited from Martin Luther King, Nelson Mandela and Mohammed Ali Jinnah. This is the philosophy of nonviolence that I have learned from Gandhi, Bacha [Badshah] Khan and Mother Teresa.

This is a truly radical (that is, down-to-the-root) way of establishing effective nonviolent campaigns. In addition to the religious assertions of this being the right thing to do, it will also make campaigns more likely to succeed, more likely to take less time to succeed, and to lead to a more permanent solution. The technique removes obstacles and melts hardness in opponents. It also invites much greater participation from the wider community of people whose support is crucial to any long-lasting success.

RELIGIOUS INSTITUTIONS AND AUTHORITY

The Milgram electroshock experiments were a way of testing under laboratory conditions how people will comply with destructive demands of authority. A man in a white lab coat would insist that the participant, as a "teacher," continue administering higher and higher levels of shock when the unseen but clearly heard "learner" got wrong answers, which happened constantly. The experiments found that around two-thirds of people would continue from small to large electroshocks at the behest of the authoritative man in the white lab coat, despite signs of harming another human being (though this was a sham). While only so much can be found in the artificial confines of a laboratory, these do offer some insights that apply to the real world and the role of religious institutions in it.

There were many variations of the design which showed under what conditions people were less likely to comply. For example, fewer people complied when the authority phoned in the orders rather than being face-to-face, allowing for "cheating." This is what happens under dictatorships when people are unwatched.

Of particular interest was when there were two different authorities—two different men in white lab coats, both of which had power over the experiment. The two of them argued over whether to continue up the scale of electroshocks, and the one who wanted to continue gave the instructions. *No one* kept going to the top. Most stopped immediately, with a few stragglers that stopped soon thereafter.

This can apply to situations in which a country has a major religious institution that holds the loyalty of the majority of the population. If a point comes when the leadership of that institution argues with the government, then the population has two authorities to consider, two clashing authorities. For example, the Catholic Church was prominent in the 1986 People Power revolution in the Philippines. Buddhist monks took the lead in a nonviolent uprising against the dictatorship in Myanmar/Burma in the Saffron Revolution of 2007.

When the ability to mobilize large numbers is necessary for noncooperation, religious institutions are often prominent in their ability to do so in practical terms. But they also have the advantage of being another authority, and so beyond merely mobilizing, they interfere with the dynamic of having the oppressive authority being the only authority.

Another variation in the Milgram electroshock experiments was when participants saw the same experiment apparently going on across a large room. In actuality, these were actors putting on a show. They presented someone in the role of a teacher, the same role as the experimental participant observing them, rebelling and refusing to comply. Given this example in front of them, only one in ten continued giving the electroshocks up to the top.

In other words, when people are already uncomfortable with a situation and not sure how to respond, seeing others responding in a way that makes sense to them serves as a model. A situation that had over two-thirds compliance dropped down to one-tenth simply with a model of noncompliance readily available. A situation where people seem to be conforming to oppression can suddenly switch to huge rallies as people see that there is a rally to join. Religious institutions, of whichever religion is prominent in the area, excel at providing models of behavior and are therefore well positioned to set the stage for noncompliance if this is what they wish to do.

THE POWER OF A SMALL GROUP

If a large mass of people refuse to cooperate, this is a social movement. What happens if there is only one person refusing to cooperate? Only a handful of people holding up protest signs, just a few who are willing to rebel in any fashion? When only a small number of people are engaged in nonviolent confrontation, there are still at least two things they can achieve for the society.

The first is the obvious point that large movements do not generally appear full-blown, any more than large-scale violence does. The same dynamic applies: it starts small and grows. While actions of a few may or may not lead to a large movement, a large movement does not come into being without first having been the actions of a few. In terms of the electroshock experiments mentioned before, just one small model of noncompliance can make a difference.

The second is what happens when the nonviolent protest remains small—it was nevertheless still there. Violent institutions commonly have the psychological problem that any dissent at all is not to be tolerated. When war fever is high, there may be very few willing to go against the prevailing hysteria—but as long as there are any at all, then war fever has failed to be entirely total. John Noonan comments on this phenomenon with the slaveholders of the American South before the U.S. Civil War, after detailing some actions they took that were not sensible from the point of view of achieving their own aims, such as the Fugitive Slave Act that had Northerners seeing people hauled off in chains so that those Northerners were aghast:

> Why did the slave-holders act as if driven by the Furies to their own destruction? . . . Why did they take such risks, why did they persist beyond prudent calculation? The answer must be that in a moral

question of this kind, turning on basic concepts of humanity, you cannot be content that your critics are feeble and ineffective, you cannot be content with their practical tolerance of your activities. You want, in a sense you need, actual acceptance, open approval. If you cannot convert your critics by argument, at least by law you can make them recognize that your course is the course of the country. (Noonan, 1979, p. 82)

Therefore, when no dissent is allowed, dissent that happens despite this achieves at the very least an ability to keep the belligerent people from having the total approval they crave.

Yet when most of a society agrees with a form of violence, going against the societal unity can be very difficult. History shows that the people who succeed in doing so will most commonly have strong roots in spiritual practices and religious institutions. Even when the full contemporary institutions do not support them, they are nourished by the religious traditions.

Conscientious objection can take place when anyone is legally required to do anything that is against their principles, most commonly violent things. Throughout history and all over the world, there have been people who were conscientious objectors to the military draft. There have also been people who refused to cooperate, whether for reasons of conscience or for their own safety; conscientious objection generally implies making a public show of the objection and perhaps going to jail or being otherwise punished.

In recent years, U.S. law has allowed "conscientious objector status" to be legally granted to people from strong peace traditions—Quakers, Mennonites, members of the Church of the Brethren, and Hopis, and occasionally people who can otherwise make an individual case for themselves. These people will usually do an alternative form of service, often one that is every bit as dangerous. Yet there are still draft resisters who refuse to register at all, on the grounds that they want to engage in more thorough noncooperation.

There has also been conscientious objection by medical people required to participate in abortions. For example, in the United States, the law protecting objection was held not to give individuals a right to sue, so a nurse who had been threatened if she did not participate in a late-term abortion had no legal recourse (Boniello, 2009). In Scotland, midwives lost in the lower courts, later won the right to object in higher courts, but finally lost in the highest court (Brooks, 2014). In Croatia, the legal protection for doctors and nurses was initially held not to apply to midwives, though a media campaign led to this being reversed (Dalmacija, 2013). In Sweden, a nurse took her case to the European Council (O'Brien, 2014). In Australia, a doctor was in danger of losing his license for refusing to perform a sex-selection late-term abortion or referring the mother to someone who would (Gye, 2013). The response has been similar to that given to draft resisters. Insisting that specific individuals must be required to participate in something against their consciences would seem to be an easy enough thing to avoid doing if there are only a few. Yet it is insisted on all the same, because not doing so requires people to admit that there is such a thing as people resisting due to conscience, and they cannot abide the idea.

As a final point, the violence against those who object to any form of injustice also frequently goes beyond jailing or unemployment and can be lethal. When people are killed, they become martyrs, which is a religious term for a common religious phenomenon. Soren Kierkegaard once remarked that when tyrants die, their rule ends, but when martyrs die, their rule begins.

WHAT ABOUT THE NAZIS?

The astonishing brutality of the Nazi regime in Germany from 1933 to 1945 has left many people with the understanding that while war may ordinarily be something to be avoided, it could not be avoided here. The damage was far too great to do anything other than to fight it militarily. This is a case that comes up most commonly as a challenge to the idea that nonviolence is effective. One could not fast and pray and expect it to impress such a monstrous entity. No chances could be taken.

This view is one that sees violence as a last resort, a common feature of any just war doctrine from any of the religions. The problem is that making it a "last resort" implies that it is a resort at all. It assumes effectiveness for violence, so that the reason for holding off on using it is only ethical, not a question of effectiveness.

Ascertaining the effectiveness of violence is often on far lower standards than those applied to nonviolent action. In this case, if a nonviolent campaign only succeeded in its goal after tens of millions were dead and whole cities destroyed, it would have a difficult time declaring itself effective. Yet that is what "victory" in the World War II meant. The war was held to a different standard than any nonviolent campaigns could ever muster.

However, this is a case where we can compare nonviolence and violence, setting aside the question of which is ethical and looking entirely at the question of which is more effective. In the case of stopping the Nazis, after all, what would be most effective *is* what is most ethical.

It is worthwhile to consider this lone case specifically as an excellent exercise in understanding the history and principles of nonviolence in other contexts as well. We need to understand how it functions in the worst of situations to have the best understanding of how it works at all.

The Nonviolence That Was Not Tried

While it took some time to realize that the Nazis were as bad as they were—the world is filled, after all, with governments that say outrageous things—and the 1935 laws that stripped Jews of citizenship in Germany were one of many concerns, it was on the night of November 9–10, 1938, that the fact that Jews were in great danger was made very clear. This was called Kristallnacht, the Night of Broken Glass, as hundreds of synagogues and thousands of businesses were attacked with sledgehammers and a few people were killed. The coverage around the world did show that people were shocked.

One of the actions to take to both protect people directly and to protest in the strongest possible terms was for countries to take in Jewish immigrants. U.S. President Franklin Roosevelt asked Congress to allow those already in the United States on visas to stay since it would be inhuman to return them—but he did not ask for the quota to be raised, so no more could come in. On May 13, 1939, the transatlantic liner St. Louis, including 937 passengers, mostly Jewish refugees, set sail from Hamburg with permission to land in Cuba. But the permission was revoked after they set sail, and all but 28 were denied entry. They begged for entry as they passed Miami and were denied. Most were sent back to Nazi Germany. Brazil actually added for its immigrants a requirement of a baptismal certificate dated before 1933.

Hitler did offer to let all the Jews under German control leave, if other countries would take them in, at the international Evian Conference held in France on July 6–15, 1938. The countries refused to expand their immigration quotas.

Hitler gloated:

> It is a shameful spectacle to see how the whole democratic world is oozing sympathy for the poor tormented Jewish people, but remains hard hearted and obdurate when it comes to helping them—which is surely, in view of its attitude, an obvious duty. The arguments that

are brought up as an excuse for not helping them actually speak for us Germans and Italians. (Baynes, 1942, p. 737)

Hitler understood the reaction of the international community as bolstering his case.

The question of whether nonviolence works with someone as vicious as the Nazis runs up first against this basic point: at the beginning, when the problem was clear enough but the slippery slope had not yet gotten past a few dozen people killed, it clearly should have been tried in the form of simple basic legislation and decency. While many people did try and did help, the response as a whole badly failed the level needed.

The Nonviolence That Was Tried

Yet nonviolence did serve to save the lives of thousands of Jews. Up until the war ended, it had a much better track record than any military techniques did. The underground railroad of a loose network of individuals hiding Jews or getting them to safety saved thousands of lives. Additionally, mass movements saved thousands more, as well as keeping the Nazis from taking full control with their military might.

Danes woke up on the morning of April 9, 1940, to find the Nazis had conquered their country. Not much could be done militarily against the huge German army, but a Freedom Council was organized. Though there was some sabotage, the Council found through experience that massive nonviolence worked better. When launching strikes brought more bloody action from the Germans, workers would go to work but then leave early, claiming they needed to tend to their gardens since the Nazi curfew did not leave them enough time. Many books and newspapers the Nazis declared illegal nevertheless got distributed secretly and widely.

The most dramatic and clearly successful part of resisting the Nazis was the rescue of Danish Jews. The Nazis knew that Jews were likely to all be home for Rosh Hashanah. They arranged to start arrests at 10 P.M. that Friday night, October 1, on into Saturday morning. But Danes got a warning that this was the plan. They sent word around so quickly that all the Jews went into hiding in other people's homes, hospitals, and other places.

So a German order on October 2 said that all non-Jews were required to turn Jews over to the authorities. Organizers knew it would not be safe to continue hiding them. They decided to send the Jews across the lake to Sweden, where the Nazis had not yet reached. During the night, about 7,200 people, almost all the Jews of Denmark, were smuggled onto anything that would float. They all made it safely to the Swedish shore.

Then word came that the Swedish king, being afraid of the Nazis, was refusing to give asylum.

But a famous Danish physicist with Jewish ancestry had previously sneaked into Sweden with his family—Neils Bohr, winner of the 1922 Nobel Prize for Physics. He sent word to the king that if the refugees were turned in to the Nazis, he would turn himself in with them. The king immediately allowed the refugees in.

The Nazis had tried hard to keep the planned grab of Jews secret so it could go smoothly, but Danes were tipped off by the Nazi naval attaché, Georg Duckwitz. This is one of many instances in which lives were saved when consciences were reached among the very people who were supposed to carry out the brutal orders.

The Bulgarian king and Parliament, on the other hand, went along with the Nazis, and offered a "Law in Defense of the Nation" that would basically outlaw Jews. The Bulgarian Orthodox Church and a large number of Bulgarians flooded them with letters not to pass it, but they did nevertheless. On January 21, 1941, it became the royal decree, starting the steps of dehumanizing the Jews with restrictions. Then came the plan to deport Jews. On May 24, 1943, there was a huge demonstration in support of those Jews who lived inside Bulgaria. It began with a rally at a synagogue in the capital city of Sofia, and then a large march that was meant to join with a march by students. It got broken up by clashes with the police, but government officials were alarmed enough that the deportations of those 8,000 never happened. The cattle cars remained empty, and further plans for more deportations were stopped. The saving of so many of the Bulgarian Jews was a massive nonviolent action by the Bulgarian people.

Nonviolence in defense of Jews also occurred in the very heart of the Nazi empire. Rosenstrasse was the name of the street in Berlin where this remarkably effective protest happened. Here is the story told by one of the Jewish men who was saved, with his wife being one of the non-Jewish women who acted:

> The Gestapo were preparing for large-scale action. Columns of covered trucks were drawn up at the gates of factories and stood in front of private houses. All day long they rolled through the streets, escorted by armed SS men . . . heavy vehicles under

whose covers could be discerned the outlines of closely packed humanity. . . .

People lowered their eyes, some with indifference, others perhaps with a fleeting sense of horror and shame. The day wore on, there was a war to be won. . . . And the public eye missed the flickering of a tiny torch which might have kindled the fire of general resistance to despotism. From the vast collecting centers to which the Jews of Berlin had been taken, the Gestapo sorted out those with "Aryan kin" and concentrated them in a separate prison in the Rosenstrasse. No one knew what was to happen to them.

At this point the wives stepped in. Already by the early hours of the next day they had discovered the whereabouts of their husbands and as by common consent, as if they had been summoned, a crowd of them appeared at the gate of the improvised detention center. In vain the security police tried to turn away the demonstrators, some 6,000 of them, and to disperse them. Again and again they massed together, advanced, called for their husbands, who despite strict instruction to the contrary showed themselves at the windows, and demanded their release.

For a few hours the routine of a working day interrupted the demonstrations, but in the afternoon the square was again crammed with people, and the demanding, accusing cries of the women rose above the noise of the traffic like passionate avowals of a love strengthened by the bitterness of life.

Gestapo headquarters was situated in the Burgstrasse, not far from the square where the demonstration was taking place. A few salvoes from a machine gun could have wiped the women off the square, but the SS did not fire, not this time. Scared by an incident which had no equal in the history of the Third Reich, headquarters consented to negotiate. They spoke soothingly, gave assurances, and finally released the prisoners. (Ullstein, 1961, pp. 338–340)

Letting the men go was not just a trick. Most of the men were found to still be alive at the end of the war (Stoltzfus, 1996). A dramatization of this event is offered in a movie available on video entitled *Rosenstrasse*.

Several quotations tell us that Hitler and other Nazis held the idea of power on which nonviolent action is based. They understood that power was not something people hold in their hands or can grab by force. It comes because other people decide to give it to them. Hitler said in *Mein Kampf* (Part II, chapter 9): "The first foundation for the creation of authority is always provided by popularity." Goebbels said that the regime "will not be content with 52 percent [of the people] behind it and with terrorizing the remaining 48 percent, but will see its most immediate task as being to win over that remaining 48 percent" (Stotzfus, 1996, p. 7).

Ironically, Hitler even said, "a National Socialist, as a means of exercising power, has a duty to disobey those in authority who are unworthy of power" (Stotzfus, 1996, p. 8). The fact that the Rosenstrasse protest was so successful this one time, in the heat of the war, shows the potential of what could have been if it had been widespread. It succeeded in part because the Nazis, as brutal as they were, did not want to spark any more resistance in the heart of Berlin.

Norway, on the other hand, did not do well by its roughly 2,000 Jews, yet they did show what can happen when the population resists takeover. The Nazis invaded Norway in 1940 and appointed Vidkun Quisling as head of government. Quisling decided that to set up the Corporate State, he would start with schoolteachers, who were required to join the Nazi-inspired teachers' organization and teach Nazi views to children. Of 12,000 teachers in the country, around 8,000 to 10,000 refused to join. They were so well organized that they did so by sending a statement concluding "I declare that I cannot take part in the new teachers' organization," signing their names, and all putting it in the mail on February 20, 1942.

The government tried closing the schools for a month on a claim that there was not enough fuel. This "fuel holiday" only fueled the opposition; fuel was wood and wood was plentiful. The Nazis could not arrest all the teachers, but they could arrest some—around 1,000 men (no women). Though they were treated brutally, they were all together. Very few broke down to the demand to sign a statement. About 500 were later shipped up north to very harsh weather by train. As the train passed the stations, groups of schoolchildren gathered and sang to them as they passed to show support.

With other strikes and noncooperation, Quisling never was able to take over. He said as much to a group of 20 teachers at Stabekk High School on May 22, 1942. In an outburst of frustration that could be heard clearly outside the building, he said, "You teachers have destroyed everything for me!" This remark passed around among the teachers quickly and cheered them up.

Only a few teachers signed the statement in order to be sent back home, mostly teachers approved by the rest of the group because they were ill. The remaining teachers were allowed to go home by November without having signed anything. On their way home, they were welcomed with flowers and free lodging at the best hotels. Hitler himself called off the project of setting up the Corporate State when he saw it would not work (Sharp, 2005, pp. 135–141).

Nonviolence vs. Violence

We cannot rerun history to see if an entirely nonviolent approach would have worked—but then, if people were acquainted with and inclined to use nonviolence at the time, the entire situation would have been different. To stop the Nazis *before* horrendous damage was done, *only* nonviolence would have worked. It was not sufficiently tried.

We do know that the military approach did not stop the Nazis until after incredible damage had already been done, with millions dead. The one military attempt to help the Jews while the war still raged was on August 24, 1944, with a bombing near Buchenwald concentration camp. The technical conditions were perfect, yet around 315 prisoners were killed, 525 seriously injured, and another 900 lightly injured (Kitchens, 1996, p. 197). Initial ideas that bombing around the death camps might be helpful reversed as people realized that the bombs themselves would likely kill Jews. The bombing also gave the Nazis the pretext of saying it was the bombing that killed the Jews rather than the Nazis themselves. Up until 1945, nonviolent action had a far better success rate of saving Jews and other targeted groups.

History is not a repeatable experiment and so we cannot say what would have happened in the event that people had behaved differently from how they did. What we do know, however, is that nonviolent action was tried, both for saving Jews and resisting occupation, and was actually successful in achieving its short-term goals. Just as we cannot know what would have happened without the violence of the war, we cannot know what would have happened without nonviolent action. It was not absent, and so the impact of its possible absence is every bit as unknowable. Conjecture that more of it would have been helpful is reasonable based on the experience of what we know did occur.

We also know that, even after all this horrific violence, the cycle of violence was stopped. Unlike World War I leading directly to World War II, Europe achieved a far more lasting state of avoiding war. This was due to several factors, including deliberate work to stop it from happening again through institutions such as the United Nations and agreements such as the Universal Declaration of Human Rights.

But we do also need to take into account that there was a huge postwar nonviolent campaign in the continent of Europe, one that was highly unusual for being run by a government rather than a people's movement. It was called the Marshall Plan. People who were still relatively affluent helped their former enemies in a massive way with food and rebuilding and otherwise meeting needs. This vast nonviolent campaign had a major impact on developments that made the defeat of the Nazis all the more thorough, and their arising again so unlikely as to be the removal of that threat. For the Nazi chapter in human history, treating what had been enemies as human beings and offering desperately needed assistance were what had the final word.

18

Coping and Healing

STRESS REDUCTION

When people are oppressed by violence, this is a major stress. Features that necessarily accompany violence include being given messages of being inferior, and this is a further source of stress. Therefore, the first positive point is that taking action with the nonviolent traditions of religion can lead to much-needed relief.

Howard Thurman, an early activist in the U.S. Civil Rights Movement who traveled to India to see firsthand how nonviolent campaigns are done, comments on this in regard to those people who had been enslaved:

> During the years of slavery in America it is said that after a hard day's work the slaves would often hold secret religious meetings. All during the working day they were addressed with unnecessary vituperations and insulting epithets. But as they gathered in these meetings they gained a renewed faith as the old unlettered minister would come to his triumphant climax saying: "you—you are not niggers. You—you are not slaves. You are God's children." This established for them a true ground of personal dignity. The awareness of being a child of God tends to stabilize the ego and bring new courage. (Thurman, 1949/1996, pp. 49–50)

This was at a time when fleeing in the Underground Railroad was the major nonviolent action option open to enslaved people; open confrontation was not workable in circumstances where even minor nonconfrontational infractions, or no infractions at all, are treated with draconian violence. Yet they neither have to engage in the danger of fleeing nor wait until the opportunity to flee came in order to gain the benefit of buffering the violence with counterviolence in the form of firm nonviolent religious principles.

When slavery was over but the "unnecessary vituperations and insulting epithets" continued along with segregation and other brutalities, the Civil Rights Movement allowed for nonviolent action to be out in the open and aimed at the entire society, rather than secret meetings held only to alleviate some of the stress for the victims. Rev. Martin Luther King Jr. noticed the stress-reduction effects after the year of the Montgomery Bus Boycott in the city of Montgomery, Alabama:

> Although the intense solidarity of the protest year has inevitably attenuated, there is still a feeling of closeness among the various classes and ages and religious denominations that was never present before. The increased self-respect of even the least sophisticated Negroes in Montgomery is evident in the way they dress and walk, in new standards of cleanliness and of general deportment. . . . There has been a decline in heavy drinking. Statistics on crime and divorce indicate that both are on the wane. (King, 1958, p. 187)

In addition, there are many religious practices that are designed for the very purpose of leading to calming people down: praying, meditation and contemplation, using rosaries and prayer beads, lighting candles, singing, doing liturgies in a group (whether quiet and dignified or loud and joyful), fellowship with others, and pastoral counseling. These are not only good stress reducers for everyday concerns but also especially crucial to those involved in high-stress activities that require courage. As Phillip Yancey put it: "For activists on the front lines, prayer serves as part oasis and part emergency room (Yancey, 2006, p. 128).

BURNOUT

Anyone who engages in any activity for human betterment needs to be aware of the psychological danger of burnout and be aware of how to recognize it and how to fix it. All the stress-reduction techniques just mentioned before apply to both prevention and treatment of burnout, but there is more.

Burnout has three components. The primary component, the one that serves as the flashing red light that indicates attention is needed, the one that most people associate with burnout, is emotional exhaustion. People feeling overwhelmed. This can lead to the second component of depersonalization. This is a feeling of being detached and callous. With uncaring actions ensuing, the third component is a feeling of reduced personal accomplishment. This is exacerbated if there is no positive feedback from others or from the situation. If too much is asked of people over an extended period of time, and too little is given to them, the problem gets worse. Burnout feels terrible, and it also interferes with the ability to do the work that helped to cause it.

Christina Maslach (1982; Leiter & Maslach, 2005) has studied burnout at length and offers several ways to avoid and cope with it. The first is to think in terms of working smarter as opposed to working harder. There are several ways to do this.

One is to set steps that are well defined and realistic. That way, when those specific things are done, progress is clear. Have daily or weekly or monthly accomplishments that can reasonably be done in a day or a week or a month.

Another way is to do the same thing differently. Find what can be varied and experiment with what is effective. Make choices rather than merely following directions. Changes might upon occasion also turn out to be improvements, and if not, the very fact of being changes has meant they have served their purpose when they are dispensed with.

An obvious way to work smarter is to take a break from the work. Besides relaxing, this gives an opportunity to get some psychological distance, and see things in perspective. All religions have the point of taking a perspective outside of the individual ego, and it can be crucial to get away from tasks that are necessarily ego-focused in order to get things done. Taking time out to meditate or pray or go to a religious service where other people are talking of other topics does not really take time away from the work. To the contrary, it is adding to the work, because it is making it more effective in the long run.

Similar to a full-fledged break is the idea of taking a "downshift." This is still doing work, but other aspects of work, ones that do not require the same level of intensity—sweeping the floor, organizing files, things of that kind. These downshifts can be scheduled, or they can be taken when a person starts to feel overwhelmed. They can have the same effect as a break in terms of lessening intensity of that which could lead to burnout. Yet because they still involve getting needed work done, they help with the sense of accomplishment and can be done more frequently. Doing low-priority work is not a way of procrastinating the high-priority work, but instead is another way of working smarter and thereby being more accomplished in both.

Pay special attention to minor accomplishments, not merely major ones. Minor ones are more frequent and more available to be admired. Indeed, before major goals are achieved, the minor achievements are all that are available to be admired. Major goals of nonviolence come only now and then, but minor ones come constantly. The religious mind that stands in awe of the beauty of a single flower and is filled with gratitude knows that minor achievements can still have cosmic significance.

In addition to strategies of working smarter, another way to avoid burnout is taking good care of one's self. The best way to help others and to keep any kind of needed work going is to be in good shape. Get plenty of sleep, eat well, exercise.

This includes accentuating the positive, because finding the good makes the bad seem less overwhelming. People working together can complement each other and otherwise give positive feedback where appropriate. Lack of positive feedback is a major cause of burnout, so even small amounts can be markedly effective in prevention.

The skills of sharing a joke or having an interesting conversation, engaging in small talk—again, all these things are not taking time away from important work, but rather are ways of making the work more effective. They may be irrelevant to the problems being worked on, but they help people manage. As mentioned in chapter 15, humor is especially important. It helps to see the bright side and lift spirits.

Finally, Maslach suggests that people need to know themselves and be in tune to inner feelings. Individuals need to use the relaxation techniques known to work best for them specifically, since people differ in what works best for them.

While psychologists are thinking of burnout in scientific and therapeutic terms, another way of looking at burnout is religious: if the work itself becomes an idol, becomes a god to be worshipped, or if one is overly attached materially to the fruit of the work. Since the work is normally understood as being in the service of God, that being the same thing as being in the service of other people, and it is good work, which if effective would accomplish great and crucial things, it becomes very easy to slip and start regarding the work itself as if it were God.

When a person's work comes to have an intensity that makes it more than mere work but practically an object of worship, then it would follow that there could be negative consequences just as there are with all idolatry or with excessive material attachments. It is easier to see the danger with work that comes from greed and callousness and hurts people, but when the work is not only helping people but giving help that is so urgently needed, the temptation to worship the work itself is all the easier to fall into. Burnout can be seen as a wake-up call: spiritually, something has gone wrong and needs attending to. The work may be urgent, but it is not God.

Prayer, meditation, and contemplation are relaxing ways of being in tune with inner feelings and keeping things in perspective. Fellowship is a common way to get social support. Places of worship are often spaces to get away from overwhelming and emotionally exhausting experiences elsewhere. For Jews and Christians, the institution of the Sabbath (Exodus 23:12) is deliberately designed as God telling us to set aside a day of rest. Religious institutions not only give people the motivation to do the kind of work that leads to burnout but also have often provided naturally the methods that help to avoid it.

COPING USING ART

Humor and Glorious Music

The literature of those in poverty is quite extensive, and the signs that it is used for coping with material deprivation and direct insults and physical violence targeted at them are often clear to see in the content:

- folk literature—stories, poetry, paintings, and so on
- music—including old ballads, blues, Southern Gospel, and Black Gospel
- artistically dramatic preaching or storytelling styles

This art has been rich in meaning, expressiveness, and themes that serve as coping mechanisms for the problems of life. They have therefore often become appreciated outside their group of origin, because the coping mechanisms involved are universally helpful.

Apocalyptic Writings

One particular literature is a religious form that is particular to the psychology of highly intense periods of violent repression of religious groups. Suppose that a group is suffering executions, torture, or massacres and the dangers are ever-present and come at arbitrary times. Under these conditions, apocalyptic literature can be quite appealing.

This literature uses heavy symbolism and cosmic themes, most especially of end times and therefore of the ultimate resolutions of current conflicts. Sometimes the symbols are needed so members of the group can communicate their points without detection by the persecuting group. The symbols are also important because they are the only way to convey how grand and universal the themes involved are.

Apocalyptic themes in ancient Hebrew literature are in the last six chapters of the book of Daniel and the entire book of Ezekiel. The Christian New Testament has its final book, the book of Revelation (all but the first three chapters).

The book of Daniel is believed by many scholars to have been written at the time the Jews were under intense pressure from the Greek king Antiochus who wanted to Hellenize them and forbid them to practice their religion; events surrounding this time period are where the Jewish celebration of Hanukkah comes from. Ezekiel was written mainly during the exile of the Jews in Babylon. Revelation was written by a man, John of Patmos, who identified himself as exiled on a penal island for his beliefs (Revelation 1:9). Many scholars place this in the 90s of the first century CE, but some place it earlier, in the year or two immediately before the destruction of the Temple (Robinson, 1976), which would be even more clearly at a time of high persecution.

One of the major concerns when people realistically fear violence and remember friends and family already victimized is that they will be strongly tempted to stop being members of the group. People might disavow their faith to avoid being tortured or killed, and naturally many did. If the values and beliefs are to be maintained under such extreme pressure, the counterpressure must also be extreme.

That counterpressure assures adherents that this is no everyday run-of-the-mill conflict. There are cosmic themes. The stakes are high. There are forces vaster and more powerful than what we see and hear directly.

In the case of the book of Revelation, while it may seem that offering a pinch of incense and saying, "Caesar is Lord" is a small price to pay to avoid torture, apocalyptic literature asserts the price is actually huge. That small act supports a system of vast structural violence, deception, and direct violence. That small act subverts the firm convictions needed by large numbers of people if violence is to be effectively opposed. It is the same as someone purchasing an item that is on boycott, or crossing a picket line rather than participating in a strike—small acts by individuals, but if enough people do them, there is no longer a nonviolent campaign. Countering violence with nonviolence requires a great deal of fortitude, not to be undermined by how small an unfaithful act is.

Because it bolsters their case, the apocalyptic literature often becomes popular among groups under great persecution. It gives them greater fortitude to face horrific violence. This imagery lets them look under the surface of everyday life and assures them they are not insignificant people facing impossible odds. Rather, they are crucial people in a cosmic drama—a drama that in the future is guaranteed to be settled in favor of their faith.

Islam also has a clear-cut understanding of the end times, with *Yawm al-Qiyāmah* (Day of Resurrection) or *Yawm ad-Dīn* (Day of Judgment; also known as Day of Reckoning or the Last Day). This is the topic of Surah 75 in the Qur'an, but is also covered many times in Qur'an and hadith; God as Lord of the Day of Judgment is in the first Surah, which also serves as the most common prayer in Islam. This idea serves as a basic understanding that ethical behavior has cosmic and long-lasting significance, but it would also serve the same function of telling people who are under great persecution—which was true of the early Muslims—that the Last Day loomed over the reality where they were suffering from violence and asserted a reality that overrides the violent people who think they are being triumphant at the moment. Their triumph is quite temporary; it is the triumph of faith that has the final word. The idea of the Last Day changes people when they understand that God is on the side of the believer.

Apocalyptic literature often comes into existence and gets into scriptures on the force of its popularity with people who find it psychologically valuable. When it is read by those from whom such experience of intense abuse is absent, it tends to be interpreted differently.

Some try to find out what kind of current events might fit the symbols to see if end times are coming. They do this despite the fact that all of the literature either leaves the scheduling murky or makes it clear that only God knows (see Gospel of Matthew 24:36; Qur'an 33:63). Since the symbols are not literal but symbols and designed to fit the dynamics of events that have common features with other historical eras in terms of the violence perpetrated, such people are practically always able to find current events that fit the symbols. Thus, the passages of scripture are scrutinized and turned into magical predictions. They lose the point for which they were written. Apocalyptic literature is not intended to assert magic, but rather be a way of turning the conflict of the time from one of apparent hopelessness to the utmost in hope.

There is also the danger that the tribulations involved against perpetrators will make readers feel vengeful, and this is true of both those who experience persecution and those who do not. It is especially true of those who use the literature in expression of their own political views. Without nonviolence as a guiding principle, the literature can easily become a weapon in the hands of the violent; this is easily done when its imagery is violent. This kind of literature is not the only form that can be misused by those who want to justify violence, however. Indeed, those bent on justifying violence have proven remarkably imaginative in finding such justifications in places the original authors would never have thought of.

HEALING

Postviolence Healing for Societies

Once institutions of massive violence have ceased, more needs to be done than giving a victory speech and going home. People will suffer the aftereffects of being victims of the institution for years to come. In the case of anxiety and depression, nonviolence requires that these be treated so that people no longer suffer from them. In the case of vengeful feelings and continued simmering resentments, nonviolence requires that these be addressed in order to avoid future violence. Neither wars nor nonviolent campaigns end neatly the way Hollywood movies do; life continues on.

One method that has been used is a societywide series of hearings in which victims and perpetrators encounter each other. The idea is that surviving victims not only can find out what happened to their family members but also can express their feelings to the perpetrators directly. The perpetrators can see the reality of the consequences of what they have done and process their own feelings and interact with surviving victims. The most famous example of using this approach is the Truth and Reconciliation Commission following the end of apartheid in South Africa (Tutu, 1999). The concept using the same term for more commissions has been copied in other places as well. It is grueling work, but well worth it as a matter of helping to heal.

When the situation is not one of divisions between perpetrators and victims, but large-scale violent conflicts in which there were clearly defined sides that people took, there is a Healing and Rebuilding Our Communities program developed by the African Great Lakes Initiative of the Friends Peace Teams (Friends being the word that Quakers call themselves; Quakers come from the Christian tradition). The program involves three-day workshops in which 20 people, 10 from each side, interact in order to restore normal relationships. The small-group atmosphere allows for more humanizing, and there are many such workshops in the hope that the work will spread throughout the communities as some of the individuals with the more intensive experience interact with others in their society. AGLI has sponsored these to great effect in Kenya, Burundi, the Democratic Republic of the Congo, Rwanda, and Uganda (see http://aglifpt.org).

Postviolence Healing for Perpetrators

A document from the Vatican (headquarters for Catholics) details various kinds of violence and concludes, "They poison human society, but they do more to harm those who practice them than to those who suffer the injury" (*Gaudium et Spes*, 27). The idea that it hurts to commit violence, even though the person chooses to do so, can be found in various religious traditions. As early as Socrates, in Plato's *Gorgias* he says, "the doer of injustice is more miserable than the sufferer." The Muslim ruler Saladin in an 1193 letter, *Instruction to His Son*, says, "Abstain from shedding blood . . . for blood that is spilt never sleeps."

The mental consequences of being a victim of violence include a pattern of symptoms called Posttraumatic Stress Disorder (PTSD). The pattern includes:

- images and memories and thoughts keep butting in;
- dreams of the event are strong, and tend to be like videotapes replaying the event;
- avoiding of reminders of the event;
- being jumpy at loud noises or having the heartbeat rise at reminders of the event;
- deadened feelings and emotional numbing;
- feeling cut off from other people; and
- having temper problems and outbursts of rage.

For the official definitions used for the diagnosis of the full-fledged disorder, see the DSM-5 of the American Psychiatric Association (2013) or the ICD-10 of the World Health Organization (1992). However, diagnoses are only necessary for those seeking professional treatment; people can have the symptoms without it being as high as the level of the disorder. Symptoms alone are disturbing.

PTSD symptoms appear to be worse for those that commit violence than for those who are merely victims of it (MacNair, 2002). So, in technical terms, the scientific psychological studies document the Vatican's and Socrates' points: more severe PTSD symptoms mean that the doer is more miserable than the sufferer. The form of PTSD symptoms that comes from being a doer is called Perpetration-Induced Traumatic Stress, also called Participation-Induced Traumatic Stress.

Those who have had to deal with this have often come to realize that the religious communities throughout the ages have good suggestions to make on how to do so. After all, all religious communities have been dealing with the phenomenon since they began. The doers of violence, if they want to find healing, need atonement, repentance, and forgiveness. At times they need to bear witness. They need to reidentify themselves as different people from the ones who did the killing, which can come with religious conversions or recommitments.

They also need to be aware that their symptoms are relatively normal for the experiences they have been through. They need pastoral counseling and fellowship with people who suffer the same way they do. There is still a lot of research that needs to be done on how best to treat people, including the spiritual aspects, and whether best treatments vary by religious background.

What happens if the healing does not happen? There are implications for the pursuit of peace and social justice. PTSD symptoms include irritable outbursts, detachment or feeling of estrangement from other people, hypervigilance looking for attacks, and flashbacks of feeling to be back in the violent situations. Any of these symptoms can lead to street crime or abuse in the home (Sontag & Alvarez, 2008). They can also support further wars, riots, executions, or lynchings. They may have helped support these things throughout history, one of the avenues that supports the old saying, "violence begets violence."

What does all this say about how we as human beings are created? People of violent proclivities have argued at length that violence and killing are inherent to the human mind. Yet if people get PTSD from committing killing or other acts of violence, if such actions can make them sick, and if the kind of sickness is trauma, then this shows the human mind is not actually well suited for killing. Is this not a crucial point in support of nonviolence as natural and healthy one that various religions have continually tried to tell us?

19

Building a Nonviolent Society

CONSTRUCTIVE PROGRAM

The term "Constructive Programme" was coined by Mohandas Gandhi to fill a need. First, while it is all very well for nonviolent campaigners to say what they are *against*, the next question is, what are they *for*? Simply be opposed to the bad is likely to be insufficient if it is not paired with promotion of the good. Second, obstruction may be necessary, but if not accompanied by construction, it may well attract fewer participants. The constructive program allows people to participate in small ways, to do so daily and as a matter of habit, and to feel more positive about the sense of accomplishment of the entire enterprise. Third, the very achievement of dispensing with one thing—in Gandhi's case, colonial rule—required that it be replaced with something better. If the replacement was not available, then the elimination of the problem could lead to chaos, the fear of which would make it more likely that the problem would not be eliminated. People may not like one form of domination, but replacing it with either a different form of domination or with instability can be too frightening to consider. So the original problem remains as "the devil you know," which is seen as better than the devil not known. Therefore, building up of alternative institutions such as schools and economic enterprises and alternative methods of arranging for infrastructure needs are common ways of allowing for a smoother transition from one system to another.

In addition to building up of institutions such as schools, universities, and hospitals, in the case of India this home-rule "Swaraj" included local growth and spinning of cotton for locally made clothing. Thus, people were employed, and those who were boycotting British textiles were not going without clothing.

Religions have always excelled at building alternative institutions and constructive options countering violent or uncaring societies. Religious organizations set up schools and universities to educate, hospitals and clinics to give medical treatment, mental hospitals to treat those suffering from mental illnesses, pregnancy resource centers and child care, prison visitation, museums and memorials to keep historical experiences alive, various services to alleviate poverty, job training and a large number of other creative approaches to get people out of poverty, and other ways of helping various groups of people. Sometimes these activities are done with support of governments, sometimes with mere acquiescence of governments, and sometimes in countering hostile governments.

BUILDING KNOWLEDGE AND EXPERIENCE

Peace Education

In addition to general education, peace education can serve during or after violent times or before they arise in the hope of preventing them. Different approaches have included:

- education directly on nonviolence, which will include such efforts as this book to get across the principles, but also direct training, which includes role-playing and other methods of gaining wisdom from experience;
- conflict resolution programs, which focus on mediation, communication, and problem-solving skills;
- human rights education to counter ethnic hatred and foster multicultural understanding;
- violence prevention programs aimed at those who have committed or are at risk of committing criminal violence, often associated with the court system, and tending to focus on anger management, learning about causes and costs of violence, self-control, personal responsibility, and support groups (see the Alternatives to Violence Project, http://avpinternational.org);
- character education, more likely to be favored by conservatives, though liberals and others also find it helpful, which can encourage the virtues of honesty and integrity, courage and patience, temperance, and concern for the well-being of others, all of which can have peace-promoting effects; and
- some forms of religious education are intended to foster peace.

Any of the approaches covered here could also be fit into religious education, especially for people more comfortable with a religious context or for whom it is more readily available. All major world religions have aspects that can be used in peace education (Brantmeier, Lin, & Miller, 2010).

Parenting

Parenting can also be seen as a constructive program for nonviolence. In psychology, much has focused on a concept of three parenting styles for socializing children, which have been called the *authoritarian*, the *permissive*, and the *authoritative*.

For the authoritarian style, rules are strict and rigid; swift and severe punishment is sure. Psychological observations show that children raised primarily this way tend to be anxious, in addition to being rigid themselves. For the permissive style, rules are lax, and what punishment comes is low and inconsistent. Children get accustomed to getting away with things and having unrealistic expectations. Learning to interact well with others becomes more of a problem.

Many times, people whose style is authoritarian are contemptuous of the permissive style. They see its problems and want to avoid them. Similarly, permissive parents are often motivated by a horror at the problems they see with the authoritarian style. Yet people do not have to choose between the two, because just as with violence and apathy, there is a third option which avoids the disadvantages of both. These three styles can be seen as analogous to the idea of nonviolence as a third way—neither fight nor flight, neither violence nor cowardice, but instead a positive alternative to both.

For the authoritative style of parenting, rules are firm, but the reasons for them are explained and they can be negotiable when that makes sense. Enforcement, rather than being harsh and punitive or done with laxity and lack of care, is warm. It takes into account the child's thoughts. Studies show children raised in this way tend to be more secure and have better skills in relating to others and making decisions—a good "constructive program" for raising adults who deal nonviolently with friends and foes all their lives, individually and as part of groups or campaigns. Children may be more likely to learn to behave nonviolently as adults if their parents model that kind of behavior for them. In short, the most nonviolent-oriented of the three parenting styles has also been shown by a good large number of psychological studies to be the best for the positive development of children.

Another concept is a "Positive Discipline," which has three criteria for methods used. Is it respectful? Is it effective not just for right now, but in the long term? Finally, does it help children develop valuable life skills, an ability to make sound decisions, a sensitivity to the needs of others, a sense of fairness, and good character? For more, see the website http://www.positivediscipline.com.

ECONOMIC CONVERSION

Sometimes people in the military have their ideas of what weapons they want and where they want bases based on their own understanding of what is most effective for their goals. Other times, however, weapons are produced or bases remain without any military justification because people have a visceral anxiety about not having people losing well-paying jobs. Yet military production is actually very poor at how many jobs it produces, because it is so capital-intensive rather than labor-intensive—that is, it uses more material resources and machines than people. If the same amount of money were spent on almost anything else, whether government services or lowering taxes and therefore left with the taxpayers to spend, that money would provide more jobs. Since the money is out of circulation because it is spent on the low-job activities, the net effect on most economies is that there are fewer jobs than there would be if the military were not taking over the money.

A nonviolent alternative is direct economic conversion. Rather than simply firing people and leaving them to their own resources to find new jobs, which is what causes the most anxiety, a weapons-building factory or base could be converted to a similar use that allows people to keep their jobs. A proposal for conversion is likely to meet less resistance than the economic dislocation people otherwise fear.

Historically, the Buddhist conversion of Emperor Ashoka led to a case of economic conversion, as reported in chapter 3. Once he decided his conquering ways were over and he would establish nonviolent rule, the government had a surplus of war chariots, elephants, and fireworks. Now these were used instead in exhibitions for popular entertainment (Nikam & McKeon, 1978, p. 31).

LIFESTYLES: EVERYDAY PEACE ACTIONS

Purchasing Decisions

While the home-spinning of one's own cloth may be more effective in India's anticolonial struggle than it is in most current situations, the same principle applies: everyday purchases and habits can have a profound influence in trying to counter violence.

There are of course specific consumer boycotts of particular items that particular organizations will promote from time to time for defined goals. In the absence of labor union organizing, or an organization with many connections, or a widespread campaign about which most of a society is excited and mobilized, these are exceedingly difficult to do well.

For everyday life and dealing with behavior of money-making corporations, letter-writing campaigns are generally more effective. A letter is a positive communication of what is understood to be wrong, whereas a decision not to purchase something could be made for any number of reasons. Letters can be impressive as being in large numbers, when the same number of people not purchasing could be so low as to not make any impression at all.

Still, the religious institutions in any country are ones that have many connections to large numbers of people and to other institutions, so may be in a good position to promote a boycott of one or two specified products for a popular reason. Strategizing is important; boycotts of products (as opposed to a one-time event with a specific date) are major campaigns and can only be done successfully occasionally. They are not normally the first tactic to think of.

On the other hand, having a lifestyle that avoids purchasing products from objectionable corporations is something that can be done separate from a campaign with a specific goal. The overall goal can be, as Gandhi put it, to be the change one wants to see in the world. One can see every unit of money one spends as a vote for what one wants to see continue. Money not spent is a vote against what one does not want to see continue. As with all voting, it would take large numbers of people to have an impact over time, but for some forms of violence, it is the only kind of impact that will be effective.

Purchases that can be avoided include those from large corporations that pollute the environment or do not pay their workers well or do not give them sufficiently safe or pleasant working conditions. In extreme cases, such as much of chocolate production, labor conditions are horrific and coerced in such a way that they could be referred to as slavery. Some corporations have other sections that produce nuclear weapons or weapons sold to dictators. Many lobby for these and other kinds of harm to occur, and the government responds to the lobbying. Practically all very large corporations are run as dictatorships; the concept of having a democracy in their business enterprise would not occur to them.

Conversely, there are enterprises—usually smaller businesses—that are very sensitive to the environment and make a point of treating their workers well; they are able to do so because they are a more personable business rather than a large-scale bureaucracy. Purchasing local, organic, mom-and-pop shop, and otherwise socially responsible is something consumers can pay attention to.

Being "pure" on this is not something current societies are well set up for. Some countries do better than other countries, but most of the world is dealing with heartless large corporate businesses now. Nevertheless, one can have a "tight wallet" in places that are less sensitive to social concerns, and a "loose wallet" in places where social concerns are well attended to. This is why the concept that each unit of money is a vote is helpful. Purity would leave a person in poverty due to a dearth of available options, but being mindful of voting with one's money is a matter of empowerment. If enough people do it, there can be long-term impact.

For a resource that gives information about which large corporations are better and which are worse on a variety of criteria, so that purchasing decisions can be influenced, see Better World Shopping Guide (www.betterworldshopper.org).

Food

One place where the "constructive program" of people making things for themselves makes sense and is gaining popularity is gardening. A full-fledged farm to make all of one's own food is beyond the desires or capabilities of most and is not necessarily a good idea for everyone to do; those people who do farm can take their produce to farmers' markets and other avenues to make good food available for purchase. But most people can grow at least some lettuce in a pot in the window, and many can do much more than that.

Any bit of food grown in a garden helps people commune with how food is actually grown, is not transported from afar, and is not grown by large corporations lacking in environmental sensitivity or mistreating workers. Having gardening skills can help buffer the gardeners from the tides of occasional recession in the economy that come about when high-finance people make an idol out of their money.

Throughout Part I, the "Forms of Violence" listed each religion's position on eating meat. Most religions have a vegetarian tradition, or at least principles that current vegetarian advocates use. In terms of violence, this is primarily an appeal based on compassion to animals, with the idea that since animals must be killed in order to make meat, avoiding the eating of meat means avoiding the killing of animals and therefore avoiding violence.

One of the problems throughout the previous centuries of vegetarian advocacy (before the word "vegetarian" was coined) has been that it has been associated with ascetic practices—that is, it is related to the virtues of giving up things that are otherwise desirable. This strain of asceticism has in many places given vegetarianism the aura of intentional deprivation of a food that is desirable, having the perverse effect of actually making that food seem more desirable. Meat is seen as a luxury to be given up by those who give up luxuries, but to be especially embraced by those who wish to have luxuries.

Additionally, vegetarianism has been associated with rigid rule-making. It would therefore fit the temperament of those who like to have rigid rules to follow, but not be so appealing to those who think more in terms of guidelines and flexibility, or who are repelled by having rules be too rigid.

Both of these features help explain why the vegetarianism common in Hinduism, Buddhism, and Sikhism are not universal in those religions. They help explain why the vegetarianism common among early Christians and throughout the centuries with monks and nuns and saints (Akers, 2000; Roberts, 2004) did not take hold, so that few Christians today are even aware of the vegetarianism within their own tradition. If one reads, for example, chapter 14 of Paul's Letter to the Romans in the New Testament with this in mind, one sees that Paul knows that some Christians avoid meat, and he would as well when he was with them, but he sees this as too much of the rigid rulemaking he opposed in other contexts, rather than the message of grace he was so keen on.

Today's vegetarians have added additional concerns to compassion to animals. Modern science is showing the vegetarian diet to be better for health (Craig & Mangels, 2009). The modern factory-farm system with huge numbers of animals has brought up a new concern about the ecology. Throughout history, meat has primarily been eaten in small amounts by most people, and in large amounts by the nobility that made up a very small portion of the population. The current practice of huge amounts of meat for most of the population in many countries is actually a fairly new phenomenon. It goes with the understanding of meat as a luxury among people who are affluent enough to want luxuries. It requires the massive factory farms that are crueler to animals than traditional methods ever were and have ecological consequences unknown to our ancestors.

Today's vegetarians tend to avoid the two pitfalls of asceticism and rigid rules. The same capabilities that produce mass meat also produce a joyous abundance of vegetarian foods; some of the foods fit the category of luxuries, and even the simple foods come in a greater variety and with greater freshness than have been previously available.

Vegetarians assure those still eating meat that having just one meal be vegetarian is better than no meals being vegetarian. Every reason to be totally vegetarian applies to reasons to be partially so as opposed to not being so at all. So while those who are inclined to rigid rules are still quite capable of doing so on a vegetarian diet and do occasionally try to commend this course to others, there is also the ability to simply enjoy the abundance of vegetarian food which in many places is now more easily available, and without worrying about strict rules.

These circumstances allow more people who commit to becoming vegetarian to remain so and to be seen as healthy rather than as deprived. They also allow people who are not committed to the full practice to nevertheless gain pleasure out of participating at least a little bit in a practice that will help build a more nonviolent society.

Ecological Habits

Lifestyles that are nonviolent to our planet will also spread out to nonviolence in many other spheres, such as treatment of workers and nonuse of massively destructive weapons. Campaigns to change public policies or business practices will therefore often include multiple reasons.

As a lifestyle matter, ecological habits are one of the most important things that can be done by individuals every day, without reference to what other large entities are doing (though having large-scale practices that make these easy for individuals to do will help). Gardening and vegetarianism as mentioned earlier are such practices, along with recycling, conserving energy, and using nontoxic methods of doing things for which toxic chemicals were used before.

This is currently such a major concern. Because religions know they are especially good at mobilizing individuals to take lifestyle actions, this being one of their specialties, there is much discussion from adherents in each religion to show how that religion's principles apply. We will cover those one by one, in the same order as in the chapters in Part I. One organization that works with several religions is the Alliance of Religions and Conservation (http://www.arcworld.org).

Judaism

A common principle applied to environmental action is *bal tashchit*, meaning "do not destroy," a long-standing principle in Jewish law. It is rooted in Deuteronomy 20:19–20, which forbids cutting down fruit trees to help in a siege. While not applying to destruction understood as justified, it has been expanded to include other senseless forms of damage or of unneeded waste. The Babylonian Talmud applies it to the wasting of lamp oil, tearing clothing, chopping up furniture for firewood, or wanton killing of animals (Talmud Shabbath 67b, Tractate Hullin 7b, Kiddushin 32a). The modern version of wasting of lamp oil would be mainly wasting of electricity, and the principles clearly apply to modern applications of conserving.

For scriptures common to Jews and Christians, there has been a passage that has been used against ecological sensitivity that when read more closely actually bolsters the case for it. This is Genesis 1:26–30, in which God creates humans to rule over the earth and master it. Those who want to have an excuse to dominate nature without regard to keeping it nurtured cite this passage, but those are people with a dominating mindset who do not understand ruling as something done with kindness. The Hebrew word for ruling in this passage is the same for how the sun and moon rule (Genesis 1:16), which is clearly a beneficial interaction and not a petulant ability to dictate irresponsibly. The very passage itself spells out that the green plants are the food and that humans are to keep things in order.

The idea of mastering the earth would apply more to figuring out how to get a living beached whale back in the water, not to doing damage and creating more chaos. Humans are to watch over nature to see that things are going well, because humans are the animals most capable of doing so. The idea that this is license to be destructive is a grotesque misreading from minds with a violent and dominating bias.

After all, God did instruct the first two people, these two rulers of nature, to exercise some self-control in what they did and did not eat. Their failure to exercise this self-control brought dire consequences (Genesis 3:14–20).

Books dealing with this topic in depth include *Judaism and Ecology* (Tirosh-Samuelson, 2002) and *Judaism and Environmental Ethics: A Reader* (Yaffe, 2001).

Hinduism

Simple living is admired and inner peace comes without material possessions. Hindus revere various parts of nature—trees, lakes, and mountains—as sacred, and so have treated them with care throughout the millennia.

Nevertheless, the government in India, as with governments elsewhere, is collaborating with large corporations who take the attitude that seeds and trees can be patented and water can be privatized, so that profits are made, but the traditional ways of caring for the environment are "modernized" out of existence. One of the groups formed to counter this is Navdanya (http://www.navdanya.org), which means "nine seeds," referring to their work in saving seeds from a large variety of plants (in the nine main categories) so the plants do not become extinct. Using the wording of Gandhi-inspired "home rule," they defend seeds from patenting in a campaign called Bija Swaraj, local sovereignty over food in Anna Swaraj, water sovereignty in Jal Swaraj, and land sovereignty in Bhu Swaraj. In their own words:

> We need a new movement, which allows us to move from the dominant and pervasive culture of violence, destruction and death to a culture of non-violence, creative peace and life. That is why in India, Navdanya started the Earth democracy movement, which provides an alternative worldview in which humans are embedded in the Earth Family, we are connected to each other through love, compassion, not hatred and violence and ecological responsibility and economic justice replaces greed, consumerism and competition as objectives of human life. (Earth Democracy, n.d.)

Its work on biodiversity has included conserving over 5,000 varieties of grains, beans, and vegetables. It is actively rejuvenating indigenous knowledge and culture with ecology and democracy in mind.

The Jains of India, with nonviolence being a major focus of their religion, also have concerns for the environment; see, for example, the book *Jainism and Ecology: Nonviolence in the Web of Life* (Chapple, 2002).

Buddhism

The basic tenet of *Pratitya Samutpada* can be translated that all beings are interconnected, and this is also a basic biological tenet of ecology. The health of the parts cannot be separated from the health of the whole.

Craving and greed are both the major underpinnings of ecological devastation and in Buddhism are understood as the major underpinnings of suffering and unhappiness for individuals. Those people who follow Buddhist recommendations for happiness will as a matter of course also be uninterested in causing ecological devastation.

This also means that simple living, or ecological living, is recommended as not merely some sort of ethical stand, but is the greatest road for the individual to avoid suffering. Foregoing desired material wealth is not a sacrifice that one makes on behalf of the environment, but rather a practice of spiritual benefit that one is well advised to follow on other grounds as well. That this has healthy ecological benefits is another thing to recommend doing such foregoing.

There is a story from Japan that the Buddha once received a donation of 500 new robes for the monks and nuns. This meant he needed to consider what to do with the old robes. They were used for bedsheets. The old sheets then would become towels, and the old towels would become cleaning rags.

One of the items on the Eight-fold Path that leads to an end to suffering is Right Livelihood. This includes not killing, and not taking more than one needs. The livelihood must avoid harming others, including any form of poisoning nature.

Zoroastrianism

Zoroastrianism claims to be the world's first proponent of caring for the environment. Human beings as the only conscious beings are to care for the Seven Creations—sky, water, earth, plants, animals, humans, and fire. Harmony of all creation, reaching perfection, is the final goal. Purity of nature is important; Zoroastrians do not enter a river to wash in it or pollute it in any other way.

There is a traditional story of how there was a time when Mother Earth was in trouble, so she asked Ahura Mazda (God) to send a prince with warriors to stop people from hurting her. But Ahura Mazda said this was not the way to do it. Instead a holy man would be sent to stop the people from hurting her. Rather than using force, this holy man would be persuasive, using words and inspirational ideas. Thus was born Zoroaster/Zarathustra.

Christianity

Environmentally oriented Christians may tend to think in terms of the need for us to repent of the damage done to God's creation; they will deal with the same passage in Genesis as covered before under Judaism. More recent concerns about the specifics of current harming of the environment have led to several official statements that make it clear that this is a crucial concern for Christians worldwide.

The Catholic branch of Christianity has this statement from Pope Benedict XVI, given in his World Day of Peace address in 2008:

> For the human family, this home is the earth, the environment that God the Creator has given us to inhabit with creativity and responsibility. We need to care for the environment: it has been entrusted to men and women to be protected and cultivated with responsible freedom, with the good of all as a constant guiding criterion. . . . Humanity today is rightly concerned about the ecological balance of tomorrow. It is important for assessments in this regard to be carried out prudently, in dialogue with experts and people of wisdom, uninhibited by ideological pressure to draw hasty conclusions, and above all with the aim of reaching agreement on a model of sustainable development capable of ensuring the well-being of all while respecting environmental balances.

The Eastern Orthodox branch had this stated by the Ecumenical Patriarchate in a 1990 statement, "Orthodoxy and the Ecological Crisis":

> We must attempt to return to a proper relationship with the Creator AND the creation. This may well mean that just as a shepherd will in times of greatest hazard, lay down his life for his flock, so human beings may need to forego part of their wants and needs in order that the survival of the natural world can be assured.

The World Council of Churches in a 1990 statement entitled "Ten Affirmations on Justice, Peace, and the Integrity of Creation" said:

> We will resist the claim that anything in creation is merely a resource for human exploitation. We will resist species extinction for human benefit; consumerism and harmful mass production; pollution of land, air and waters; all human activities which are now leading to probable rapid climate change; and the policies and plans which contribute to the disintegration of creation.

Islam

Many Qur'anic verses deal with being kind to animals and to the environment or castigate people for not doing so. Commonly cited, especially by Muslim environmental activists, are:

- "There is no animal in the earth, nor a bird that flies on its two wings, but that they are communities like yourselves" (first part of Quran 6:38);

- "Do not corrupt the land once it has been set right" (middle part of Qur'an 7:56); and
- "Corruption has appeared on land and sea because of what people's hands have earned. He will make them taste part of what they have committed; perhaps they will turn back" (last part of Qur'an 30:41).

That last verse is essentially saying that when we pollute or otherwise mess up our environment, God will give us a taste of our own medicine in the hope that we will turn away from the wrong direction.

One website with more information on Islamic principles and practical advice for lifestyles is The Eco Muslim (http://www.theecomuslim.com).

First Nations of North America

The closeness to the land and its sacredness that has for millennia been a feature of most Native American religions has always meant great sensitivity to the well-being of the environment. This feature is common to indigenous religions that remain active worldwide, since one of the attractions of remaining with an original religion is the harm to the environment seen as being done by those following outside religions.

When Indians, especially in the 19th and 20th centuries, were sent off to marginal areas to live, they were also sent off to the areas most likely to be used for mining of coal, uranium, and other material toxic to the local environment. Therefore, campaigns against this form of pollution are a major concern among contemporary indigenous nonviolent activists.

Sikhs

Sikhism follows 300-year cycles that have names. The last one started in 1699 and ended in 1999, and it was named the "Cycle of the Sword." This time period included a great deal of persecution of Sikhs. The next cycle goes from 1999 to 2299. The name the Sikh leaders chose was the "Cycle of Creation." There has accordingly been a dramatic increase in environmental practices by Sikh temples and individuals.

The Sikh understanding is that human beings create their surroundings by their inner state. Therefore, the increasing barrenness of the earth is a reflection of an emptiness within human beings. If human beings improve their spiritual state of mind with prayer and humility before the divine will of God, then seeing the divine spark within oneself makes it easy to see and cherish it in others.

A simple life free from conspicuous waste has always been the Sikh ideal, and vegetarianism is a strong tradition for many.

Bahá'ís

The sense that the world is all one country and that all of humanity is united has the natural corollary that the natural world is to be protected and that we are all stewards of seeing that this is so. The restructuring of the educational, social, economic and political systems needed to reflect the understanding of human unity will also cause a more ecologically sustainable world.

The Tables of Bahá'u'lláh say, "Nature is God's Will and is its expression in and through the contingent world" (p. 142). All things are interconnected; the way the universe works is that things flourish according to the law of reciprocity. In a spiritually based civilization, science and religion would work in harmony, and both would preserve the ecological balance.

Revived Paganism

One of the major reasons behind the idea of reviving ancient pagan beliefs is that the religions that overrode them were harmful to the planet due to philosophies of domineering and disconnection from the natural world. Reconnecting with and taking good care of the natural world is therefore one of the major themes of the various forms of revived paganism.

Tenrikyo

The Tenri Citizens Network for Ecology was founded in 1997 to facilitate cooperation for the city of Tenri, where worldwide church headquarters are, and to focus on ecological concerns for developing nations. They are aware that much of the pollution comes from cars that are produced there in Japan.

CONCLUSION ON BUILDING NONVIOLENCE

Despite the word "nonviolence" being based on what it is not—it is not violence—because it means *countering* violence it is a very positive word as to what kind of society is peaceful and healthy for all.

The "constructive program" may be building a better society while the "obstructive program" of noncooperation with what is wrong with nonviolent confrontations and rebellions opposes rather than builds. Yet such noncooperation is a positive thing for the human community all the same, because its obstruction is attempting to remove the obstruction that is in the way of being constructive for a healthier community.

Removing or mitigating the various sins that religions critique both individuals and whole societies with may sound like a negative—getting rid of something—but getting rid of the underpinnings of violence means getting rid of violence itself, and that is a positive.

Along with building virtues and finding creative ways to transform conflicts, all these things contribute to greater nonviolence in the world and therefore to building nonviolent societies. This last chapter has covered aspects that are more directly related to such building, but all of the chapters in Part II contribute to aspects that are important for this positive goal.

All of the religions in Part I are long-lasting human communities with brilliant and crucial insights that help build a nonviolent society as well. They will do so all the better if people (such as readers of this book) are well educated on what those brilliant and crucial insights are, along with the long centuries of experience of which the religions are the prime historical foundations and current carriers.

The subtitle of this book is "The Rise of Effective Advocacy for Peace." Over the course of time, the principles of nonviolence have become more established and the experience of nonviolence has grown and matured. Yet the cover depicts a sunrise, because while the book documents how this has in the past grown over time, the growing is only at the beginning. In the future, there is plenty more rising to do.

References

Abdalla, Amr, & Arafa, Yasmine. (2013). Egypt: Nonviolent resistance in the rise of a nation-state, 1805–1922. In Macie J. Bartkowski (Ed.), *Recovering nonviolent history: Civil resistance in liberation struggles* (pp. 125–142). Boulder, CO: Lynne Rienner Publishers.

Abu-Nimer, Mohammed. (2003). *Nonviolence and peace building in Islam: Theory and practice*. Gainesville: University Press of Florida.

Ahmad, Sheheryar. (2014, February 16). Islam's mark on racial equality. *Las Vegas Sun*. Retrieved from http://lasvegassun.com/news/2014/feb/16/islams-mark-racial-equality/.

Ackerman, Peter, & Duvall, Jack. (2000). *A force more powerful: A century of nonviolent conflict*. New York: St. Martin's Press.

Akers, Keith. (2000). *The lost religion of Jesus: Simple living and nonviolence in early Christianity*. New York: Lantern Books.

Ali, Maulana Muhammad. (1995). *The holy Qur'an: Arabic text, English translation and commentary*. Columbus, OH: Ahmadiyya Anjuman Isha'at-e-Islam Lahore, USA.

American Psychiatric Association. (2013). *Diagnostic and statistical manual of mental disorders* (5th ed.). Washington, DC: Author.

Ammar, N. (2001). Restorative justice in Islam: Theory and practice. In Michael L. Hadley (Ed.), *The spiritual roots of restorative justice* (pp. 161–180). New York: State University of New York Press.

Armstrong, Karen. (2006). *The great transformation: The beginning of our religious traditions* (1st ed.). New York: Knopf.

Arner, Rob. (2010). *Consistently pro-life: The ethics of bloodshed in ancient Christianity*. Eugene, OR: Wipf and Stock Publishers.

Banta, Bruce. (1997). Cooperation and competition in peaceful societies. *Psychological Bulletin, 121*(2), 299–320.

Bartoli, Andrea. (2004). Christianity and Peacebuilding. In Harold Coward & Gordon S. Smith (Eds.), *Religion and peacebuilding*. New York: State University of New York Press.

Basarke, Alice. (2006). Origins of nonviolence. Retrieved from http://searchsikhism.com/origins-of-non-violence-movement-in-india

Bauckham, R. (1993). *The Theology of the Book of Revelation*. New York: Cambridge University Press.

Baynes, N. H. (Ed.), (1942). *The speeches of Adolf Hitler*. London: Oxford University Press.

Berling, Judith A. (2004). Confucianism and Peacebuilding. In Harold Coward & Gordon S. Smith (Eds.), *Religion and peacebuilding*. New York: State University of New York Press.

Berrigan, Daniel. (1983). *The nightmare of God: The book of Revelation*. Portland, OR: Sunburst Press.

Bickerman, Elias. (1949). *From Ezra to the last of the Maccabees: Foundations of Post-Biblical Judaism*. New York: Schocken Books.

Bond, George. (2003). *Buddhism at work: Community development, social empowerment and the Sarvodaya Movement*. West Hartford, CT: Kumarian Press.

Boniello, Kathianne. (2009, July 26). Nurse forced to help abort. *New York Post*. Retrieved from http://nypost.com/2009/07/26/nurse-forced-to-help-abort/

Borg, Marcus. (1997). *Jesus and Buddha: The parallel sayings*. Berkeley, CA: Seastone.

Boyce, Mary. (1992). *Zoroastrianism: Its antiquity and constant vigour*. Columbia: University of Michigan.

Brantmeier, E. J., Lin, J., & Miller, J. P. (2010). *Spirituality, religion, and peace education*. Charlotte, NC: Information Age.

Bristow, John T. (1988). *What Paul really said about women: The apostle's liberating views on equality in marriage, leadership and love*. New York: HarperCollins.

Brooks, Libby. (2014, December 17). Catholic midwives' abortion ruling overturned by supreme court. *The Guardian*. Retrieved from http://www.theguardian.com/world/2014/dec/17/catholic-midwives-abortion-ruling-overturned

Cahill, Thomas. (1998). *The gifts of the Jews*. New York: Doubleday.

Chapple, Christopher Key. (2002). *Jainism and ecology: Nonviolence in the web of life*. Cambridge, MA: Harvard University Press.

Chenowith, Erica, & Stephan, Maria. (2012). *Why civil resistance works: The strategic logic of nonviolent conflict*. New York: Columbia University Press.

Chopra, Deepak. (2005). *Peace is the way: Bringing war and violence to an end*. New York: Harmony Books.

Churchill, Ward. (1993). *Indians are us? Culture and genocide in Native North America*. Monroe, ME: Common Courage Press.

Clark, Howard. (2013). Kosovo: Civil resistance in defense of the nation, 1990s. In Macie J. Bartkowski (Ed.), *Recovering nonviolent history: Civil resistance in liberation struggles* (pp. 143–160). Boulder, CO: Lynne Rienner Publishers.

Conway, Moncure Daniel. (1904). *Autobiography, memories and experiences of Moncure Daniel Conway*. London, New York: Cassell.

Coward, Harold, & Smith, Gordon S. (Eds.). (2004). *Religion and peacebuilding*. New York: State University of New York Press.

Craig, W. J., & Mangels, A. R. (2009). Position of the American Dietetic Association: Vegetarian diets. *Journal of the American Dietetic Association, 109*(7), 1266–1282.

Dalmacija, Slobdna. (2013, August 3). Midwife fired for refusing to assist in abortion. The Protection of Conscience Project. Retrieved from http://consciencelaws.org/blog/?tag=jaga-stojak

Dawkins, Richard. (1986). *The blind watchmaker*. New York: W.W. Norton & Company, Inc.
de la Boétie, Etienne. (1548). *Discourse de la servitude volontaire*. Retrieved from http://www.constitution.org/la_boetie/serv_vol.htm
Deloria, Vine. (1992, Spring). Is religion possible? An evaluation of present efforts to revive traditional tribal religions, *Wicazo Sa Review, 8*, 37.
Derr, M.K., MacNair, R.M., & Naranjo-Huebl, L. (2005). *ProLife feminism: Yesterday & today*. Philadelphia, PA: Feminism & Nonviolence Studies Association.
Dhar, Sujoy. (2007). Sikhs worldwide campaign for death penalty abolition. Death Penalty Information Center. Retrieved from http://www.deathpenaltyinfo.org/node/2226
Dixie, Quinton, & Eisenstadt, Peter. (2011). *Visions of a better world: Howard Thurman's pilgrimage to India and the origins of African American nonviolence*. Boston, MA: Beacon Press.
Douglass, Frederick. (1857/1985). The Significance of Emancipation in the West Indies. Speech, Canandaigua, New York, August 3, 1857; collected in pamphlet by author. In John W. Blassingame (Ed.), The Frederick Douglass Papers. Series One: Speeches, Debates, and Interviews. Vol. 3: 1855–63. New Haven: Yale University Press.
Dymond, Jonathan. (1824). *An inquiry into the accordancy of war with the principles of Christianity*. Philadelphia, PA: Friends Bookstore. Retrieved from http://www.qhpress.org/texts/dymond/
Earth Democracy. (n.d.). Retrieved from http://www.navdanya.org/earth-democracy
Easwaran, Eknath. (1984). *A man to match his mountains: Badshah Khan, nonviolent soldier of Islam*. Petaluma, CA: Nilgiri Press.
Edgerton, William (1951). The strikes in Ramses III's twenty-ninth year. *Journal of Near Eastern Studies, 10*(3), 137–145.
Eduljee, K.E. (2014). Were ancient Iranians & Zoroastrians vegetarian? Retrieved from http://zoroastrianheritage.blogspot.com/2011/07/were-ancient-iranians-zoroastrians.html
Ellsberg, Robert. (1991). *Gandhi on Christianity*. Maryknoll, NY: Orbis Books.
Follett, Mary Parker. (1924). *Creative experience*. New York: Longmans Green.
Frandsen, Paul J. (1990). Editing reality: The Turin strike papyrus. In Sarah Israelit-Groll (Ed.), *Studies in Egyptology, 1*. Jerusalem, Israel: Magnes Press, Hebrew University.
Frankl, V. E. (1984). *Man's search for meaning*. New York: Washington Square Press.
Gandhi, Mohandas K. (1924, May 28). *Young India*, p. 178.
Gandhi, Mohandas K. (1958). *Hindu dharma*. Ahmedabad, India: Navajivan Press.
Gandhi, Mohandas K. (1980). *All men are brothers: Autobiographical reflections*. New York: Continuum.
Gandhi, Rajmohan. (2004). Hinduism and peacebuilding. In Coward, H. & Smith, G.S. (Eds.), *Religion and peacebuilding* (pp. 45–68). Albany: State University of New York Press.
Gaventa, Beverly Roberts. (2010). *Paul among the people: The apostle reinterpreted and reimagined in his own time*. New York: HarperOne.
Gnoli, Gherardo. (2000). *Zoroaster in history*. New York: Bibliotheca Persica Press.

Guoping, Jiang, & Garris, Christopher Paul. (2011). The compatibility between restorative justice and Islamic law: The case of Saudi Arabia. *Crime and Criminal Justice International, 16*, 102. Abstract retrieved from http://www.ntpu.edu.tw/gradcrim/temp/P_220120502194948.pdf

Gye, Hugo. (2013, October 8). Australian doctor could be struck off after refusing to carry out abortion on woman who didn't want to have a girl. *UK Daily Mail Online*. Retrieved from http://www.dailymail.co.uk/news/article-2449568/Doctor-Mark-Hobart-struck-refusing-abortion.html

Hadley, Michael L. (2001). *The spiritual roots of restorative justice*. Albany: State University of New York Press.

Hanh, Thich Nhat. (1993). *Love in action: Writings on nonviolent social change*. Berkeley, CA: Parallax Press.

Hanh, Thich Nhat. (1995). *Living Buddha, Living Christ*. New York: Riverhead Books.

Hanh, Thich Nhat. (2002). *Anger: Wisdom for cooling the flames*. New York: Riverhead Trade.

Harris, Rabia Terri. (n.d.). On Islamic nonviolence. Retrieved from http://forusa.org/fellowship/2010/spring/islamic-nonviolence/11639

Hascall, Susan C. (2012). Restorative justice in Islam: Should *Qisas* be considered a form of restorative justice? *Berkeley Journal of Middle Eastern & Islamic Law*. Retrieved from http://scholarship.law.berkeley.edu/cgi/viewcontent.cgi?article=1018&context=jmeil

Hoig, Stan. (1980). *The peace chiefs of the Cheyenne*. Norman: University of Oklahoma Press.

Hornby, Helen. (1988). *Lights of guidance: A Bahá'í reference file*. New Delhi, India: Bahá'í Publishing Trust.

Hossain, Ishtiaq. (2013). Bangladesh: Civil resistance in the struggle for independence, 1948–1971. In Macie J. Bartkowski (Ed.), *Recovering nonviolent history: Civil resistance in liberation struggles* (pp.199–216). Boulder, CO: Lynne Rienner Publishers.

Iftikhar, Arsalan. (2011). *Islamic pacifism: Global Muslims in the post-Osama era*. CreateSpace: Author.

Islamic Supreme Council of Canada. (2012, February 14). *Honour killings, domestic violence, and misogyny are un-Islamic and major crimes*. Retrieved from http://www.islamicsupremecouncil.com/fatwa-honour-killings-misogyny-domestic-violence.pdf

Jaspers, Karl. (1953). *The origin and goal of history* (Michael Bullock, Trans.). London: Routledge & Keegan Paul. Originally published as Jaspers, Karl. (1949). *Vom Ursprung und Ziel der Geschichte* [The origin and goal of history] (in German) (1st ed.), München: Piper.

Jaspers, Karl. (2003). *The way to wisdom: An introduction to philosophy*. New Haven, CT: Yale University Press. (Original work published in 1951.)

Jerryson, Michael K., & Juergensmeyer, Mark. (2010). *Buddhist warfare*. Oxford, UK: Oxford University Press.

Jocks, Christopher Ronwanièn:te. (1997). Spirituality for sale: Sacred knowledge in the consumer age. In Lee Irwin (Ed.), *Native American spirituality: A critical reader* (pp. 61–77). Lincoln: University of Nebraska Press.

Kabbani, Shaykh M. Hisham, & Ziad, Homayra. (2011). The prohibition of domestic violence in Islam. Retrieved from http://www.worde.org/wp-content/uploads/2011/09/DV-Fatwa-Online-Version.pdf.

Kamenetz, Roger. (1994). *The Jew in the lotus: A poet's rediscovery of Jewish identity in Buddhist India*. San Francisco, CA: HarperSanFrancisco.
Keddie, Nikki R. (2013). Iran: Nonviolent revolts, 1890–1906. In Macie J. Bartkowski (Ed.), *Recovering nonviolent history: Civil resistance in liberation struggles* (pp. 143–160). Boulder, CO: Lynne Rienner Publishers.
Kelly, Thomas. (1941). *Testament of devotion*. New York: HarperCollins.
Kennedy, R. Scott. (1984). The Druze of the Golan: A case of non-violent resistance. *Journal of Palestine Studies, 13*(2), 48–64.
Kephart, Horace. (1936). *The Cherokees of the Smoky Mountains*. Ithaca, NY: The Atkinson Press.
Khanneh, M., & Salameh, N. (2006). *Islam and peace* (Walid Shomali, Trans.). Bethlehem, Palestine: Center for Conflict Resolution and Reconciliation.
Kidwell, Carla Sue, Noley, Homer, & Tinker, George E. (2001). *A Native American theology*. Maryknoll, NY: Orbis Books.
Kimelman, Reuven. (trans.). (1970). *Netivot Olam, Netiv Hatochecha*, in The Rabbinic ethics of protest, *Judaism 19*, 1.
King, Martin Luther Jr. (1958). *Stride toward freedom*. New York: Harper & Row.
King, Martin Luther Jr. (1959). My trip to the land of Gandhi. Retrieved from http://mlk-kpp01.stanford.edu/primarydocuments/Vol5/July1959_MyTriptotheLandofGandhi.pdf
King, Martin Luther Jr. (1963). *Letter from a Birmingham jail*. Retrieved from http://www.africa.upenn.edu/Articles_Gen/Letter_Birmingham.html
Kitchens, James H. (1996). The bombing of Auschwitz reexamined. In Vern W. Newton (Ed.), *FDR and the Holocaust*. New York: St. Martin's Press.
Konko Churches of North America (n.d.). Retrieved from http://foxmeister.net//kcnahacked/view/beliefs.php?id=4
Korejo, Muhammad Soaleh. (1993). *The Frontier Gandhi: His place in history*. Karachi, Pakistan: Oxford University Press.
Kushner, Harold S. (1981). *When bad things happen to good people*. New York: Avon.
Lacouture, Jeane, & Lacouture, Simonne. (1958). *Egypt in transition*. New York: Criterion Books.
Laws, Rita. (1994, September). History of vegetarianism: Native Americans and vegetarianism. *The Vegetarian Journal*. Retrieved from http://www.ivu.org/history/native_americans.html
Leiter, M.P., & Maslach, C. (2005). *Banishing burnout: Six strategies for improving your relationship with work*. San Francisco, CA: Jossey-Bass.
Linn, D., Linn, S. F., & Linn, M. (1997). *Don't forgive too soon: Extending the two hands that heal*. Mahwah, NJ: Paulist Press.
Long, Michael G. (2011). *Christian peace and nonviolence: A documentary history*. Maryknoll, NY: Orbis Books.
Loy, David R. (1997). *The great awakening: A Buddhist social theory*. Boston: Wisdom Publications.
Mabee, Carleton. (1970). *Black freedom: The nonviolent abolitionists from 1830 through the Civil War*. Toronto, Canada: The Macmillan Company.
MacNair, Rachel M. (2002). *Perpetration-Induced Traumatic Stress: The psychological consequences of killing*. Westport, CT: Praeger Publishers.
Mann, B., & Fields, J.L. (1997). A sign in the sky: Dating the League of the Haudenosaunee. *American Indian Culture and Research Journal, 21*, 105–163.
Mann, Charles C. (2005). *1491: New revelations of the Americas before Columbus*. New York: Alfred A. Knopf.

Marder, Ian. (2014). *Opportunities to use restorative justice in the Moroccan criminal justice process*. Souissi, Rabat, Morocco: Search for Common Ground-Morocco. Retrieved from https://www.sfcg.org/wp-content/uploads/2014/07/Opportunities-to-use-Restorative-Justice-in-the-Moroccan-Criminal-Justice-Process.pdf

Martin, James. (2013). The humor of St. Teresa of Avila. Retrieved from http://www.carmelites.net/news/the-humor-of-st-teresa-of-avila/.

Maslach, C. (1982). *Burnout: The cost of caring*. Englewood Cliffs, NJ: Prentice-Hall, Inc.

Moore, Hannah. (1811). On the comparatively small faults and virtues. *Religion of the heart*, Chapter 11. Retrieved from http://gracegems.org/Books2/more11.htm

Morgan, Diane. (2001). *The best guide to eastern philosophy and religion* (1st ed.). Los Angeles: Renaissance Books.

Moser-Puangsuwan, Yeshua. (2013). Burma: Civil resistance in the anticolonial struggle, 1910–1940. In Macie J. Bartkowski (Ed.), *Recovering nonviolent history: Civil resistance in liberation struggles* (pp.183–198). Boulder, CO: Lynne Rienner Publishers.

Mullen, T. (1989). *Laughing out loud, and other religious experiences*. Richmond, IN: Friends United Press.

Muni, Jagdish. (2006). Capital punishment: Time to abandon it? *Hinduism Today*. Retrieved from http://www.hinduismtoday.com/modules/smartsection/item.php?itemid=1451

Nikam, N. A. & McKeon, Richard (Eds.). (1978). *The edicts of Asoka*. Chicago, IL: University of Chicago Press.

Noonan, J. T. (1979). *A private choice*. New York: The Free Press.

O'Brien, Mariola. (2014, February 19). Swedish nurse takes a stand on conscience rights. *Mercatornet*. Retrieved from http://www.mercatornet.com/articles/view/swedish_nurse_takes_a_stand_on_conscience_rights

Open Letter to Al-Baghdadi. (2014). Retrieved from http://lettertobaghdadi.com/index.php

Paige, Glenn D., Satha-Anand, Chaiwat, & Gilliatt, Sarah. (2001). *Islam and nonviolence*. Center for Global Nonviolence. Retrieved from http://nonkilling.org/pdf/b3.pdf

Pal, Amitabh. (2011). *"Islam" means peace: Understanding the Muslim principle of nonviolence today*. Santa Barbara, CA: Praeger.

Paris, Ginette. (1986). *Pagan meditations*. New York: Spring Publications.

Paris, Ginette. (1992). *The sacrament of abortion*. New York: Spring Publications.

Peat, F. D. (1994). *Blackfoot physics: A journey into the American Indian universe*. London, UK: Fourth Estate Ltd.

Pew Research Center. (2008, February). U.S. Religious Landscape Survey. Retrieved from http://religions.pewforum.org/pdf/report-religious-landscape-study-full.pdf

Pew Research Center. (2011). *The future of the global Muslim population*. Retrieved from http://www.pewforum.org/2011/01/27/the-future-of-the-global-muslim-population/

Pew Research Center. (2012, December 18). *The global religious landscape: Buddhists*. Retrieved from http://www.pewforum.org/2012/12/18/global-religious-landscape-buddhist/
Prabhavananda, Swami. (1963). *The Sermon on the Mount according to the Vedanta*. Hollywood, CA: The Vedanta Press.
Prete, Anthony. (2006). A God of surprises. In Buckley & Angell (Eds.), *The Quaker Bible reader*. Richmond, IN: Earlham School of Religion Publications.
Pyarelal, Nayar. (1966). *Thrown to the wolves: Abdul Ghaffar Khan*. Kolkata, India: East Light Book House.
Qafisheh, Mataz M. (2012). Restorative justice in the Islamic penal law: A contribution to the global system. *International Journal of Criminal Justice Sciences, 7*(1), 487–507. Retrieved from http://www.sascv.org/ijcjs/pdfs/mutazaicjs2012istissue.pdf
Queen, Christopher S. (1988). The Peace Wheel: Nonviolent activism in the Buddhist tradition. In D. L. Smith-Christopher (Ed.), *Subverting hatred: The challenge of nonviolence in religious traditions* (pp. 25–48). Maryknoll, NY: Orbis Books.
Rahal, Malika. (2013). Algeria: Nonviolent resistance against French colonialism, 1830s–1950s. In Macie J. Bartkowski (Ed.), *Recovering nonviolent history: Civil resistance in liberation struggles* (pp. 107–123). Boulder, CO: Lynne Rienner Publishers.
Rahami, M. (2007). Islamic restorative traditions and their reflections in the post revolutionary criminal justice system of Iran. *European Journal of Crime, Criminal Law and Criminal Justice*, 227–248.
Rahman, Jamal, Elias, Kathleen Schmitt, & Redding, Ann Holmes. (2009). *Out of darkness into light: Spiritual guidance in the Quran with reflections from Christian and Jewish sources*. Harrisburg, NY: Morehouse Publishing.
Religion & Ethics Newsweekly. (2014, October 24). China, Buddhism, and the environment. Public Broadcasting System. Retrieved from http://www.pbs.org/wnet/religionandethics/2014/10/24/october-24-2014-china-buddhism-environment/24431/
Roberts, Holly H. (2004). *Vegetarian Christian saints: Mystics, ascetics & monks*. Sequim, WA: Anjeli Press.
Robinson, John A. T. (1976). *Redating the New Testament*. Eugene, OR: Wipf and Stock Publishers.
Rosenberg, Marshall B. (1999). *Nonviolent communication: A language of compassion*. DelMar, CA: PuddleDancer Press.
Rosenberg, Marshall B. (2004). *Practical spirituality: Reflections on the spiritual basis of nonviolent communication*. Encinitas, CA: PuddleDancer Press.
Ross, Janet L. R. (2006). Hidden manna, hidden meanings: Unveiling Revelation. In P. Buckley & S. W. Angell (Eds.), *The Quaker Bible reader*. Richmond, IN: Earlham School of Religion Publications.
Rothberg, D. (1998). Responding to the cries of the world: Socially engaged Buddhism in North America. In C. S. Prebish & K. K. Tanaka (Eds.), *The faces of Buddhism in America* (pp. 266–268). Berkeley: University of California Press.
Sa'id, Jawdat. (1964). *The doctrine of the first son of Adam*. Retrieved from http://www.jawdatsaid.net

Satha-Anand, Chaiwat. (1993). Core values for peacemaking in Islam: The Prophet's practice as paradigm. In Elise Boulding (Ed.), *Building peace in the Middle East: Challenges for states and civil society*. Boulder, CO: Lynn Rienner.

Sayers, Dorothy. (1941). *The mind of the maker*. London, UK: Methuen.

Schaaf, Gregory. (1988). From the Great Law of Peace to the Constitution of the United States: A revision of America's democratic roots. *American Indian Law Review, 14*(2), 323–331.

Schaefer, Robert W. (2008). *Insurgency and Chechnya*. Washington, DC: Potomac Books.

Schwartz, Richard H. (2001). *Judaism and vegetarianism* (Rev. ed.). New York: Lantern Books.

Seager, Richard Hughes. (2006). *Encountering the Dharma: Daisaku Ikeda, Soka Gakkai, and the globalization of Buddhist humanism*. Berkeley, CA: University of California Press.

Seibert, Eric A. (2012). *The violence of scripture: Overcoming the Old Testament's troubling legacy*. Minneapolis, MN: Fortress Press.

Shah, Indries. (1996). *Learning how to learn: Psychology and spirituality in the Sufi way*. New York: Penguin Compass.

Shareef, Simon. (2008, December). Democratic dawn. *Himal Southasian*. Retrieved from http://old.himalmag.com/component/content/article/1045-.html

Sharma, Arvind. (2011). The Bhagavadgita and war: Some early anticipations of the Gandhian Interpretation of the Bhagavadgita. In A. Sharma (Ed.), *The world's religions: A contemporary reader*. Minneapolis, MN: Fortress Press.

Sharp, Gene. (1973). *The politics of nonviolent action*. Boston, MA: Porter Sargent Publishers.

Sharp, Gene. (2005). *Waging nonviolent struggle: 20th century practice and 21st century potential*. Boston, MA: Extending Horizon Books.

Shastri, S.Y., & Shastri, Y.S. (1998). Ahimsa and the unity of all things: A Hindu view of nonviolence. In D.L. Smith-Christopher (Ed.), *Subverting hatred: The challenge of nonviolence in religious traditions* (pp. 67–84). Maryknoll, NY: Orbis Books.

Shih, Hu. (1963). *The development of the logical method in ancient China*. New York: Paragon Book Reprint Corporation.

Sinclair, Upton. (1918). *The profits of religion: An essay in economic interpretation*. Pasadena, CA: Author.

Singh, Nikki. (2009). Jesus through Sikh eyes. Retrieved from http://www.bbc.co.uk/religion/religions/sikhism/people/jesus.shtml

Smith, Hannah Whitall. (1906). *The God of all comfort*. Retrieved from http://pastorpauley.com/books/comfort.pdf

Smith-Christopher, Daniel L. (Ed.). (1998). *Subverting hatred: The challenge of nonviolence in religious traditions*. Maryknoll, NY: Orbis Books.

Sontag, D. & Alvarez, L. (2008, January 13). War torn: Across American, deadly echoes of foreign battles. *New York Times*.

Squire, J.C. (1916). *The survival of the fittest and other poems*. London, UK: George Allen & Unwin Ltd.

Starhawk. (1999). *The Spiral Dance: A rebirth of the ancient religion of the Great Goddess*. New York: HarperCollins.

Stark, Rodney. (2007). *Discovering God: The origins of the great religions and the evolution of belief.* New York: HarperCollins.
Stoltzfus, Nathan. (1996). *Resistance of the heart: Intermarriage and the Rosenstrasse Protest in Nazi Germany.* New Brunswick, NJ: Rutgers University Press.
Tagore, Rabindranath. (1916). *Adhana: The realization of life.* New York: Macmillan.
Tarbiyat Community. (n.d.). Frequent questions. Retrieved from http://www.tarbiyatcenter.org/FAQ.html
Teasdall, Wayne. (1999). *The mystic heart: Discovering a universal spirituality in the world's religions.* Novato, CA: New World Library.
Tendulkar, Dinanath. (1967). *Abdul Ghaffar Khan: Faith is a battle.* Mumbai, India: Times of India Press.
Tenrikyo Online. (2012, November 1). Tenrikyo attends international meeting for peace in Sarajevo. Retrieved from http://online.tenrikyo.or.jp/?p=1530
Tenrikyo Online. (2013, November 6). Tenrikyo's representative speech by Rev. Yoshihiko Shirokihara at International Meeting for Peace in Rome. Retrieved from http://online.tenrikyo.or.jp/?p=2198
Tenrikyo Online. (2014, January 28). A symposium on the overseas mission held. Retrieved from http://online.tenrikyo.or.jp/?p=2416
Thistlethwaite, Susan Brooks (Ed.). (2012). *Interfaith just peacemaking: Jewish, Christian, and Muslim perspectives on the new paradigm of peace and war.* New York: Palgrave MacMillan.
Thurman, Howard. (1949/1996). *Jesus and the disinherited.* Boston, MA: Beacon Press.
Tirosh-Samuelson, Hava (Ed.). (2002). *Judaism and ecology.* Cambridge, MA: Harvard University Press.
Tonstad, S. K. (2006). *Saving God's reputation: The theological function of Pistis Iesou in the cosmic narrative of Revelation.* New York: T&T Clark International.
Tutu, D. M. (1999). *No future without forgiveness.* New York: Doubleday.
Ullstein, Hans. (1961). *Spielplatz meines Lebens.* Munich, Germany: Kinkler.
Umbreit, M., Lewis, T., & Burns, H. (2003). A community response to a 9/11 hate crime: Restorative justice through dialogue. *Contemporary Justice Review, 6*(4), 383–391.
Umbreit, M. & Ritter, R. (2006). Arab offenders meet Jewish victim: Restorative family dialogue in Israel. *Conflict Resolution Quarterly, 24*(1), 99–109.
United Nations. (2006). *Handbook on restorative justice programmes.* New York: United Nations. Retrieved from http://www.unodc.org/pdf/criminal_justice/06-56290_Ebook.pdf
Wagner, Sally Roesch. (1996). *The untold story of the Iroquois influence on early feminists.* Aberdeen, SD: Sky Carrier Press.
Walker, Polly O. (2009). Singing a new song: The role of music in indigenous strategies of nonviolent social change. In Ralph V. Summy (Ed.), *Nonviolent alternatives for social change* (pp. 130–155). EOLSS Publishers Co. Ltd. . . Retrieved from http://www.eolss.net/Sample-Chapters/C04/E6-120-07.pdf
Washington, James Melvin (Ed.). (1986). *A testament of hope: the essential writings of Martin Luther King, Jr.* San Francisco, CA: Harper & Row.
World Health Organization. (1992). *The ICD-10 classification of mental and behavioural disorders: Clinical descriptions and diagnostic guidelines.* Geneva, Switzerland: World Health Organization.

Wright, N. T. (2003). *The resurrection of the Son of God*. Minneapolis, MN: Fortress Press.

Wright, N. T. (2011). *Revelation for everyone*. Louisville, KY: Westminster John Knox Press.

Yaffe, Martin D. (Ed.). (2001). *Judaism and environmental ethics: A reader*. Lanham, MD: Lexington Books.

Yancey, Philip D. (1999). *The Bible Jesus read*. Grand Rapids, MI: The Zondervan Corporation.

Yancey, Philip D. (2006). *Prayer: Does it make any difference?* Nashville, TN: Zondervan.

Yogananda, Paramahansa. (2004). *The Second Coming of Christ: The resurrection of the Christ within you*. Los Angeles: Self-Realization Fellowship.

Yogananda, Paramahansa. (2013). *The Bhagavad Gita: God talks with Arjuna*. Los Angeles, CA: Self-Realization Fellowship.

Zaehner, R. C. (1956). *The Teachings of the Magi*. London, UK: George Allen & Unwin Ltd.

Zunes, Stephen. (1999). Unarmed resistance in the Middle East and North Africa. In S. Zunes, L. R. Kurtz, & S. B. Asher (Eds.), *Nonviolent social movements: A geographical perspective*. Malden, MA: Blackwell Publishers.

Subject Index

Aaron, 18, 26
'Abdu'l-Baha, 178, 181–82, 185
Abhinavagupta, 55–56
Abolition of slavery, 117–18, 120
Abortion, 103, 113, 213–14, 263–64. *See also* Feticide
Abraham, 18, 26, 33, 36, 123, 126
Abrogation, 145–46
Abu-Nimer, Mohammed, 134, 241
Adams, John, 159
Agamas, 61
Agnosticism, 206–14, 249
Ahmadiyya, 135
Ahura Mazda, 82–83, 86, 88, 292
Aisha, 133
Akbar, 43
Akhenaten, 17
Al Ahsai, Shaykh Amad, 178
Algeria, 140
Ali, Maulana Muhammad, 233–34
Ali, Mirza Husayn, 188. *See also* Bahá'u'lláh
Allegories, 122
Al-Wathbah, 142
Ambedkar, Bhimrao Ramji, 79
Amesha Spentas, 83–84
Amritsar massacre, 172, 173
Andrews, C. F., 172–73

Anger, 226–27, 238–39
Angra Mainyu, 82–83
Angulimala, 76, 251–52, 254
Animal sacrifice. *See* Blood sacrifice; Meat consumption
Antiochus, 30, 277
Apartheid, 47, 235, 239, 279
Apocalyptic writings, 276–79
Aquinas, Thomas, 121, 188
Arab Spring, 136, 143
Argentina, 119
Aristophanes, 104
Aristotle, 96, 188
Ariyaratne, A. T., 75
Arjuna, 41, 55–56
Arkhipov, Vasili, 213
Armstrong, Karen, 97
Arner, Rob, 114
Art, 276–79
Asceticism, 62, 170, 288–89
Ashoka, 64, 68–69, 76, 78, 79, 285
Asser, Tobias Michel Karel, 21
Astrology, 210
Atheism, 6, 8, 61, 114, 206–14, 221, 249
Atom bomb. *See* Nuclear weapons
Augustine of Hippo, 121, 240
Aung San, 71–72, 79, 243, 261
Aung San Suu Kyi, 66, 72

Aurangzeb, 43, 168
Australia, 70, 151, 166, 264
Australian aborigines, 166
Avatars, 57
Avesta, 82
Axial Age, 24, 82, 96–97, 217
Ayonwatha, 158
Azad, Abul Kalam, 142
Aztec, 154

Baal Shem Tov, 23
Báb, The, 177–78
Bahá'ís, 6, 177–86, 149–50; ecology, 295; relations with other religions, 92
Bahá'u'lláh, 92, 177–80, 183, 184, 186, 295
Bangladesh, 79, 131, 140–41
Banta, Bruce, 244
Banyacya, Thomas, 160
Barlas, Asma, 133
Bartoli, Andrea, 119
Baptism, 120
Berrigan, Daniel, 124
Bhave, Vinoba, 45, 52
Bhutan, 76
Bible composition, 18–19, 107
Bilal, 134
Biology, 67, 152–53, 183, 207, 221, 291
Bismallah, 245
Blasphemy, 236
Blavatsky, Helena, 188
Blood sacrifice, 18, 83, 86, 105, 109, 163–64, 187; ancient religion positions, 33, 53, 75, 87, 120, 143; recent religion positions, 173, 184, 191–93, 202
Blood sports, 144
Bodhisattvas, 65, 224
Bohr, Neils, 267
Bowen, Charles, 230
Boycott, Charles, 47
Boycotts: campaigns, 116–17, 137, 138, 140, 171, 273, 277; strategy, 3, 47, 286
Buddha: life story, 62–63, 76, 77, 101; quotes, 64, 68, 75

Buddhism, 62–80; ecology, 291–92; relations with other religions, 36, 56–57, 125, 148
Bulgaria, 267
Burma, 66, 71–73, 79, 243, 261
Burnout, 236, 273–76

Cahill, Thomas, 23
Cahokia, 155, 164
Calendars, 11–12, 129, 154
Caligula, 31
Cambodia, 73, 76, 205
Canada, 146, 151, 152
Cao Dai, 79–80
Carlin, George, 220–21
Cassin, René, 21
Caste system, 45, 64, 79, 87, 175
Celibacy, 221
Changing the script, 251–52
Chechnya, 141
Chelcisky, Peter, 114
Chenoweth, Erica, 5, 12
Cherokee/Tsigali, 154, 163, 165, 166
Cheyenne, 163
Chieu, Ngo Va˘n, 79–80
Childbirth, 194, 202
Chile, 118–19
China, 6, 65, 67, 96, 97–103 211, 213
Chocktaw, 165
Chocolate, 286
Chopra, 45
Christianity, 106–27; ecology, 292–93; relations with other religions, 36–37, 57, 78, 91, 165
Civil Disobedience, 109, 119, 141, 243
Civil Rights Movement, U.S., 8, 47, 117, 119, 134, 212, 243, 272–73
Clare of Assisi, 114
Clement of Alexandria, 125
Cochin Jews, 58–59
Colombia, 119
Comenius, Jan Amos, 115, 250
Communion, 120
Competition, 244, 291
Community policing, 254
Conflict resolution, 4, 246–54, 283
Confucianism, 96, 99
Confucius/K'ung Fu Tze, 96, 99, 240

Subject Index

Connecting, 251–52
Conscience, 4, 218–29, 267
Conscientious objection, 3–4, 34, 160, 263–64
Constantine, 36, 108–9, 133, 125
Constructive Program, 282–96
Conway, Moncure, 118
Cooperation, 165, 180, 244
Council of Christians and Jews, 37, 127
Cyprian, 242
Creationism, 209
Creation stories, 21–23, 165
Croatia, 263–64
Crones, 190
Crucifixion, 114, 120, 126, 147
Crusades wars, 114, 148, 210
Cuba, 118–19, 211, 213, 265
Cuban missile crisis, 4, 213
Cyrus, 84
Czechoslovakia, 114–15

Daijin, Konko, 203–5
Daimoku, 72–73
Dalai Lama, 36, 66, 79, 245
Dalit, 45, 79
Daniel, Biblical book, 277
Dawkins, Richard, 209
Darwin, Charles, 209
Day, Dorothy, 234
Deception, 29
Death Penalty, 103, 114; ancient religion positions, 34, 53–54, 60, 88, 121, 144; recent religion positions, 174, 184–85, 202
Deganawidah, 157–58
de la Boétie, Etienne, 256–57
Deming, Barbara, 239
Demonstrations: against Nazis, 267, 268; Chinese, 213; Druze, 150; Islamic, 137, 138, 141, 143; Judean, 32, 109; strategy, 3
Denmark, 266–67
de Nobili, Roberto, 125–26
Devil, 37, 88, 91, 92, 125, 234
Dharam Yudh, 174
Dharma, 49, 60, 69, 70, 147, 243
Dialecticians, 100

Divine Reminder, 204
Diwali, 42
Diem, Ngo Dinh, 74
Dionysius the Short, 11
Domestic violence, 146
Dominican Republic, 119
Douglass, Frederick, 220
Downshift, 274
Draft, military, 4, 115, 160, 263–64
Druids, 188, 191
Druze, 149–50
Duckwitz, Georg, 267
Dust of the mind, 196, 199, 202
Dyer, E. H., 172
Dylan, Bob, 222
Dymond, Jonathan, 116, 257, 259

Ebadi, Shirin, 131, 133
Ecology, 67, 86, 167, 201, 203, 187–93, 289–95
Economic conversion, 69, 285
Ecumenism, 8–9
Effendi, Shoghi, 178, 185, 186
Egypt, 17, 28, 114, 131, 136–38
Eichhorn, J. G., 209
Eichmann, Adolph, 34, 223
Eid al-Adha, 143
Eightfold Path, 63, 292
ElBaradei, Mohamed, 131
Elections, 2
Elijah, 96
Elizabeth II, 172
El Salvador, 119
Emetan, Atrupat-e, 88
Emperor worship, 7, 31, 73, 187, 211
Empedocles, 103
Engaged Buddhism, 70–75
Enslaved people, 18, 117, 222–23, 272–73. *See also individual names*
Enuma Elish, 22
Epicurus, 208
Equality, gender. *See* Women's equality
Eucharist, 120
Euthanasia, 103
Evolution, 209–10
Ezekiel, 82, 89, 96, 277

Fa-Hsien, 76
Ferdowsi, 88
Feticide, 103, 114; ancient religion positions, 34, 54, 76, 89, 121, 144; recent religion positions, 174–75, 185, 202; sex-selection, 45, 54, 64, 112–13, 132–33
Feuerbach, Ludwig, 209
Finn, Huckleberry, 157
First Nations, 6, 151–67, 294
Follett, Mary Parker, 247
Forgiveness, 237–39
Four Noble Truths, 63, 219
Fox, George, 259
Francis of Assisi, 114
Frankl, Victor, 237
Friedd, Alfred Hermann, 21
Fundamentalism, 210

Gage, Matilda Joslyn, 159
Gaius, 31–32
Gandhi, Mohandas: attitude on scriptures, 55, 58; authority, 142, 174; explanations, 1, 219, 224, 282; life story, 46–47, 56, 71, 141; quotations, 4, 52, 136, 222, 226, 237, 242, 259
Gandhi, Rajmohan, 56
Ganges River, 42
Gardening, 287, 289
Gardner, Gerald Broussaeu, 189
Gayoom, Maumoon Abdul, 139–40
Georgia, 92, 140
Gladiator games, 111, 113
Goebbels, 268–69
Golden Rule, 97, 245
Goldman, Emma, 225
Graham, Sylvester, 118
Greece, ancient, 96, 103–5, 188
Greed, 224–26
Green Movement, 130
Guatemala, 119
Gurdwaras, 169, 175
Guru Granth Sahib, 169, 170
Gurus, Sikh, 168–69, 175

Hadith, 129–30, 133, 134, 144, 146, 177, 227
Hanh, Thich Nhat, 67, 70, 218, 220–21, 227, 258–59

Haiti, 119
Hajj, 42, 129, 132, 141, 142
Halal, 144
Hare Krishna, 45, 54
Harris, Rabia Terri, 130, 131, 132, 134, 137
Harrison, George, 44
Hatred, 226–27
Haudenosaunee/Iroquois, 118, 157–60
Heaven, 68, 102, 124, 220, 240, 247
Heaven and hell, 37, 83, 90, 91, 92, 179, 204, 231
Hell, 9, 53, 77, 78, 83, 122–23, 147, 210, 218, 226–27
Heretics: ancient religion positions, 36, 56, 78, 89, 124–25, 147; recent religion positions, 175, 186, 202
Herod, King, 11
Hertz Joseph, 37
Hiawatha, 158
Hibakusha, 73
Hijra, 129, 131–32
Hillel, Rabbi, 245
Hinduism, 39–61; ecology, 290–91; relations with other religions, 37, 78–79, 90–91, 148–49
Hindutva, 56
Hinokishin, 196, 202
Hippocratic Oath, 103
Hiroshima, 73
Hitchens, Christopher, 211
Hitler, Adolf, 265–66, 268–70
Hobbes, Thomas, 209
Holocaust, 20–21, 79, 127, 264–71
Holy Experiment, 116–17
Honorius, emperor, 113
Hope, 234–36
Hopis, 160, 263
Hopper, Isaac, 252
Hui Shih, 100
Humanism, 206–14
Human sacrifice. See Blood sacrifice
Humility, 9, 236, 239–41
Humor, 236–37, 275, 276
Husain, 142

Subject Index 311

Idolatry, 18, 132, 219–21, 228, 236, 275–76, 287
Ikeda, Daisaku, 73
Incarnation of God, 41, 57, 107, 148
Independence movement, 71, 135–36, 272, 282, 285
India: Axial Age, 96; Buddhism, 79; Government, 291; Islam, 141, 142. *See also* Ashoka; Hinduism; Jainism; Parsis; Sikhs
Indians, American. *See* First Nations *and individual names and nations*
Indigenous, 7, 94–96, 151–67, 187–88, 294
Indonesia, 58, 79
Infanticide, 45, 112–13, 113, 114, 132–33; ancient religion positions, 34, 54, 76, 88, 121, 144; recent religion positions, 174–75, 185, 202
Integrative solutions, 247
Interconnectedness, 67
Iran, 59, 82, 85, 92, 131, 138–39, 177, 254
Iraq, 25, 73, 92, 142
Irenaeus, 124–25
Iroquois/Haudenosaunee, 118, 157–60
Isaac, 18, 33, 126, 143
Ishmael, 126, 143
Islam, 128–50; ecology, 293–94; relations with other religions, 37, 58, 79, 91–92, 126
Islamic State (ISIS), 92–93
Israel: ancient, 18–20, 24, 38, 51, 107, 126, 163; modern, 21, 34, 36–38, 149, 150
Isnad, 130

Jacob, 18
Jaspers, Karl, 96
Jainism, 6, 40, 59–61, 88, 96, 186, 208, 291
Japan, 65, 71, 72–73, 76, 79, 194–206, 292, 296
Jerome, saint, 125
Jesus: attitudes of Bahá'ís, 177; attitudes of Buddhism, 78, 125; attitudes of First Nations: 155–56, 166; attitudes of Hinduism, 57; attitudes of Judaism, 36; attitudes of Islam, 126, 128, 148; female imagery, 93; impact, 114, 223, 260; life story, 11–12, 91, 106–7; teachings, 109–12, 120, 122, 226–27, 230
Jiba, 195
Jinas, 60–61
Jinja Honcho, 203
Jobs, 285
Jobs, Steve, 44
Jocks, Christopher Ronwanièn:te, 162–63
John of Damascus, 126
John of Patmos, 123–24, 277
John the Baptist, 177
Josephus, 30–32, 34
Joy, 236–37
Judaism, 17–38; ecology, 290; relations with other religions, 58–59, 79, 89–90, 126–27, 149
Just peacemaking, 121
Just war doctrines, 2, 34, 53, 60, 77–78, 84, 120, 144, 174, 264
Just-World View, 229–31

Ka'aba, 129
Kamenetz, Roger, 36
Kami, 203–5
Kara, 199–200
Karma: rejected, 203, 208; religious beliefs, 40–42, 60–61, 63, 170; use of doctrine, 8–9, 54, 76, 77, 217
Karman, Tawakkol, 131, 133
Kazim-i-Rashti, Siyyid, 178
Kellogg, John Harvey, 118
Kelly, Thomas, 220
Khadija, 128, 133
Khalsa community, 169
Khan, Abdul-Ghaffar/Badshah, 128, 135–36, 142, 241, 260
Khudai Khidmatgars, 135–36
King, Martin Luther, 119, 125, 132, 212, 234, 243, 260, 273
Kishiev, Kunta-haji, 141
Kitab-i-Aqdas, 177
Kitab-i-Iqan, 177
Knots, 196–97
Konkokyo, 203–5
Kosher, 34–35, 121, 144

Kosovo, 141
Krishna, 41–42, 45, 49, 55–56, 57, 232
Kumbh Mela Festival, 42
Kung-Shu Pan, 98
Kung-sun Lung, 100
Kushner, Harold, 230
Kwanzaa, 167
Kyoten-Gorikai, 205

Langar, 170
Lao-Tzu, 101
Last Day, 149, 233, 278
Law of Peace, 156, 157–58
Laws, Rita, 165
Lazarus, 123
Lifestyles, 4, 46, 60, 103, 170–71, 285–96
Livy, 94–95
Lotus Sutra, 65, 72, 73
Lucretius, 208

Mabee, Carleton, 252
Maccabaeus, Judas, 30
Maccabees, 30
Magi, 81, 91, 127
Magic, 106, 189–90, 231, 236, 278
Magna Carta, 114
Mahabharata, 41, 49, 55
Mahaprabhu, Chaitanya, 46
Maharal of Prague, 1, 27
Maharishi, Ramana, 51
Mahavira, 59, 61
Mahraspandan, Adarbad, 88
Maimonides, Moses, 34
Makiguchi, Tsunesaburo, 73
Malaysia, 79
Malcolm X, 132, 134
Maldives, 139–40
Mandela, Nelson, 260
Mann, Charles, 156
Marcion, 126
Marshall Plan, 271
Martyrs: Christian, 108, 124, 242; Muslim, 132; general, 264; Sikh, 172, 174
Marx, Karl, 211, 237
Marx, Groucho, 237
Mary, mother of Jesus, 148, 190

Maslach, Christina, 274–75
Meat consumption, 46, 103–4, 113, 143, 164–65; ancient religion positions, 23–24, 54, 77, 88–89, 121, 144–45, 287–88; recent religion positions, 175, 185–86, 192, 202
Mecca, 42, 128–29, 132, 141, 145
Medina, 129, 132, 145
Mehta, Lekh Raj, 60
Melek Taus, 92
Mencius/Meng Tzu, 99
Mennonites, 114, 263
Messiah, 19, 36, 106, 110
Metta, 66
Mikagura-uta, 197
Miki, Nakayama, 194. See also Oyasama
Milgram, Stanley, 223
Milgram electroshock experiments, 223, 227, 260–62
Mill, John Stuart, 210
Milosevic, Slobodon, 141
Mindfulness, 63, 66, 74, 78, 196, 239
Miriam, 18
Mishnah, 36, 149
Miwoks, 161
Moksha, 42
Money, 182, 220, 224, 285, 286–87
Mongols, 69
Montgomery Bus Boycott, 273
Moore, Hannah, 228, 239
Moral jiu-jitsu, 3–4
Morocco, 254
Moses: in the Bible, 18, 26, 27, 36; as historical figure, 63, 177, 209; in the Qur'an, 147, 149
Mo Tse, 6, 96, 97–100
Mother Teresa, 245, 260
Mott, Lucretia, 159, 252
Muhammad: attitudes of Bahá'ís, 147; life story 128–29, 133; final prophet, 147–48; impact, 130–31, 140, 149; teachings, 130, 134, 144 T, 146
Mullen, Tom, 236–37
Muni, Jagdish, 54
Murti, Vasu, 41
Music, 74, 161, 166, 197, 276
Musharraf, 142

Subject Index 313

Mystery, 189, 241
Mysticism, 43, 58, 126, 134–35

Naganuma, Myoko, 73
Nagasaki, 73
Nagrela, Samuel ibn, 28
Nanak, Guru, 168
Nasheed, Mohamed, 139–40
Native Americans, 151–67
Nazism, 4, 7, 21, 127, 223, 264–71
Nichiren, 72–73
Nirvana, 41, 64, 65
Niwano, Nikkyo, 73
Noah, 35, 149
Nobel Peace Prize: nominees, 75, 136; winners, 21, 45, 66, 72, 131, 133, 260
Nonattachment, 60, 219
Nontheism, 207, 208, 214
Nonviolent army, 135–36
Nonviolent communication, 4, 250–51
Noonan, John, 262–63
North Korea, 7, 211
Norway, 269–70
Nuclear weapons: impact, 213, 286; Nobel Peace Prize for opposing, 21, 131; religious opposition, 72–73, 160, 183, 191

Ofudesaki, 197
Origen, 55
Original Sin, 9, 210
Open Letter to Baghdadi, 93, 143–44, 146
Osashizu, 197
Ottama, U, 71
Oyasama, 194–95, 197–99, 202

Paganism: ancient, 7, 94–105; revived, 6, 187–93, 295
Pali Canon, 65
Pakistan, 58, 92, 131, 136, 140–41, 142, 148, 168
Palm Sunday, 108
Paramahamsa, Ramakrishna, 43, 48
Parenting, 284–85
Parliament of the World's Religions, 43, 51, 165
Paris, Ginette, 192

Parsis, 59, 82–83, 85, 87, 89, 90, 92
Participation-Induced Traumatic Stress, 280–81
Patience, 241–44
Patrick, saint, 120
Patricians, 94–95
Paul, saint, 112, 288
Peace Chiefs, 163
Peace education, 283–84
Peace Villages, 163
Peace Wheel, 64
Penn, William, 115–16
Penn, Thomas, 116
People Power, 2–3, 119, 256, 261,
Perpetration-Induced Traumatic Stress, 280–81
Persia, 96–97
Persecution, 128–29, 150, 162, 198, 276–79
Petronius, 31–32
Pilate, Pontius, 30–31
Philippines, 2, 119, 140, 205, 261
Philo, 32
Physics, 67, 207, 267
Plato, 96, 105, 280
Plebeians, 94–95
Poland, 119, 213
Posttraumatic Stress Disorder, 280–81
Poverty: ancient religion positions, 35, 54–55, 77, 89, 121, 145; recent religion positions, 175, 186, 202. *See also* Structural violence
Power, 2–3, 64, 95, 221, 256–58, 268–69
Prabhavananda, 45, 57, 58, 227
Prabhupada, 45
Prabhu, Sharath, 208
Pratitya Samutpada, 67, 291
Prete, Anthony, 22–23
Progressive revelation, 179
Prophets: Bahá'í, 178–79; Judean, 18–19, 24–25, 33, 35, 96, 225, 242; Muslim, 92, 128, 148, 233
Puah, 28
Pythagoras, 6, 82, 96, 103–4

Quisling, Vidkun, 269
Qur'an composition, 129–30

Rabia al-'Adawiyya, 231, 235
Rahula, 63
Ramadan, 129, 132, 145, 179
Rana, Jadi, 90
Randolph, A. Philip, 212
Rape, 153, 166, 221, 229
Rehoboam, King, 18
Reincarnation, 190. *See also* Karma
Restorative justice, 253–54
Resurrection, general, 89, 91, 119, 278
Resurrection of Jesus, 107, 110, 112, 126
Revelation, Biblical book, 122–24, 277
Romans, ancient: Christians, 36, 106, 108, 110, 112–14, 124; in Judea, 19, 30, 31–32; plebeian revolt, 94–95
Roosevelt, Franklin, 265
Rosenberg, Marshall, 250
Rosenstrasse protests, 267–69
Ross, 124
Rotblat, Joseph, 21
Rugova, Ibrahim, 141
Rumi, 147
Russia, 47, 141, 178, 256

Sabbath, 276
Sacredness of life, 2
Sadducees, 20, 110
Sa'id, Jawdat, 135
Saffron Revolution, 72, 261
Saladin, 280
Salat, 131
Samaritans, 38, 112, 162
Saoshyant, 91
Saraswati, Sivananda, 52
Sarvodaya movement, 74
Satan, 90, 230, 234
Satha-Anand, Chaiwat, 131
Satyagraha, 2
Satyarthi, Kailash, 45
Saudi Arabia, 254
Savitsky, Valentin Grigorievitch, 213
Sawm, 132
Sazuke prayers, 196, 197
Scotland, 263
Sea of Silence, 137
Secularism, 67, 207, 211, 214
Secular humanism, 207, 214

Self-control, 49, 233, 244, 283, 290
Septuagint, 19, 30, 193
Serbia, 140, 141
Sermon on the Mount, 58, 226
Sex, 221
Shahadah, 131, 224
Shah, Indries, 237
Shammai, Rabbi, 245
Sharp, Gene, 5, 12, 95
Sheol, 90, 122
Shinto, 64, 73, 194, 195, 198, 203
Shiphrah, 28
Shomu, emperor, 76
Sikhs, 6, 168–76; ecology, 294–95; relations with other religions, 59, 149
Simons, Menno, 115
Sinclair, Upton, 225
Singh, Jagmohan, 174
Singh, Manmohan, 170
Singh, Ram, 171
Singh, Ranjit, 169, 174
Sivaraksa, Sulak, 70
Slaves. *See* Enslaved people
Slavery, 164, 243–44; abolition of slavery, 117–18, 120; ancient religion positions, 33–34, 53, 75–76, 87, 120, 143–44, 164; recent religion positions, 173, 184, 202
Slippery slope, 227–29, 266
Smith, Hannah Whitall, 235
Socially responsible spending, 4, 285–89
Socrates, 96, 105, 280
Songs, 74, 161, 166, 197, 276
South Africa, 47, 235, 238–39, 279
South Korea, 195
Soviet Union, 4, 6, 211, 212, 213
Squire, J.C., 7
Sramana traditions, 96
Sri Lanka, 65, 74, 76
Stanton, Elizabeth Cady, 159
Starhawk, 191
Stark, Rodney, 17, 41, 112
Strikes, 2

Structural violence, 35, 74, 220, 225–26, 244, 277. *See also* Poverty
Suddhodana, 63
Sufis, 43, 58, 92, 134–35, 141, 218, 237
Sukthankar, V. S., 56
Sung Keng, 99
Sweden, 264, 267
Sweet Medicine, 163
Synagogues, 20, 37, 122, 265, 267

Tadodaho, 158
Tagore, Rabindranath, 234, 244
Taliban, 136, 260
Talmud, 20, 26, 27, 28, 30, 35, 228, 240, 290
Tanakh, 35
Taoism, 64, 80, 96, 100–103, 224, 247, 257, 259
Tao Te Ching, 100–103
Telemachus, 113
Temple, William, 37
Ten Commandments, 218, 221, 222
Tenrikyo, 6, 194–205, 295
Tenri-O-no-Mikoto, 195
Teresa of Avila, 234, 237
Teruo, 70
Thailand, 70, 76, 79, 205
Thakin movement, 71
Theodicy, 208
Thoreau, Henry David, 256
Thurman, Howard, 126, 222–23, 272
Tibet, 69, 79
Toda, Josei, 73
Toland, John, 188
Tolstoy, Leo, 47, 256
Transcendental Meditation, 45
Trinity, 107–8
Tsukihi, 195, 200–201, 202
Tsuji, Shinichiro, 201
Tunisia, 136, 143
Turiyananda, Swami, 240
Tutu, Desmond, 235, 239
Twain, Mark, 157

Underground railroad, 117, 127, 266, 272
Ukraine, 140

United Nations, 21, 160, 254, 260, 270
United States: Buddhism, 70, 72, 73; First Nations, 151–67; Hinduism, 43, 45, 58; slavery, 33, 117–18, 120, 184; wars and violence, 191, 198, 254, 265. *See also* Civil Rights Movement, U.S.
Universal Declaration of Human Rights, 21, 270
Universal House of Justice, 178, 183, 185
Upanishads, 40, 53, 55, 57, 96

Vedas, 39–40, 42, 53, 55
Vegetarianism, 8, 34–35, 46, 60, 69, 118, 145, 165, 288–89. *See also* Meat consumption
Veils, 133
Veto power, 94–95, 160
Vietnam, 70, 74–75, 79–80, 211
Virtues, 232–45, 296. *See also individual types*
Vivekananda, 43, 44, 45, 51, 58

War: ancient religion positions, 34, 53, 76, 87, 121, 144; recent religion positions, 174, 184, 202
War opposition, 25–26, 97–100, 182–84
Whistle-blowers, 3
Wicca, 6, 189–91
Wiesel, Elie, 21
Wilberforce, William, 117
Witchcraft, 189
Withdrawal: American, 117, 157; ancient Rome, 94–95; Islamic, 132, 128, 140; strategy, 3, 251; Zoroastrian, 85
Women's equality: Bahá'ís, 181, 183; Buddhism, 64, 69, 70; Christianity, 108, 112–13, 118, 121; First Nations, 159–60; Islam, 131, 132–33, 137; Pythagoreans, 103; revived paganism, 188, 193; Taoism, 100; Zoroastrianism, 86
Wright, Tom (N. T.), 110, 124
Wu Wei, 100

Yancey, Phillip, 24–25, 273
Yin and Yang, 100
Yoga, 42, 50
Yogananda, 44, 56, 57–58, 218, 244
Yogaswami, Siva, 51
Yogi, Maharishi Mahesh, 45
Yasodhara, 63
Yazidis, 92–93
Yoboku, 196
Yonaguska, 166

Yousafzai, Malala, 131, 133, 260
Yunus, 131

Zakat, 131, 143, 145
Zikrism, 141
Zoroaster/Zarathustra, 63, 81, 92, 96–97, 186, 292
Zoroastrianism, 81–93; ecology, 292; relations with other religions, 37, 59, 127, 149

Scripture Index

Jewish Tanakh/Christian Old Testament

Genesis 1:1–2:4 22
Genesis 1:16, 290
Genesis 1:26–30, 290
Genesis 1:27, 193
Genesis 1:29, 34
Genesis 3:1–13, 224
Genesis 3:14–20, 280
Genesis 9:3, 34
Genesis 9:20–27, 35
Genesis 18, 26, 36
Genesis 22, 33

Exodus 1:15–21, 28
Exodus 20:7, 222
Exodus 21:1–11, 33
Exodus 23:12, 276
Exodus 32, 36

Leviticus 15:19, 112
Leviticus 17:3–4, 34
Leviticus 18:21, 18, 228

Numbers 16:20–22, 26
Numbers 35:11–14, 163

Deuteronomy 5:14–15, 18
Deuteronomy 7:1–2, 35
Deuteronomy 12:31, 33
Deuteronomy 13:2–19, 35
Deuteronomy 15:14–15, 18
Deuteronomy 16:11–12, 18
Deuteronomy 18:10, 18, 33, 228
Deuteronomy 20:16–17, 35
Deuteronomy 20:19–20, 290
Deuteronomy 24:17–22, 18
Deuteronomy 32:11–12, 193
Deuteronomy 32:18, 193

Joshua chapters 6–11, 35
Joshua 20:2, 163

Judges 11, 33

1 Samuel 22:17, 29

1 Kings 12:1–16, 18
1 Kings 18:3–4, 29

2 Kings 16:3, 18, 228
2 Kings 17: 15–17, 219
2 Kings 17:17, 18, 33, 228
2 Kings 21:6, 18, 228
2 Kings 23:10, 18, 33, 228

Esther 4 and 5, 39

Job 1:8–11, 230
Job 42:7, 26

Psalms 13:2, 5, 6, 234
Psalms 16:8–10, 234–35
Psalms 20:7–8, 25
Psalms 33:16–19, 25
Psalms 42:9, 26
Psalms 85:8–10, 26
Psalms 104:35, 28
Psalms 106:37–38, 33
Psalms 115: 4–5, 135, 219
Psalms 123:2–3, 193
Psalms 131:2, 193
Psalms 135:15–16, 219
Psalms 147:10–11, 26

Proverbs 1:20–33, 193
Proverbs 3:13–18, 193
Proverbs 4:5–9, 193
Proverbs 8, 193
Proverbs 9:1–6, 193
Proverbs 12:18, 249
Proverbs 13:23, 225
Proverbs 14:31, 225
Proverbs 15:1, 249, 258
Proverbs 15:18, 242
Proverbs 17:14, 228, 249
Proverbs 17:22, 237
Proverbs 24:17, 28
Proverbs 25:21, 28, 258
Proverbs 25:21–22, 28, 258
Proverbs 28:3, 225
Proverbs 29:7, 225

Ecclesiastes 5:8–10, 35

Isaiah 1:11–17, 33
Isaiah 2:4, 25
Isaiah 2:8, 219
Isaiah 11:6–9, 25
Isaiah 31:7, 219
Isaiah 42:14, 193
Isaiah 46:1–2, 219
Isaiah 49:15, 193
Isaiah chapter 53, 106
Isaiah 57:5, 33
Isaiah 61:1–2, 122
Isaiah 66:13, 193

Jeremiah 6:13–14, 226
Jeremiah 7:22–23, 33

Jeremiah 7:31, 18, 228
Jeremiah 19:3, 18, 228
Jeremiah 19–4–5, 219
Jeremiah chapter 19, 24
Jeremiah 32:6–15, 24
Jeremiah 32:35, 33

Ezekiel 5:8–10, 225
Ezekiel 16:20–21, 33
Ezekiel 20:31, 33
Ezekiel 23:37–39, 33
Ezekiel chapter 34, 225
Ezekiel 45:9, 35, 225

Daniel 1:8–15, 35
Daniel chapters 3 and 6, 224
Daniel 3:17–18, 29
Daniel 12:2, 90, 110

Hosea 2:18, 25
Hosea 6:6, 33, 120
Hosea 11:3–4, 193
Hosea 13:2, 219
Hosea 13:8, 193

Amos 5:21–24, 33
Amos 6:1–6, 225

Micah 2:1–2, 225
Micah 4:3, 25
Micah 6:8, 238

Habakkuk 2:18, 219

Zechariah, 4:6, 30

Malachi 2:10, 23

Hindu Scriptures

Rig Veda 6.75:15, 53
Rig Veda 7.36.9, 54
Rig Veda 10, 47–48

Atharva Veda 3:24–25, 55
Atharva Veda 6.113.2, 54
Atharva Veda 7.52:1–2, 48
Atharva Veda 10.191:4, 48

Dharma Shastras 6, 48–49
Dharma Shastras 10, 49

Mahabharata 18.113:8, 49
Mahabharata 18.115:8, 49
Mahabharata 18.116:37–41, 49

Kaushitaki Upanishad, 3.1, 54

Sandilya Upanishad, 49

Bhagavad Gita 4:7–8, 42, 57, 107
Bhagavad Gita 5:18, 41
Bhagavad Gita 10:4–5, 49–50, 55, 232
Bhagavad Gita 10:20, 49
Bhagavad Gita 16:1–3, 50, 232
Bhagavad Gita 16:21, 224

Bhagavata Purana 1.5.15, 55

Yoga Sutras of Patañjali, 50

Tiru Kural, Verse 312, 50
Tiru Kural, Verse 321, 50

Thirumanthiram, Verse 197, 50–51

Buddhist Scriptures

Dhammapada 1:5–6, 67
Dhammapada 1:163, 243
Dhammapada 17:3, 1, 67
Dhammapada 26:399, 400, 405, 68

Digha-Nikaya [Lion's Roar Sutra], 3:65, 228

Sutta Nipata 1.8, Karaniya Metta Sutta, 68

Anguttaranikaya 3:185, 66

Patisambhida 2:130, 66

Nirvana Sutra chapter 19, 77
Nirvana Sutra chapters 22, 24, 34, 39, and 40, 78

Sadharmapundarika Sutra 5, 230–31

Karaniya Metta Sutta: Loving-Kindness, Sn. 1.8, 232–33

Kakacupama Sutta, Majjhima Nikaya 21, 252

Zoroastrian Scriptures

Songs 3, 4, and 10, p. 87

Vendidad 15:9–16

Yacht, 86

Yasna 32:3, 87
Yasna 32:8, 87

Zend-Avesta, 86

Taoism

Tao Te Ching 30, 101
Tao Te Ching 31, 102
Tao Te Ching 37, 102
Tao Te Ching 39, 257
Tao Te Ching 46, 224
Tao Te Ching 67, 102
Tao Te Ching 68, 250
Tao Te Ching 78, 102–3
Tao Te Ching 79, 247

Chuang Tzu, 99
Chuang Tzu 33, 100

Christian New Testament

Matthew 5:9, 107
Matthew 5:21–24, 227
Matthew 5: 29–30, 123
Matthew 5:38–40, 244
Matthew 5:43, 230
Matthew 5:43–44, 1, 111, 258
Matthew 5:45, 230
Matthew, chapters 5–7, 58
Matthew 8:12, 123
Matthew 9:13, 120
Matthew 10:28, 123

Matthew 12:7, 120
Matthew 13:41–43, 123
Matthew 18:9, 123
Matthew 21:24, 11
Matthew 22:13, 123
Matthew 23:37, 193
Matthew 24:1–32, 106
Matthew 24:14, 109
Matthew 24:36, 278
Matthew 25:30, 123
Matthew 25:40, 111
Matthew 27:55, 112
Matthew 28:1–10, 112

Mark 5:25–34, 112
Mark 7:25–30, 12
Mark 9:45–47, 123
Mark 13:1–30, 106
Mark 13:10, 109
Mark 15:40, 112

Luke 4:18, 122
Luke 4:20, 122
Luke 5: 27–36, 111
Luke 6:29, 244
Luke 8:1–3, 112
Luke 10:38–42, 112
Luke 12:5, 123
Luke 15:8–10, 193
Luke 16:19–31, 123
Luke 21:5–32, 106
Luke 22:49–51, 111
Luke 23:24, 111
Luke 24:1–11, 112
Luke 24:27, 109
John 20:1–18

John 4:7–27, 112
John 20:1–18, 112

Acts 5:27–29, 224
Acts 17:4, 112

Romans 5:3–4, 242
Romans 12:14–18, 11
Romans 12:14–21, 258
Romans, chapter 14, 121–22, 288
Romans 15:13, 235
Romans 16:1–3, 112

1 Corinthians 1:11, 112
1 Corinthians 7:3–5, 113

Galatians 5:22–23, 233

Colossians 3:2–13, 111

1 Timothy 6:10, 224

Hebrews 10:32–34, 111

James 1:19–20, 111, 249
James 3:6, 123
James, 5:1–6, 225
James 5:7–8, 242
James, 5:10–12, 242

2 Peter 2:4, 123

Revelation 1:1, 123
Revelation 1:3, 123
Revelation 1:9, 277
Revelation 17:2, 124
Revelation 14:6, 220
Revelation 15:8, 124
Revelation 17:18; 124
Revelation 18:3, 124
Revelation 19:19, 124
Revelation 20:14, 122

Septuagint/Catholic Deuterocanonical

The Book of Wisdom 6:12–17, 193
The Book of Wisdom 7:7–14, 193
The Book of Wisdom 7:22–30, 193
The Book of Wisdom 8:1–18, 193
The Book of Wisdom 9:9–11, 193
The Book of Wisdom 10:1–21, 193
The Book of Wisdom 11:1–26, 193

Ecclesiasticus/Sirach 4:12–18, 193
Ecclesiasticus/Sirach 6:18–31, 193
Ecclesiasticus/Sirach 14:20–27, 193
Ecclesiasticus/Sirach 15:1–10, 193
Ecclesiasticus/Sirach 24:1–29, 193
Ecclesiasticus/Sirach 41:13–22, 193
Baruch 2:29–38, 193
Baruch 4:1–4, 193

Islam

Qur'an 2:45, 242
Qur'an 2:62, 149
Qur'an 2:106, 146
Qur'an 2:153, 242
Qur'an 2:177, 143, 145, 233
Qur'an 2:213, 249
Qur'an 2:215, 145
Qur'an 2:256, 234
Qur'an 3:180, 224–25
Qur'an 3:186, 242
Qur'an 3:200, 242
Qur'an 4:34, 146
Qur'an 4:36, 225
Qur'an 4:92, 143
Qur'an 4:124, 133
Qur'an 5:8, 133–34, 249
Qur'an 5:27–29, 135, 136
Qur'an 5:32, 147
Qur'an 5:33, 147
Qur'an 5:38, 146
Qur'an 5:89, 143, 145
Qur'an 6:38, 145, 293
Qur'an 7:56, 294
Qur'an 7:123–124, 147
Qur'an 9:5, 145
Qur'an 9:29, 145
Qur'an 9:60, 143
Qur'an 10:19, 249
Qur'an 10:109, 242
Qur'an 11: 115, 242
Qur'an 16:58–59, 132, 144
Qur'an 16:90, 133
Qur'an 16:97, 133
Qur'an 16:126–127, 242
Qur'an 17:31, 144
Qur'an 17:86, 146
Qur'an 20:71, 147
Qur'an 20:130–132, 242
Qur'an 23:91, 128
Qur'an 24:33, 143
Qur'an 24:41, 145
Qur'an 25:43, 219
Qur'an 25:63, 129
Qur'an 30:41, 294
Qur'an 33:63, 278
Qur'an 40:40, 133
Qur'an 40:55, 77, 242
Qur'an 41:34, 1, 259
Qur'an surah 42, 249
Qur'an 42:15, 133
Qur'an 42:36, 39–43, 238
Qur'an 42:42, 133
Qur'an 47:4, 143
Qur'an surah 42, 249
Qur'an 50:39, 242
Qur'an 53:23, 219
Qur'an 58:3, 143
Qur'an 59:7, 145
Qur'an surah 75, 278
Qur'an 81:8–9, 132, 144
Qur'an 90:12–14, 143

Sikh

Guru Arjun Dev Ji, 171

Guru Nanak Hymn, 171

Guru Granth Sahib page 74, 174
Guru Granth Sahib page 1159, 175

Baha'i

Kitab-i-Aqdas 72, 184

Tenrikyo

Ofudesaki 1:19–20, 199
Ofudesaki 1:33–36, 199
Ofudesaki 1:52–53, 199
Ofudesaki 3:57–58, 199–200
Ofudesaki 3:120–125, 200
Ofudesaki 4:15–17, 200
Ofudesaki 4:90–93, 198
Ofudesaki 4:104, 196
Ofudesaki 4:131, 202
Ofudesaki 8:43–50, 200–201

Osashizu, December 11, 1897, 196

Konkokyo

GII: Sato Mitsujiro, 27:1–2, 205

About the Author

RACHEL M. MACNAIR, PHD, is director of the Institute for Integrated Social Analysis. She has served as editor-in-chief for the Feminist and Nonviolence Studies Association, as president of the American Psychological Association's Division 48, Peace Psychology, and as the division's membership chair. A dedicated follower of the Quaker tradition, MacNair holds an interdisciplinary Ph.D., in psychology and sociology. She serves as a reviewer for *Peace and Conflict: The Journal of Peace Psychology, Peace and Change: A Journal of Peace Research, American Psychologist, Political Psychology, Journal of Peace Education*, and *PsycCRITIQUES*, the journal of the American Psychological Association. MacNair's previous books with Praeger are *Perpetration-Induced Traumatic Stress: The Psychological Consequences of Killing* (2002), *The Psychology of Peace: An Introduction, 1st and 2nd editions* (2003 and 2012), and *Consistently Opposing Killing* (2008).

www.ingramcontent.com/pod-product-compliance
Lightning Source LLC
Chambersburg PA
CBHW050619300426
44112CB00012B/1565